Pro PHP-GTK

Scott Mattocks

Pro PHP-GTK

Copyright © 2006 by Scott Mattocks

Softcover re-print of the Hardcover 1st edition 2006

ISBN-13: 978-1-4302-1191-4

ISBN-10: 1-4302-1191-4

Lead Editor: Jason Gilmore
Technical Reviewers: Christian Weiske, Steph Fox
Editorial Board: Steve Anglin, Dan Appleman, Ewan Buckingham, Gary Cornell, Jason Gilmore, Jonathan Hassell, James Huddleston, Chris Mills, Matthew Moodie, Dominic Shakeshaft, Jim Sumser, Matt Wade
Project Manager: Kylie Johnston
Copy Edit Manager: Nicole LeClerc
Copy Editors: Marilyn Smith, Jennifer Whipple
Assistant Production Director: Kari Brooks-Copony
Production Editor: Ellie Fountain
Compositor: Kinetic Publishing Services, LLC
Proofreader: Dan Shaw
Indexer: Valerie Perry
Cover Designer: Kurt Krames
Manufacturing Director: Tom Debolski

For information on translations, please contact Apress directly at 2560 Ninth Street, Suite 219, Berkeley, CA 94710. Phone 510-549-5930, fax 510-549-5939, e-mail info@apress.com, or visit http://www.apress.com.

The source code for this book is available to readers at http://www.apress.com in the Source Code section.

To my wife Cristina:
Thanks for giving me the courage to start this book
and for having the patience to let me finish.

Contents at a Glance

v

Contents

■CHAPTER 8   Using Multiline Text 153

■CHAPTER 9   Working with Trees and Lists 179

About the Author

SCOTT MATTOCKS is a PHP developer with OnForce.com. Scott has been working with PHP and PHP-GTK for almost his entire career. Not only has Scott been working with these tools, but he has also been contributing back to the community in many ways. Scott spent many hours to help improve the first set of documentation for PHP-GTK and is listed as one of the authors for the PHP-GTK 2 documentation. He has also contributed several PHP-GTK classes to PEAR and added code to more traditional PEAR packages such as PHPUnit and Console_Getargs. Scott can be contacted at scottmattocks@php.net. Read more about what he's up to at http://www.crisscott.com.

About the Technical Reviewer

CHRISTIAN WEISKE is student of Information Technologies in Leipzig, Germany. He has been a member of the PHP-GTK documentation team for several years and is a regular contributor to the PEAR project.

In his spare time, Christian works on various PHP-GTK 2 tools, translates programs into his native German language, and writes articles for *PHP Magazine*. He also works as a freelancer, creating PHP-GTK applications for those who need them. You can reach him by email at cweiske@cweiske.de or at his website, http://www.cweiske.de.

Introduction

The PHP-GTK extension is a powerful solution for creating stand-alone GUI applications. It takes the benefits of programming with PHP and combines them with the visual capabilities of GTK (the GIMP Toolkit). The goal of this book is to get you started developing your own desktop applications with PHP-GTK.

This book isn't just a rehashing of PHP-GTK's documentation. There is really no point in that. The documentation does a perfect job of providing an API reference. If you want to know the interface for a given method, then the online documentation is the best place for you. If, however, you want to know which is the best widget for displaying a list of airline reservations that can be sorted by departure or arrival times, the documentation isn't going to be much help.

Here, I'll give you problem-based analysis of PHP-GTK, as opposed to the function-based analysis you get with the documentation. I may refer you to the documentation from time to time, because in some situations, it is the best resource around. But in other situations, the documentation just isn't designed to allow you to understand the why behind a decision.

I feel the best way to learn is by getting your hands dirty and experiencing things for yourself. Throughout this book, I'll ask you to implement the examples that I talk about to see for yourself exactly what is happening. PHP-GTK is designed to interact with the user. You need to click certain places in the application and drag things around the screen. Only when you see firsthand how parts of a program react can you be ready to make an informed decision.

This book is packed full of examples and screenshots, but I beg you to not be satisfied with just what I have provided. You should always be asking, "Well, what if I changed this part . . . ?" The more you question what I am trying to explain, the deeper your understanding will be. If you just read through this book, you will be ready to make some pretty decent applications. But if you implement the examples and see what happens when you change a few values, there won't be anything you can't accomplish within the limits of PHP-GTK.

Who This Book Is For

This book is intended for PHP developers of all skill levels who want to break free from the web browser and create desktop applications. You'll find it easier going if you're familiar with PHP 5.1 and are comfortable with the principles of object-oriented programming.

What You'll Find in This Book

Pro PHP-GTK guides you through PHP-GTK's key capabilities, beginning with an introduction to fundamental aspects of building desktop applications and a discussion of how PHP-GTK implements these features. Subsequent chapters explain how to lay out and manage widgets such as windows, labels, buttons, and text fields; manage events to control the behavior of an application; and accept and manipulate user input. You will also learn how to customize an application's look and feel, implement drag-and-drop capabilities, and package an application for distribution to users.

Throughout the book, you'll develop a real-world project to help you learn how to use PHP-GTK to satisfy critical business needs. The source code for all of the examples is available from the Source Code section of the Apress website (http://www.apress.com).

Here's a quick rundown of the chapter contents:

- Chapter 1 discusses the basics of GUI, PHP, and PHP-GTK. It also introduces the sample application you will work with throughout the book.

- Chapter 2 covers installing and configuring the software you need to begin developing applications with PHP-GTK.

- Chapter 3 examines how the pieces of PHP-GTK interoperate to allow you to build a complete working application.

- Chapter 4 goes over how a PHP-GTK application interacts with the user. These topics are crucial to making an application react to both user and application requests.

- Chapter 5 talks about setting up the basics of an application. After that chapter, you'll have an application that brings up a window, shows some data, and shuts down cleanly.

- Chapter 6 deals with designing the application. It demonstrates how to lay out the application so you can work on one piece at a time and add features as they are ready.

- Chapter 7 shows you how to display and collect simple data. You'll start small with single lines.

- Chapter 8 describes how to work with multiline text and PHP-GTK's powerful text-editing capabilities.

- Chapter 9 focuses on displaying large sets of data, like trees and lists, which often overflow the space they are given.

- Chapter 10 goes over the details of making scrollable spaces on the screen to accommodate data that can't be shown all at once.

- Chapter 11 looks at how to organize user tasks with menus and toolbars.

- Chapter 12 covers creating and displaying images.

- Chapter 13 tackles one of the more advanced features of PHP-GTK: drag-and-drop. It will show you how to make objects on the screen draggable and allow other elements on the screen to accept those objects.

- Chapter 14 provides information pertaining to selectors and dialogs. These are windows that are used for things like selecting files or verifying that a user wants to delete some data.

- Chapter 15 talks about ways to make applications more efficient by doing work in the background. This allows the user to keep working while time-consuming processes are handled by the application.

- Chapter 16 shows you how to change the look and feel of an application, not only to customize the application, but also to improve its usability.

- Chapter 17 talks about how to get an application into the user's hands. You'll learn about PHP "compilers" and different distribution methods.

■■■

## CHAPTER 1

Introducing PHP-GTK

This book takes a problem-based approach to learning. Each chapter discusses a particular issue, and then shows which tools can be used to solve that issue. You will also walk through a real-world project to help you learn how to use PHP-GTK to develop a desktop application to solve the problem of a fictional company. This first chapter introduces the sample project, and then discusses the basics of graphical user interface (GUI) applications, PHP, and PHP-GTK.

A Real-World Project

Learning about programming through a book can sometimes be difficult. Oftentimes, a book will break down the problems into such tiny pieces that it is hard to put them back together to understand how they are related. You want to learn how to solve problems, not determine what problems exist to be solved. Keeping that in mind, you are going to work with a real-world project to help you learn how to use PHP-GTK to satisfy critical business needs. You are going to go through the entire process of developing a desktop application for a fictional online retailer, Crisscott, Inc. We will start out with a brief analysis of the retailer's problem and move on to designing a solution, then implementing the solution, and, finally, distributing and maintaining the application.

I am not just going to throw a list of classes and methods at you, and expect you to be able to put together an enterprise-level application. Instead, I am going to look at the problems and help you make the right choices for solving them. I am not going to say, "If you find yourself in situation A, use widget X." That helps only if you are trying to do exactly what I have done before. What happens if you find that you need a slightly different solution? By the time you're finished with this book, you will be able to recognize which tools are best for your needs, not mine. You will be able to build a solution designed specifically to solve the problems you are facing. Together, we will look at all the ways something can be done and discuss the advantages and disadvantages of each.

In order to help keep us on the right track, this book is going to focus on the development of a distributed product inventory management system, or PIMS, for Crisscott, Inc. At the conclusion of the book, you will have an entire application that is ready for use in the real world.

You will pretend to be a developer hired to help Crisscott, Inc. with product management issues. You will assume that Crisscott is an online shop that sells goods for PHP-GTK programmers. Its products range from books, such as this one, to downloadable applications, such as integrated development environments (IDEs) or documentation browsers.

Crisscott is having a problem managing its product information. It sells products from many different suppliers, all of which currently report their data and inventories in different ways. Managing this data is a real problem for Crisscott. It has to spend too much time fixing data problems and trying to track inventory. To solve this, Crisscott is putting the data in the hands of the people who know it best, the suppliers. It wants to distribute a tool to all of its suppliers that will allow them to quickly and easily make changes, add products, remove products, and update inventory levels. If the tool isn't easy to set up and use, the suppliers will never accept it. Crisscott doesn't just want to offload its work onto the suppliers; it wants to make life easier for everyone. Preserving relationships with the suppliers is a high priority of the project.

The PIMS application must provide a user-friendly interface for updating product information. It also needs to be compatible with any platform the suppliers are using and cannot be dependent on the suppliers having any particular third-party software installed. The application should allow the suppliers to work online or off. They must be able to edit data, save it, and upload it later. The application needs to be able to grab data for the supplier from multiple sources. It needs to get the latest information from Crisscott, pull information from a file, or get data from a database. The application also needs to be easily updated when bug fixes are found or new features are added. Finally, the application needs to be able to display news and announcements that Crisscott may wish to pass on to its suppliers.

As you develop this application for Crisscott, Inc., you will learn how to use PHP-GTK to make a seemingly difficult task relatively easy. You will analyze all the tools PHP-GTK provides and determine when each tool is most suitable. You will also learn how PHP-GTK easily interacts with "normal" PHP code. You will need to generate XML, get and display RSS news feeds from a central location, send the product data to a web service using SOAP, connect to a local database, and do many other tasks. It does not stop there, though. As with any project, development is not the end of the line. Finally, we will discuss techniques for distributing and updating the application once the implementation stage is finished.

GUI Applications

Applications involving a GUI have helped to bring computers to the masses. It is much easier to click a button than it is to remember which command to type on a command line. GUI applications also make computers more usable by presenting information in an organized visual context. Yet many people take for granted the computer applications they use on a daily basis. All they know is that they type into a little box, hit the Send button, and, magically, Grandma has an email message waiting for her. Few people ever stop to wonder how that Send button is able to get that message from the box and send it to Granny, let alone how that button even got on the screen. This chapter lays the groundwork for this book, helping you understand some of the fundamental aspects of these GUI-based applications, introducing PHP and PHP-GTK, and discussing what will be covered in later chapters.

Unlike web applications, which function within the context of a web browser, stand-alone GUI applications function in their own context, and they are often developed to organize tasks and data that might be too cumbersome or too confusing to represent through a web browser. Analyzing and organizing complex data into an understandable format is the goal of most computer applications. If the data were simple, you wouldn't need a program to help you out. Think about all the things you use GUI applications for on a daily basis. Web browsers, email clients, text editors, and even your file system browser are all GUI applications designed to present data in a format that is more productive and easier to understand. Being able to create objects on the screen that can help users get more out of their data is a powerful tool for any programmer. But you probably already know this. That is why you've got this book in your hands. Either that or you really like the cover art.

Most people think GUI applications are only for large, complicated tasks and require complex libraries that are only available for compiled languages such as C++ or Visual Basic .NET. This simply isn't true. GUI applications come in all sorts of different sizes and shapes. There are simple applications such as calculators and clocks, and there are complex applications such as Photoshop and PowerPoint. They also come in different languages, such as Java, C++, PHP, and Python. Regardless of what they do or how they are written, GUI applications all share a common goal: they represent tasks and data in a graphical way. Applications written in PHP-GTK are no different. They are written to make complicated tasks easier to manage and understand. Applications written with the PHP-GTK scripting language can be just as powerful as those written in compiled languages.

Figures 1-1 and 1-2 show screenshots from two text-editing applications. The first image you might recognize as WordPad, an application written in C++, from a typical Windows installation. The second is Tulip, a text editor written with PHP-GTK. The two applications are remarkably similar, even though the underlying technology is different.

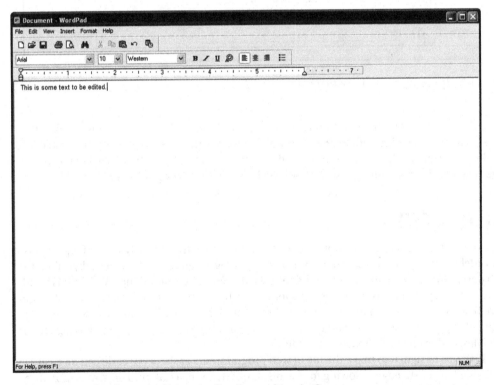

Figure 1-1. *WordPad, a text editing application written in C++*

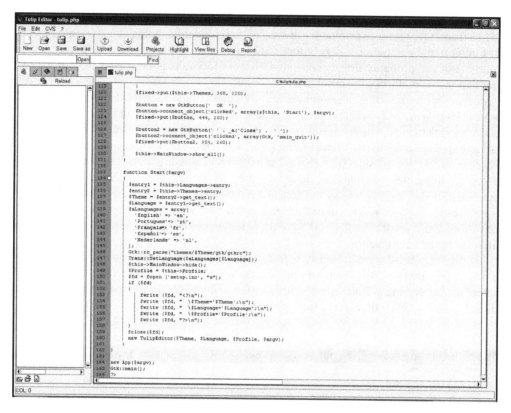

Figure 1-2. *Tulip, a text editor written with PHP-GTK*

PHP-GTK is a powerful solution for creating stand-alone GUI applications. It takes the benefits of programming with PHP and combines them with the visual capabilities of GTK. To get the most out of PHP-GTK, you must understand the technologies that have been brought together. In the next couple of sections, we will look at what pieces make up PHP-GTK.

What Is PHP?

According to the PHP documentation, PHP (a recursive acronym for PHP Hypertext Preprocessor) is a widely used, open source, general-purpose scripting language that is especially suited for web development and can be embedded into HTML. You may be thinking, "Well, if it is good for web development, why am I reading about it in a book on desktop applications?" PHP may have been developed with the Web in mind, but it is also a very powerful tool for other uses. Using PHP, you can easily read and write from the file system, connect to a database, generate PDF files, and even create images on the fly.

PHP was designed to make the life of web programmers easier. PHP code can be easily embedded in HTML pages allowing for the display of dynamic content. The syntax of PHP is very easy to understand, and therefore PHP has a very short learning curve. In many cases, a web developer with little prior knowledge of PHP can be up and running with a simple dynamic page in a matter of hours. Such a low barrier of entry has given PHP unprecedented acceptance in the open source community. Once people started realizing how easy it is to use PHP for web development, they began to wonder why they couldn't use it for other types of development. So, as of version 4.2.0, PHP broke free from the Web with the introduction of the command-line interface, or CLI.

The CLI allows scripts to be executed directly by the operating system without having to be passed through a web server. I've written CLI scripts for parsing incoming email messages, generating sales reports, and importing batches of product data. One of the most popular CLI tools is the PEAR installer. PEAR shows how far PHP has come since its beginnings as a tool for web development.

Part of what has made PHP so widely accepted is that it is an interpreted language. This means that any system that has the PHP engine installed can run the same PHP script. (In Chapter 17, we will throw that out the window and show how you don't even need the PHP engine.) This makes PHP a cross-platform language. A well-designed script written on a machine with Linux installed will work just as well on a server running Windows. Please note that the script must be "well-designed." It is quite possible to write a script that won't run on both a Linux and a Windows server, but this is actually harder than writing a cross-platform script. PHP makes it incredibly easy to create well-designed scripts and applications. It is up to you to make sure you take advantage of these features.

Object-Oriented PHP

This book expects you to have at least a basic understanding of PHP already. You don't need to be a PHP master but you should at least be able to recognize valid syntax. PHP-GTK is heavily object-oriented (OO). The release of PHP 5 has introduced a much more powerful object model than its predecessor, allowing for cleaner, faster running code. Everything in PHP-GTK uses objects in one way or another. If you aren't instantiating a class and calling one of its methods, then you are calling some class method statically. As a result, all of the code examples throughout this book will be written in the OO programming style. As a quick refresher, consider Listing 1-1.

Listing 1-1. *Inheritance in PHP*

```php
<?php
class Ralph {
    public    $name   = 'Ralph';
    protected $suffix = 'Sr';

    public function __construct()
    {
        echo 'My name is ' . $this->name . ' ' . $this->suffix . ".\n";
    }

    public function giveBirth()
    {
        echo "It's a boy!\n";
        return new Ralph_Jr();
    }
}
```

```php
class Ralph_Jr extends Ralph {
    protected $suffix = 'Jr';

    public function giveBirth()
    {
        throw new Exception('Ralph Jr. can\'t have kids!');
    }
}

$senior = new Ralph();
$junior = $senior->giveBirth();

try {
    $junior->giveBirth();
} catch (Exception $e) {
    echo $e->getMessage() . "\n";
}
?>
```

```
My name is Ralph Sr.
It's a boy!
My name is Ralph Jr.
Ralph Jr. can't have kids!
```

■**Note** The code throughout this book was written and tested on Linux. Depending on your operating system of choice, the code samples may require some minor changes such as using \r\n for newlines instead of just \n.

This simple example defines two classes. The first class, Ralph, simply defines one public member variable, one protected member variable, a constructor, and one method. When the class is instantiated, it prints out a simple message. The second class, Ralph_Jr, extends the first and redefines one of the class members. Ralph_Jr also redefines the giveBirth method. For the purposes of this example, we aren't instantiating Ralph_Jr directly. Instead, we are creating an object by calling a method of Ralph. Notice the difference in the output when you run the example. The suffix on the names is different depending on the class you instantiate. Also, Ralph is capable of having kids; Ralph_Jr is a bit too young.

■**Note** For more details on PHP 5, take a look at *Beginning PHP 5 and MySQL 5: From Novice to Professional, Second Edition* by W. Jason Gilmore (Apress, 2006).

Exceptions

When we try to call the giveBirth method on Ralph_Jr, an exception is thrown. An *exception* is an error-handling mechanism that requires the calling code to catch it and handle it. When something unexpected happens, or some important piece of data is missing, well-designed code should throw an exception. Exceptions are themselves objects and have methods and properties, and can be instantiated and extended.

When calling code can possibly throw an exception (when connecting to a database, for example), it is a good idea to wrap the code in a try-catch block. Look at the last few lines of Listing 1-1. Before we call junior's giveBirth method, we wrap it in a try block. This tells PHP that there may be an exception thrown, and it should be ready in case that happens. When an exception is thrown, execution will leave the try block and jump to the catch block.

You can have multiple catch blocks for a given try block. In our example, this catch block will catch any Exception class instance or any exception class that extends the Exception class. In our case, we are just going to output the message from the exception. Depending on the situation, you may want to take some more drastic measures, such as halting execution all together.

If you do not wrap code that can throw an exception in a try-catch block, the exception will "bubble up" to the next level. If an exception bubbles all the way up and is never caught, a fatal error will be thrown, and execution of the code will halt.

PHP's DOM and SOAP Extensions

Aside from looking at simple object creation and access, we will also examine some of the PHP extensions and wrappers around them. In particular, we will use the DOM and SOAP extensions for PHP 5. The DOM extension makes reading and creating XML documents using SAX much easier than the old callback method. The SOAP extension lets you access web services on remote systems. The SOAP extension basically builds a SOAP client or server based on an XML document that describes the web services known as a WSDL.

Don't worry if you aren't that familiar with DOM or SOAP. I won't leave you high and dry. When it comes time to put them into your application, I'll show you how to use them. If you just can't wait that long, see the "Further Resources" section later in this chapter for some excellent resources.

Throughout this book, we will also be making extensive use of some PEAR classes. Using a PEAR class is no different from using any other PHP class. Installing the classes is what may be new to you. The next chapter will show you how to install all of the extensions and PEAR classes that we will be using throughout this book.

What Is GTK?

GTK is an acronym for the GIMP Toolkit (http://www.gtk.org/). It is a library of structures and functions written in C to make developing GUI applications easier. GTK provides the tools to create windows, buttons, and text that are viewable without the assistance of another program, such as a web browser or a text editor.

GTK works with GDK, the GTK Drawing Kit, to interface with the underlying windowing system. Having a separate code base for interacting with the operating system allows GTK to support multiple operating systems. That is, by keeping the two code bases separate, GTK does not have to worry about which operating system the code is running on. All of the windowing system interactions are handled by GDK, leaving GTK free to specialize in the user interface.

Along with the visual representations, GTK provides a means for interacting with the visual objects that are created by making it possible to listen for and react to user-triggered events. This means that instead of just having a pretty button, you have a clickable pretty button. Your code can tell when a button is clicked and take a specific action. This is an important piece of the programming puzzle. After all, users need to be able to make the application do something; otherwise, they just have an image on the screen. Because of its importance, two entire chapters are devoted to this feature. Chapter 3 explains how these structures relate to each other, and Chapter 4 explains how to write code that interacts with them.

Just like PHP, GTK has undergone many iterations and releases. At the time of this writing, GTK+ 2.8.10 was the most current stable release. GTK+ 2.x offers a much more powerful set of tools than its predecessor. The most significant improvements over GTK+ 1.x are in its text handling and representation abilities and its use of trees and lists. In fact, the main widget for creating editable text in GTK+ 1.x is "broken" and will never be fixed. With the version 2 branch, working with text is not only simpler, but also gives the developer greater control over how the text looks and acts within the application. The latest offering also makes manipulating individual elements of trees, lists, and tables less cumbersome than before. GTK+ 2.x gives the developer greater control over atomic pieces of data that make up an application. When combined with the advanced object model of PHP 5, GTK+ 2.x gives you a very powerful tool that is remarkably easy to use.

What Is PHP-GTK?

Simply put, PHP-GTK is a PHP wrapper for the GTK library. It allows the creation of stand-alone GUI applications written in PHP. PHP-GTK makes it possible to call the GTK library functions from the context of a PHP script by creating PHP classes and methods that hook into the native C code at runtime. That sounds pretty complicated, so how about this for an answer: you can create windows, buttons, text, images, and other objects on the screen using PHP. In more traditional PHP applications, the task of presentation falls on HTML and a web browser. With PHP-GTK, it is possible to create stand-alone applications that do not need support from other pieces of software, such as the PHP-GTK manual browser shown in Figure 1-3.

The presentation layer of an application is handled entirely by PHP, just like the rest of the application. This isn't to say that your presentation layer needs to be tied to your business logic, just that the same engine takes care of both tasks. PHP-GTK 2, the version this book focuses on, combines the power of GTK+ 2.6 with the ease of programming and advanced object model of PHP 5.1. Listing 1-2 gives you a quick look at the syntax needed for creating a PHP-GTK application.

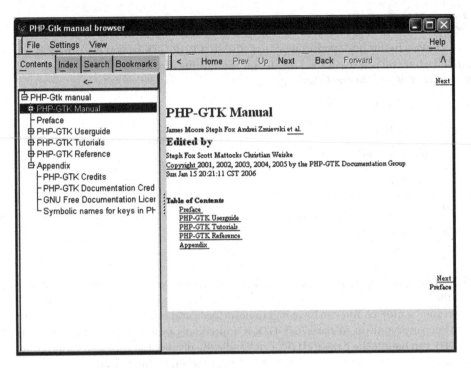

Figure 1-3. *A PHP-GTK documentation browser*

Listing 1-2. *A Simple PHP-GTK Application*

```php
<?php
$window = new GtkWindow();
$window->connect_object('destroy', array('gtk', 'main_quit'));

$dateTime = new GtkLabel(date('Y-m-d H:i:s'));

$window->add($dateTime);
$window->show_all();
gtk::main();
?>
```

While the ability to create objects on the screen is a nice feature of PHP-GTK, the ability to interact with those objects supplies the real power. PHP-GTK allows you to define specific actions that should take place in response to user events. This makes your applications more than just pretty sets of data. It makes them functional. Being able to click buttons, drag objects, and cut and paste text are the things that differentiate your application from just a PNG or a JPEG image. PHP-GTK frees the typical PHP developer from the confines of the Web. It allows interaction that a website just can't offer. You can do a lot of great things with a website and PHP, but there are some things that are better suited for a desktop application.

Why Use PHP-GTK?

Now that you have a better understanding of exactly what PHP-GTK is, you are probably asking yourself what you can use it for. The answer is anything and everything. I've seen PHP-GTK applications such as the following:

- Content management system (CMS) tools

- Documentation browsers

- Internet relay chat (IRC) clients

- Network monitors

- News feed viewers

- Statistical analysis

- Text editors

The list goes on and on. For instance, if you don't like the way your web browser handles bookmarks, then create your own web browser. You can create a special calendar application for your open source project. You can have it grab news feeds and important dates from a central server to keep everyone up-to-date. PHP-GTK is limited only by the technologies on which it is built. If PHP can handle the data and GTK can handle the display, then you can create your application with PHP-GTK. I have yet to think of a situation where either fell short.

Of course, PHP-GTK is not always the right tool for the job, but it does expand the range of possibilities for PHP and PHP developers. When someone approaches you with a problem, such as collecting product registration information from thousands of users all over the world, you probably say, "Easy, get yourself a website, a database, and a short PHP script." But if someone were to say, "I need to be able to enter maintenance data in the field and create custom invoices on the fly," the typical PHP programmer may respond with, "OK. Go talk to that guy." A programmer with PHP-GTK in his programming toolbox will say, "No problem. Come back this time tomorrow." Alright, maybe not tomorrow, but you get my point. PHP-GTK makes PHP and PHP developers more versatile.

PHP-GTK lets you accomplish tasks that you can't do with PHP alone. A normal PHP application is based on a send-and-response system. The user sends some data, and then the PHP script does something with the data and responds with a new page. Some may argue that PHP-GTK also uses this send-wait-receive method, and I can see how they might come to that conclusion. But they are missing one important part. The user doesn't have to be involved. The application itself can do some work and change the presentation itself. There is no need for the user to make any request. By clicking a button, the user can start some data processing in action. The user is then free to go and do some other task. When the system is finished processing the data, it can trigger an event that notifies the user, start some other process, or even close the application.

Another reason to use PHP-GTK comes from PHP itself. PHP is remarkably simple to learn and easy to code. Take a look at Listing 1-3. In five lines of code, I have loaded the extension, created a window, set up the window for a clean shutdown, and displayed the window.

Listing 1-3. *A Simple Application in PHP-GTK*

```php
<?php
$window = new GtkWindow();
$window->connect_object('destroy', array('gtk', 'main_quit'));
$window->show();
gtk::main();
?>
```

Now take a look at Listing 1-4. This does the same exact thing but it is written in Java using the Swing package. The Java Swing example takes twice as many lines of code, plus the naming conventions are restricted. In my opinion, PHP-GTK is one of the cleanest and easiest to write languages around for making desktop applications.

Listing 1-4. *A Simple Application in Java Swing*

```java
import javax.swing.*;
public class listing1_4 {
    public static void createAndShowGUI() {
        JFrame frame = new JFrame();
        frame.setDefaultCloseOperation(JFrame.EXIT_ON_CLOSE);

        frame.setVisible(true);
    }

    public static void main(String[] args) {
        javax.swing.SwingUtilities.invokeLater(
        createAndShowGUI();

        );
        createAndShowGUI();
    }
}
```

PHP-GTK is a powerful tool, but it isn't perfectly suited for everything. Before spending a lot of time developing your application, make sure PHP-GTK is really what you need. If it isn't obvious by looking at your problem whether a desktop application is the best solution, ask yourself a few simple questions:

- Does the application need to work without the aid of another application such as a web browser?

- Does the application need to be able to listen for and react to events from sources other than the primary user?

- Does the application need to be run directly on the user's computer?

If you answered no to all of these questions, then a desktop application may not be the best solution for your problem.

Even after deciding that you do need to develop a desktop application, you should make sure that PHP-GTK is the best language to use. There are several other scripting language wrappers for the GTK library, such as PyGTK (http://www.pygtk.org/) and Ruby-GNOME2 (http://ruby-gnome2.sourceforge.jp/). There are also other graphical libraries all together. As I already mentioned, you could use Java Swing. You could also use Mozilla's XUL.

Why do I use PHP-GTK? Because I am a PHP guy. I can write PHP code quickly and easily. You may be better at writing Java code. By all means, use the language that you feel most comfortable with. If you stick around though, I will show you how easy it can be to create some pretty neat pieces of software without too much struggle.

Further Resources

Before wrapping up this chapter, I want to make you aware of some other resources that can help you write and debug your code. First and foremost there is the PHP-GTK website (http://gtk.php.net/). Here, you will find the online API documentation. The documentation describes every class and every function that exists in PHP-GTK. If you need to know which parameters are optional for a given method, this is the place to go.

You will also find a wiki with some helpful tips and code snippets contributed by PHP-GTK users from all over the world. The wiki also lists several sites dedicated to PHP-GTK that are in languages other than English.

If you have trouble finding your answers directly on the site, take a look at the Resources section. There, you will find the next great tool, the PHP-GTK general mailing list. Please don't ever hesitate to ask a question on this list. The worst thing that can happen is that someone might send you a link to a previous thread that discusses the issue.

Another good place to turn for help is some of the regular PHP publications. Every so often, *PHP | Architect* or *PHP Magazine* will publish an article relating to PHP-GTK. These are usually aimed at entry PHP-GTK programmers to help people get started with GUI programming.

There are also several places online to find PHP-GTK code. One of the best resources, along with the PHP-GTK wiki, is PEAR (http://pear.php.net). PEAR is a repository of high-quality, well-documented PHP code. Few people realize that PEAR has several PHP-GTK classes. Later in this book, we will take a look at some of these classes that can make your life a little easier. It doesn't get much easier than installing a class and being all set to go.

If you want some hard copy to read over, I recommend *Beginning PHP 5 and MySQL 5: From Novice to Professional, Second Edition* by W. Jason Gilmore (Apress, 2006) and *GTK+ Programming in C* by Syd Logan (Prentice Hall, 2001).

Summary

Let's recap what we have talked about so far. PHP-GTK is a powerful tool for creating stand-alone GUI applications that can make presenting and interacting with data quick and easy. PHP-GTK allows you to create applications that not only have excellent presentations, but also listen for and react to user actions. PHP-GTK is capable of listening for actions because it is a combination of the PHP language wrapped around the GTK library. The GTK library allows you to create and interact with images on the screen. While PHP-GTK is an excellent choice for some developers, it isn't the only choice. Many other technologies are available for creating GUI applications.

In walking through the development of a pretty complicated product inventory management system for our fictional company, you will learn about all the tools that are available to a developer and we will discuss which tools are best in which situations.

The next chapter talks about getting everything ready to start developing with PHP-GTK. It covers installation and setup of all the software needed. It starts with GTK and PHP, and then discusses downloading and installing the needed PEAR and PECL (`http://pecl.php.net`) packages.

CHAPTER 2

■ ■ ■

Installing PHP-GTK

Before getting too involved in trying to understand how PHP-GTK works, it would be a good idea to install it first. Installing PHP-GTK can be a tricky process because of all the different pieces that make up the PHP-GTK extension. First, you need to install GTK, then PHP, then PHP-GTK, and, finally, all of the classes and extensions you will need for your application. For Windows users, most of what you need comes packed in the downloadable binary file. For Linux users, it may be a little more difficult to find all of the necessary packages.

Prerequisites

Aside from PHP-GTK and its supporting packages, you need to set up a few other items before the application is ready to go.

First, you will need some sort of development environment where you can edit files, install new software, and basically have run of the file system. The development environment should also have access to the Internet. As your product inventory management system (PIMS) application starts to take form, you will want to test it. To do a full test, you will need to send and receive data over HTTP and FTP.

You will also need access to a relational database. You will be creating tables and manipulating data, so make sure you have the correct permissions. Which database system you use is up to you, because you will be using PEAR::DB (http://pear.php.net/DB/), a database abstraction layer, which supports a wide range of database implementations. I prefer to use PostgreSQL (http://www.postgresql.org/), but feel free to use any other database supported by PEAR::DB.

Last, but certainly not least, you will need a text editor or an integrated development environment (IDE). Several options are available, and publicly endorsing one over another is never a good idea. Emacs and vi usually come standard on most Linux distributions, and WordPad usually does the trick on Windows systems. If you prefer an IDE, you might use Eclipse or Zend Studio. Of course, there is also Tulip, which is written in PHP-GTK, as you saw in Chapter 1.

With all of these requirements satisfied, you are now ready to install PHP-GTK.

Installing PHP-GTK 2 on Windows

As I mentioned at the beginning of this chapter, installing PHP-GTK on Windows is very simple. Everything you need to get PHP-GTK up and running is all in one downloadable file.

Even if you don't have PHP installed on your machine, you'll be fine. The Windows version of PHP-GTK comes with PHP included. Thanks to the work of Frank Kromann and Steph Fox, all you need to do is download the precompiled binaries from the PHP-GTK website (http://gtk.php.net/) and unzip the files to the proper location. If PHP 5 is already installed on your computer, you should already have a c:\php5 directory. If not, you should create that directory. After downloading and unpacking the files, simply copy the \php5 directory of the zip file to the c:\php5 directory.

The last step in installing PHP-GTK on Windows is setting up the php.ini file. If PHP was not previously installed on your machine, you can just copy \winnt\php.ini to c:\php5. If, on the other hand, PHP (4 or 5) was installed, before adding the PHP-GTK files, be sure to back up the php.ini, and don't be so quick to copy things. Blindly replacing the php.ini file will erase any specific configuration changes that were made to your original php.ini file.

Depending on how you typically use PHP, it may be a good idea to keep two separate INI files to allow for different settings for web applications and desktop applications. For instance, you may want to log PHP-GTK errors in a different file than web application errors. If you decide to use only one php.ini file, be careful not to overwrite any changes in the original file. The \winnt directory contains a php.ini-gtk file that has only the configuration directives related to PHP-GTK. It is usually safe to append these directives to an existing php.ini file.

Once you have all of the files copied into the right place, you should try running a few tests. Copy the \demos directory from the PHP-GTK zip file to the \php5 directory on your hard drive and run the following command:

```
$> c:\php5\php c:\php5\demos\phpgtk2-demo.php
```

Tip The preceding command should be entered at a command-line prompt. To bring up the command-line prompt, click the Start button and then select Run. In the window that pops up, type cmd, and then press Enter. This will bring up a DOS prompt. Type the command in the newly opened DOS and press Enter.

If all goes according to plan, you will see an application that demonstrates several features of PHP-GTK 2, as shown in Figure 2-1.

Note PHP 5.1 comes with a php_win.exe executable. Running PHP or PHP-GTK scripts with this command does not pop up a console or DOS window. This executable can be associated with a particular extension such as .phpw (the w stands for "windowed application"). Associating the executable with an extension makes scripts executable by double-clicking them.

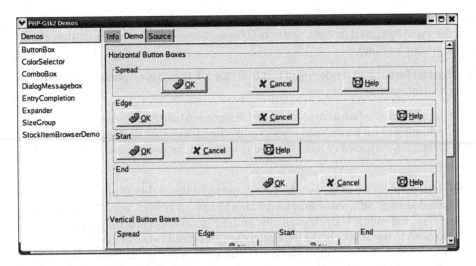

Figure 2-1. *The PHP-GTK demo application*

The next section discusses installation on Linux systems. If you are a Windows user, you can skip to the "Using PEAR and PECL Packages" section.

Installing PHP-GTK 2 on Linux

The first step in getting PHP-GTK running on a Linux system is installing GTK. Most systems these days come with GTK+ 2.*x* already installed. Chances are your system already meets the minimum requirements for PHP-GTK, which is GTK+ 2.6.0.

Before downloading and configuring anything, double-check that your system doesn't already have the necessary files. To verify that you have the right packages and versions, use the pkg-config utility, which comes standard on most Linux distributions. Try running the following command:

```
$> pkg-config --modversion gtk+-2.0
```

If your version number is lower than 2.6.0, you will need to upgrade GTK before you can go any further. If you see something to the effect of "Package gtk+-2.0 was not found . . .", then you'll need to do a complete installation of GTK+ 2.

GTK has several dependencies, each of which must be installed before you can get GTK working. Fortunately, there are no major conflicts with the dependencies for PHP-GTK. You will need the following packages:

GNU make: Used to compile the source code into working executables. make uses makefiles, written by the application developers, to determine which pieces of source code need to be compiled and linked together to produce a working application like PHP-GTK. While there are many different versions of make available, GTK installation requires some features of GNU make that may not be available in other versions. See http://www.gnu.org for more information about the GNU Project.

Glib: The base libraries for GTK. Glib provides the interfaces for things such as the object system, the event loop, and threads. See http://www.gtk.org/ for more information about the GIMP Toolkit and Glib.

Pango: Used for layout and rendering of text in GTK+ 2.0. Pango is responsible for font handling and internationalizing text.

ATK: The Accessibility Toolkit, a set of interfaces designed to help applications interact with assistive technologies such as screen readers and alternative input devices. ATK makes it possible for visually impaired or handicapped users to get the most out of a GTK-based application.

A few other dependencies exist, but the vast majority of Linux distributions will have these files installed already. Still, some may be missing from your system. For all of these packages, including GTK, the source is freely available, and the installation process is pretty much the same. If you need to install any of the dependencies, you should start at the top of the list and work your way down. That will avoid any wasted time, since one of the packages may be a dependency for some of the other packages. Once you have downloaded and unpacked the source code, follow the typical installation procedure:

```
$> cd /path/to/package/dir/
$> ./configure
$> make
$> make install
```

Once all the packages are installed, use the pkg-config utility one more time. If everything looks good, you are ready to move to the next step.

PHP-GTK 2 requires a working PHP 5.1+ installation. Installing PHP is very similar to installing GTK, except you need to do a little extra configuration to get things set up right. Start off by downloading and unpacking the source code for PHP 5.1 or higher. Once you have moved to the PHP directory, you can start setting up the configuration.

PHP-GTK requires PHP to be compiled with CLI mode. CLI mode is enabled by default, but some developers also like to explicitly disable CGI mode. Doing so helps to avoid some confusion. If CGI mode is not disabled, two command-line executables will be created: one for command-line scripts, php-cli, and the other for CGI scripts, php-cgi. If CGI is disabled, only one executable will be created, php. Therefore, you need to pass the --disable-cgi option.

Next, add a few extensions you will need for development. For this book's sample application, we will be using the DOM XML extension, some variety of a relational database management system (RDBMS), SOAP, and FTP. When you configure PHP, you need to make sure these features are turned on. You also want to make sure that PEAR gets installed. A few of these options are already set by default, but it doesn't hurt to specify them again. When you configure PHP you need to run the following command:

```
$> ./configure --with-pgsql --enable-soap --disable-cgi --enable-cli ➡
--enable-ftp --enable-dom --with-pear
```

Depending on the results of the configure command, you may need to specify a directory for your RDBMS or PEAR installation. You may also need to specify the location of you LibXML and zlib installations.

To specify the location of a directory, you simply add the directory after the `configure` command. For example, to tell `configure` that PEAR should be installed in `/usr/share`, you pass `--with-pear=/usr/share`. The same can be done for your database or XML or zlib extensions.

Chances are you also want to use this same PHP installation for your web applications. That's not a problem. Just add the `configure` commands for your web server.

Once `configure` has run successfully, continue with the normal build process by running `make` and then `make install`. As usual, you will probably need to have root permissions to run `make install`.

Note Different Linux distributions, package versions, and installation methods can put files in different places. For instance, some systems may have MySQL installed in `/usr/lib/`, while others may have it installed in `/usr/local/lib/`. The `configure` tool is usually pretty good about locating files, but sometimes it may need help finding the files on your particular system. That is why it may be necessary to pass the path to an installation directory or extension, such as `--with-libxml=/usr/lib`.

So you have PHP 5.1 installed and GTK+ 2 ready to go. You can install PHP-GTK now, right? Not exactly. While you could go ahead and install PHP-GTK, the installation would be somewhat limited. Don't misunderstand. You could write some pretty nice applications with a basic installation of PHP-GTK, but that would be like installing PHP without any database functions. To get the most out of your PHP-GTK installation, you also need a few supporting packages. You can install all of these packages using the typical `configure`, `make`, `make install` process. The desired packages include the following:

`Libglade-2.0`: A package to help make designing the layout easier.

`Scintilla`: A powerful text-editing widget.

`GdkPixbuf`: A package for manipulating and drawing images in a GTK-based application.

`GtkHTML`: A widget for displaying HTML like a web browser. GtkHTML has a number of dependencies. Make sure you install all of those first.

Once all of these packages are installed, it's time to install PHP-GTK. As is the process with most installations, first you need to download the sources and unpack them. Make sure you have retrieved the correct version of PHP-GTK. Version 1 will not work with PHP 5 or GTK+ 2.

Building PHP-GTK is slightly different from most Linux installations. After downloading the sources, you would normally run the `configure` command. With PHP-GTK, you must build the `configure` utility first. To do this, run the `buildconf` command. This builds a `configure` utility specifically tailored for your system. Next, run the `configure` command.

If you decided not to install any of the recommended support packages, you will need to turn them off by using `--disable-<feature>`. If you did install these packages, turn them on with `--enable-<feature>`. Next, run `make` and `make install`.

After running these commands, you will need to update the `php.ini` file. PHP must load the PHP-GTK 2 extension so the applications can be run. If you don't update the `php.ini` file, you'll get an error about nonexistent classes, such as `GtkWindow`. Simply add `extension=php_gtk2.so` (or `.dll` for Windows) to the Extensions section of your `php.ini` file. Listing 2-1 shows what the Extensions section looks like and has some simple instructions.

Listing 2-1. *The Extensions Section of php.ini*

```
;;;;;;;;;;;;;;;;;;;;;;;;;
; Dynamic Extensions ;
;;;;;;;;;;;;;;;;;;;;;;;;;
;
; If you wish to have an extension loaded automatically, use the following
; syntax:
;
;    extension=modulename.extension
;
; For example, on Windows:
;
;    extension=msql.dll
;
; ... or under UNIX:
;
;    extension=msql.so
;
; Note that it should be the name of the module only; no directory information
; needs to go here.  Specify the location of the extension with the
; extension_dir directive above.
```

Next, test your installation by running one of the demo applications. You can do this by running the following command:

```
$> php demos/phpgtk2-demo.php
```

Now that you have PHP-GTK up and running, you can install a few supporting packages.

Using PEAR and PECL Packages

Regardless of whether you are using Windows or Linux, the remainder of the installation process is essentially the same. To make your life easier, you are going to use some PEAR packages.

PEAR packages are collections of PHP classes designed to be easily installed, upgraded, and used by a wide range of users. They are aimed at solving a common problem in the best and most general way possible. For instance, PEAR::DB is a PEAR package that allows a developer to change the underlying database for an application without having to change more than one line of code. You may be pondering the frequency in which you might swap out application databases. Frankly, the answer is probably never. But if you're planning on distributing applications to other users, it would be nice to offer users the flexibility of using their database of choice. By using PEAR::DB, you can give users the freedom to use whichever database system they like without requiring them to rewrite any parts of the application. We are going to use PEAR::DB so the code you write will work just as well on a server running MySQL as it will on a server running PostgreSQL. This will help make your applications easier to install and use, because there will be fewer restrictions for the end user.

Aside from providing cross-platform capabilities, many PEAR packages have solved common problems in a very efficient manner. The Gtk_FileDrop package makes it easy to add drag-and-drop functionality to a PHP-GTK driven application. Using this package saves you the trouble of having to reimplement that functionality every time you write an application.

PEAR packages are installed, updated, and removed using the PEAR installer, which is a command-line utility bundled with PHP. Unless you specifically said not to install PEAR during the PHP 5 installation process, you already have the PEAR installer and a few core packages on your system. You can see which packages have been installed by running the following command:

```
$> pear list
```

You'll see a list all of the packages that have been installed from the default channel server, pear.php.net.

A *channel* is a server that offers PEAR-installable packages. To see which packages have been installed from another server, you need to pass -c <channel> after the list command. Just because a package is PEAR-installable doesn't make it an official PEAR package. The only real PEAR packages are those that come from the pear.php.net channel. Channels also have short names to make life a little easier. The short name for pear.php.net is simply pear.

To install a package using the PEAR installer you simply type the following command:

```
$> pear install <channel>/<package_name>
```

Substitute the short or long channel for <channel> and the name of the package for <package_name>. If you are installing a package from your default channel (usually pear), you can leave out <channel>/ and just use the package name.

Installing PEAR Packages

First, make sure that all the current packages are up-to-date. To do this, execute the following command:

```
$> pear upgrade-all
```

This will check for any packages that have new versions and will update them. PEAR packages are updated and released much more frequently than PHP, so there is a good chance that one or more of your PEAR packages will need an upgrade.

Next, install a few additional packages. You will install only two now, but you will install more as the need arises. You'll install the following packages:

Mail_Mime: A package for sending MIME-encoded email. It makes creating and sending complex email messages a breeze. Adding attachments or sending email with HTML and plain text are relatively simple tasks with Mail_Mime.

Console_Getargs: A package designed for letting the user pass command-line arguments. You will be using it to tell your application to start up in certain states or to provide help for the user.

To install these packages, type this:

```
$> pear install -a Mail_Mime
$> pear install -a Console_Getargs
```

You don't need to add the pear channel first because the PEAR installer defaults to the pear channel. The -a flag tells the PEAR installer to also get all of the dependencies and install them. Both of these commands should end with a message similar to this:

```
Install <package_name> ok
```

If you run into any trouble, execute pear help or pear help install for additional help.

Installing PECL Packages

Next, you want to install two PECL (pronounced "pickle") packages. PECL packages are similar to PEAR packages, in that they exist to solve common problems for a wide user base, but they are not PHP code.

PECL packages are PHP extensions (just like PHP-GTK) that are written in C. PECL packages are compiled once and loaded dynamically when PHP is run.

To install the PECL packages, use the PECL installer, which is exactly the same as the PEAR installer, except that it defaults to the PECL channel. The PECL channel is pecl.php.net. Its short name is pecl. Instead of typing pear install pecl/<package_name>, type this:

```
pecl install <package_name>
```

The first package, bcompiler, is used to turn PHP code into bytecode. This will allow your application to run without requiring the user to install PHP first. This means that you can distribute your application without worrying about whether the user has done any setup work. bcompiler can also make your code closed source instead of open source. Many businesses rely on the sale of their software to stay in business. If they cannot protect their source code, their business model will not be very effective.

The next package, pdflib, is a library for creating PDF files on the fly. We will use this package to produce a catalog based on the supplier's inventory information.

To build the packages, execute the following commands:

```
$> pecl install bcompiler
$> pecl install pdflib
```

With these commands, you should see much more output. You will see some configuration messages, and in the end you should see an "Install OK" type message, just as in the PEAR installations.

Running PHP-GTK Applications

You run PHP-GTK applications from the command line. You have already run at least one PHP-GTK program if you ran the demo application to test the installation.

Running a PHP-GTK application is just like running any other PHP command-line script. For Linux systems, simply type the following:

```
$> php <filename>.php
```

For Windows systems, type this:

```
$> c:\php5\php.exe <filename>.php
```

PHP-GTK applications will freeze the console window unless you tell them to run in the background. Usually, you do this by using & after the command.

You'll find several demo applications in the /demos directory. Give them a try so you can get a feel for how PHP-GTK programs are run, what they typically look like, and how users interact with them.

Summary

This chapter was rather short, because there really isn't too much to the PHP-GTK installation process. You may have heard horror stories about people fighting with PHP-GTK for days before getting it to install right, but those stories are about PHP-GTK 1. With that version, installation was difficult at best. With PHP-GTK 2 those problems have largely been resolved and installation is much simpler.

Installation of the dependencies and supporting packages is also pretty straightforward. Of course, there are a lot of configuration options you can set and plenty of customization, but not all of that is necessary to get a smooth-running PHP-GTK 2 installation.

Now that everything is up and running, we can start looking at what makes PHP-GTK work the way it does. Chapter 3 describes the basic building blocks of PHP-GTK. You will learn about the base classes and how all of these classes interact with each other. Once you understand how the pieces of your application interact with each other, you can look at how they interact with the user.

Understanding PHP-GTK Basics

In the previous chapter, you installed and tested a PHP-GTK environment, setting the stage for writing some code. However, before rushing into creating an application, you should understand the basic relationships between PHP-GTK classes.

PHP-GTK is a complex hierarchy of classes. If you want to understand why your Save As window isn't showing up properly, you need to know what its base classes are doing.

Inheritance isn't the only relationship in PHP-GTK. Classes can be wrappers around other classes; some classes will have instances of another class as properties; and other classes may exist only to manipulate other objects. It is important to know how these classes interact, because changing one object can have a profound effect on many others.

PHP-GTK defines many class families, which are based on the libraries that the classes hook into. The two most important families from a developer's standpoint are Gdk and Gtk. The Gdk family of classes consists of low-level classes that interact very closely with the windowing system. These classes are responsible for displaying windows and showing colors on the screen.

The Gtk family is a grouping of higher-level objects. These objects represent application components such as text, menus, or buttons.

The Gtk classes will often contain one or more Gdk classes as members. Although it does happen, it is rare that a developer works directly with a Gdk class. In most cases, manipulation of a Gdk instance is done through a Gtk class. The Gtk classes are the ones that create and manage the pieces of an application that you are used to seeing. If Gtk is the movie star of PHP-GTK, Gdk is the personal assistant. Gdk does half of the work, while Gtk gets all of the attention.

Widgets and Objects

The Gtk family tree starts with one class: GtkObject. Every class in the Gtk family extends GtkObject. Some classes extend directly from GtkObject, while others are grandchild classes. Members of the Gtk family can basically be broken into two major groups: objects and widgets.

The GtkObject Class

GtkObject defines a few basic methods and declares a few signals (We'll talk more about signals in the next chapter; for now, just keep in mind that a signal is used to let PHP-GKT know that some important event has occurred). Having one base class is nice not only for the GTK developers, but also for the users. We know that any class we instantiate that extends from GtkObject will have these few methods that we can call when needed.

Let's take a look at what the class definition for this object might look like if it were written in PHP. Then we can talk about how it works and what role it plays in our development. Take a look at Listing 3-1.

Listing 3-1. *Definition of GtkObject*

```php
<?php
class GtkObject {

    private $flags;
    private $refCounter;

    public function destroy()
    {
        unset($this);
    }

    public function flags()
    {
        return $this->flags;
    }

    public function set_flags($flags)
    {
        $this->flags = $this->flags | $flags;
    }

    public function sink()
    {
        if (--$this->refCounter < 1) {
            $this->destroy();
        }
    }

    public function unset_flags($flags)
    {
        $this->flags = $this->flags & ~$flags;
    }
}
?>
```

As you can see, the class defines a handful of public methods. These public methods are available to all other classes in the Gtk family. Just because they are available, however, doesn't mean that you will ever use them. Most of the methods defined by GtkObject are used primarily by PHP-GTK itself. We will still take a closer look at them, though, because it is important to know why PHP-GTK calls them.

The destroy Method

The destroy method is probably the only GtkObject method you will ever call explicitly in your code. It does exactly what you would expect: destroys the object. This method will be overridden by some classes that extend GtkObject.

Some classes, known as *containers*, exist just to group other objects logically and visually. When you destroy a container, it will destroy all of the objects it contains. For instance, destroying the main window of your application will basically delete every class in your application.

The sink Method

The destroy method is called by PHP-GTK when an object is no longer needed. Determining when an object is no longer needed (or wanted) is done in two ways.

The first way is by tracking the reference counter. The reference counter is the number of objects (including the object itself) that reference a given object. When the reference counter hits zero, it pretty much means that no one cares about the object anymore. Since no one cares, PHP-GTK destroys the object. This type of action is pretty rare. The reference counter is maintained using the sink method. Calling the sink method decrements the reference counter. Usually, PHP-GTK does this during the execution of an application. Incrementing the counter is always done by PHP-GTK. There is no method for "unsinking" an object.

The other way PHP-GTK knows that an object isn't needed is when someone or something tells it to kill the object. For example, let's say an instance of class A contains an instance of class B. When you destroy the class A instance, you no longer need the class B instance. While object A is in the process of deconstructing, it is going to tell PHP-GTK to get rid of the class B instance. Another example is when the user clicks the *x* in the upper-right corner of a window. That tells your application that the user is finished using it. Under most circumstances, the application will shut down. It does this by destroying the main window. When the main window is destroyed, it destroys everything contained within it.

The flags, set_flags, and unset_flags Methods

The flags, set_flags, and unset_flags methods do exactly what their names suggest: they return, set, and unset flags associated with an object, respectively. Flags are used to track object attributes, such as whether or not the object is visible, or whether or not it can accept drag-and-drop objects. They offer a simple way to track object properties without using a lot of memory.

If you wanted to know the current status of an object, you could call the flags method and compare the result to some known state. In practice, though, you probably won't ever use this method. Similarly, you probably won't use the set_flags or unset_flags method either. In fact, setting the flags doesn't mean you have changed any object properties. Setting or unsetting flag values will likely just confuse your application.

On the other hand, PHP-GTK will use these methods. Before it does any operation that requires the object to be in a certain state, such as displaying the object on the screen, it will compare the current set of flags. If they aren't right, PHP-GTK will call the method needed to get the object in the right state. For instance, before a button can be shown on the screen, it must be inside a window. PHP-GTK uses the flags method to quickly check if the button is ready to go. Any method that changes an object's state will call set_flags or unset_flags as needed. The parameter that is passed to set_flags and unset_flags is an integer, and it's used to change the value of the object flags through bitwise operations. PHP-GTK will call set_flags when you show or realize an object. PHP-GTK will call `unset_flags` when you hide that object later. Before PHP-GTK does either of these operations, it will check the flags, using the `flags` method, to verify whether it actually needs to do any work.

The object flags allow PHP-GTK to quickly and easily manage object properties. These few simple methods are integral to being able to control and manipulate all of the classes that inherit from `GtkObject`.

Objects

Objects are the classes that extend directly from `GtkObject` and their children, except for `GtkWidget` and classes that extend from it, as described in the next section.

Objects are usually considered helper classes. They don't have any visual components that can be shown on the screen. A buffer for holding and manipulating text is an example of an object.

Objects cannot receive direct user interactions. Since they have no visual components, there is nothing for the user to click on or select.

Objects typically store data such as number ranges or text. They are used to encapsulate data and provide a consistent interface for manipulating that data. It is much easier to pass around a bundle of numbers than it is to pass around several numbers while trying to keep them organized.

Widgets

Widgets are classes that extend from `GtkWidget` (which extends from `GtkObject`). Widgets technically are objects because they inherit from `GtkObject`, but they deserve special treatment in the world of GTK.

Widgets are objects with visual representations and can react to user input. Widgets are the classes you are familiar with through your use of GUI applications. A button is a widget, as are labels, menus, and windows. Widgets are the objects with which your application's users will be directly interacting. They can listen for interaction events, such as user clicks, resizing, and even dragging and dropping.

Widgets can be shown or hidden. They can be given keyboard focus or have it taken away. You can also control the look and feel of an individual widget or all widgets of a certain type.

Widgets and objects need each other to make an application work. Data that no one can see or interact with isn't very useful. A button that doesn't have a label or change any data doesn't do much good either. Widgets and objects must work together to make a successful application.

Widgets, being visual objects, can be shown on the screen. This isn't always what you want, though, and it isn't how they start. For instance, you may not want a button to show up until the user enters some data in a text field. You don't have to show the button until you are ready. To help you manage what is shown and what isn't, widgets have three basic states: *realized*, *unrealized*, and *shown*. These three states represent the visual status of a widget, and we'll take a closer look at them here.

■**Note** I apologize for the confusing naming conventions. It is true that all widgets are objects, but they are a special and quite large subset of objects. Keep in mind that when I refer to *objects* in PHP-GTK, I am talking about those classes that do not inherit from GtkWidget.

The Realized State

A realized widget is a widget that has valid window and allocation properties. It isn't yet visible on the screen, but it is ready to be shown. The window property of a widget is a GdkWindow instance. Remember that the Gdk classes are the ones that actually take care of the visual representations on the screen. The allocation property, an instance of the GdkAllocation class, holds the location and dimensions of a widget. It has value for the x and y coordinates, and the height and width of the widget. The window and allocation properties are responsible for telling PHP-GTK how the widget is going to be displayed and where.

The realized state may also be called the *hidden* state. This is because it is pretty similar to a widget in the shown state, but it just isn't shown on the screen. Only realized widgets can be shown. Fortunately, the GtkWidget base class is smart enough to realize a widget before you try to show it.

Listing 3-2 shows how you can move from one state to another.

Listing 3-2. *Changing Widget States*

```php
<?php
$widget = new GtkWindow();

// If you try to grab the window before realizing
// the object, you will get nothing.
var_dump($widget->window);
var_dump($widget->flags());

$widget->realize();

// Now that the widget is realized, you can grab
// the window property.
var_dump($widget->window);
var_dump($widget->flags());

$widget->show();

// Showing and hiding a widget changes the value
// of its flags.
var_dump($widget->flags());

$widget->hide();
```

```
var_dump($widget->flags());

$widget->unrealize();

// Now that the widget is realized, you can grab
// the window property.
var_dump($widget->window);
var_dump($widget->flags());
?>
```

Some appropriately named methods help you change a widget's state. The realize method tells PHP-GTK to make room in memory for the widget, because you plan on showing it soon. If you call the realize method of a widget, the widget will be moved into the realized state but will be hidden; that is, PHP-GTK will assign it a valid GdkWindow and GdkAllocation. The widget will not be displayed on the screen, though.

We talked earlier about how widgets may be members of other widgets and how the destroy method can affect those members. The realize method can also have an effect on widgets other than the calling widget. A widget cannot be realized until its parent widget is realized. If you think about it logically, there is pretty good reason for this. Realizing a widget tells you where it will be on the screen. But how can you know where it will be if you don't know where its parent will be? If you try to realize a widget whose parent hasn't yet been realized, PHP-GTK will help you out by realizing that parent also. It will do this recursively, all the way up to the top-level widget, which is usually a window.

In most applications, the realize method doesn't need to be called directly. The exception is when you need to know where a widget will be on the screen or how much space it will take up before it is displayed. For instance, say you wanted to print the dimensions of an image as a caption. Before the image is displayed on the screen, you can get its size and location by calling the realize method and then checking the value of its allocation property.

The Unrealized State

When you first create a widget, it is unrealized. *Unrealized* means that no memory has been allocated for the visual parts of the widget. The unrealized widget doesn't have a size, and it doesn't have a position. The most important thing to know about an unrealized widget is that it doesn't have a valid value for its window property. As noted in the previous example of printing the dimensions of an image as a caption, you cannot get those dimensions from an unrealized object.

Just as there is a realize method, there is an unrealize method. Calling unrealize removes the widgets window and allocation properties. If a widget is shown when unrealize is called, it will first be hidden, and then unrealized.

Just like the realize method, the unrealize method has an effect on widgets other than the calling widget. If a widget that is unrealized has children, they will be unrealized, too. The positioning and size information are no longer relevant if the parent doesn't contain any position or size information. These rules do not apply in reverse, however. Realizing a parent does not realize the child, just as unrealizing the child does not unrealize the parent.

Look at the simple example in Listing 3-3. It shows how realizing and unrealizing have a recursive effect on multiple widgets.

Listing 3-3. *Recursively Realizing and Unrealizing Widgets*

```php
<?php
$window = new GtkWindow();
var_dump($window->window);
var_dump($window->flags());

$button = new GtkButton();
$window->add($button);

$button->realize();
var_dump($window->window);
var_dump($window->flags());

$window->unrealize();
var_dump($button->window);
var_dump($button->flags());
?>
```

First, we show the window in its initial unrealized state. Then, after adding a button and realizing the button, we check the window's state again. The presence of a window property is evidence that the window has been realized, even though we didn't call the realize method explicitly. Next, we show the button in its realized state, and then unrealize the window. When we try to view the button's window property again, it is gone.

The Shown State

To arrive at the shown state, all you need to do is call the show method of a widget. If the widget hasn't yet been realized, PHP-GTK will realize the widget first.

When you no longer want the widget to be shown, you can call the hide method. That will move the widget back to the realized or hidden state. The widget will still have its window and allocation properties, but will not be displayed on the screen.

Showing or hiding a widget doesn't have quite the same recursive effect that realizing a widget does. If you show a widget whose parent has not been shown, nothing seems to happen. The parent isn't realized, and neither is the child. PHP-GTK will queue up this request and show the widget when the parent is ready.

Try changing the realize call in Listing 3-3 to a call to show. You will see that the window property of our window object is still null. If you then change the unrealize call to show, you will see that the window property for both the window and the button will be objects. Also try showing the window without showing the button. That will demonstrate that showing widgets is not recursive. The button is not shown unless you call show explicitly for the button; that is, unless you use the show_all method.

The show_all method shows the calling widget, and then recursively shows all of the widget's children. The corollary to the show_all method is the hide_all method. Calling hide_all will hide the calling widget and all of its children recursively. Keep in mind that hide and hide_all are just moving the widget back to the realized state. They are not unrealizing the widgets. The widget will still have its window and allocation properties.

Parents and Children

We've been talking a lot about parent widgets and child widgets, but we haven't given this relationship much attention. As you have seen from the previous examples, the parent-child relationship is very important to any application. Making changes to a parent can have effects that trickle down to many other pieces of the application. Understanding the implications of making a change will save you countless hours of debugging.

In the parent-child relationship, a widget that has another widget as a member is a *parent*. A widget that is a member of another is a *child*. The parent doesn't just provide a place for the child to hang out while waiting for the code to be executed. The parent provides a visual context in which the child will appear. In some cases, the child widget exists only to assist the parent with some critical function. The nodes of a tree, for instance, exist only to represent data in the tree and don't have a use elsewhere. Without the nodes, the tree would be useless. Without the tree, the nodes would be unorganized and be almost impossible to manage.

Containers

While most widgets may be children, a few widgets may be parents. Only those widgets that extend from the GtkContainer class may be parents. These widgets are called *containers*, of which there are many types. Here are a few examples:

- Bin containers, such as GtkWindow, GtkFrame, and GtkButton, can have only one child at a time.

- Box containers, such as GtkHBox and GtkVBox, display their children one after the other in a given direction.

- Special containers, like GtkTable and GtkTree, manage their children in unique ways, such as rows and columns for tables and nodes for trees.

How a container manages its children is often a function of how the container is used. GtkWindow, for instance, is designed to provide a window for all the other widgets in the application. It isn't designed for laying out or organizing any data. Because of this, it accepts only one child. It relies on the addition of a widget designed specifically to control the layout.

The GtkWindow class extends the GtkBin class. GtkBin is a specialized class for all containers that accept only one child. Any class that inherits from GtkBin is known as a *bin*. If you try to add two children to a bin, you get a warning message. Try executing Listing 3-4 by saving the code to a file, and then running php filename.php. If you try running the example with a GtkHBox instance instead of a GtkWindow instance, you won't see the warning.

Listing 3-4. *Adding Two Children to a Bin*

```php
<?php
$window = new GtkWindow();
$window->add(new GtkButton());
$window->add(new GtkButton());
/*
 Prints a warning:
 Gtk-WARNING **: Attempting to add a widget with type GtkButton to a
 GtkWindow, but as a GtkBin subclass a GtkWindow can only contain one
```

```
widget at a time; it already contains a widget of type GtkButton
*/
?>
```

The number of children that a container may have varies depending on the role of the container. But the number of parents a widget may have is much more controlled.

Top-Level and Parent Widgets

A widget either may not have any parents or it may have one. Widgets that cannot have a parent are called *top-level widgets*. GtkWindow is a top-level widget, because it doesn't make sense to put a window inside another widget. A window provides a framework for the application. Putting a window inside another widget would be like putting your garage inside your car.

If a widget is not a top-level widget, it may have one and only one parent. Remember that the parent not only keeps the children organized, but also provides a visual context for the child. If a widget had two parents, it wouldn't know where to show up. If you try to assign two parents to a widget, as shown in Listing 3-5, a rather informative message will be printed to the terminal. The message tells you exactly what you did wrong. You can't put a widget directly into a container while it is still inside another container. You can, however, put the first container into the second with the child still in it, because each widget will still have only one parent.

Listing 3-5. *Trying to Give a Widget Two Parents*

```
<?php
// Create some containers.
$window = new GtkWindow();
$frame  = new GtkFrame();
// Create our test widget.
$button = new GtkButton('Button');

// Try giving the widget two parents.
$window->add($button);
$frame->add($button);

/*
Prints a warning message:
 Gtk-WARNING **: Attempting to add a widget with type GtkButton to a
 container of type GtkFrame, but the widget is already inside a
 container of type GtkWindow, the GTK+ FAQ at http://www.gtk.org/faq/
 explains how to reparent a widget.
*/
?>
```

Adding a widget to a container doesn't mean that the widget is stuck there, as you'll learn next.

Adding and Removing Widgets

Containers and widgets have some handy methods to help you move widgets into and out of containers. Some are specialized for the container type, and we will cover those in later chapters. For now, we will look at the methods that come with the base GtkContainer, GtkBin, and GtkWidget classes.

The add, remove, and reparent Methods

You have already seen one of the methods for adding a child in some of the previous examples. The appropriately named add method will take a widget and make it a child of the container. add is a method of the base class GtkContainer. Because it is part of the base class, it needs to be very generic. add doesn't worry about placement or positioning; it simply puts the widget into the container. It is up to the classes that extend GtkContainer to worry about positioning and ordering. We will go into much more detail about how to lay out children inside a container in Chapter 6.

The equally well-named remove method will remove a given widget from the container. For both of these methods, you need to know the container and the widget that you want to add or remove. With adding, obviously, you need to know which widget you want to add, but removing may be different. You may just want to remove a bin's child so that you can put something else in that container.

Containers have a children method that returns the children of the container in an array. There is also a get_children method which has the same result. Bins have an extra method for getting the child. Since a bin can have only one child, it is kind of silly to return an array. You can use the get_child method to return the container's child widget. Once you know what is in the container, you can then remove its contents.

If you just want to move a widget from one container to another, you don't have to go through the process of removing the widget from one container and adding it to the other. There is a neat little helper method that makes changing the widget's parent, or "reparenting" the widget, a simple one-step process. The reparent method removes the widget from its current parent container and adds it to the container that you pass as the method's only parameter. reparent does all of the dirty work for you behind the scenes.

Tip If your container is a bin, you can also add a child using the set_child method. For bins, add and set_child do the same thing, so I usually just stick with add all of the time to avoid confusion.

Let's take a look at how you can control the parent-child relationship with container methods. Listing 3-6 is a simple script that demonstrates the use of add, remove, and reparent.

Listing 3-6. *Adding and Removing Widgets from a Container*

```php
<?php
function testForParent($widget)
{
        $parent = $widget->get_parent();

        echo 'The ' . get_class($widget) . ' has ';
        if (isset($parent)) {
                echo 'a ' . get_class($parent);
        } else {
                echo 'no';
        }
```

```
        echo " parent.\n";
}

// Start with three widgets.
$window = new GtkWindow();
$frame  = new GtkFrame('I am a frame');
$button = new GtkButton("I'm a button");

testForParent($button);

$frame->add($button)
testForParent($button);

// What if we want the button to be added directly to
// the window?
$frame->remove($button);
$window->add($button);
testForParent($button);

// Now switch it back to the frame.
$button->reparent($frame);
testForParent($button);
?>
```

The function at the top, testForParent, is used to show which type of container is the parent of the widget that is passed in. You might use a method like this to figure out what role a widget is playing in your application. Say you have a method that changes a label's text. You may want to know if the label is just text from the application or is part of a button. If it is part of a button, you may want to shorten the text that you set for the label. It prints out a simple message that tells the class of the widget you are testing and the class of its parent, if it has one. In the rest of the script, we use this function to report the parent information every time we add, remove, or reparent a widget.

When you run the script, you will see that the button starts off with no parent. This is what you would expect, since we did the first test immediately after creating the button. Next, we call the frame's add method and pass in the button. When we test for the parent this time, the function tells us that the button has a frame for a parent. After removing the button from the frame and adding it to the window, we test again. This time, as expected, the button's parent is a window object. Finally, we add the button back to the frame using the reparent method. The test again shows that the frame is the button's parent.

Notice that when we moved the button to the window, we had to first remove it from the frame. In this simple example, it isn't that big of a deal, because we know which container is the button's parent. In a real-world situation, you probably won't know which container is the widget's parent. You would probably need to use a function similar to testForParent, which returns the parent container. Using reparent, all we needed to do was pass in the new parent container. PHP-GTK took care of tracking down the old parent and removing the widget first.

The set_parent and unparent Methods

Adding a widget to a container using the add method isn't the only way to accomplish the task. A few methods that belong to widget can be used to create a parent-child relationship.

Calling set_parent and passing the container has a similar effect to calling the container's add method and passing the widget. It adds the calling widget as a child of the container. Similarly, the unparent method will remove a child widget from its container. The unparent method doesn't need any parameters, because a widget can have only one parent.

These widget methods for controlling the parent-child relationship should be used with caution. While it is true that they have the same effect on the widget, they also have some side effects that can make debugging difficult. If you use set_parent to set a widget's parent, trying to remove the widget from the container using the container's remove method will not work. If you use add to assign a widget to a container, calling unparent will not work.

In short, if you set a widget's parent with a widget method, you must remove the widget from the container with a widget method. If you use a container method to add the widget, you must use a container method to remove the widget. However, there is an exception to the rule. In Listing 3-6, we used reparent to move the button back into the frame. reparent is really just a shortcut method for calling remove on the widget's parent container and then adding it to the new container. Since reparent uses the container methods internally, you can't use it when you have used set_parent.

Listing 3-7 is a reworked version of Listing 3-6. It uses set_parent and unparent instead of add and remove. At the end, there is a call to reparent.

Listing 3-7. *Using set_parent and unparent*

```php
<?php
function testForParent($widget)
{
        $parent = $widget->get_parent();

        echo 'The ' . get_class($widget) . ' has ';
        if (isset($parent)) {
                echo 'a ' . get_class($parent);
        } else {
                echo 'no';
        }
        echo " parent.\n";
}

// Start with three widgets.
$window = new GtkWindow();
$frame  = new GtkFrame('I am a frame');
$button = new GtkButton("I'm a button");

testForParent($button);

$button->set_parent($frame)
testForParent($button);
```

```
// What if we want the button to be added directly to
// the window?
$button->unparent();
$button->set_parent($window);
testForParent($button);
$button->unparent();
testForParent($button);
$button->set_parent($frame);

// This line will throw an error message.
$button->reparent($window);
?>
```

As you can see, the call to reparent will throw an error, saying something to the effect that you are trying to give a widget two parents. Since the button was added using set_parent, when reparent calls the container's remove method, nothing happens. Then when reparent calls add on the new container, PHP-GTK balks, as it should. Under no circumstances can a widget have two parents. Because of this little problem, I recommend that you use only add, remove, and reparent. It will make your life just a little easier.

Summary

PHP-GTK is a well-structured hierarchy. The classes that make up PHP-GTK all have a relationship to one another and all depend on each other to make an application a success. Some classes are designed to organize data (objects); others are created specifically to interact with the user (widgets).

Aside from their class definitions, widgets also relate to each other through a parent-child relationship. Containers provide a context for their child widgets and give them an area in which to be displayed. The parent also plays a key role in whether or not the child is displayed at all. The parent-child relationship is one of the key elements in the makeup of a PHP-GTK application.

In Chapter 4, we will look at another fundamental principle of PHP-GTK: events. We will discuss what exactly an event-driven model is and how it is used in PHP-GTK. We will start to look at how your application will be able to respond to the user's actions. By the end of the next chapter, you will have all of the pieces you need to make a fully interactive application.

CHAPTER 4

■ ■ ■

Handling Events and Signals

Web-based applications operate based on a *request-driven architecture*. The user requests a piece of information, and the application returns it. The request is very specific and deliberate. The user clicks a link, which tells the application, "I want to see the information contained on the pages that this link points to." That's it. That is all a web application can do. With a request-driven architecture, the application cannot do anything until the user submits a properly formatted request.

An *event-driven architecture*, on the other hand, is one that can listen for and react to user events other than simple requests. Event-driven architectures allow an application to do more than simply present information. For instance, an event-driven system can offer fine-grained control over how an application reacts to the user. An event-driven model allows the application to react to events such as mouse clicks, key presses, or even changing the property of a certain object. An event-driven system doesn't even need the user to do anything. It can react to events that it creates itself.

Events and Signals

Using PHP-GTK, you can easily react to user actions, or events. An *event* is just that. It is something that happens. Here are a few examples:

- Pressing a key, a `key-press-event`

- Changing a widget's value, a `value-change` event

- Setting a widget's parent, a `parent-set` event

- Pressing a mouse button, a `button-press-event`

- Releasing a mouse button, a `button-release-event`

Events can be triggered by either the user or the application. The beauty of PHP-GTK is that it will recognize these events and tell you about them by firing a signal.

A *signal* is an indication to your code that something has happened. You can set up your application to let you know when something happens. You can instruct a widget to let you know when a specific action occurred. Your application might say, "Hey, the user hit the Tab key. Didn't you want to do something when that happens?" Then you can check a widget's value, hide a section of the application, or do anything else you want. By listening for events and emitting signals, your application interacts with the user.

Being able to quickly respond to a wide range of events makes PHP-GTK a very powerful tool. It is the last fundamental piece that you need to begin working with PHP-GTK to create interactive, stand-alone applications.

Signal Handlers

To make an application interactive, you not only need to listen for events, but you also need to do something when the event occurs. Knowing that a button was clicked doesn't really accomplish anything unless the code can also perform a specific reaction to the event. Reacting to an event is done by "connecting" a piece of code, either a function or a method, to a signal.

If you connect a method to a signal, that method will be invoked every time the signal is emitted. A method (or function) connected to a signal is known as a *signal handler* or *callback*. A signal handler is the connection between a given method or function and a specific signal emitted from a specific widget. Signal handlers are the key to making an application not only listen for user interactions, but also to making the application react to them.

Interacting with Signal Handlers

Let's look at a simple example that illustrates a signal handler. Listing 4-1 builds on the examples in Chapter 3.

Listing 4-1. *Creating a Signal Handler*

```php
<?php
function setParentFunction($widget)
{
    // Get the widget's parent.
    $parent = $widget->get_parent();

    // Echo a message about the widget.
    echo 'The ' . get_class($widget) . ' has ';

    if (isset($parent)) {
        // Echo the class of the parent widget.
        echo 'a ' . get_class($parent);
    } else {
        // The widget doesn't have a parent.
        echo 'no';
    }
    echo " parent.\n";
}
```

```php
// Start with three widgets.
$window = new GtkWindow();
$frame  = new GtkFrame('I am a frame');
$button = new GtkButton("I'm a button");

// Connect the event to our test function
$button->connect('parent-set', 'setParentFunction');


// Now set some parents.
// Note: I am using set_parent and unparent for example only
// you should always use add/remove/reparent.
$button->set_parent($window);
$button->unparent();
$frame->add($button);


$button->reparent($window);
?>
```

In this listing, we have three widgets. Two of them are containers (a window and a frame), and the other is a button. At the top of the listing is a function that takes a widget as its only argument. This function takes the widget passed in and reports what kind of widget was given and the class of its parent, if it has one. This is pretty simple and shouldn't be too confusing if you understood the concepts presented in the previous chapter. The bottom half of code should also be pretty easy to follow. The last few lines of code simply set, unset, and change the button's parent container.

The important piece for this example is the call to the connect method. The button's connect method is telling PHP-GTK that every time the button's parent changes, we want to call the setParentFunction function. More specifically, we are saying that every time this button emits a parent-set signal—which happens whenever an event occurs that causes the button to be added or removed from a container—we want to call setParentFunction.

When you run the code, you will see that you get five messages providing updates about the button's parent. Sometimes it says the button has a window for a parent; other times it says the button has a frame; and sometimes it says that the button has no parent.

Notice that at no point did we explicitly call setParentFunction anywhere in the code. PHP-GTK called the function for us when it found out that the button's parent had been changed. All we do is set up the signal handler and wait for the correct signal to be emitted.

Before digging into the details of how to create signal handlers, consider another example. This time, instead of the code triggering the event, we will have the user click a button to trigger the event. Listing 4-2 shows the source code. Give it a try and click the button a few times. Each time you click the button, you should see a message telling you that the button was pressed.

Listing 4-2. *Using a Signal Handler to React to User-Triggered Events*

```php
<?php
function buttonPressed($widget)
{
    // Output a simple message indicating which type of widget was clicked.
    echo 'The ' . get_class($widget) . " was clicked.\n";
}
```

```
// Create a new window.
$window = new GtkWindow();
// Create a new button with the lable 'Click Me'.
$button = new GtkButton('Click Me');

// Create a signal handler for the clicked signal.
$button->connect('clicked', 'buttonPressed');
// Set up the window to close cleanly.
$window->connect_simple('destroy', array('Gtk', 'main_quit'));

// Add the button to the window.
$window->add($button);
// Show the window and the button.
$window->show_all();
// Start the main loop.

Gtk::main();
?>
```

Alright, so that is how you interact with signal handlers, but how exactly do you create them?

Creating Signal Handlers

You create signal handlers by using the connect family of methods. The connect methods connect a specific signal to a specific method or function. Listing 4-2 includes two calls to connect methods. The first is to a plain old connect, and the second is to connect_simple. Both methods have the same result, they create a signal handler. However, you can use two other methods to create signal handlers: connect_after and connect_simple_after. All of these methods take the same arguments, but they create the handlers in slightly different ways. Let's take a closer look at each of these methods, so that you will understand the advantages of each method. We will start with the simplest method: connect.

The connect Method

connect creates a signal handler by connecting the event that is passed as the first argument to the function or method that is passed as the second argument. When connect calls the callback, the widget that emitted the signal is automatically passed to the callback.

In both of the examples so far, the function expected a parameter called $widget to be passed in, but we never called the function explicitly, so where did the parameter value come from? It was passed automatically to the callback by PHP-GTK. How does PHP-GTK know which widget emitted the signal? It knows because we connected a specific signal from a specific widget to the callback. In Listing 4-2 it was the clicked signal from the $button instance of the GtkButton class.

You may be wondering, "But if we connected a specific signal from a specific widget, why do we need to pass in the widget that emitted the signal anyway? We already know which widget emitted the signal." For starters, having the widget passed in automatically saves us from having to declare all of the widgets in our application that we want to use in the callback as globals.

Second, one of the basic principles of OO programming is code reuse. We can create one, two, three, or ten thousand signal handlers that all call the same callback method. By passing in the widget that emitted the signal, we have that widget there ready to be worked on, and we can take the same action on a different widget.

Listing 4-3 is a slightly more complicated example, which demonstrates a much more OO approach using two buttons and the same callback method.

Listing 4-3. *Two Buttons Using the Same Callback*

```php
<?php
class ExtendedButton extends GtkButton {

    // Text for one state of the button.
    var $label1 = 'Click Me';
    // Text for the other state of the button.
    var $label2 = 'Thank You';

    public function __construct()
    {
        // Call the parent constructor with the first label.
        parent::__construct($this->label1);
    }

    public function changeLabel($button1, $button2)
    {
        // Change the label of the button that was pressed.
        $button1->child->set_text($this->label2);
        // Change the label of the other button.
        $button2->child->set_text($this->label1);
    }
}

// Start with four widgets.
$window    = new GtkWindow();
$buttonBox = new GtkHButtonBox();
$buttonA   = new ExtendedButton();
$buttonB   = new ExtendedButton();

// Create a signal handler for buttonA's clicked signal.
// Pass buttonB as the second argument for changeLabel.
$buttonA->connect('clicked', array($buttonA, 'changeLabel'), $buttonB);

// Create a signal handler for buttonB's clicked signal.
// Pass buttonA as the second argument for changeLabel.
$buttonB->connect('clicked', array($buttonB, 'changeLabel'), $buttonA);
```

```
// Set up the window to close cleanly.
$window->connect_simple('destroy',
                                array('Gtk', 'main_quit'));

// Add the button box to the window.
$window->add($buttonBox);

// Add the buttons to the button box.
$buttonBox->add($buttonA);
$buttonBox->add($buttonB);

// Show the window and all of its children and grandchildren.
$window->show_all();

// Start the main loop.
Gtk::main();
?>
```

Figure 4-1 shows what this simple application looks like.

Figure 4-1. *A simple application with two buttons using the same callback*

In this example, we are extending the GtkButton class to add some extra functionality. The main part that we added is the changeLabel method. It expects two buttons and changes both of their labels. The parts to focus on, however, are the two calls to connect.

Both calls to connect are connecting the clicked signal from a button to that button's changeLabel method. The first parameter, again, is the signal we are listening for. The second parameter is an array. When most people see this, they think it is some kind of special PHP-GTK syntax for registering callback methods of instances, but this is standard PHP syntax. By passing an array with an object instance as the first element and a string as the second, we are telling PHP to call the method identified by the second element of the object identified by the first element. If we passed a class name string as the first element, PHP would try to call the method statically.

The last argument that we passed to connect is an extra parameter that will be passed to the callback. Any number of extra arguments can be passed to connect. The extra parameters are passed in order to the callback after any arguments that are supplied automatically. In this case, we are passing the other button. Each time you click a button, the other button is passed to the callback as $button2.

■**Note** When extra parameters are passed to a `connect` call, they are evaluated at the time the initial call to `connect` is processed. I have seen plenty of people spend hours trying to figure out why the value of a widget is stuck at its startup value. Actually, it isn't. They tried passing a method as an extra parameter to the callback. If you need the real-time value from a widget, pass the entire widget and grab the value in your callback.

The connect_simple Method

Listing 4-3 is kind of silly when you think about it. We are passing an object to itself in order to change its label. That doesn't really make a whole lot of sense, but what choice do we have, since the widget that emitted the signal is passed to the callback automatically? Well, that is where `connect_simple` comes in.

`connect_simple` has the same result as `connect`, but it doesn't pass the widget that emitted the signal to the callback. Listing 4-3 can be reworked using `connect_simple` instead of `connect` to make a more elegant application. I'll leave that as an "exercise" and focus on something slightly more interesting.

The widget that emitted the signal is not always the only thing passed to the callback automatically. Depending on the signal emitted, other information may also be passed. For instance, when a widget is added to a container, the container emits an add signal. When an add signal is emitted, it tells PHP-GTK to pass not only the container that had something added to it, but also the child that was added. If you create a signal handler for the add signal using `connect`, the callback method must accept at least two parameters: the container and the child. If you create a similar signal handler with `connect_simple`, the callback needs to accept only the child as an argument. The container itself will not be passed. Using `connect_simple` doesn't mean that no arguments will be passed automatically. It just means that the widget that emitted the signal will not be passed.

Listing 4-4 shows an example of using `connect_simple`. Try running it and see if you can tell what is happening.

Listing 4-4. *Using connect_simple to Reduce the Arguments for the Callback*

```php
<?php
class ExtendedContainer extends GtkHBox {

    // A variable to keep track of the number of children.
    public $counter = 0;

    public function __construct()
    {
        // Call the parent constructor.
        parent::__construct();

        // Create a signal handler for the ExtendedContainer's add signal.
        $this ->connect_simple('add', array($this, 'checkLimit'));
    }
```

```php
    public function checkLimit($child)
    {
        // Check to see how many children have been added so far.
        if (++$this->counter > 1) {
            echo "Whoa! Too many children.\n";
            // Remove the newly added child.
            $this->remove($child);
            // Update the counter.
            $this->counter--;
        }
        return;
    }

    public static function quit($msg)
    {
        echo $msg . "\n";
        Gtk::main_quit();
    }
}

// Create a new window.
$window    = new GtkWindow();
// Create a new instance of the ExtendedContainer class.
$container = new ExtendedContainer();
// Create a button to put in the ExtendedContainer.
$button    = new GtkButton('Close Window');

// Create a signal handler that will close the application when the
// button is clicked.
$button->connect_simple('clicked', array('ExtendedContainer', 'quit'), ➥
'Button Pressed');

// Create a signal handler that will call the container's quit method when
// the container is destroyed.
$window->connect_simple('destroy', array('ExtendedContainer', 'quit'), 'Window
Closed');

// Add the button to the container.
$container->add($button);

// Try to add a new label to the container also.
$container->add(new GtkLabel('label'));

// Add the container to the window.
$window->add($container);

// Show the window and its contents.
$window->show_all();
```

```
// Start the main loop.
Gtk::main();
?>
```

Here, we are extending the GtkHBox and basically turning it into a bin (a container that can hold only one child). We've modified the class so that it can have only one child at a time. We have created a signal handler that calls the checkLimit method whenever a child is added to the container.

Even though we used connect_simple, we still need to be prepared to accept the new child as an argument for our callback. The callback checks the number of children in the container, and if it is too high, it prints a message, removes the child, and updates the counter.

We created two other signal handlers in this example. The first handler connects the clicked signal of the button to the quit method of the container. The quit method is called statically and expects one argument to be passed in. The clicked signal, by default, passes the button, and only the button, that was clicked to the callback, but we used connect_simple so it doesn't pass anything. The argument that is passed in is the string that we passed as the third parameter for our connect_simple call. When the method is called, it outputs a message and quits the main GTK loop.

The other connect_simple call is similar. It connects the window's destroy signal to the statically called quit method. Just like the button's clicked signal, a widget's destroy signal passes only the widget that emitted the signal. This time, when we created the signal handler, we passed a different string as the message. When you run the code, try clicking the button one time and the x in the upper-right corner of the window the next time. Both actions shut down the application, but they produce different messages.

The connect_after and connect_simple_after Methods

Using connect_simple, you can make your callback methods a little simpler, but what about controlling the order in which they are called? In our simple examples so far, we pretty much know which signal handlers are going to be called first, because we know the order in which they were created.

In real-life applications, however, the signal handlers may not be created in the order we expect. Some of them may not be created until after the user selects some menu option. For example, consider a text-editing application. Applications like OpenOffice.org and Microsoft Word have real-time spell checking, which can highlight misspelled words as the user is typing them. When you type a letter, there may be one signal handler that is used to put the words into the document and another signal handler that checks for spelling errors. Obviously, you want the letters to appear in the document before the application checks for spelling mistakes. To help with this issue, PHP-GTK lets you separate signal handlers into two groups. The callbacks in the first group will always be called before the callbacks in the second group. Using this strategy, you can be certain that words will appear on the screen before they are spell-checked.

So far, we have been putting all of our signal handlers into one group using connect and connect_simple. To put handlers into the group that is called after the first group, you need to use two new methods: connect_after and connect_simple_after. These methods are identical in form and function to connect and connect_simple, respectively, except that they ensure that the callbacks will be put into the second group.

Let's look at a simple but practical example of why you might want to ensure that one signal handler is called before another. For our PIMS application, we will want to check that the users have saved their work before allowing them to close the application. To do this, we will create two signal handlers: one for the destroy signal and one for the delete-event signal. The signal connected to the destroy signal will close the application, and the other signal handler will check that all progress has been saved. Listing 4-5 presents the code.

Listing 4-5. *Using connect_simple_after to Ensure a Callback Is Called Second*

```php
<?php
class Editor {

    public $window;
    public $button;
    public $saved = false;

    public function __construct()
    {
        // Create a new window.
        $this->window = new GtkWindow();
        // Create a button with the label 'Save'.
        $this->button = new GtkButton('Save');

        // Add the button to the window.
        $this->window->add($this->button);

        // Set up the window to close cleanly after the other signal
        // handlers have been called.
        $this->window->connect_simple_after('destroy', ➥
            array('Gtk', 'main_quit'));

        // Create a signal handler to check if the user has saved their
        // work before allowing the application to be closed.
        $this->window->connect_simple('delete-event', ➥
            array($this, 'checkSaved'));

        // Create a signal handler that calls the saveFile method when the
        // user clicks the Save button.
        $this->button->connect_simple('clicked', ➥
            array($this, 'saveFile'));
    }

    public function start()
    {
        // Show the window and its contents.
        $this->window->show_all();
```

```php
        // Start the main loop.
        Gtk::main();
    }

    public function saveFile()
    {
        // For now, just set the saved flag to true.
        $this->saved = true;
    }

    public function checkSaved()
    {
        // Check the value of the saved flag.
        if (!$this->saved) {
            // Echo a warning message.
            echo "File not saved.\n";
            // Return true to prevent the window from closing.
            return true;
        }
    }
}

// Create a new editor.
$editor = new Editor();

// Start the application.
$editor->start();
?>
```

Because we don't want to close the application until after we check that the user has saved her work, we create the signal handler for the Gtk::main_quit method using connect_simple_after. Now we are assured that the application will not exit until after our check has run.

Try running the application a few times. First, click the Save button before closing the application. Next, close the application without clicking the Save button. The second time, you will see a warning message appear in the terminal.

This listing doesn't implement the entire process, but just enough to show the relationship between signal handlers created with connect_simple and those created with connect_simple_after. For now, we are just checking if the user has saved recently. In the next section, we will prevent the application from closing if she hasn't saved her work.

Blocking and Destroying Signal Handlers

Events are great because they let you interact with the user. But sometimes you may not want the user to interact with your application.

If you have ever developed an e-commerce website, you have undoubtedly run into the problem of user impatience. We have all been guilty of it, too. You go to a website and try to buy a book. You click the checkout button, but the site is slow to react. Well, maybe it didn't hear you the first time, so you click it again . . . and again. And before you know it, you have just bought 12 copies of *Harry Potter*.

Nowadays, developers have gotten a bit wiser. Sure, you can't make users more patient, but you can take away their tools for self-destruction. For instance, these days, most sites take you to some sort of processing page or simply remove the checkout button. That way, you can't do any more damage. That is what signal handler *blocking* is all about.

When you block a signal handler, you are saying, "I know I gave you the ability to click this button before, but for right now, I am going to ignore any clicks I hear." Blocking a signal handler prevents the callback from being called when the signal is emitted. It doesn't prevent the signal from being emitted. It just prevents that signal from calling the particular callback. If you blocked the signal completely, all of the signal handlers connected to it would be blocked as well.

In the previous section, you learned about creating signal handlers using the connect method and its sister methods. I must apologize because I left out one minor detail. All four of those methods return an integer value known as the signal handler ID. The number returned is used to uniquely identify the signal handler just created. Each signal handler created will return a different number, even if a second signal handler for the exact same widget, signal, and method is created. Most of the time, the signal handler ID return value is just ignored because the callback needs to be called reliably every time the event occurs. In some cases, however, you may want to temporarily or permanently block a particular signal handler. In these cases, you need to know the signal handler ID number.

Using a few methods, you can temporarily block a signal handler, bring it back "online," or destroy it all together. These are the block, unblock, disconnected, and is_connected methods. Let's look at how each of these works.

The block Method

Most aspects of an application are all about empowering the user; that is, when a feature is added, it is often designed to be used. However, sometimes you need to take away features. A feature may be disabled because the user hasn't yet completed a given set of tasks, or perhaps the system is busy processing information.

Blocking a signal handler takes some previously defined connection between a signal and an event and temporarily disables it. It doesn't kill the connection. It is just makes it temporarily unavailable. Picture a drag race. Two cars are sitting at the starting line waiting for the green light. Now let's say that just as the green light turns on, a large bird flies in front of the car in lane two, blocking the driver's view. Since the driver doesn't see the green light, he doesn't hit the gas. In our drag race, there is an event (the start of the race), a signal (the green light), an action (the cars go down the track), and a signal handler (the driver). The car in lane one represents a normal connection. The event occurred, a signal was emitted, and the signal handler took action. The car in lane two represents a blocked signal handler. The event occurred and the signal was emitted, but the signal handler was not made aware of it. Therefore, the signal handler took no action. The same things happen in PHP-GTK when a signal handler is blocked. Even though the event occurs and the signal is emitted, the signal handler takes no action.

Blocking a signal handler in PHP-GTK is a pretty simple process. You call the block method, passing the signal handler ID number, which is returned by the connect method. Listing 4-6 shows a simple example of blocking a signal handler.

Listing 4-6. *Blocking a Signal Handler*

```php
<?php
class ClickOnce extends GtkButton {

    public $handlerId;

    public function __construct($label)
    {
        // Call the parent constructor
        parent::__construct($label);

        // Set up the signal handler and capture the handler id.
        $this->handlerId = $this->connect_simple('clicked',
                            array($this, 'checkClicked'));

        // Spit out the handler id.
        var_dump($this->handlerId);
    }

    public function checkClicked()
    {
        // Change the label of the button.
        $this->child->set_text('Thanks');

        // Block the signal handler id.
        $this->block($this->handlerId);
    }
}

// Create a new window.
$window = new GtkWindow();

// Create a new ClickOnce button with the label 'Press Me'.
$button = new ClickOnce('Press Me');

// Add the buton to the window.
$window->add($button);

// Show the window and its contents.
$window->show_all();

// Set up the window to close cleanly.
$window->connect_simple('destroy', array('Gtk', 'main_quit'));

// Start the main loop.
Gtk::main();
?>
```

We start off by extending the GtkButton class to add some functionality. The constructor does some setup work, including creating a signal handler for the clicked signal. Notice that the return value of connect_simple is captured in the handlerId member variable. It is important that this value isn't ignored, because without it, there is no way to block the signal handler.

The class in the example is named ClickOnce because nothing happens the second, third, or billionth time the button is clicked. When the user clicks the button the first time, the checkClicked method will be called. checkClicked first changes the button's label to say Thanks, and then blocks the signal handler. With the signal handler blocked, checkClicked won't be called when the user clicks the button a second or third time. The signal is still being emitted, but the handler is ignoring it because it is blocked.

The unblock Method

If blocking a signal handler is only temporary, then obviously there must be a way to unblock a signal handler. Unblocking a signal handler simply means that the signal handler will begin to call its callback method again the next time the signal is emitted.

When a signal handler is blocked, requests that come in are simply thrown out. Requests are not queued up waiting to be processed. Unblocking a signal handler will not unleash a flood of previous user actions that took place while the signal handler was blocked. Unblocking a signal handler simply allows the callback method to be called when the given signal is emitted.

Unblocking a signal handler is as easy as blocking one. All it takes is the unblock method and the signal handler ID number. Take a look at Listing 4-7, which extends the previous listing.

Listing 4-7. *Unblocking a Signal Handler*

```php
<?php
class OnOff extends GtkButton {

    // The id of the signal handler.
    public $handlerId;
    // A counter to show how many times the button has been pressed.
    public $counter = 0;

    public function __construct($label)
    {
        // Call the parent constructor
        parent::__construct($label);
    }

    public function setUp($otherButton)
    {
        // Set up the signal handler.
        $this->handlerId = $this->connect_simple('clicked',
                        array($this, 'turnOff'), $otherButton);
    }

    public function turnOff($otherButton)
    {
        // Turn this button off.
        $this->block($this->handlerId);
```

```php
        // Change the text to process and add the number of times the
        // button has been pressed.
        $this->child->set_text('Processing (' . $this->counter++ . ')');

        // Turn the other button on.
        $otherButton->unblock($otherButton->handlerId);

        // Change the text to press me and add the number of times the
        // button has been pressed.
        $otherButton->child->set_text('Press Me (' .
                                      $otherButton->counter . ')');
    }
}

// Create a new window.
$window  = new GtkWindow();

// Create two new OnOff buttons.
$button1 = new OnOff('Press Me');
$button2 = new OnOff('Press Me');

// Create a new box to hold the buttons.
$box     = new GtkHBox();

// Set up the connections.
$button1->setUp($button2);
$button2->setUp($button1);

// Add both buttons to the box.
$box->add($button1);
$box->add($button2);

// Add the box to the window.
$window->add($box);

// Show the window and its contents.
$window->show_all();

// Set up the window to close cleanly.
$window->connect_simple('destroy', array('Gtk', 'main_quit'));

// Start the main loop.
Gtk::main();
?>
```

Figure 4-2 shows the simple application created by Listing 4-7.

Figure 4-2. *An application that blocks a signal handler when a button is pressed*

In the previous example, we had a button that could be clicked only once. In this example, we have two buttons. When clicked, each button will block its own signal handler, preventing it from being clicked again. Each button will also unblock the other button's signal handler. Basically, when a button turns itself off, it turns the other button back on. This example brings up two important points.

First, notice that we needed to change our class a little. Since each button is responsible for the other, the call to connect_simple had to be moved outside the constructor. This is pretty simple and should be obvious.

The other point is a little more subtle but also has to do with passing in the other button. Notice the entire button, not just the handler ID, was passed to the callback. This isn't because the handler ID can change and we need to get its value in real time. As long as a signal handler exists, its ID number will always be the same. The button was passed in because only the widget that created the signal handler can block or unblock it. This wasn't a big deal in Listing 4-6, where there was only one widget, but here there are two widgets. If $button1 tried to block the signal handler for $button2, a message saying something similar to the following would be output to the screen:

```
GLib-GObject-WARNING **: gsignal.c:1768: ➥
instance '0xa3a1788' has no handler with id '6'
```

This requirement makes blocking and unblocking signal handlers a little more difficult. Instead of simply maintaining a list of handler IDs, you must also maintain a relationship between the handler and the widget that created it. Fortunately, using OO programming, this isn't too difficult.

Note If you haven't yet given Listing 4-7 a try, you really should. You will see a message about a handler not being blocked yet. This is because every time a button is pressed, it tries to unblock the handler for the other button. But when the first button is pressed, no handlers have been blocked yet. Obviously, a handler can't be unblocked if it isn't blocked. Unfortunately, it is up to your application to keep track of whether or not a signal handler has been blocked. You can keep track of this in your code using a simple Boolean flag.

The disconnect Method

Using the block method will temporarily disable a signal handler, which can be brought back to life using the unblock method. Signal handlers don't always need to be brought back, though.

Consider a demonstration version of a calendar application. The developers may have decided that until the user pays the license fee, he may add only one event every time the application is loaded. The user can still use the calendar but cannot add more events. In this case, the application would have a signal handler that adds the event when the user clicks the New Event button. After adding the first event, the signal handler should stop processing new event requests. Unlike the previous examples, the application doesn't want to allow the user to add new events again. Instead of blocking the signal handler, the better solution is to get rid of it.

Connecting signal handlers is done with the connect method or one of its sister methods. Disconnecting a signal handler is done using the disconnect method. disconnect will permanently destroy the signal handler identified by the signal handler ID that is passed as the only argument.

Once a signal handler is disconnected, it is not possible to bring it back. If you need the functionality of that signal handler again, you must create a new signal handler. As with block and unblock, only the widget that created the signal handler may destroy it.

The is_connected Method

The block, unblock, and disconnect methods all require that the widget that created the signal handler be the one to block, unblock, or destroy it. Trying to use one of these methods on a signal handler created by another widget produces a warning message that is difficult to hide. To avoid such an error message, you can check that the signal handler belongs to the widget before trying to block, unblock, or disconnect it. That is where the is_connected method comes into play.

By passing is_connected a signal handler ID, you can determine if the calling widget is the owner of the signal handler. If the widget is the owner of the signal handler, is_connected returns true, regardless of whether or not the signal handler has been blocked.

Remember that once a signal handler has been destroyed with disconnect, the signal hander no longer exists, even though the callback still does. Calling is_connected and passing the ID of a signal handler that has been disconnected will return false. See the following code for a quick example.

```
if (!$this->is_connected($this->handlerId))
    trigger_error('The signal handler is not connected.', E_USER_WARNING);
```

Listening for New Events

Each widget that is used in an application comes with a certain set of events that it watches for by default. Depending on the function of the widget, the set of events can be greatly varied. In most cases, the events that come with a widget are more than enough for any given task. But sometimes the best widget for the job may not react to all of the events your application requires. That is why PHP-GTK has the flexibility to allow widgets to listen for new events that they do not listen for by default.

You can make a widget more responsive in two ways:

- Wrap the widget in a special container called a GtkEventBox. This container listens for a wide range of events and can be used to make normally inactive widgets appear to listen for events.

- Tell a widget to start listening for a particular set of events, such as making an image clickable.

We'll look at both techniques.

Using the GtkEventBox Container

The easiest way to make a widget listen for a new event is to put the widget inside a GtkEventBox. The GtkEventBox is designed specifically to hold a child widget and listen for a user event within that child's screen space. Unfortunately, the name GtkEventBox is a little misleading. It isn't a box at all—it's a bin. As a bin, it can have only one child. This makes its life a little easier, since you just need to worry about one child.

Normally, containers exist only to hold and align children. You can't interact with them, because the children take up all of the available screen space. The typical container might be better thought of as a stand instead of a box. The stand is just big enough to hold the widget in place but not big enough to be seen or touched. On the other hand, a GtkEventBox might be considered more of a tight-fitting glass case. The event box holds the child widget but also wraps around it. Now when you go to touch the widget inside, you hit the glass instead of the widget. The glass case can now react to your actions.

In Listing 4-8, a GtkEventBox changes the label that appears in a window when the user moves the mouse over it. Labels by themselves do not listen for any events by default. We are simulating their responsiveness by putting them inside an event box.

Listing 4-8. *Making a Widget More Responsive with GtkEventBox*

```php
<?php
class ChangingLabel extends GtkEventBox {

    public $mouseOverLabel;
    public $mouseOutLabel;

    public function __construct($mouseOverText, $mouseOutText)
    {
        // Set up the labels.
        $this->mouseOverLabel = new GtkLabel($mouseOverText);
        $this->mouseOutLabel  = new GtkLabel($mouseOutText);

        // Call the parent constructor.
        parent::__construct();

        // Add the mouse out label to start.
        $this->add($this->mouseOutLabel);

        // Connect the mouse over and out events.
        $this->connect_simple('enter-notify-event', array($this, ➥
            'switchLabels'));
        $this->connect_simple('leave-notify-event', array($this, ➥
            'switchLabels'));
    }

    public function switchLabels()
    {
        // Check to see which label is currently set.
```

```php
        if ($this->child === $this->mouseOverLabel) {
            // Remove the current label.
            $this->remove($this->mouseOverLabel);
            // Add the other label.
            $this->add($this->mouseOutLabel);

        } else {
            // Remove the current label.
            $this->remove($this->mouseOutLabel);
            // Add the other label.
            $this->add($this->mouseOverLabel);

        }

        // Make sure that the contents of the event box are shown.
        $this->show_all();
    }
}

// Create a window and add our new class to it.
$window = new GtkWindow();
$window->add(new ChangingLabel('Whoo Hoo!', 'Move the mouse here.'));

// Set up the window to close cleanly.
$window->connect_simple('destroy', array('Gtk', 'main_quit'));

// Show the window and its contents.
$window->show_all();

// Start the main loop.
Gtk::main();
?>
```

The event box listens for mouse enter and leave events, called enter-notify-event and leave-notify-event, respectively. These two events are triggered when the mouse enters or leaves the screen space taken up by the child of the event box.

In this example, we have extended the GtkEventBox class. Our new version, ChangingLabel, changes the event box's child label when the mouse moves over the label area. When the mouse moves out of the area again, the label returns to its original value.

It is important to understand that we are not making the labels listen for the mouse-over events. The labels themselves have not changed; they are just as boring and unresponsive as they were when they were created. It is the event box itself that is responding to the user's actions. We used the connect_simple method of our extended class, not of the labels.

Just to see what happens to a widget inside an event box, try changing the mouseOverLabel widget from a GtkLabel to a GtkButton. Make sure to connect a method to the button's clicked signal. Then try clicking the button. GtkEventBox acts as an interceptor for all user-triggered events. The button cannot be clicked anymore. When you put the mouse over the button and click, you are actually clicking the event box. You have basically put the button behind a glass case. You can see it, but you can't touch it.

Note Listing 4-8 is just an example. In a real application, there would be no reason to put a GtkLabel inside a GtkEventBox just to achieve a mouse-over effect. Chapter 16 shows a more appropriate method for achieving a mouse-over effect.

Because putting a widget inside an event box basically cuts it off from the user, it may not always be the best solution. Sometimes you need to keep the responsiveness of a widget. Also, a GtkEventBox does not automatically listen for some events.

Adding Events to a Widget

A vast majority of the times a widget is used in an application, it already listens for all of the signals that it will need. However, you may need to add another event to the set of events that will cause a widget to react to the user. You have seen that using an event box can add functionality to a widget, but that it also blocks off the widget from the user. If a widget needs to listen for a new set of events and retain its current level of responsiveness, you can add new events with the add_events method. add_events will make the widget listen for new signals generated by the events that are passed to it.

Before adding events to a widget, you should know which events the widget already listens for. *Signal reflection*—knowing which signals a widget listens for by default—is one of the built-in features of PHP-GTK. Because signals are not part of PHP proper, the reflection class is not able to grab or display them. Therefore, PHP-GTK must handle this on its own.

The signal_list_ids and signal_list_names methods list the IDs and names, respectively, of the signals that a widget listens for immediately after it is constructed. These methods expect either a class name or a class instance as the only parameter. Each returns an array of the signal data. Both methods are defined by the GObject class and can be called statically. signal_list_ids is not really that useful of a method. It can be used to programmatically compare a list of signal IDs with the signals that a widget listens for, but using it requires you to know which signal names match with which signal IDs. Usually, it is much easier to compare names. Using signal_list_names is a little easier because you know the names of the signals. The names are the values that are passed to connect.

Listing 4-9 shows the use of signal_list_names, as well as add_events. Before any new events are added, the code checks to see that the events are not listed in the array returned by signal_list_names. If not, the events are added. add_events is called with an integer passed as the only argument. The integer value is used as a mask to tell PHP-GTK which events should be captured by the widget. The values are more easily represented by Gdk constants. The masks make it easy to do bitwise comparison and track all of the events that a widget listens for in one value.

Listing 4-9. *Using signal_list_names and add_events to Enhance an Entry's Functionality*

```php
<?php
class EchoEntry extends GtkEntry {
```

```php
    public function __construct()
    {
        // Call the parent constructor.
        parent::__construct();
    }

    public function addKeyPress()
    {
        // Loop through the signal the GtkEntry listens for.
        foreach (GObject::signal_list_names('GtkEntry') as $signal) {
            if ($signal == 'key-press-event') {
                // If key-press-event is found, echo the name of the signal
                // and return false. This should not happen since GtkEntry
                // doesn't listen for key-press-event by default.
                echo $signal . "\n";
                return false;
            }
        }
        // Make the entry listen for a key press.
        $this->add_events(Gdk::KEY_PRESS_MASK);

        // Create a signal handler for the key-press-event signal.
        $this->connect_simple('key-press-event', array($this, 'echoText'));

        return true;
    }

    public function echoText()
    {
        // Echo the current text of the entry.
        echo $this->get_text() . "\n";
    }
}

// Build some widgets
$window = new GtkWindow();
$vBox   = new GtkVBox();
$label  = new GtkLabel('Type something in the entry field');
$entry  = new EchoEntry();

// Pack them all together.
$window->add($vBox);
$vBox->add($label);
$vBox->add($entry);

// Set up the window to close cleanly.
$window->connect_simple('destroy', array('Gtk', 'main_quit'));
```

```
// Show the window and its contents.
$window->show_all();

// Add the key-press-event signal to the signals that the EchoEntry listens
// for.
$entry->addKeyPress();

// Start the main loop.
Gtk::main();
?>
```

Figure 4-3 shows this simple application.

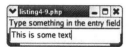

Figure 4-3. *A simple application that echoes the text entered*

Notice in this example that the widget was realized, by calling show_all on the window, before add_events was called. Recall from Chapter 3 that interaction with the operating system is handled by Gdk. Since events are often notices from the operating system that something has happened, Gdk is ultimately responsible for handling the events. Therefore, before any events can be added to a widget, the widget must have its Gdk-related properties set, namely, GdkWindow and GdkAllocation.

Also recall from Chapter 3 that the way to initialize a widget's Gdk properties is to call realize. Once the widget is realized, it is safe to call add_events. In this example, Gdk::KEY_PRESS_MASK is passed to add_events. This will make the widget react when the user presses any key on the keyboard while the entry has the keyboard focus (which is all of the time in this simple example). After setting up the widget to listen for key press events, the key-press-event signal is connected to the echoText method.

key-press-event is one of many event types that can be added. Table 4-1 summarizes the event masks and the corresponding signals that will be emitted by each.

Table 4-1. *Event Masks and Corresponding Signals*

Event Mask	Signal	Description
EXPOSURE_MASK	expose-event	An event occurred that has to do with exposing the widget, such as when it is shown or hidden.
POINTER_MOTION_MASK	motion-notify-event	The mouse was moved within the screen space of the widget.
POINTER_MOTION_HINT_MASK	motion-notify-event	The mouse was moved, and is still moving, within the screen space of the widget.
BUTTON_MOTION_MASK	motion-notify-event	The mouse was moved across the screen space of the widget while one of the mouse buttons was pressed.

Event Mask	Signal	Description
BUTTON1_MOTION_MASK	motion-notify-event	The mouse was moved across the screen space of the widget while the first mouse button was pressed.
BUTTON2_MOTION_MASK	motion-notify-event	The mouse was moved across the screen space of the widget while the second mouse button was pressed.
BUTTON3_MOTION_MASK	motion-notify-event	The mouse was moved across the screen space of the widget while the third mouse button was pressed.
BUTTON_PRESS_MASK	button-press-event	A mouse button was pressed on the widget.
BUTTON_RELEASE_MASK	button-release-event	A mouse button was released over top of the widget.
KEY_PRESS_MASK	key-press-event	A keyboard key was pressed while the widget had keyboard focus.
KEY_RELEASE_MASK	key-release-event	A keyboard key was released while the widget had keyboard focus.
ENTER_NOTIFY_MASK	enter-notify-event	The mouse pointer has entered the screen space of the widget.
LEAVE_NOTIFY_EVENT	leave-notify-event	The mouse pointer has left the screen space of the widget.
FOCUS_CHANGE_MASK	focus-in-event/ focus-out-event	The widget has either had keyboard focus given to it or taken away from it.
STRUCTURE_MASK	map-event/unmap-event/ destroy-event/ configure-event	An event relating to the underlying properties of a widget occurred.
PROPERTY_CHANGE_MASK	property-notify-event	A property of the widget has been changed, such as $widget->style.
VISIBILITY_NOTIFY_MASK	visibility-notify-event	The widget has become visible or has been hidden from view.
PROXIMITY_IN_MASK	proximity-in-event	The mouse pointer has come close to the widget.
PROXIMITY_OUT_MASK	proximity-out-event	The mouse pointer has moved away from the widget.
SUBSTRUCTURE_MASK	map-event/unmap-event/ destroy-event/ configure-event (from a child widget)	A change has been made to the underlying properties of one of the widget's children.
ALL_EVENTS_MASK	All events	This mask adds the ability to listen for any and all of the event types.

In PHP-GTK 1, it was necessary to call add_events any time that a widget needed to listen for a signal outside its default set. Fortunately, PHP-GTK 2 has taken a step forward and made it much easier to add new event types. Instead of requiring you to go through the tedious process detailed in Listing 4-9, PHP-GTK 2 will automatically call add_events for a widget when a signal that the widget does not listen for is used in a call to connect or one of the other connect methods. While Listing 4-9 is technically correct, and is an example of a best practice for adding events, Listing 4-10 works just as well.

Listing 4-10. *A Simpler Approach to Adding Events*

```php
<?php
class EchoEntry extends GtkEntry {

    public function __construct()
    {
        // Call the parent constructor.
        parent::__construct();
    }

    public function addKeyPress()
    {
        // Create a signal handler for the key-press-event signal.
        // add_events will be called automatically.
        $this->connect_simple('key-press-event', array($this, 'echoText'));
    }

    public function echoText()
    {
        // Echo the current text of the entry.
        echo $this->get_text() . "\n";
    }
}

// Build some widgets
$window = new GtkWindow();
$vBox   = new GtkVBox();
$label  = new GtkLabel('Type something in the entry field');
$entry  = new EchoEntry();

// Pack them all together.
$window->add($vBox);
$vBox->add($label);
$vBox->add($entry);

// Set up the window to close cleanly.
$window->connect_simple('destroy', array('Gtk', 'main_quit'));

// Show the window and its contents.
$window->show_all();

// Create the signal handler for the key-press-event signal.
$entry->addKeyPress();

// Start the main loop.
Gtk::main();
?>
```

Summary

PHP-GTK gives an application the ability to react to the user quickly and efficiently. The system of signals and events turns an unresponsive window on the screen into a functional and flexible application. Using the connect family of methods, user and system events emit signals that trigger callback methods that can then perform a designated task. When a signal is connected to a method, a signal handler is created. Signal handlers are the key to making an application respond to the user. Signal handlers can be created, blocked, unblocked, or destroyed, allowing for a constantly changing set of user-application interactions.

Now that we have covered all of the basics, in the next chapter, you'll start creating a real PHP-GTK application. Chapter 5 will focus on getting the Crisscott PIMS application off the ground. The chapter will start with creating a GtkWindow to hold the application. Next, we will look at setting some of the basic window properties and connections.

CHAPTER 5

■■■

Getting an Application Up and Running

Bringing a simple application to life can be a pretty easy process with PHP-GTK, but you also have a lot of flexibility. For instance, instead of just displaying a window on the screen and exiting, you can customize your application to place the window in a particular location, set a specific size, set a certain title, and tailor a whole host of other features. More important than any of these features, however, is making sure that the application starts and exits cleanly. In this chapter, you will learn how to do all of this, but first you must understand exactly what a window is.

Windows and Other Top-Level Widgets

All PHP-GTK widgets need to have a top-level widget. A top-level widget is one that is capable of existing on its own without the need to be embedded within a parent widget. GtkWindow is the most common top-level widget. Others include GtkFileChooserDialog, GtkAboutDialog, GtkMessageDialog, and GtkColorSelectionDialog.

Each dialog widget has a specific purpose and is actually just a window containing other widgets. A dialog is used to draw the user's attention to something or to get confirmation of some behavior. Figure 5-1 offers an example GtkMessageDialog widget, which is made up of an icon, a label, and a button. All of these top-level widgets can exist alone, floating around the user's screen.

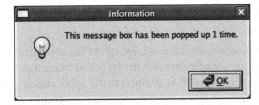

Figure 5-1. *A GtkMessageDialog widget*

Widgets that are not top level must be embedded within a top-level widget. They may be nested several layers down, but the trail of widget parents must lead back to a top-level widget eventually. If not, the widgets cannot be *realized* (displayed), which means they will never have an impact on the application.

It is safe to say that the vast majority of PHP-GTK applications use a GtkWindow as the main top-level widget, providing the framework for most applications. The window gives everything else in the application a starting point and a frame of reference. The window is also usually the controlling widget for the application. That isn't to say that the window is how the user controls the application, but the window is a sort of master widget for the application. For instance, when widgets are shown, it is usually because show_all was called on the main window. When the application is shut down, it is usually because the main window was destroyed.

Figure 5-2 is an example of a typical PHP-GTK application. The GtkWindow contains several other widgets, including labels, a list, and a GtkNotebook (a widget that displays its information on multiple tabs, as discussed in Chapter 6). The window provides a context for the rest of the application. It gives the other pieces a structure in which they can be shown.

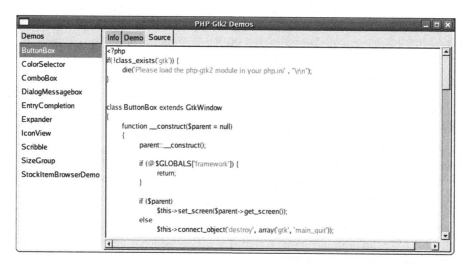

Figure 5-2. *A typical GtkWindow widget*

Types of Windows

GtkWindow widgets come in two varieties. The most commonly used version of GtkWindow is the normal window with a border and title bar. The title bar usually contains the standard minimize, maximize, and close buttons that appear in the upper-right corner, in addition to the application's title. Widgets within this type of window are nicely framed and easy to recognize as a group.

The other type of window is called a *pop-up window*. As you'll soon learn, the naming is a tad misleading, because it doesn't represent what one typically thinks of as a pop-up window. A pop-up window is the same as a regular GtkWindow, except that it doesn't have a border or title bar. The widgets inside a pop-up window appear to be floating free on the screen.

You can determine the type of window when the window is constructed. The constructor for GtkWindow takes one argument, which is the window type. The window type should be either Gtk::WINDOW_TOPLEVEL or Gtk::WINDOW_POPUP. The following two lines show how to create each type of window.

```
$window = new GtkWindow(Gtk::WINDOW_TOPLEVEL);
$window = new GtkWindow(Gtk::WINDOW_POPUP);
```

From a coding perspective, the argument passed to the constructor is the only difference between these two types of windows. They are both the same class, and you can use the same methods with both instances. If no value is passed to the constructor, the window will default to a top-level window. Figures 5-3 and 5-4 show the same simple application, first as a normal top-level window and next as a pop-up window.

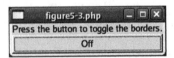

Figure 5-3. *A simple application with a Gtk::WINDOW_TOPLEVEL window*

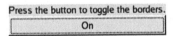

Figure 5-4. *The same application with a Gtk::WINDOW_POPUP window*

The Gtk::WINDOW_POPUP type is not designed to be used when an application needs to hide the border and title bar. It is designed to house pieces of an application that may not appear to be windows at first glance.

For instance, menus need to appear in their own window on top of the existing application. When a user clicks File in a typical application, the File menu appears, giving the user options such as Open, Save, and Exit. The menu isn't embedded in the application. It appears in front of the rest of the application. This is because the menu is actually its own top-level window. Obviously, you don't want a border and title to appear in the application menus, so you use a pop-up window.

Tooltips are another good example. Tooltips are the messages that appear when the mouse hovers over an icon in the toolbar. For example, in many text editors, a disk icon appears in the toolbar. Clicking the disk icon will save the file. Usually, if the mouse hovers over this icon, a small text box that says "Save" will appear. The tooltip needs to appear over the current window, not within it. Therefore, the tooltip "pops up" in a new window. Do you see how pop-up windows got their name now?

Window Decorations

A window that is displaying its border and title bar is considered *decorated*. A window that is not showing the border and title bar is *undecorated*. All GtkWindow widgets of type Gtk::WINDOW_TOPLEVEL are decorated by default.

The proper way to remove a window's border and title bar is to use the set_decorated method. Passing false to set_decorated will turn the border and title bar off. Passing true will turn them back on.

Note that turning off the borders will not make them instantly disappear. The borders will remain until the window is redrawn. However, if set_decorated is called before the window is displayed, the borders will be hidden (or displayed, depending on the argument passed to set_decorated) when the window appears on the screen. If the window is displayed before set_decorated is called, the borders will be shown until the GUI is updated.

Listing 5-1 shows a simple application (the same application as displayed in Figure 5-3) that allows the user to turn the borders off and on. Notice that each time set_decorated is called, hide_all and show_all are also called. This forces the window to be redrawn with the new decorated value. In the "The GTK Loop" section later in this chapter, you'll see a much more elegant way to refresh the GUI.

Listing 5-1. *Toggling Window Borders with set_decorated*

```php
<?php
function toggle($button, $window)
{
        // Toggle the borders and title bar.
        $window->set_decorated(!$window->get_decorated());

        // Update the button.
        if ($window->get_decorated()) {
                $button->child->set_text('Off');
        } else {
                $button->child->set_text('On');
        }

        // Hide and show the window.
        $window->hide_all();
        $window->show_all();
}

// Create the widgets.
$window = new GtkWindow();
$vBox   = new GtkVBox();
$label  = new GtkLabel('Press the button to toggle the borders.');
$button = new GtkButton('Off');

// Put everything together.
$window->add($vBox);
$vBox->add($label);
$vBox->add($button);

// Call the toggle function when the button is clicked.
$button->connect('clicked', 'toggle', $window);
```

```php
// Set up the application to close cleanly.
$window->connect_simple('destroy', array('Gtk', 'main_quit'));
// Show all pieces of the application.
$window->show_all();
// Start up the main loop.
Gtk::main();
?>
```

Toggling window decorations is a little more common than it may seem at first glance. An application in full-screen mode is basically an undecorated window that takes up the entire screen space. More commonly, window decorations are removed to make a splash screen.

A splash screen is an undecorated window that appears while the main application is loading. Splash screens are usually used to show the user an application's progress during loading. It is possible that the Crisscott PIMS application may take a few moments to load, so a splash screen would probably be a good idea. This way, the user will know what the application is doing while it loads. Listing 5-2 is a first run at a simple Crisscott PIMS splash screen.

Listing 5-2. *A Simple Splash Screen*

```php
<?php
class Crisscott_SplashScreen extends GtkWindow {

    // A widget to show a status message.
    public $status;

    public function __construct()
    {
        // Call the parent constructor.
        parent::__construct();

        // Turn off the window borders.
        $this->set_decorated(false);

        // Set the background color to white.
        $style = $this->style->copy();
        $style->bg[Gtk::STATE_NORMAL] = $style->white;
        $this->set_style($style);

        // Call a helper method to create the pieces of the splash screen.
        $this->_populate();

        // Set up the application to shut down cleanly.
        $this->connect_simple('destroy', array('Gtk', 'main_quit'));
    }

    private function _populate()
    {
```

```php
        // Create the containers.
        $frame = new GtkFrame();
        $hBox  = new GtkHBox();
        $vBox  = new GtkVBox();

        // Set the shadow type.
        $frame->set_shadow_type(Gtk::SHADOW_ETCHED_OUT);

        // Create title label.
        $titleText = '<span foreground="#000060"><b>Crisscott ' .
                    'Product Information Management System</b></span>';
        $title = new GtkLabel($titleText);
        // Use markup to make the label blue and bold.
        $title->set_use_markup(true);

        // Create an initial status message.
        $this->status = new GtkLabel('Initializing Main Window');

        // Stack the labels vertically.
        $vBox->pack_start($title,        true, true, 10);
        $vBox->pack_start($this->status, true, true, 10);

        // Add a logo image.
        $logoImg = GtkImage::new_from_file('Crisscott/images/logo.png');

        // Put the image and the first box next to each other.
        $hBox->pack_start($logoImg, false, false, 10);
        $hBox->pack_start($vBox,    false, false, 10);

        // Put everything inside a frame.
        $frame->add($hBox);

        // Put the frame inside the window.
        $this->add($frame);
    }
    public function start()
    {
        // Show all the pieces of the application
        $this->show_all();
        // Start the main loop.
        Gtk::main();
    }
}
```

```
// Instantiate the splash screen.
$splash = new Crisscott_SplashScreen();
// Start up the splash screen.
$splash->start();
?>
```

As shown in Figure 5-5, Listing 5-2 creates an undecorated window that gives some basic information about the application. This version isn't perfect, but it is a good start. The next few sections introduce a few more tools to spice things up and make the splash screen look a little more professional.

Figure 5-5. *An overly simple splash screen*

Window Positioning and Sizing

One of the problems with this version of the splash screen is that it appears wherever the operating system wants it to appear. The location where the operating system puts the window usually depends on what other windows are open at the time. Fortunately, PHP-GTK applications aren't slaves to the window manager.

An application can start up with its window anywhere on the screen you please. To accomplish this, you use the set_uposition method. set_uposition positions the window's upper-left corner *x* pixels from the left edge of the screen and *y* pixels from the top edge of the screen. The *x* and *y* values are integers that are passed as arguments.

Rarely will you want an application to always appear in a fixed position, such as 300 pixels from the top edge and 200 from the left. More likely, if the application is to be positioned at all, you'll want the application to appear some relative distance from the upper-left corner of the screen, such as in the center of the screen.

Since it is impractical to expect all users of an application to have the same screen dimensions, the screen height and width must be grabbed at runtime. To get values related to the user's screen, the code must call on GDK for a little help. Two static GDK methods return the needed information: Gdk::screen_width and Gdk::screen_height provide the size of the screen in pixels. Using these values, you can position an application so that it appears in the same relative position for all users.

Listing 5-3 shows a slightly modified version of the splash screen's constructor. This version calls set_uposition, passing half of the screen width and half of the screen height. Therefore, the window should be positioned in the center of the screen.

Listing 5-3. *Positioning a Window with set_uposition*

```php
<?php
    public function __construct()
    {
        // Call the parent constructor.
        parent::__construct();

        // Turn off the window borders.
        $this->set_decorated(false);

        // Set the background color to white.
        $style = $this->style->copy();
        $style->bg[Gtk::STATE_NORMAL] = $style->white;
        $this->set_style($style);

        // Move the window to the center of the screen.
        $this->set_uposition(Gdk::screen_width() / 2, Gdk::screen_height() / 2);

        // Call a helper method to create the pieces of the splash screen.
        $this->_populate();

        // Set up the application to close cleanly.
        $this->connect_simple('destroy', array('Gtk', 'main_quit'));
    }
?>
```

■**Tip** The move method is a synonym for set_uposition. It takes the x and y coordinates for the upper-left corner of the window and positions it there.

Figure 5-6 shows the new splash screen as it appears on the screen. After implementing the new version of the splash screen, you'll see that the result is better than before, but it is still not perfect. The window does exactly what it is told: it puts the upper-left corner dead center in the middle of the screen. It would be better if the center of the window appeared in the center of the screen. To do this, you need to know the height and width of the window.

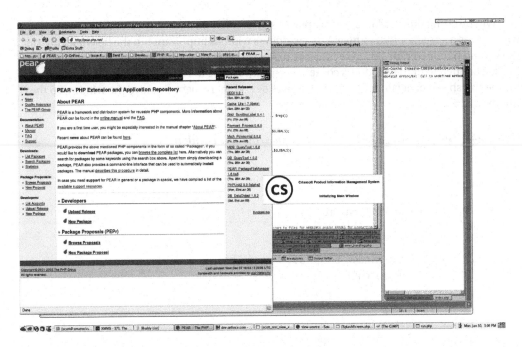

Figure 5-6. *The splash screen almost centered on the screen*

Getting and Setting the Window's Height and Width

To center the window vertically on the screen, the upper-left corner of the window needs to be moved down half the screen height and then back up half the window height. To center the window horizontally, the window needs to move to the right half the screen width and then moved back to the left half the window width. Unfortunately, there are no convenient methods for obtaining the window's height and width. However, you have two ways to obtain this information.

The first method involves realizing the window and then grabbing the height and width from the GdkAllocation property. This method is not so elegant, because it requires you to dig around in the inner workings of a widget. It also requires the widget to be realized, which can have unwanted effects, depending on the application configuration. For example, realizing the window may trigger signal handlers before they need to be triggered. The following lines of code show how to get the width of a widget from its GdkAllocation. Getting the height is very similar.

```
$widget->realize()
$width = $widget->allocation->width;
```

The second method for retrieving the screen size is to explicitly set the size and just remember it. This is not only easier, but it also provides more control over the application. You can set the height and width by using set_size_request, passing these dimensions in as pixel values. Again, you can use Gdk::screen_height and Gdk::screen_width if the window needs to be sized relative to the user's screen.

When setting the window's size for reasons other than positioning, you may not care if the window has a specific width or height. If a window's width is important but the height is not, set the second parameter for set_size_request to -1. This tells PHP-GTK to allow the window to be just tall enough to fit the window's content vertically. Listing 5-4 shows the constructor method for the splash screen again, but this time it uses set_size_request to move the window to the middle of the screen.

Listing 5-4. *Using set_size_request to Control the Window's Position*

```php
<?php
    public function __construct()
    {
        // Call the parent constructor.
        parent::__construct();

        // Turn off the window borders.
        $this->set_decorated(false);

        // Set the background color to white.
        $style = $this->style->copy();
        $style->bg[Gtk::STATE_NORMAL] = $style->white;
        $this->set_style($style);

        // Set size of the window.
        $this->set_size_request(300, 100);
        // Move the window to the center of the screen.
        $width  = Gdk::screen_width() / 2 - 150;
        $height = Gdk::screen_height() / 2 - 50;
        $this->set_uposition($width,$height);

        // Call a helper method to create the pieces of the splash screen.
        $this->_populate();

        // Set up the application to close cleanly.
        $this->connect_simple('destroy', array('Gtk', 'main_quit'));
    }
?>
```

Caution Calling set_size_request doesn't just set the window's current size. It also sets the window's minimum size. If a window is set to 300 pixels by 200 pixels, for example, users will not be able to adjust the size of the window to make it any smaller, although they can make it larger. The application can still adjust the window size by calling set_size_request again, but the new values will become the new limits.

Centering a Window

Using set_uposition and set_size_request, you can place a window in any desired location, but this is a little cumbersome. If you need exact, absolute positioning of a window, these two methods make a powerful team, but often you don't need such a degree of control. More likely, one of two relative positions is sufficient.

PHP-GTK provides a way to easily center the window on the screen or center the window under the user's mouse. The set_position method (note the missing u) will automatically set the position for the window, and then adjust it based on the window's height and width. When you pass this method the Gtk::WIN_POS_CENTER constant, the window will be positioned in the center of the screen. To position the window under the user's mouse, call the same method but pass Gtk::WIN_POS_MOUSE. Passing the Gtk::WIN_POS_CENTER_ALWAYS constant will force the window back to the center of the screen whenever the window is redrawn.

Using set_position is much cleaner and easier than trying to do the math needed to position the window yourself, but you can use it only to center the window or position it under the user's mouse. If the window needs to be positioned somewhere else, say relative to another window that has already been created, you need to use set_uposition instead.

Listing 5-5 shows the splash screen centered using set_position.

Listing 5-5. *Centering a Window with set_position*

```php
<?php
    public function __construct()
    {
        // Call the parent constructor.
        parent::__construct();

        // Turn off the window borders.
        $this->set_decorated(false);

        // Set the background color to white.
        $style = $this->style->copy();
        $style->bg[Gtk::STATE_NORMAL] = $style->white;
        $this->set_style($style);

        // Set size of the window.
        $this->set_size_request(300, 100);

        // Move the window to the center of the screen.
        $this->set_position(Gtk::WIN_POS_CENTER);

        // Call a helper method to create the pieces of the splash screen.
        $this->_populate();

        // Set up the application to close cleanly.
        $this->connect_simple('destroy', array('Gtk', 'main_quit'));
    }
?>
```

Tip Even though Listing 5-5 doesn't use the screen size for positioning, it is still considered good practice to set the screen size anyway. It provides a cleaner, more consistent user experience. If the size is not set, the window will default to the size of its contents.

Maximizing Windows

Just because a window's size has been set once doesn't mean that the window can't undergo further changes. It is always possible to change the window's dimensions using set_size_request. There are other ways to set the window size, however.

In most windowed applications, three icons reside in the upper-right corner of the title bar:

The first icon is used to minimize the application, and the last icon is used to close the application. The middle icon is often represented in one state as a single box, and in another state as two overlapping boxes. The middle icon is used to maximize the application; that is, make the application take up the entire screen but maintain its borders and title bar.

Maximizing a window can be controlled by the application as well as by the user. The maximize method will resize the application so that it fills the screen. maximize will not hide the borders or title bar, so the usable space within the window is not actually the entire screen. Taskbars and other fixtures can prevent the application from taking up the entire screen, but the window will expand to take up as much space as it is allowed. Using maximize is pretty simple:

```
$window->maximize();
```

To make the area inside the window the same size as the user's screen, the window decorations need to be turned off. This could be done by calling set_decorated and maximize in succession, but there is an easier way. The fullscreen method does exactly the same thing as maximize, except it also turns off the window decorations. The area within the window will now take up the entire area of the user's screen. To see an example of full-screen mode in action, open Internet Explorer and press F11. The page you're viewing will take up the entire screen.

To return the window to its previous size and location, the application should call unmaximize or unfullscreen. It may seem logical that calling fullscreen followed by unmaximize will turn off the decorations, maximize the window, and then return it to its original size and position without the decorations, but this doesn't work. The only way to return a window that has been maximized to its original size and location is to use unmaximize. The same goes for windows for which you've called fullscreen. After calling fullscreen, the only way to get a window out of full-screen mode is to call unfullscreen. Keep in mind that when a window is in full-screen mode, the window is undecorated. Users cannot unfullscreen a window quite as easily as they can unmaximize it.

Setting the Z-Index

One last piece to window positioning often goes overlooked. Most often, a computer screen is thought of as a two-dimensional workspace. Positioning is normally considered in terms of x and y coordinates. However, today's modern windowed operating systems can display objects in relation to each other with a z coordinate.

Windows can appear to be in front of or behind other windows in the application. This is often referred to as the *z-index*. The greater the z-index, the closer to the user the window appears. A window with a z-index of 1 will appear in front of a window with a z-index of 0, but behind a window with a z-index of 2.

With PHP-GTK, setting the z-index is either all or nothing. A window can be told to always remain on top of all other windows, or it can be told to always remain below all other windows. When a window is told to always remain on top of or below other windows, it doesn't mean the window must stay there for the life of the application. It means the window must remain on top until the application tells it otherwise. If another application starts up, its window will appear below the current window. If another window is maximized, it, too, will remain below the window that was set to remain on top.

Telling a window to stay in front of all other windows is a simple matter of calling set_keep_above and passing true as the only argument. If a window is already set to stay above all other windows, passing false to set_keep_above will allow the window to slip behind other windows again. The window will not instantly fall behind other windows on the screen, but newly created or raised windows will have a greater z-index than the current application window.

The splash screen we've been working on in this chapter should always remain on top of other windows until the main application window is ready to take over. Otherwise, important messages may be missed. Other parts of the application may not be so important. For instance, when the PIMS application transfers product data to the main server, it would be nice to keep the user updated as to the overall progress, but forcing this information in front of other parts of the application would be frustrating and detract from the more important parts of the application. It would be better to keep information relating to background tasks in the background. Calling set_keep_below and passing true as the only argument forces the window to have the lowest z-index of all the windows currently on the screen. Calling the same method again but passing false will allow the window to slip in front of other windows again.

Listing 5-6 shows yet another slightly modified version of the splash screen. This version looks exactly the same as the previous version, but uses set_keep_above to make sure that no other windows appear in front of the splash screen. This way, all of the important messages will be seen by the user, regardless of what else happens on the screen. When you run this example, try to bring other windows in front of the splash screen.

Listing 5-6. *Forcing a Window to Stay in Front of All Other Windows with set_keep_above*

```php
<?php
    public function __construct()
    {
        // Call the parent constructor.
        parent::__construct();

        // Turn off the window borders.
        $this->set_decorated(false);
```

```
        // Set the background color to white.
        $style = $this->style->copy();
        $style->bg[Gtk::STATE_NORMAL] = $style->white;
        $this->set_style($style);

        // Set size of the window.
        $this->set_size_request(300, 100);
        // Move the window to the center of the screen.
        $this->set_position(Gtk::WIN_POS_CENTER);

        // Keep the splash screen above all other windows.
        $this->set_keep_above(true);

        // Call a helper method to create the pieces of the splash screen.
        $this->_populate();

        // Set up the application to close cleanly.
        $this->connect_simple('destroy', array('Gtk', 'main_quit'));
    }
?>
```

■**Tip** Most splash screens don't need to appear in the taskbar while the application is loading. You can prevent the splash screen in Listing 5-6 from showing up in the taskbar by adding `$this->set_skip_taskbar_hint(true);` to the constructor.

Modal Windows

A common reason for keeping a window on top of another is to make sure that the user takes some action before continuing. For example, when a file is saved in a text editor, the user is normally not allowed to edit the file while the save dialog window is open. This is because the save dialog window is *modal*.

A modal window prevents the user from interacting with the other windows in the application while the modal window is open. You can make a window modal by passing true to set_modal.

Modal windows should usually remain on top of the other windows in the application. You can tell the window manager to keep the modal window above the parent window by making the modal window *transient* for the parent. Making one window transient for another makes the window manager aware that the two windows are related and that one is the parent of the other. The following two lines of code would make the window $window2 modal and transient for window $window1.

```
$window2->set_modal(true);
$window2->set_transient_for($window1);
```

Now that $window2 is modal and transient for $window1, the window manager will keep $window2 on top of $window1. Also, the user will not be able to interact with $window1 until $window2 has been closed by the application or the user.

> **■Tip** A transient window may not have much meaning without its parent. Therefore, the transient window may be destroyed when the parent is destroyed. `$window2->set_destroy_with_parent(true)` would close `$window2` if the user or application closed `$window1` while `$window2` was still open.

Window Titles

When a window is decorated, it will have a title bar. The title bar is used to identify the application. The title is also used as the text that appears in the taskbar on most modern operating systems.

If a title is not set for a window, the title will default to the name of the file that was executed. For example, if you executed the command php example.php, the window's title would be example. php. This is true even if the window itself is created in another file. Setting the title to the name of the application is usually much better than using the default.

Setting the title on a window that isn't decorated still has its purpose. The title will appear in the taskbar and when the user tries to switch applications using Alt+Tab.

You can set the window title by using the set_title method. set_title expects one string argument and sets the title to that value. Listing 5-7 implements a new window that will be decorated and have its title set. This listing will become the basis for the Crisscott PIMS application. This new window combines several of the methods discussed so far, including set_title and maximize.

Listing 5-7. *Setting the Title and Maximizing a Decorated Window*

```php
<?php
class Crisscott_MainWindow extends GtkWindow {

    public function __construct()
    {
        // Call the parent constructor.
        parent::__construct();

        // Set the size of the window.
        $this->set_size_request(500, 300);
        // Move the window to the center of the screen.
        $this->set_position(Gtk::WIN_POS_CENTER);
        // Add a title to the window.
        $this->set_title('Criscott PIMS');
        // Maximize the window.
        $this->maximize();

        // Set up the application to shut down cleanly.
        $this->connect_simple('destroy', array('Gtk', 'main_quit'));
    }
}
?>
```

Notice that even though the window is maximized, the size is still set. This ensures that the window will be a reasonable size if it is unmaximized.

The GTK Loop

So far, you have seen several examples of simple applications, but as of yet, we haven't really discussed what makes a piece of code a working PHP-GTK application. Close inspection of the code shown so far reveals that all of the listings that create windows on the screen have a few lines of code in common: the show_all, main, and main_quit methods. These few lines are essential to any working PHP-GTK application, as they're responsible for starting up and shutting down the application.

As you've already learned, show_all displays the main window on the screen and also displays the widgets contained in the window. The main and main_quit methods are arguably the two most important methods in PHP-GTK, and we'll cover them here.

Starting the Loop

An application created with PHP-GTK is able to continuously react to user events because it runs in a continuous loop. Every fraction of a second, PHP-GTK checks to see if any events have occurred, emits any needed signals, and calls any needed callback methods. It does this repeatedly for as long as the application is running. This repeated action is what makes PHP-GTK work the way it does.

Several of the examples you've seen so far include a call to Gtk::main, which starts the GTK loop. This begins the process of listening for events and calling callbacks.

The GTK loop is similar to any other PHP loop, but it does have some fundamental differences. For instance, in a script, any code that appears after the call to Gtk::main will not be executed until the loop finishes. This is what one would expect from a for or a while loop. However, unlike the typical looping structures, what occurs during the loop can change drastically. The loop is interactive and, depending on what events occur, one iteration may crunch a large set of numbers while the next may do nothing at all. Program execution may take a wildly different path during each iteration, but in the end, execution always comes back to the loop.

The loop will continue indefinitely until the application exits the loop. Exiting the loop is accomplished by calling the Gtk::main_quit method. Gtk::main_quit emits a sort of internal signal that tells PHP-GTK it is time to stop the continuous looping. When the loop exits, execution of the script continues.

In most OO applications, the call to Gtk::main is wrapped within a class method called start or something similar. Doing so allows the application one last chance to execute any code or check some values before the loop is started.

Regardless of how Gtk::main is called, there is one important thing to remember for every application: before Gtk::main is called, the main window for the application should at least call show, if not show_all. Remember that Gtk::main starts the main GTK loop. The loop allows the application to be interactive, but if the code hasn't shown the window, there is no way for the user to interact with the application. Since the program is executing in a loop, the program cannot get inside and make any changes. Therefore, if the window isn't shown before the loop is started, the application is stuck.

Stopping the Loop

Stopping the loop is a simple matter of calling Gtk::main_quit, but deciding how to call it is not quite as simple. While the call to Gtk::main is usually done automatically when the script is run, the call to exit the loop is normally done in reaction to a user event. Automatically shutting down the application probably isn't the best idea, so most applications usually wait for the user to close the window or select an exit option from a menu.

Since shutting down an application is normally triggered by the user, Gtk::main_quit is used as a callback for the destroy signal of the top-level window. Take a look at the listings in this chapter so far. Every one of them has the following line (except Listing 5-1, which contains a similar line):

```
$this->connect_simple('destroy', array('Gtk', 'main_quit'));
```

This line says that when the main application is destroyed, the loop should exit. This method simply kills the loop. No checks are run to verify that users want to close the application or to give them one last chance to save their work. For most simple applications, this is probably enough. Others may need to wrap the call to Gtk::main_quit inside another method or create two signal handlers for the destroy signal, as you saw in Chapter 4.

Calling Gtk:main_quit while the last widget is being destroyed is essential. If all widgets are destroyed before the loop exits, there will be no way to call Gtk::main_quit from within the loop. As you saw with Gtk::main, if you are outside the main loop, you cannot interact with it. If there is no way to interact with the loop, there is no way to stop it. If the loop can't be stopped, the script can't be stropped. If the main loop is stopped before all of the widgets are destroyed, it will be up to the script that called Gtk::main to clean up the other widgets.

Creating a signal handler that calls Gtk::main_quit, or a wrapper method, is really the best practice for terminating the GTK loop.

Stepping Through the Loop

GTK loops may be nested, meaning one loop may start up another. For each call to Gtk::main, there must be a call to Gtk::main_quit. Each call to Gtk::main_quit exits one level of looping. To be honest, I have yet to encounter a case where nested loops are needed, but they are possible.

Much more likely is the chance that only one iteration of the loop should be executed. In effect, running one iteration of the loop updates the application GUI. This might be done to update a progress bar while the application is involved in some long process, such as uploading a file via FTP. To execute only one iteration of the loop, use the Gtk::main_iteration method.

The splash screen we've been developing in this chapter can make excellent use of methodically stepping through the loop. Each time some part of the application setup starts or completes, such as connecting to the database, the splash screen can be updated so that the user knows exactly what is happening. Unfortunately, Gtk::main_iteration doesn't quite do the trick by itself. It needs help from another method called Gtk::events_pending.

The Gtk::events_pending method tells PHP-GTK if any events that need to be handled have happened since the last iteration of the loop. When Gtk::events_pending is used in a while loop, along with Gtk::main_iteration, the GUI will be updated anytime something has happened, such as a label's value being changed. If an iteration of the GTK loop goes by without anything significant happening, the while loop will be terminated.

Listing 5-8 is a combination of the previous two listings. This example puts the splash screen to work. First, the splash screen is created and shown. When the splash screen is instantiated, we create a signal handler that will call the startMainWindow method when the splash screen is shown. Since the show signal cannot be emitted until the main GTK loop starts up, this signal handler is basically a way to set up a method call so that it happens as soon as the loop begins executing. It is kind of a way to cheat and get inside the loop before the loop starts. When called, the startMainWindow method instantiates a Crisscott_MainWindow instance and calls a few setup methods. In between each method, a new status message is set, and the GUI is updated by calling Gtk::main_iteration. The simple while loop found with each Gtk::main_iteration call makes checks to see if something has happened since the last iteration that needs to be handled.

Listing 5-8. *Using Gtk::main_iteration to Update the GUI*

```php
<?php
class Crisscott_SplashScreen extends GtkWindow {

    public $status;

    public function __construct()
    {
        // Call the parent constructor.
        parent::__construct();

        // Turn off the window borders.
        $this->set_decorated(false);

        // Set the background color to white.
        $style = $this->style->copy();
        $style->bg[Gtk::STATE_NORMAL] = $style->white;
        $this->set_style($style);

        // Set the size of the window.
        $this->set_size_request(300, 100);
        // Move the window to the center of the screen.
        $this->set_position(Gtk::WIN_POS_CENTER);

        // Keep the splash screen above all other windows.
        $this->set_keep_above(true);

        // Call a helper method to create the pieces of the splash screen.
        $this->_populate();

        // Set up the application to shut down cleanly.
        $this->connect_simple_after('show', array($this, 'startMainWindow'));
    }

    private function _populate()
    {
```

```php
    // Create the containers.
    $frame = new GtkFrame();
    $hBox  = new GtkHBox();
    $vBox  = new GtkVBox();

    // Set the shadow type.
    $frame->set_shadow_type(Gtk::SHADOW_ETCHED_OUT);

    // Create title label.
    $titleText = '<span foreground="#000060"><b>Crisscott ' .
                 'Product Information Management System</b></span>';
    $title = new GtkLabel($titleText);
    // Use markup to make the label blue and bold.
    $title->set_use_markup(true);

    // Create an initial status message.
    $this->status = new GtkLabel('Initializing Main Window');

    // Stack the labels vertically.
    $vBox->pack_start($title,        true, true, 10);
    $vBox->pack_start($this->status, true, true, 10);

    // Add a logo image.
    $logoImg = GtkImage::new_from_file('Crisscott/images/logo.png');

    // Put the image and the first box next to each other.
    $hBox->pack_start($logoImg, false, false, 10);
    $hBox->pack_start($vBox,    false, false, 10);

    // Put everything inside a frame.
    $frame->add($hBox);

    // Put the frame inside the window.
}


public function start()
{
    // Show all the pieces of the application
    $this->show_all();
    // Start the main loop.
    Gtk::main();
}

public function startMainWindow()
{
    // Create an instance of the main window.
    $main = new Crisscott_MainWindow();
```

```php
        // Update the status message.
        $this->status->set_text('Connecting to server...');
        // Update the GUI.
        while (Gtk::events_pending()) Gtk::main_iteration();

        // Try connecting to the server.
        if ($main->connectToServer()) {
            // Update the status message.
            $this->status->set_text('Connecting to server... OK');
        }
        // Update the GUI.
        while (Gtk::events_pending()) Gtk::main_iteration();
        sleep(1);

        // Update the status message.
        $this->status->set_text('Connecting to local database...');
        while (Gtk::events_pending()) Gtk::main_iteration();

        // Try connecting to the local database.
        if ($main->connectToLocalDB()) {
            // Update the status message.
            $this->status->set_text('Connecting to local database... OK');
        }
        // Update the GUI.
        while (Gtk::events_pending()) Gtk::main_iteration();

        $main->show_all();
        // Update the GUI.
        while (Gtk::events_pending()) Gtk::main_iteration();
        sleep(1);

        // Hide the splash screen.
        $this->hide();
    }
}

class Crisscott_MainWindow extends GtkWindow {

    public function __construct()
    {
        // Call the parent constructor.
        parent::__construct();

        // Set the size of the window.
        $this->set_size_request(500, 300);
        // Move the window to the center of the screen.
        $this->set_position(Gtk::WIN_POS_CENTER);
```

```php
    // Add a title to the window.
    $this->set_title('Criscott PIMS');
    // Maximize the window.
    $this->maximize();

    // Set up the application to shut down cleanly.
    $this->connect_simple('destroy', array('Gtk', 'main_quit'));
  }

  // ...
}

// Create a new splash screen instance.
$splash = new Crisscott_SplashScreen();
// Start up the application.
$splash->start();
?>
```

Now that the two windows are combined into one application, you get a more complete view of how the splash works. From the user's perspective, when Listing 5-8 is executed, the splash screen appears, a few messages flash by, the main window for the application loads, and then the splash screen disappears. The sleep calls are just temporary and give a more realistic user experience. This approach is much more user-friendly than just loading the application without notifying the user that something is happening.

We will update both of these classes as the application continues to take form, but for right now, these should be sufficient.

Summary

This chapter looked at what it takes to get an application up and running. We paid a great deal of attention to setting up the main application window because it is the starting point of most applications. The high level of customization possible for a window allows you a great degree of control over how the application looks and behaves. While the customizations that can be done to a window may not have a huge effect on the overall function of the application, they do have a significant impact on the user experience, and that can be just as important.

Another very important factor in starting up an application is the GTK loop. The GTK loop continuously cycles while an application is running, checking for user interactions and events from the operating system. Without the GTK loop, an application would not be able to react to the user. A noninteractive application doesn't do anyone much good.

In the next chapter, we will continue to bring the PIMS application to life. Now that we have a main window, we can start putting widgets inside. Chapter 6 will focus on the wide variety of containers that are available and highlight which containers are best for holding certain types of widgets. At the end of the next chapter, our PIMS application will be ready to get to work managing some product data.

CHAPTER 6

▪▪▪

Laying Out Applications

In the previous chapter, we looked at creating and setting up windows to provide a framework for an application. In this chapter, we will begin looking at how to add other widgets to the newly created windows.

PHTP-GTK provides various specialty widgets that give you control over not only their placement within the container, but also how they react when the container is resized. This chapter introduces the GtkFrame, GtkVBox, GtkHBox, GtkButtonBox, GtkTable, GtkFixed, and GtkNotebook widgets. We will also begin to implement the Crisscott PIMS application, focusing on setting up the application so that the functional pieces can just be dropped into place.

The Sample Application Layout

The Crisscott PIMS application needs to have the following elements as part of the main window:

- A menu for opening and saving files, changing settings, and so on

- A toolbar for quick access to commonly used commands

- An area for navigating to individual products

- An area to display a summary of the current inventory data

- An area to display a summary of the currently selected product

- An area to display news and important messages

- An area for adding and editing product information

- An area for displaying status messages

Adding these eight areas to the window is more involved than it appears. We need to do more than simply decide which pieces go where. We need to consider the relative size and importance of each section, as well as whether or not an area should be able to shrink or grow with the application. These decisions are often made by considering what the final product might look like and how it will be used.

For instance, what type of information will the news section include? Will it just show headlines, or will it also display article bodies? If the news section will show summaries of the articles, or even the full articles, it will need to be much larger than it would if it were to simply show headlines. This decision of how to size and place the news section will have a significant impact on the user experience. Whereas a large prominently displayed news section will draw the user's attention, it is more likely that Crisscott, Inc. wants the suppliers to remain focused on the product information instead of the news and updates.

Figure 6-1 shows one possible skeleton layout for the PIMS application. Different interpretations of the importance and role of each section of the application will result in widely varied final products, but the layout in Figure 6-1 is what we will try to achieve by the end of this chapter.

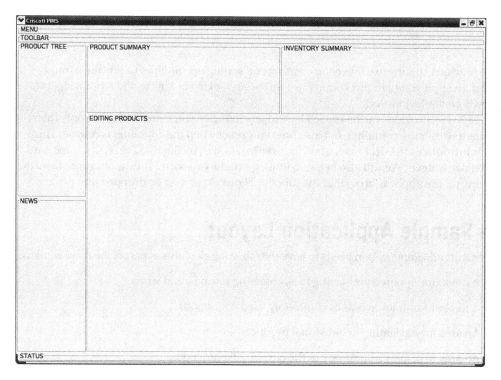

Figure 6-1. *One possible layout for the PIMS application*

Discussion of application layout revolves mainly around containers, which provide the framework and structure for the application by holding and positioning the other elements on the screen. The choice of which container to use depends greatly on the needs of the application and can vary from one section of the application to another. Before deciding which route to go, you must determine levels of priority for the program. Influencing factors are the expected size of the application's window, whether or not certain elements should shrink or grow when the window changes size, and the space between elements on the screen.

Frames

A GtkFrame widget is a simple container that exists mostly for decoration purposes, but also allows related content to be grouped together on the screen. GtkFrame widgets are bin containers, meaning they can contain only one child widget. As far as providing structure for an application, a GtkFrame plays no role. However, it is useful for enhancing usability.

The GtkFrame has a thin border and a label at the top. The border helps to group the frame's contents as a single unit. The label is most often used to describe the contents of the frame.

Most containers do not take up space or have any size without having children added first, but because GtkFrame has a border and a label, it is able to take up screen space on its own. This makes GtkFrame an excellent choice as a placeholder during development. Throughout the next several sections, we'll use frames to hold the place of application elements while we develop the layout. Figure 6-2 shows GtkFrames in action as part of the PHP-GTK 2 demo application.

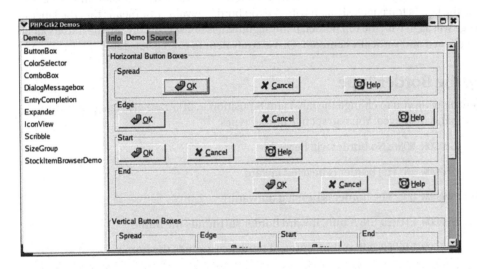

Figure 6-2. *GtkFrames in action*

Creating and using a GtkFrame is simple. The constructor takes the label to be displayed. You can add a child with the add method.

Setting the Label Section

While frames may be simple, they are flexible. Even though technically GtkFrame is a bin container, it is really more of a bin-and-a-half, because the label section of the frame can be set with either a string value or a widget.

You can add any type of widget as the frame's label. This opens up a whole world of possibilities—both good and bad. For example, adding a button to the frame's label area can increase the functionality of an application but can also distort the layout. So, you need to understand exactly what may happen if you add a widget as the frame's label.

To add a widget as the label, call set_label_widget and pass the new label widget. If all you want is a simple string, you can call set_label, passing the new label string. The following line uses set_label to change a frame's label from its current value to the string 'Buttons'.

```
$frame->set_label('Buttons');
```

And to set the frame's label to a GtkButton, you can use the following:

```
$frame->set_label_widget(new GtkButton('Click Me'));
```

You can also move the label around within the top edge of the frame, aligning it both horizontally and vertically. By using set_label_align, you can move the label left or right and up or down. The two values passed to set_label_align determine the label's relative distance from the upper-left corner of the frame. The values must be decimal numbers between zero and one, inclusive. The numbers represent a percentage of the frame's width. If .5 is passed as the first argument, the label will appear centered along the top edge of the frame. If 1 is passed, the label will be aligned to the right. The second argument determines the vertical positioning. A value of 0 means the label's top edge will align with the top border. A value of 1 means that the label's bottom edge will align with the top border. If the alignment is not specifically set, the frame's label will be left aligned and vertically centered. This is equivalent to calling set_label_align(0, .5).

Setting the Border Type

Aside from allowing you to change the label and reposition it, GtkFrame also lets you control the border that is displayed. You can set five border types:

- Gtk::SHADOW_NONE: No border will be visible.

- Gtk::SHADOW_IN: The border is beveled inward.

- Gtk::SHADOW_OUT: The border is beveled outward.

- Gtk::SHADOW_ETCHED_IN: A thin, inward border surrounds the frame.

- Gtk::SHADOW_ETCHED_OUT: A thin, outward border surrounds the frame.

To set the frame's border, use set_shadow_type. By default, a frame's border is set to Gtk::SHADOW_ETCHED_IN. Figure 6-3 shows five simple frames with varying borders and label positions.

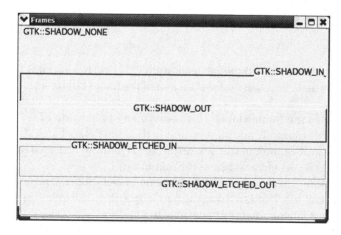

Figure 6-3. *Several GtkFrames with different alignments and border types*

Boxes

The box container is one of the simplest types of containers available to PHP-GTK, and it is also one of the most versatile. PHP-GTK offers three types of box containers, each designed to fulfill a specific need:

- GtkVBox: Used to display widgets in a vertical column.

- GtkHBox: Used to display widgets in a horizontal row.

- GtkButtonBox: Used to display a set of buttons.

Creating Vertical and Horizontal Boxes

GtkVBox and GtkHBox are probably the two most commonly used containers in PHP-GTK. Their simplicity and ability to be nested makes them extremely powerful tools for laying out an application. Part of the power in these two classes is that they are not picky about what types of widgets are added to them, meaning any widget that does not require a specific type of parent can be added to a GtkVBox or GtkHBox. This includes buttons, labels, trees, text entries, and even other boxes. In fact, after creating the main application window, most applications immediately add either a GtkVBox of GtkHBox to the main GtkWindow, and then add boxes within the box. Actually, that is the fastest way to achieve the layout shown earlier in Figure 6-1.

Let's start from the outside and work our way in. Remember from the previous chapter that almost all applications start with a GtkWindow. Also remember that GtkWindow is a bin, meaning that it can have only one child directly. Therefore, to place more than one widget inside a window, the window's only child must be a container. The container can then take one or more children, which themselves can be containers, and so on. Nesting containers allows an application to be built up from a single-child widget to a collection of containers and children that work together as an application. The quickest way to fill a window with multiple widgets is to add a widget that is not a bin—namely, a GtkVBox or GtkHBox.

Look at Figure 6-1 again. We can break down the application into four main rows. The first two are the menu and toolbar. The last row is the status bar. The third row is everything in between. While rows tend to make you think of horizontal displays, rows are actually created by stacking items one on top of another vertically. Since the rows are elements stacked vertically, they must be packed into a GtkVBox.

Packing Widgets into a Box

While to most people, the terms *packing* and *adding* may have the same meaning, in the PHP-GTK world, *packing* has a slightly different connotation. Think about how you get ready for a vacation. Sure you add items to your suitcase, but things are not just haphazardly thrown in. They are placed neatly and with a purpose. The items are packed, not just added. The same thing can be said about adding widgets to a box. They can be simply added, but more commonly they are packed. This means that their order is carefully considered and thought is given to how they will react within the container.

You pack widgets into a box by using the pack_start method. Each call to pack_start adds its widget to the container, starting at the top and working down toward the bottom of the box. The first call to pack_start places its widget at the top of the box, the second call to pack_start adds the widget passed as the second element from the top, and so on. There is no limit to how many elements can be added this way.

A similar method is called pack_end. It works in the same way as pack_start, except that the widgets are packed from the bottom up. The first element added with pack_end will be the last element in the container, the second element added with pack_end will be the second to last element in the container, and so on.

Regardless of what order the method calls are made, elements added to a GtkVBox with pack_start will always appear above elements added with pack_end.

Listing 6-1 shows the code that will create four rows within our sample application's window. GtkFrame widgets are used as temporary placeholders. The frames are packed using the pack_start method.

Listing 6-1. *Creating Rows Within a Window*

```php
<?php
class Crisscott_MainWindow extends GtkWindow {

    public function __construct()
    {
        // Call the parent constructor.
        parent::__construct();

        // Set the size of the window.
        $this->set_size_request(500, 300);
        // Position the window.
        $this->set_position(Gtk::WIN_POS_CENTER);
        // Give the window a title.
        $this->set_title('Criscott PIMS');

        // Add window's children
        $this->_populate();

        // Make the window expand to the limits of the screen.
        $this->maximize();

        // Set up the application to close cleanly.
        $this->connect_object('destroy', array('Gtk', 'main_quit'));
    }

    private function _populate()
    {
        // Create a vertical box.
        $vb1 = new GtkVBox();

        // Pack some frames in the box.
        $vb1->pack_start(new GtkFrame('MENU'), false, false, 0);
        $vb1->pack_start(new GtkFrame('TOOLBAR'), false, false, 0);
        $vb1->pack_start(new GtkFrame('MAIN'), true, true, 0);
        $vb1->pack_start(new GtkFrame('STATUS'), false, false, 0);
```

```
            // Add the box to the window.
            $this->add($vb1);
      }
      // ...
}
?>
```

A closer look at the calls to pack_start shows that there are four arguments passed, instead of just the widget that is added. The following three optional parameters allow pack_start and pack_end to be more powerful than the generic add method:

- expand: A Boolean value that determines whether or not the widget will take up all of the space available to it.

- fill: A Boolean value that determines whether or not the widget will shrink and grow along with its parent.

- padding: The amount of padding, in pixels, that will surround the child widget.

As I mentioned, packing implies consideration of how widgets will react within their parent container. A child widget will be given the opportunity to interact with its parent container at two times: first, when the child is added, and then when the container is resized. When these events occur, the children of the container will be given the opportunity to automatically adjust their size or the amount of space each occupies within the box.

When a widget is packed into a box, by default, it tries to take up as much room as is available. Also by default, the widget will try to resize itself to fill in that space. Taking up space and filling in space are not necessarily the same thing.

Taking up space simply means that the widget reserves a given amount of space for itself. It tells other widgets, "This area is mine. Stay out!"

Filling up the space means that the widget shrinks or grows to fit within the space it has reserved. If the widget is only 50 pixels square, but the space available is 100 pixels wide by 200 pixels high, the widget will try to expand to fit the 100×200 space. When more than one widget wants to take up all the space available, just as with children on a long car trip, the parent steps in. The parent splits up the available space evenly among the children that want to occupy as much screen space as possible.

The second and third arguments to the pack_start and pack_end methods determine whether a widget may reserve the maximum amount of available space, known as *expanding*, or resize itself to fill the space allotted to it, known as *filling*, respectively. By default, both of these arguments are passed as true. This means that when a widget is packed into a box, it will be automatically resized to be as big as the box and other children will allow.

However, in cases where a widget has been specifically sized, allowing the widget to fill the available space may have undesired effects. Passing false as the second argument tells the container that the given child widget does not want more space than it needs to display its content. Passing false as the third argument tells the application that the widget being packed should not be resized to fill the space available. Both of these requests are honored when the child is packed and when the container is resized. If when the child was packed, it was allowed to fill the available space, it will resize itself again when the container is resized and more (or less) space is available.

In Listing 6-1, most parts of the application should take up as little space as needed to allow for the more important pieces to be the focus of the application. That is why only the frame labeled MAIN is allowed to expand and fill the space available to it. All other sections of the application are forced to remain just large enough to show their contents.

Tip All boxes have a set_homogeneous method, which makes the box's children share the space equally. This is the same as setting all of the fill arguments (the third argument) to true for every widget packed into the box. If set_homogeneous is passed true, all children will share the space equally, regardless of what options were passed when the widget is packed.

The final argument that may be passed to pack_start and pack_end is an integer that defines the amount of padding that will surround the child widget. The padding that surrounds a child is given in pixels. In a box container, padding exists only in the direction of the box. So, for a GtkVBox, padding will appear only above and below the child widget. For a GtkHBox, padding will appear only to the left and right of the widget. Padding between widgets does not collapse. If widget A is packed with a padding of 10 pixels and widget B is packed with a padding of 20 pixels, the total space between the two widgets will be 30 pixels. Figure 6-4 shows several widgets packed into a GtkHBox with different padding values. In Listing 6-1, the maximum amount of screen space is used by setting all of the padding to 0.

Figure 6-4. *Different padding values*

Nesting Boxes

Nesting boxes is the practice of putting one box inside another box. Box classes are highly specialized, as this makes managing their children easier. While specialization may be good for managing children, it makes layout a little more difficult. For instance, creating rows *or* columns is easy, but creating rows *and* columns with boxes requires a little patience and planning.

To create rows within a column, a GtkVBox must be placed inside a GtkHBox. To create columns within a row, simply do the opposite—put a GtkHBox inside GtkVBox. While this may not sound very complicated, it can become quite difficult to track all the different boxes when the levels go beyond one or two deep.

Listing 6-2 shows a reworked version of the _populate method used in Listing 6-1. The new method uses GtkVBox and GtkHBox widgets nested inside one another to add more sections to the application.

Listing 6-2. *Nesting Boxes*

```php
<?php
//...
private function _populate()
{
```

```
    // Create several boxes for nesting.
    $vb1 = new GtkVBox();
    $vb2 = new GtkVBox();
    $vb3 = new GtkVBox();
    $hb1 = new GtkHBox();
    $hb2 = new GtkHBox();

    // Add some frames to the first vBox.
    $vb1->pack_start(new GtkFrame('MENU'), false, false, 0);
    $vb1->pack_start(new GtkFrame('TOOLBAR'), false, false, 0);

    // Nest an hBox inside the vBox.
    $vb1->pack_start($hb1);

    // Add another frame after the hBox.
    $vb1->pack_start(new GtkFrame('STATUS'), false, false, 0);

    // Nest a vBox inside the hBox
    $hb1->pack_start($vb2, false, false, 0);

    // Nest another vBox inside the hBox.
    $hb1->pack_start($vb3);

    // Pack some frames into one of the nested vBoxes.
    $vb2->pack_start(new GtkFrame('PRODUCT TREE'));
    $vb2->pack_start(new GtkFrame('NEWS'));

    // Set the size of the vBox.
    $vb2->set_size_request(150, -1);

    // Nest an hBox inside one of the nested vBoxes.
    $vb3->pack_start($hb2, false, false, 0);

    // Add a frame after the nested box.
    $vb3->pack_start(new GtkFrame('EDITING PRODUCTS'));

    // Add a few frames to the nested hBox.
    $hb2->pack_start(new GtkFrame('PRODUCT SUMMARY'));
    $hb2->pack_start(new GtkFrame('INVENTORY SUMMARY'));

    // Set the nested hBox's size.
    $hb2->set_size_request(-1, 150);

    // Add the vBox to the window.
    $this->add($vb1);
}
// ...
?>
```

Figure 6-5 shows the new layout using nested boxes.

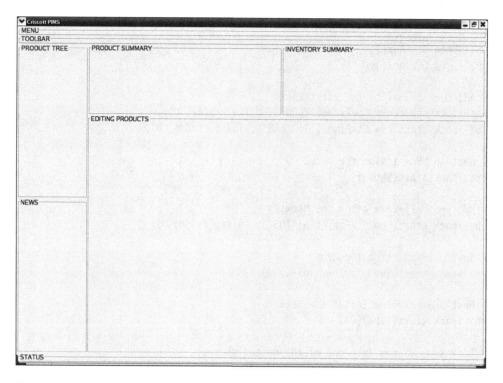

Figure 6-5. *Using nested boxes for layout*

In Listing 6-2, the third row, which used to have a title of MAIN, is now split into two columns. The third row was changed from a simple frame to a GtkHBox. A GtkHBox was used because the application needs to display things next to each other horizontally. By placing two GtkVBox widgets next to each other, you can create columns.

The items packed into the GtkVBox widgets will be separated distinctly into items on the left and items on the right. Notice that the first GtkVBox packed is told not to expand or fill. The box also has its size explicitly set using set_size_request. The combination of proper packing and set_size_request ensures that the box will appear just as you intended. The box will not shrink or grow within its parent box, and its size is not dependent on other children in the container.

Within each of the two columns are two rows. Since $vb2, the column on the left, is very simple, two frames are added directly to the GtkVBox. $vb3, on the other hand is slightly more complex. Its first row contains two columns again. Once again, the rows are created by nesting GtkHBox widgets inside the GtkVBox.

Pay close attention to when and how the extra arguments for pack_start are used in this listing. Try switching the values from true to false and vice versa, and add a little (or a lot) of padding here and there. Changing one Boolean value can have a huge impact on the rest of the application.

Note In Listing 6-2, because the child box was packed into a GtkHBox, the expand and fill arguments apply only in the horizontal direction. The vertical expand and fill arguments trickle down from the parent when it was packed into the GtkVBox. Since the parent was told that it may expand and fill within the GtkVBox, the child will shrink and grow vertically depending on the size of its parent.

Button Boxes

The application isn't quite ready to start adding buttons, but this is a good point to discuss button boxes. GtkButtonBox is a descendant of GtkBox, just like GtkVBox and GtkHBox. The difference is that button boxes can use special layouts that are often helpful when displaying a group of buttons.

There are two varieties of GtkButtonBox: GtkVButtonBox and GtkHButtonBox. Each type functions in the same way as its regular box counterpart. Widgets are packed into a GtkButtonBox using pack_start and pack_end.

The advantage to using a button box is in the set_layout method. set_layout determines how the buttons will be shown within the box. The layout can be one of four values:

- spread: The buttons will be distributed evenly in the box.

- edge: The buttons will be as far apart as possible. The first button will be against the beginning edge of the box, and the last button will be against the ending edge of the box. All of the buttons in between will be as far apart from each other as they can.

- start: The buttons appear toward the starting edge of the box.

- end: The buttons appear toward the ending edge of the box.

For a better understanding of how to use button boxes, take a look at phpgtk2-demo.php, located in the demos directory of the PHP-GTK source. The button box demo shows the many different layouts of a GtkButtonBox, as you can see in Figure 6-6.

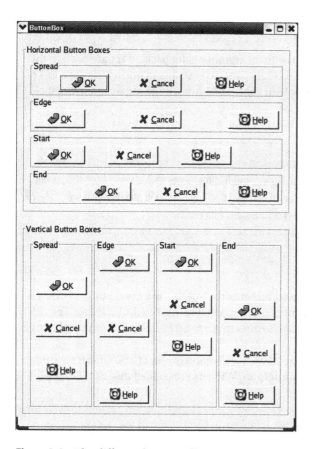

Figure 6-6. *The different layouts of button boxes*

Tables

It is often possible to achieve the desired layout of an application using nested boxes, but setting up the application and keeping things organized gets more and more difficult as the levels of nesting get deeper. As with most things in life, there is more than one way to reach the same result.

GtkTable is a container class designed specifically for laying out an application, unlike its HTML counterpart, which is designed for organizing data. A GtkTable can be used to more easily display widgets in rows and columns. A GtkTable container is similar to a table in HTML. It has rows and columns made up of individual cells, and each cell can span more than one row and/or column. While the contents of each cell are independent, the dimensions of a row or column are determined by the largest cell in that row or column.

Listing 6-3 is an implementation of the _populate method from the earlier listings, but it uses a GtkTable instead of nested boxes. At first glance, the new version appears to be quite complicated because of all of the integers floating around, but once these numbers are explained, the picture clears up rather quickly.

Listing 6-3. *Laying Out an Application Using GtkTable*

```php
<?php
// ...
private function _populate()
{
    // Create a new table with 5 rows and 3 columns.
    $table = new GtkTable(5, 3);

    // Make it easier to set both expand and fill at the same time.
    $expandFill = Gtk::EXPAND|Gtk::FILL;

    // Attach two frames to the table.
    $table->attach(new GtkFrame('MENU'), 0, 2, 0, 1, $expandFill, 0, 0, 0);
    $table->attach(new GtkFrame('TOOLBAR'), 0, 2, 1, 2, $expandFill, 0, 0, 0);

    // Create a new frame and set its size.
    $productTree = new GtkFrame('PRODUCT TREE');
    $productTree->set_size_request(150, -1);

    // Attach the frame to the table.
    $table->attach($productTree, 0, 1, 2, 3, 0, $expandFill, 0, 0);

    // Create a new frame and set its size.
    $news = new GtkFrame('NEWS');
    $news->set_size_request(150, -1);

    // Attach the frame to the table.
    $table->attach($news, 0, 1, 3, 4, 0, $expandFill, 0, 0);

    // Create a subtable.
    $table2 = new GtkTable(2, 2);

    // Create a new frame and set its size.
    $productSummary = new GtkFrame('PRODUCT SUMMARY');
    $productSummary->set_size_request(-1, 150);

    // Attach the frame to the subtable.
    $table2->attach($productSummary, 0, 1, 0, 1, $expandFill, 0, 1, 1);

    // Create a new frame and set its size.
    $inventorySummary = new GtkFrame('INVENTORY SUMMARY');
    $inventorySummary->set_size_request(-1, 150);

    // Attach the frame to the subtable.
    $table2->attach($inventorySummary, 1, 2, 0, 1, $expandFill, 0, 1, 1);
    $table2->attach(new GtkFrame('EDITING PRODUCTS'), 0, 2, 1, 2,
                    $expandFill, $expandFill, 1, 1);
```

```
    // Attach the subtable to the main table.
    $table->attach($table2, 1, 2, 2, 4, $expandFill, $expandFill, 0, 0);

    // Attach another frame to the main table.
    $table->attach(new GtkFrame('STATUS'),  0, 2, 4, 5, $expandFill, 0, 0, 0);

    // Add the table to the window.
    $this->add($table);
}
// ...
?>
```

Figure 6-7 gives an idea of what the end result of this section looks like. Notice that even though the code has changed, the result is the same.

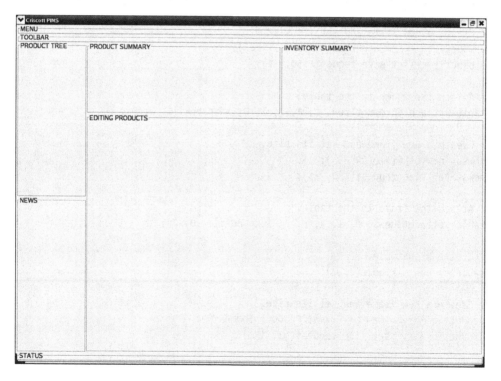

Figure 6-7. *The Crisscott PIMS application using a GtkTable for layout*

Constructing the Table

The first step in using a GtkTable is to create a new instance. The constructor for a GtkTable widget takes three optional parameters.

- rows: The number of rows the table should have initially. The value must be an integer between 1 and 65535, inclusive. It defaults to 1.

- columns: The number of columns the table should have initially. The value must be an integer between 1 and 65535, inclusive. It defaults to 1.

- homogeneous: A Boolean value that if set to true will force all cells to be the same size. It defaults to false.

The first two parameters are the number of rows and columns that the table should have. If at some point the table needs an additional row or column, you can easily change the dimensions of the table using resize. resize sets the new number of rows and columns to the two integer values passed. In both the constructor and resize, the first argument is the number of rows and the second argument is the number of columns.

Note It isn't strictly necessary to resize the table when a new row or column is added. If a child is added into a cell that doesn't exist, the row and/or column needed for that cell will be added automatically.

The final argument for the GtkTable constructor is the Boolean homogeneous value. This value defaults to false and has the same effect that set_homogeneous has for boxes. If the homogeneous argument is set to true, all cells in the table will be the same size. In Listing 6-3, the table is created with five rows and three columns, for a total of fifteen cells. No value is passed to tell the table whether or not the cells should be homogeneous, so they will default to being as tall as the tallest cell in their row and as wide as the widest cell in their column. The height and width of the largest cell in a row or column are determined by the cell's content.

Attaching Children

The next step in laying out the application is adding children to the table. Just as boxes have their own terminology for adding children, so does GtkTable. In a table, children are not added— they are *attached*, and this is accomplished with the attach method.

Attaching a child gives greater control over the location and the way the child reacts within the table. The first priority in attaching a child to a table is putting it in the right place. When putting a widget in a table, all four sides of the widget must be specifically positioned. The attach method takes a whopping nine arguments:

- child: The widget to be added to the table.

- col_start: The starting column to attach the child to.

- col_end: The ending column to attach the child to.

- row_start: The starting row to attach the child to.

- row_end: The ending row to attach the child to.

- x_options: Whether or not the child should expand and fill in the x direction.

- y_options: Whether or not the child should expand and fill in the y direction.

- x_padding: The amount of padding on the left and right of the child widget.

- y_padding: The amount of padding on the top and bottom of the child widget.

The first argument to attach is the widget that will be added to the table. The other arguments specify the child's placement within the cell, whether it expands and fills, and its padding.

Cell Placement

After the child argument, the next four arguments to the attach method correspond to the four sides of the child widget. The col_start argument tells the table in which column the left side of the child should start. If the col_start argument is 0, the child will be in the leftmost column. If the col_start argument is 1, the child will start in the second column. The col_end argument tells the table where the child should stop. The value passed is one greater than the column in which the widget should end.

For instance, if a child should be in only the first column of a table, the col_start and col_end arguments should be 0 and 1. If a child should span the second and third columns, the col_start and col_end arguments should be 1 and 3. This tells the table that the child should start in column 1 (rows and columns are indexed starting with 0, just like most things in programming) and end before column 3.

The row_start and row_end arguments to attach are similar to col_start and col_end, except they determine the row or rows that the child will occupy.

The first call to attach in Listing 6-3 places a GtkFrame in the first row of the table, spanning all three columns. This is done by telling the child to start in column 0 and end just before column 3. The child is also told to start in row 0 and end just before row 1. With these four values, you can place a child in any cell and have it span as many rows and/or columns as needed.

Expanding and Filling

Assigning a widget to a cell in a table is only half the goal. The other half involves explaining how the widget should react within the table. Similar to packing items in boxes, attaching widgets to a table also involves determining whether or not the child should expand and fill the maximum amount of space available.

With boxes, the space for each element is either part of a row (GtkHBox) *or* part of a column (GtkVBox). A table cell is the intersection of both a row *and* a column. Therefore, the expand and fill attributes need to be set for both the row, or x-axis, and column, or y-axis.

The x_options argument passed to attach tells the table whether the child should expand and/or fill the cell in the x direction. The value passed should be made up of one or more constant values. If the widget should expand but not fill the cell, the value should be Gtk::EXPAND. If the widget should fill the cell but not expand, the value should be set to Gtk::FILL. If the widget should both expand and fill the cell, the value should be Gtk::EXPAND|Gtk::FILL.

The y_options argument sets the same values for the y-axis. Passing 0 to either of these values tells the table not to allow the child to expand or fill the cell in that direction. By default, a child will expand and fill a cell in both directions. In Listing 6-3, the menu and toolbar frames are told to expand and fill their cells only along the x-axis. The product tree frame is told to expand and fill only along the y-axis. Because the product tree frame is set to 150 pixels wide and is told not to expand or fill on the x-axis, it will always remain 150 pixels wide. The height of the frame is set to -1, which means that its height is not to be strictly controlled. Coupled with the expand and fill properties for the y-axis, this allows the frame to stretch when the window is resized.

Padding

The final task when attaching a widget to a table is setting the amount of padding that each cell should have. When packing a widget in a box, the padding is set equally on two sides to the value of the last argument passed to pack_start or pack_end (which two sides depends on the type of box). When attaching a widget to a table, padding can be set for both the x and y directions, just as with the expand and fill properties.

The x_padding and y_padding arguments passed to attach determine the x and y padding, respectively. If either of these values is omitted, the padding for that direction will default to 5 pixels.

Tables vs. Boxes

You can use tables and boxes in a similar manner to create similar output. Listing 6-3 even has a table nested inside another table to show how similar the two can be. Despite their similarities, GtkTable is often a better choice when setting up an application.

Using tables gives you more control over the placement of children within the application than creating the layout with boxes. With tables, it is possible to have a good idea of where the widgets will appear before the application starts up. Boxes usually require much more trial and error.

Tables also lend themselves better to more readable code. It is easy to tell where in the application a table cell will be by looking at the row and column to which it is attached. With boxes, it is usually more difficult and requires a little bit of tracing through the code.

While tables may have several advantages over boxes, they are not the only other choice. An alternative is to use a fixed container, as described next.

Fixed Containers

GtkTable is very effective in lining up widgets into rows and columns. But sometimes the relationships between children in the same row or column can be a problem, because the dimensions of a cell in a table are determined by the largest cell in a cell's row and column. That is where GtkFixed comes in.

Like GtkTable, GtkFixed allows for precise positioning, but it does not strictly align elements with each other. The elements in a GtkFixed container have no influence on one another. The height and width of a given child do not depend on another element, because each child is placed independently of the other children.

A GtkFixed widget is similar to a bulletin board. Each child is put in a specific location and stays there, somewhat oblivious to its surroundings. Free-form layout is quick and easy with a GtkFixed widget. Simply put a widget in its place, and that is it.

Listing 6-4 re-creates Figure 6-1, but this time uses a GtkFixed container instead of boxes or tables. The end result is exactly the same in appearance.

Listing 6-4. *Using GtkFixed to Lay Out the Application*

```php
<?php
// ...
private function _populate()
{
    // Create a GtkFixed container.
    $fixed = new GtkFixed();

    // Create a frame, set its size, and put it in the fixed container.
    $menu = new GtkFrame('MENU');
    $menu->set_size_request(GDK::screen_width() - 10, -1);
    $fixed->put($menu, 0, 0);

    // Create a frame, set its size, and put it in the fixed container.
    $toolbar = new GtkFrame('TOOLBAR');
    $toolbar->set_size_request(GDK::screen_width() - 10, -1);
    $fixed->put($toolbar, 0, 18);

    // Create a frame, set its size, and put it in the fixed container.
    $pTree = new GtkFrame('PRODUCT TREE');
    $pTree->set_size_request(150, GDK::screen_height() / 2 - 54);
    $fixed->put($pTree, 0, 36);

    // Create a frame, set its size, and put it in the fixed container.
    $news = new GtkFrame('NEWS');
    $news->set_size_request(150, GDK::screen_height() / 2 - 54);
    $fixed->put($news, 0, GDK::screen_height() / 2 - 18);

    // Create a frame, set its size, and put it in the fixed container.
    $status = new GtkFrame('STATUS');
    $status->set_size_request(GDK::screen_width() - 10, -1);
    $fixed->put($status, 0, GDK::screen_height() - 72);

    // Create a frame, set its size, and put it in the fixed container.
    $pSummary = new GtkFrame('PRODUCT SUMMARY');
    $pSummary->set_size_request(GDK::screen_width() / 2 - 90, 150);
    $fixed->put($pSummary, 152, 36);

    // Create a frame, set its size, and put it in the fixed container.
    $iSummary = new GtkFrame('INVENTORY SUMMARY');
    $iSummary->set_size_request(GDK::screen_width() / 2 - 75, 150);
    $fixed->put($iSummary, GDK::screen_width() / 2 - 90 + 154, 36);
```

```
    // Create a frame, set its size, and put it in the fixed container.
    $edit = new GtkFrame('EDIT PRODUCTS');
    $edit->set_size_request(GDK::screen_width() - 150, GDK::screen_height() - 262);
    $fixed->put($edit, 152, 190);

    // Add the fixed container to the window.
    $this->add($fixed);
}
// ...
?>
```

To create this version of the application, each child widget needs to be sized and placed individually. This is different from the other examples. In the previous two listings, only a few widgets were specifically sized, and even then, it was either their height or width, not both.

With a GtkFixed, children are not able to react to their surroundings. Children cannot expand or fill an area. They simply get put into the container and remain there. Therefore, if a child should take up a certain amount of the screen space, its size must be explicitly set.

Putting Widgets in a Fixed Container

When you use boxes, you *pack* widgets, which implies that the widgets are added to the container one after another. When you use tables, you *attach* widgets, which implies that they become part of the table. When you use a fixed container, the widgets are *put*, which implies that a location was selected and the widget was placed in that specific spot.

To put a widget into a GtkFixed container, call the put method and pass the x and y coordinates for the upper-left corner of the child. The child will be put directly into the container at the location given. Its size will remain the same as it was before it was added. If the container is resized, the child will not change. It will still be *x* pixels from the left and *y* pixels from the top of the container.

In Listing 6-4, each element is sized and put individually. Calculating the position for a given element can be difficult and often requires some advance knowledge of the other children in the container.

Using Fixed Containers

Fine-grained control is the strong point of GtkFixed; however, as the name implies, flexibility is its weakness. Listing 6-4 is admittedly a poor use of GtkFixed. The PIMS application does not need such complete control over the application layout. Instead, it needs less control and more flexibility.

Run the application using the _populate method from Listing 6-4. When the application has loaded, try unmaximizing or resizing the window. The elements within the GtkFixed do not resize. As you can see in Figure 6-8, the product edit area quickly gets cut off when the window is resized even slightly smaller. This obviously is a bad design.

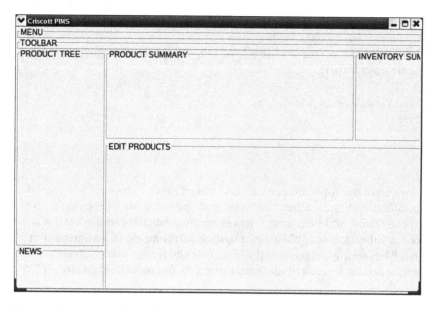

Figure 6-8. *An example of the issues inherent in GtkFixed*

GtkFixed has its uses, but laying out a large application probably isn't one of them. GtkFixed should instead be used in places where position is much more important than size or where the container cannot be resized. For instance, the splash screen might make good use of a GtkFixed container. The user cannot resize the window, and the splash screen will likely show a corporate logo. Corporations often have specific rules about their logos, which define sizes and distances between the logo and other elements. A GtkFixed container can be used to ensure that the corporate rules are followed.

For the Crisscott PIMS application, Listing 6-3 is probably the best solution. Because of the complexity of the layout, the box approach is just too much work to keep organized. The desire to keep the application highly usable and flexible rules out the GtkFixed approach.

Notebooks

Now that the general layout for the application is set, it is time to think about how to best fit all the varying pieces into the limited real estate. For several parts of the application, this is a simple matter. The menu goes in the area we blocked out for the menu, and the news section goes where the news frame is. But the main reason for building this application is not to show a menu or to distribute news; it is to manage product data. That means we are going to need one or more areas to modify product data and other information. Trying to show all of the tools in the product-editing area at the same time would be difficult at best. Additionally, it would make the application rather confusing to use.

One approach could be to make the product-editing area scroll to give elements more room, but that wouldn't really improve the usability. A more helpful approach would be to show only one set of tools at a time. Tools that are not in use should be hidden to avoid confusion and brought to the forefront when needed. Hiding and displaying groups of widgets may sound difficult, but there is a highly specialized container widget that makes it easy. That widget is GtkNotebook.

Figure 6-9 shows the PHP-GTK 2 Dev_Inspector (http://cweiske.de/phpgtk2_devinspector. htm). This application uses a GtkNotebook widget to organize reflection data.

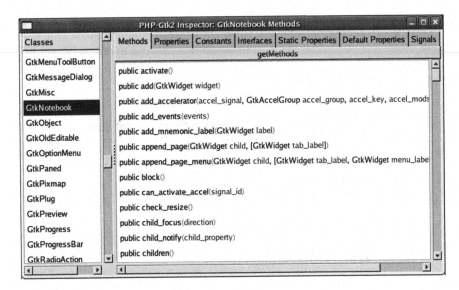

Figure 6-9. *GtkNotebook in the PHP-GTK 2 Dev_Inspector*

GtkNotebook is a container that organizes its children into pages. Each page is itself a bin container and can hold one child. What makes GtkNotebook so powerful is that at any given time, a specific page can be brought to the front of the screen. Only the selected page will be seen by the user. All other pages will remain intact but out of view. The GtkNotebook can have tabs that allow the user to select a given page, or the tabs can be hidden. If the tabs are hidden, the application will control which page is currently displayed.

GtkNotebook is very good for organizing groups of widgets into task-oriented blocks. Being able to control which group of widgets is currently visible also allows you to force the user to step through a process in an ordered manner. The user will not be able to skip ahead, because the next step is not yet available.

GtkNotebook should be thought of more as a three-ring binder than an actual notebook. It consists of pages that can be added, removed, and reordered. The GtkNotebook can have all of its pages marked, or tabbed, or the tabs can be hidden. If the tabs are visible, a user can click one to jump to that page. The tabs can also be moved to any side of the page.

A GtkNotebook widget can have as many pages as needed. Each page holds any arbitrary data and exists independently of the other pages. While the notebook may have more than one child page, the pages themselves are bins and may only have one child each. Just as with GtkWindow and GtkFrame, to have more than one widget show up in the page, another container must be added as the page's child.

In the Crisscott PIMS application, the main area in the application will serve multiple purposes. It will be used to add and edit product information, update supplier data, transmit inventory data, and perform a few other tasks. Figure 6-10 shows what the application will look like with the GtkNotebook widget added. To keep these tasks organized, the main area will use GtkNotebook, with each task assigned to one or more pages. This approach will maximize the amount of space available and will also help improve usability by forcing the user to focus on one task at a time.

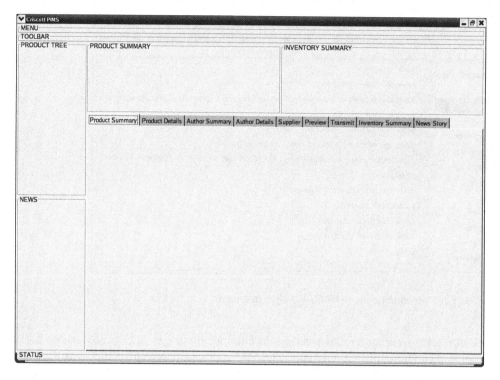

Figure 6-10. *The PIMS application with a simple notebook*

The amount of effort that must be put into organizing widgets with GtkNotebook is considerably less than trying to group, hide, and show widgets by hand. In Listing 6-5, the GtkFrame widget that was labeled EDITING PRODUCTS has been replaced with a custom object that extends GtkNotebook. The custom class helps to make the PIMS-specific organization a little easier. Note also that the notebook is stored as a member variable. This is because items will need to be added, removed, and accessed by other parts of the application.

Listing 6-5. *Adding GtkNotebook to the Application*

```php
<?php
// ...
private function _populate()
{
    // Create a new table.
    $table = new GtkTable(5, 3);
```

```php
// Make it easier to set both expand and fill at the same time.
$expandFill = Gtk::EXPAND|Gtk::FILL;

// Attach a few frames to the table.
$table->attach(new GtkFrame('MENU'),    0, 2, 0, 1, $expandFill, 0, 0, 0);
$table->attach(new GtkFrame('TOOLBAR'), 0, 2, 1, 2, $expandFill, 0, 0, 0);

// Create a new frame and set its size.
$productTree = new GtkFrame('PRODUCT TREE');
$productTree->set_size_request(150, -1);

// Attach the frame to the table.
$table->attach($productTree, 0, 1, 2, 3, 0, $expandFill, 0, 0);

// Create a new frame and set its size.
$news = new GtkFrame('NEWS');
$news->set_size_request(150, -1);

// Attach the frame to the table.
$table->attach($news, 0, 1, 3, 4, 0, $expandFill, 0, 0);

// Create a new subtable.
$table2 = new GtkTable(2, 2);

// Create a new frame and set its size.
$productSummary = new GtkFrame('PRODUCT SUMMARY');
$productSummary->set_size_request(-1, 150);

// Attach the frame to the subtable.
$table2->attach($productSummary, 0, 1, 0, 1, $expandFill, 0, 1, 1);

// Create a new frame and set its size.
$inventorySummary = new GtkFrame('INVENTORY SUMMARY');
$inventorySummary->set_size_request(-1, 150);

// Attach the frame to the subtable.
$table2->attach($inventorySummary, 1, 2, 0, 1, $expandFill, 0, 1, 1);

// Create a new instance of the main notebook.
require_once 'Crisscott/MainNotebook.php';
$this->mainNotebook = new Crisscott_MainNotebook();

// Attach the notebook to the subtable.
$table2->attach($this->mainNotebook, 0, 2, 1, 2,
                $expandFill, $expandFill, 1, 1);

// Attach the subtable to the main table.
$table->attach($table2, 1, 2, 2, 4, $expandFill, $expandFill, 0, 0);
```

```php
    // Attach a new frame to the main table.
    $table->attach(new GtkFrame('STATUS'),  0, 2, 4, 5, $expandFill, 0, 0, 0);

    // Add the table to the window.
    $this->add($table);
}
// ...
?>
```

Defining the Notebook

The next step is defining the Crisscott_MainNotebook class. To start, the notebook will be very simple and use the default settings. Then we will look at customizing the notebook to better suit our needs.

Listing 6-6 is a first run at putting the notebook together. The Crisscott_MainNotebook class is a simple wrapper around GtkNotebook that adds a few pages and tracks them using an array. The constructor for GtkNotebook takes no arguments and returns a notebook that has no pages. The idea behind the Crisscott_MainNotebook class is just to make development a little more organized. Each page is given a text label, which is also used as the array index. Now instead of having to search for a page by number, you can search a small array by its label.

Listing 6-6. *Organizing Tools with GtkNotebook*

```php
<?php
class Crisscott_MainNotebook extends GtkNotebook {

    public $pages = array();

    public function __construct()
    {
        // Call the parent constructor.
        parent::__construct();

        // Create an array of tab labels.
        $titles = array(
                        'Product Summary',
                        'Product Details',
                        'Author Summary',
                        'Author Details',
                        'Supplier',
                        'Preview',
                        'Transmit',
                        'Inventory Summary',
                        'News Story'
                        );

        // Add a page for each element in the array and put
        // it in the pages array for easier access later.
```

```
        foreach ($titles as $title) {
            $pageNum = $this->append_page(new GtkVBox(), new GtkLabel($title));
            $page    = $this->get_nth_page($pageNum);
            $this->pages[$title] = $page;
        }
    }
}
?>
```

Adding, Moving, and Removing Notebook Pages

Each page of a notebook has two elements: the tab and the content. The page tab is usually a string that describes the contents of the page. The tab is the main method by which a user will select a page. The content of the page can be anything. Usually, the content that is added directly to the page is some sort of container.

A page can be added at the beginning of a notebook, at the end of a notebook, or anywhere in between using the methods prepend_page, append_page, and insert_page, respectively. All require a widget for the page body and a widget for the page tab. In Listing 6-6, several pages are appended to the notebook. Each page is added in turn to the back of the notebook with append_page. The pages could have just as easily been added to the front of the notebook with prepend_page. To insert a page in any arbitrary position, use insert_page, passing the body widget, the tab widget, and the page position. Pages are indexed starting from 0, so the first page in the notebook is actually page 0.

When a page is added to a GtkNotebook widget, its page index is returned. The value returned from append_page is always the total number of pages minus one. The return value from prepend_page is always 0. The return value from insert_page is not always the same as the position passed to it. If a page is inserted with a position of 12 but there are only eight pages in the notebook, the new page will be added as the last page. The page indexes are always collapsed. For example, the newly inserted page may be inserted in position 12, but it will immediately be moved to position 8. If no position value is passed to insert_page, the position will default to –1, which means the page should be appended to the back of the notebook. The value that will be returned will be the same as if append_page were used.

Knowing the page index is useful because you can use it to retrieve a page from the notebook. Listing 6-6 uses the get_nth_page method to return the page body widget after it has been added to the notebook. This is done to make accessing the page contents easier later on.

Once the page is found, it can then be used to grab the label or the label text. get_tab_label takes a notebook child, usually returned by get_nth_page, and returns the tab widget. get_tab_label_text will return just the text string for the same page if passed the same child widget. Just as you can get a tab label or its text, you can set a tab label or its text. set_tab_label and set_tab_label_text work in much same way as their get counterparts. Each expects a widget that has already been prepended, appended, or inserted into the notebook as the first argument and either a tab widget or a string of text to be set as the tab label. The index of a page is the key to being able to make changes.

Tip To get the total number of pages, use get_n_pages. Keep in mind that this is the total number of pages, not the index of the last page. The index of the last page is get_n_pages() - 1.

While the index of a page is the key to accessing the page, the index may change. If a new page is prepended or inserted in front of a given page, the index will be incremented. If a page in front of a given page is removed or moved to the back of the notebook, the page's index will be decremented. To get the index of a specific child, use the page_num method. page_num takes a widget as the only argument and returns the page index. Regrabbing the index this way comes in handy when pages in the notebook are moved.

You can reorder pages by using the reorder_child method. reorder_child takes the child given as the first argument and puts it in the position given by the second argument. The page that previously occupied the position will be moved backward in the notebook. If the position passed to reorder_child is greater than the total number of pages, the page will be moved to the back of the notebook.

You can also remove pages from the notebook. To do this, call remove_page and pass the page index.

Whenever either the reorder_child or remove_page method is called, the pages are reindexed. This means, for example, that the page that was previously in position 5 may now be in position 4, 5, or 6, even though that particular page was never moved. Because of this reindexing, the code in Listing 6-6 uses a separate array with associative keys to keep track of the pages. Without this separate array, finding a particular page may require cycling through all the pages in the notebook.

Navigating Notebook Pages

In reality, a GtkNotebook widget can do only three things: go back one page, go forward one page, or jump to a particular page. What makes GtkNotebook such an excellent tool is the number of ways in which these three simple tasks can be accomplished. The most obvious method to get from one page to another is by clicking the tab for a given page. This is a simple user interaction and requires no special programming.

GtkNotebook containers are powerful because of their ability to bring a particular group of widgets to the front while hiding all others. While showing and hiding groups is a nice feature, it is the ease with which the top page can be changed that makes GtkNotebook so powerful.

In some cases, an application may need to display a given page of the notebook. For instance, when a user wants to edit a product in the Crisscott PIMS application, the page that is currently being shown should be hidden, and the product-editing page should be brought to the screen. Likewise, if there were a page specifically for error messages, that page would be shown whenever an error is encountered.

Moving to the Next, Previous, or Specific Page

Another reason to change a page automatically is to step through a process. GtkNotebook makes it easy to move through a series of steps that together make up one complete process. The way to step through something is to complete the requirements for one page, and then go to the next. Moving to the next page is done by calling next_page. The next_page method hides the current page and shows the page with the next index. The previous_page method is similar to next_page, except it goes to the previous page. If there is not a previous page, the first page is shown again. Neither next_page nor previous_page will cycle around the pages.

Listing 6-7 rewrites the constructor of the Crisscott_MainNotebook class and adds two buttons to each page. One is connected to the previous_page method, while the other is connected to the next_page method.

Tip If next_page is called and the last page of the GtkNotebook is already being shown, nothing happens. This can be shown by creating a signal handler for the switch-page signal and trying to go past the end of the GtkNotebook. When trying to go beyond the last page, the signal handler will not be called.

Listing 6-7. *Moving to the Next or Previous Page*

```php
<?php
// ...
public function __construct()
{
    // Call the parent constructor.
    parent::__construct();

    // Create an array of tab labels.
    $titles = array(
                    'Product Summary',
                    'Product Details',
                    'Author Summary',
                    'Author Details',
                    'Supplier',
                    'Preview',
                    'Transmit',
                    'Inventory Summary',
                    'News Story'
                    );

    // Add a page for each element in the array and
    // put it in the pages array for easier access
    // later.
    foreach ($titles as $title) {
        $pageNum = $this->append_page(new GtkVBox(), new GtkLabel($title));
        $page    = $this->get_nth_page($pageNum);
        $this->pages[$title] = $page;

        // Create a previous page button.
        $button = new GtkButton('PREVIOUS');

        // Create a signal handler that will bring the previous page to the
        // front of the notebook when the button is clicked.
        $button->connect_object('clicked', array($this, 'prev_page'));

        // Pack the button into the page.
        $page->pack_start($button, false, false);
```

```php
        // Create a next button.
        $button = new GtkButton('NEXT');

        // Create a signal handler that will bring the next page to the front of the
        // notebook when the button is clicked.
        $button->connect_object('clicked', array($this, 'next_page'));

        // Pack the button into the page.
        $page->pack_start($button, false, false);
    }
}
// ...
?>
```

Moving to the next or previous page is good enough for stepping through a process, but there are cases when relative movements are not enough. Sometimes it is necessary to jump to a particular page. To jump to a particular page, use set_current_page. When passed an integer, set_current_page will bring the page with that index to the screen. If an index of -1 is passed, the last page will be shown.

set_current_page has a corresponding get_current_page method. This method returns the page index of the page that is currently visible. Listing 6-8 shows a method that can be connected to any signal, such as the clicked signal of a button, and jumps to a random page in the notebook. This method is not all that practical, but it does show how the $pages array can be used with set_current_page to easily navigate to any page in the notebook.

Listing 6-8. *A Method for Jumping to a Random Page*

```php
<?php
public function goToRandomPage()
{
    // Pick an array key at random and jump to that page.
    $rndIndex = array_rand($this->pages);
    $this->set_current_page($this->page_num($this->pages[$rndIndex]));
}
?>
```

So, to summarize, the following methods can be used to access pages in GtkNotebook:

- prev_page: Brings the previous page to the front of the notebook.

- next_page: Brings the next page to the front of the notebook.

- set_current_page: Brings the page with the given index to the front of the notebook.

Using a Pop-Up Menu

Navigating in a notebook is easy because of the many ways there are to get from one page to another. Not only are there plenty of class methods to switch pages, but there are also multiple ways for the user to get from one page to the next.

Normally, a user clicks the page's tab to bring that page to the front of the screen, but if the notebook is set up properly, another method may be available to the user. If popup_enable is called, a menu will pop up when the user right-clicks in the tab area. This pop-up menu will have an entry for each page in the notebook. When a user selects an entry from this menu, a built-in signal handler is fired and shows the corresponding page. To see this menu, the user doesn't actually need to click a tab. If there is empty space in the tab area, the user can click there as well. If at some point the menu is no longer needed or shouldn't be available, popup_disable will make the menu unavailable.

By default, the text that is used for the pop-up menu is copied from the tab label. If you want to use different text or a different type of widget for a particular page in the menu, use the *_page_menu methods. You can prepend, append, and insert pages with the methods discussed earlier, but you can also perform the same tasks with the menu sister methods: prepend_page_menu, append_page_menu, and insert_page_menu. The *_page_menu methods can take an additional parameter that is not available with their nonmenu counterparts: a widget that will be used as the menu label. The widget for the menu is usually a GtkLabel widget, but it could be any type of widget.

At this point, you might be thinking, "What is the point of having a pop-up menu when the user can just click one of the tabs?" That is a valid question and one that will be answered in the next section.

Decorating a Notebook

The power of GtkNotebook is not only in the way it shows and hides different pages, but also in the amount of customization it allows. Having tabs at the top of the notebook may not work for an application. You can put the tabs at the bottom. If that doesn't work, you can move the tabs to one of the sides. You can even get rid of them entirely. Maybe that isn't good enough. Maybe all of the tabs need to be the same size. Maybe the tabs need some padding. Or there may even be too many tabs to show at once. GtkNotebook has methods to help with each of these situations.

First, let's tackle moving the tabs away from the top of the notebook.

Repositioning the Tabs

Having the tabs at the top of the notebook may be popular on web pages, but many desktop applications move the tabs to another side. For instance, Microsoft Excel uses tabs at the bottom of the notebook for accessing worksheets within a workbook.

Repositioning the tabs is a simple matter of calling set_tab_pos and passing a GtkPositionType. A GtkPositionType is just a constant value that defines a position such as top, right, bottom, or left. The names of the constants are Gtk::POS_TOP, Gtk::POS_RIGHT, Gtk::POS_BOTTOM, and Gtk::POS_LEFT. When the tabs are moved to another side of the notebook, they keep their order and orientation; that is, on the left and right the tab for the first page is on the top, and the tab for the last page is on the bottom.

Because the tabs keep their orientation, moving the tabs to the left or right of the notebook may not have the desired effect. The tabs will appear to stick out from the side of the notebook instead of lying along it. This may be nice if the notebook has many pages, but in most cases, it won't be the intended result. It is possible to make the tabs lay flat against the side of the notebook by angling text so that it will run vertically, as discussed in the next chapter.

Hiding the Tabs

Just because you're using GtkNotebook doesn't mean that you must show the tabs. When using a notebook to control a user's movement through a step-by-step process, it probably isn't a good idea to allow the user to jump around using the notebook tabs. In that case, you may want to hide the tabs.

When the tabs are hidden, all built-in user navigation is taken away. Because the pop-up menu requires the user to click the tab area, if the tabs are hidden, there is no way for the user to access the menu.

You turn off the tabs by calling the set_show_tabs method and passing false. Passing true to the method turns the tabs back on. Unfortunately, with GtkNotebook, it is either all or nothing. There is no way to turn off a particular tab while leaving the rest visible.

Adjusting the Border and Sizing the Tabs

The all-or-nothing rule applies to other aspects of tabs as well. You can adjust the padding, or border, around the contents of a tab on all four sides. The border can be changed for the top and bottom independently of the left and right, but individual sides cannot be manipulated. Also, setting the tab border changes the border for all tabs, not just the tab for a specific page.

To change the border on all four sides of every tab at once, use set_tab_border. To change the border for just the left and right, use set_tab_hborder. To change the padding on the top and bottom of the tabs, use set_tab_vborder. All three methods take one argument that defines the number of pixels of padding that should be set. The default border for all sides of the tabs is 2 pixels.

Setting a larger border value will increase the dimensions of all tabs, regardless of their contents. Normally, the contents of the tab determine its width because the tab shrinks to fit the contents so that it takes up as little space as possible. Using set_homogeneous_tabs and passing true, will make all of the tabs the same width. The space that is available for the tabs will be divided equally and shared by every tab. The border on the left and right (or top and bottom depending on where the tabs have been positioned) will be automatically adjusted. If a new page is added to the notebook, the tabs will be readjusted to account for the new tab. When set_homogeneous tabs is passed true, all tabs will be the same size. This is true even if one tab's text is much longer than the text on the rest of the tabs. If one tab takes up more than its fair share of real estate, the width of that tab (plus any border) will become the new width of all tabs.

But how can the width of the tabs be more than the width of the notebook? Normally, the notebook simply stretches to accommodate the extra width, but this can lead to unwanted results. Depending on how the notebook was added to its parent container, it may stretch out the window and throw off the layout. If the notebook isn't able to stretch the window, one or more of the tabs may simply be cut off and not be accessible to the user. This is obviously a problem, but not one without a solution.

Using Scrolling Tabs

The set_scrollable method sounds like it would make the pages within a notebook scroll when the contents are too much to show on one screen, but that is not quite what it does. set_scrollable applies only to the tab area of the notebook.

Calling set_scrollable and passing true will allow some of the tabs to be hidden yet accessible through the use of two scrolling icons. Take a look at Figure 6-11. Notice the two icons to the left and right of the tabs. Clicking one of these arrows will select the next page in the notebook. If the tab for the next page is hidden, the tabs will be shifted so that the new current page's tab is shown. In fact, any time a page is shown, the tabs will be shifted so that the tab for that page is shown. This is where the pop-up menu comes in handy again. Scrolling through the pages requires the users to move one by one through every page until they reach their destination. Using the pop-up, the users can quickly jump directly to the desired page.

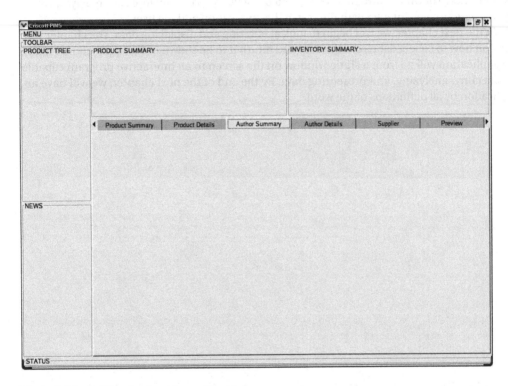

Figure 6-11. *GtkNotebook with scrolling tabs*

The Crisscott PIMS application can certainly make good use of GtkNotebook. There are several distinct and independent tools that the application will have that can benefit from the organization GtkNotebook offers. The tools in the application need to be somewhat controlled, so the tabs should probably be hidden. Other features, such as buttons or menus, can serve to bring pages to the screen when they are needed.

Summary

Containers are arguably the most essential pieces of an application. They provide structure and organization for an application. Aside from these two very important features, you simply can't build a PHP-GTK application without using at least one container.

In this chapter, you learned how to lay out an application through the use of containers. There is the fast and free method of using boxes, which is good for smaller applications with less rigid design constraints. Then there is the extremely structured GtkFixed approach, where everything has a place and that place doesn't change. And there is a compromise between the two using GtkTable. GtkTable provides a good balance between structure and flexibility. Widgets are easy to align, but are also free to shrink or grow as the application needs.

Finally, we looked at GtkNotebook. This handy widget makes organizing an application a snap. Tools within the application can be organized into pages, which can then be accessed in a variety of ways.

The choice of which container to use for a particular piece of an application plays a very big role in how it will interact with the rest of the application and the user.

In the next chapter, we will begin to look at entering and displaying data. The chapter will focus on how to collect data from the user and return it to be shown in the application. Finally, the application will go from a static window on the screen to an interactive program capable of collecting, analyzing, and presenting data. By the end of the next chapter, we will have an application by all definitions of the word.

CHAPTER 7

∎∎∎

Displaying and Collecting Simple Data

Now that there is a place for all the pieces of our application, it is time to start implementing some of the core features. The most essential feature of our PIMS application is the ability to create and modify product data. This requires the application to be able to present the user with some data and also to accept data input by the user.

This chapter will focus on the different ways that you can present and collect smaller pieces of information. First, we will look at how to communicate simple messages using labels. Then we will examine how to collect data from the user using text entries, combo boxes, scales, and spin buttons. Finally, we will cover how to add buttons to indicate data processing should begin.

Labels

GtkLabel is the simplest widget for displaying data. It is used primarily, as the name suggests, to label other parts of the application. Many widgets create GtkLabel widgets automatically when certain methods are passed a string. For instance, GtkFrame takes a string on construction and creates a GtkLabel widget to label the frame.

Labels come in handy when you want to identify text-entry fields or sections of an application, or when you want to print some simple text to the screen. Other, more complicated widgets for text display can be overkill when you need to show only a handful of words.

Just because GtkLabel excels at simple text display doesn't mean that it isn't versatile. In its simplest form, a label can just pass a string to the constructor and then add it to a container. However, you can also do the following with a label:

- Use a label with marked-up text.

- Make a label selectable.

- Have a label rotate text.

- Have a label automatically shorten text that is beyond a certain length.

GtkLabel widgets come in two main forms: simple and complex.

Simple Labels

In most circumstances, a label is used to identify some other piece of an application, and standard text reading from left to right is all that is needed. That is what GtkLabel creates by default: a plain label. Simple labels do not contain any markup or mnemonics, are not automatically truncated, are not selectable, and do not appear at an angle. It may sound like there are not many simple label features to discuss, but you can set the label's line wrap, width, and alignment. In fact, simple labels are sufficient for the needs of most applications.

As with every widget you've seen so far, discussion of GtkLabel begins with the constructor. The constructor for GtkLabel is very simple. All that is required is the string that the label should show. Once constructed, the label can be placed into a container and shown on the screen. Nothing else needs to be done. Of course, that doesn't mean that nothing else *can* be done.

Setting and Getting Text

Labels may be simple widgets for displaying small pieces of information, but that doesn't mean they must be static. You can change a label's text at any time. set_text will change the label's value from its current state to the text passed in.

The value that the label should be changed to may often depend on the label's current value. To get the current value, use the appropriately named get_text method. Because there is no method for appending text, get_text is often used as a sort of .= operator; that is, it is called inside set_text. Here is an example:

```
$label->set_text($label->get_text() . ' text to append.');
```

get_text has other valuable uses when the label is used within another widget. For instance, you may be able to determine which of several buttons was clicked by looking at the value of the button's label.

Tip A better way to determine which button was clicked is to give the button a name using set_name. Later, you can use get_name to determine which button the user clicked. Using set_name and get_name allows a button to be identified even when the label changes.

The remaining features pertaining to simple use of GtkLabel all deal with how the text is displayed.

Wrapping Label Text

GtkLabel is useful to display a small amount of text, but *small amount* is a relative term. Specifically, this means text that does not contain any hard line breaks. This could be anything from one or two words to an entire paragraph. The number of lines a block of text requires depends not only on the length of the string, but also on the properties of the GtkLabel widget.

By default, all labels contain one line of text only. The dimensions of the label stretch to fit the text on one line. If the label's size has been set with set_size_request or the label's size is restricted by its parent container, the text will be cut off. The best way to avoid this is to wrap the text to the next line when it exceeds the label's width.

Allowing a label to wrap text is a simple matter of calling set_line_wrap and passing it the value of true. This tells the widget to wrap the text at the last possible word break to avoid cutting off text. Passing false to set_line_wrap will put the label back into single-line mode.

Even if the text is allowed to wrap lines, some characters may still get cut off. If a single word is too large for the widget to display within its constraints, the word will appear on its own line, but characters will still be hidden. set_line_wrap is not absolute. The label will make a best effort attempt to wrap the text and make it as readable as possible, but there are other label methods and settings that can override set_line_wrap or cause it to behave unexpectedly.

Setting the Label's Width

A GtkLabel widget's width may be set explicitly in pixels using set_size_request, or may be requested as a number of characters. The key word in that last sentence is *requested*. Using set_max_width_chars, you can set a requested size of the label widget. The label will be sized to the given number of characters, provided no other method or setting has made a conflicting size request.

The width is not set in stone. By resizing the widget, it is possible to show more characters than were originally requested. Frankly, set_max_width_chars really should be named, set_max_chars_to_show, because it tells the label not that each line should be *n* characters long, but that only *n* characters of the string should be shown. However, because it shows only a certain number of characters from the string and does not set the label's dimensions, set_max_width_chars doesn't work quite as one would expect. set_max_width_chars sets the label's dimensions so that only one line of at most *n* characters is shown.

Setting the width in characters allows an application to limit the size of the message a label displays. It helps to prevent individual characters from being cut in half, although characters may still be truncated in some cases. In many cases, it is better to show only part of a word instead of part of a letter. But, keep in mind that using set_max_width_chars implicitly forces a label to be one line only.

Tip If a label doesn't fit within the allotted space, an alternative is to have it show an ellipsis. See the "Ellipsizing Text" section later in this chapter for details.

As with most set methods in PHP-GTK, set_max_width_chars has a corresponding get_max_width_chars. As you would expect, it returns the requested maximum width in characters for the label. If set_max_width_chars was not called, -1 will be returned.

Aligning Text in a GtkLabel

Whether text appears on one line or thirty lines, you can control the way it aligns within the label by using set_justify. set_justify expects one of the following justification type constants to be passed as the only argument:

- Gtk::JUSTIFY_LEFT
- Gtk::JUSTIFY_RIGHT
- Gtk::JUSTIFY_CENTER
- Gtk::JUSTIFY_FILL

The first three are self-explanatory, but Gtk::JUSTIFY_FILL may not be so obvious. In word processing applications, such as OpenOffice.org Writer and Microsoft Word, this setting is more commonly known as *justified*. Characters on both the left and right sides of the block of text will appear flush with the margins.

When you use set_justify by itself or with set_line_wrap, the results are rather predictable. But when you throw set_max_width_chars into the mix, the labels may not behave quite as you would expect. When set_justify is used with set_max_width_chars, the label may appear to be misaligned. This is just another side effect of the conflicting efforts of the two methods. set_justify and set_max_width_chars (or set_width_chars) should not be used together.

Using Simple Labels

The product summary section of the PIMS application is designed to display a brief summary of a product selected from the product tree. Figure 7-1 shows the product summary section. Displaying a summary first allows the users to double-check that the product they selected is actually the product they want to edit.

Figure 7-1. *The product summary area of the PIMS application*

The product summary is a simple tool that displays five small pieces of information: the product name, type, group, price, and a thumbnail image (if it is available). The first four items are perfect candidates for simple labels.

Listing 7-1 is an implementation of Crisscott_Tools_ProductSummary. This class is responsible for showing the product summary. For now, a GtkFrame is used as a placeholder for the thumbnail. The product summary area actually contains eight GtkLabel widgets: four for the data items, and four to tell the users what those data items represent.

Listing 7-1. *Simple Labels in the Product Summary Section*

```php
<?php
class Crisscott_Tools_ProductSummary extends GtkTable {

    public $productName;
    public $productType;
    public $productGroup;
    public $productPrice;
    public $productImage;
```

```php
public function __construct($product = NULL)
{
    // First call the parent constructor.
    // Create four rows and three columns.
    parent::__construct(4, 3);

    // Create labels for the attributes.
    $name  = new GtkLabel('Name');
    $type  = new GtkLabel('Type');
    $group = new GtkLabel('Group');
    $price = new GtkLabel('Price');

    // Set the width of each label to create a uniform appearance.
    $name->set_size_request(50, -1);
    $type->set_size_request(50, -1);
    $group->set_size_request(50, -1);
    $price->set_size_request(50, -1);

    // Next align each label within the parent container.
    $name->set_alignment(0, .5);
    $type->set_alignment(0, .5);
    $group->set_alignment(0, .5);
    $price->set_alignment(0, .5);

    // Attach them to the table.
    $expandFill = Gtk::EXPAND|Gtk::FILL;
    $this->attach($name,  0, 1, 0, 1, 0, $expandFill);
    $this->attach($type,  0, 1, 1, 2, 0, $expandFill);
    $this->attach($group, 0, 1, 2, 3, 0, $expandFill);
    $this->attach($price, 0, 1, 3, 4, 0, $expandFill);

    // Create the labels for the attributes.
    $this->productName  = new GtkLabel();
    $this->productType  = new GtkLabel();
    $this->productGroup = new GtkLabel();
    $this->productPrice = new GtkLabel();

    // Allow the labels to wrap.
    $this->productName->set_line_wrap(true);
    $this->productType->set_line_wrap(true);
    $this->productGroup->set_line_wrap(true);
    $this->productPrice->set_line_wrap(true);

    // Left align them.
    $this->productName->set_alignment(0, .5);
    $this->productType->set_alignment(0, .5);
    $this->productGroup->set_alignment(0, .5);
    $this->productPrice->set_alignment(0, .5);
```

```
        // Attach them to the table.
        $this->attach($this->productName,  1, 2, 0, 1);
        $this->attach($this->productType,  1, 2, 1, 2);
        $this->attach($this->productGroup, 1, 2, 2, 3);
        $this->attach($this->productPrice, 1, 2, 3, 4);

        // Attach a placeholder for the image.
        $this->productImage = new GtkFrame('Image');
        // The image's size can be fixed.
        $this->productImage->set_size_request(100, 100);
        $this->attach($this->productImage, 2, 3, 0, 4, 0, $expandFill);

        // Now that everything is set up, summarize the product.
        if (!empty($product)) {
            $this->displaySummary($product);
        }
    }

    public function displaySummary(Crisscott_Product $product)
    {
        // Set the attribute labels to the values of the product.
        $this->productName->set_text($product->name);
        $this->productType->set_text($product->type);
        $this->productGroup->set_text($product->group);
        $this->productPrice->set_text($product->price);
    }
}
?>
```

Most of the lines in Listing 7-1 actually deal with setting up the product summary area. The area is laid out using a GtkTable, which requires quite a few lines to get things where we want them (as you learned in the previous chapter). Relatively few lines actually deal with GtkLabels.

In the constructor, eight labels are created. Four are saved as class members so that they can be accessed more easily later. These four represent the product information. These four labels are also set to allow their text to wrap lines using set_line_wrap. This will help if a product has a rather long name, or even a short name if the window has been resized considerably smaller. The other four labels in the constructor are used to identify each piece of information. In this project, the text within these labels will not change. Therefore, there is not much point in holding on to them as member variables.

Notice the use of the set_alignment method with these labels. set_alignment is a method of GtkMisc. GtkMisc is the parent class to GtkLabel. set_alignment does not align the text within the label, but instead aligns the label within its parent container. This method functions just the same as the set_label_align method of GtkFrame, which was discussed in the previous chapter.

The only other lines in Listing 7-1 that deal with GtkLabel are within the displaySummary method. When a new product is to be displayed in the summary area, this method changes the label text. The Crisscott_Product class has a property for each label in the summary area. This method simply grabs those values and uses set_text to update the label.

Simple labels serve their purpose well. They are easy to create and use. They offer a modest yet powerful set of features, which makes them a perfect fit for most uses. Previous listings (especially those dealing with GtkNotebook) have shown how useful GtkLabel widgets can be in their default state.

The next section deals with complex labels, which go beyond simple line wrap and justification settings. These labels expand on the features you've seen so far. In the listings that follow, notice how some of the simple features of GtkLabel are used in conjunction with some of the more advanced features.

Complex Labels

Complex labels use some of the more advanced features that GtkLabel has to offer. These features include the ability to automatically shorten text that doesn't fit in a given area, show text at an angle, provide markup, and make text selectable. Using these features, you can transform a label into colorful, powerful text.

Complex labels can call more attention to a message. Consider how error messages are often displayed. A simple label would probably get lost in the application, but text that is big, bold, and red stands out and gets noticed. When displaying a table of data, complex labels may also come in handy. Instead of displaying column headers horizontally, they can be displayed vertically. This will improve readability by allowing all of the columns to be shown at once. We'll use some complex labels in our PIMS application.

Using Pango for Markup

Pango is a package used by GTK to help internationalize and mark up text. You can use Pango to format text, similar to how you use HTML. Pango can make pieces of text bold, colored, underlined, and so on. For a listing of Pango markup elements, visit http://www.pango.org.

We'll use Pango to mark up labels used in one of our PIMS application's tools: the contributor editing tool. This tool provides a way for the user to manage information related to people or businesses that help to create, produce, or distribute an item. Because this tool allows the user to enter information, it will need a way to notify the user if some data is not valid. Using Pango, we can easily format the text of the label to draw attention to pieces of information that may have invalid data, as shown in Figure 7-2.

Figure 7-2. *Using a bold label to indicate an error*

Listing 7-2 is the first step in creating the contributor editing tool (ContributorEdit). It simply lays out the application and adds labels for all of the properties that the tool will allow the user to edit. Some of the information, such as the contributor's address, is not really important for Crisscott's business, but it is put in the application as a value-added feature for the end users. If they can manage contributor information in the same place as they manage their products, the users are more likely to adopt the application more quickly.

Listing 7-2. *Using Pango to Make a Label Red*

```php
<?php
class Crisscott_Tools_ContributorEdit extends GtkTable {

    const ERROR_MARKUP_OPEN  = '<span foreground="#F00">';
    const ERROR_MARKUP_CLOSE = '</span>';

    public  $contributor;
    private $firstNameLabel;
    private $middleNameLabel;
    private $lastNameLabel;
    private $websiteLabel;
    private $emailLabel;
    private $street1Label;
    private $street2Label;
    private $cityLabel;
    private $stateLabel;
    private $countryLabel;
    private $postalLabel;

    public function __construct($contributor = null)
    {
        // Call the parent constructor.
        parent::__construct(7, 4);

        // Lay out the tool.
        $this->_layoutTool();

        // Connect the needed callbacks.

        // Prepopulate the fields if a contributor is given.
        if (!empty($contributor) && is_a($contributor, 'Crisscott_Contributor')) {
            $this->populateFields($contributor);
        }
    }

    private function _layoutTool()
    {
        // First create the labels that identify the fields.
        $this->firstNameLabel  = new GtkLabel('First Name');
```

```php
        $this->middleNameLabel = new GtkLabel('Middle Name');
        $this->lastNameLabel   = new GtkLabel('Last Name');
        $this->emailLabel      = new GtkLabel('Email Address');
        // Continue for the rest of the labels...

        // Next add the labels to the table.
        // The labels will be added in two columns.
        // First column.
        $this->attach($this->firstNameLabel,  0, 1, 0, 1, Gtk::FILL, 0);
        $this->attach($this->middleNameLabel, 0, 1, 1, 2, Gtk::FILL, 0);
        $this->attach($this->lastNameLabel,   0, 1, 2, 3, Gtk::FILL, 0);
        $this->attach($this->emailLabel,      0, 1, 3, 4, Gtk::FILL, 0);
        $this->attach($this->websiteLabel,    0, 1, 4, 5, Gtk::FILL, 0);

        // Second column.
        $this->attach($this->street1Label, 2, 3, 0, 1, Gtk::FILL, 0);
        $this->attach($this->street2Label, 2, 3, 1, 2, Gtk::FILL, 0);
        $this->attach($this->cityLabel,    2, 3, 2, 3, Gtk::FILL, 0);
        $this->attach($this->stateLabel,   2, 3, 3, 4, Gtk::FILL, 0);
        $this->attach($this->countryLabel, 2, 3, 4, 5, Gtk::FILL, 0);
        $this->attach($this->postalLabel,  2, 3, 5, 6, Gtk::FILL, 0);

        // Right align all of the labels.
        $this->firstNameLabel->set_alignment(1, .5);
        $this->middleNameLabel->set_alignment(1, .5);
        $this->lastNameLabel->set_alignment(1, .5);
        $this->emailLabel->set_alignment(1, .5);
        // Continue for the rest of the labels...
    }

    public function reportError(GtkLabel $label)
    {
        $label->set_label(self::ERROR_MARKUP_OPEN .
                        $label->get_label() .
                        self::ERROR_MARKUP_CLOSE);
    }

    public function clearError(GtkLabel $label)
    {
        $text = $label->get_label();
        $text = str_replace(self::ERROR_MARKUP_OPEN,  '', $text);
        $text = str_replace(self::ERROR_MARKUP_CLOSE, '', $text);

        $label->set_label($text);
        $label->set_use_markup(true);
    }
}
?>
```

Each label in Listing 7-2 is created in the same way as all the other labels you've seen so far. In fact, when the labels are added to their parent table, they are still just simple labels. The `reportError` and `clearError` methods of `Crisscott_Tools_ContributorEdit` take the simple labels and turn them into complex labels by adding and removing Pango markup.

Once the user has entered and submitted the contributor's values, the contributor editing tool will assign the values to the contributor and try to validate the new data. If the data is not valid, the label that identifies that piece of data will be made red using the `reportError` method. The `reportError` method adds Pango markup to the text of the label. The Pango markup that is added is `<span foreground="#F00"></span>`, which colors the text within the tags red.

Adding markup to a label is not quite enough. If the code stopped at just adding markup, the label's text would not change color. Instead, the characters of the tags would be shown directly in the label. The label must be told that it has Pango markup in order to format the text properly. To inform the label that its text contains markup tags, we call the `set_use_markup` method. Passing `true` to this method treats markup elements as formatting tags. If `false` is passed, any markup elements will be treated as regular characters. You can find out if a label is using markup by calling the `get_use_markup` method.

By making a label red when all others are black, the user's attention will be immediately drawn to that section of the screen. This quickly notifies the user that something is not right.

Removing Markup

The whole point of highlighting a label is to let the user know that something needs to be fixed. When the user has successfully fixed the data in question, the text should be returned to normal. This will give the user a visual cue that the particular piece of data is now valid. You can remove the markup from a `GtkLabel` widget in a few different ways. Passing `false` to `set_use_markup` is not one of them. Remember that this will just tell the label to treat the tags as normal text. This means that the email label will end up showing `<span foreground="#F00"> Email Address</span>` instead of Email Address. This is obviously not acceptable.

One method that will work is to use the `get_label` method, strip the tags using regular expressions, and set the text again using either `set_text` or `set_label`. The `get_label` method is very similar to the `get_text` method. When used with simple labels, the two methods are exactly the same. `get_text` actually returns the text as it appears on the screen. `get_label`, on the other hand, returns the text as it was set. Any embedded markup or mnemonics (also known as shortcuts, as described shortly) will be stripped out of the label when `get_text` is called. `get_label` will preserve these elements and return them along with the label text.

The `set_text` method implicitly turns off markup in the label. When `set_text` is called, `set_use_markup` is passed `false` automatically. Using `set_label` preserves the value that has previously been passed to `set_use_markup`.

Another slightly less complicated way to strip out the formatting is to take advantage of the fact that `get_text` returns the text as it appears on the screen, and use its return value as the argument to `set_label`. This works nicely if the only special treatment the text has undergone is Pango formatting.

The `clearError` method of Listing 7-2 takes a middle-ground approach by replacing the previously defined markup constants with empty strings. It isn't as powerful as a regular expression, but it is much easier to read and serves our needs nicely.

Ellipsizing Text

You can accommodate large labels in several ways, such as by wrapping lines and allowing the label's parent container to shrink and grow. But at some point, these options may not be enough. It may be necessary to lose some characters from the label.

Ellipsizing text is not the process of shaping text into an ellipse. Ellipsizing text means removing characters and replacing them with three periods, or an ellipsis. An ellipsis implies that there is more to the text, but it cannot be shown at the moment.

GtkLabel can automatically determine if its text is too big for the given area, and if so, drop some characters and replace them with an ellipsis. Calling set_ellipsize will tell the label to ellipsize the text if it is too large to fit in its parent container. set_ellipsize needs one argument that tells the label which characters should be dropped:

- Pango::ELLIPSIZE_START: Tells the label to put the ellipsis at the beginning of the label and to preserve the characters at the end of the label.

- Pango::ELLIPSIZE_END: Preserves the characters at the beginning of the label and puts the ellipsis at the end of the label.

- Pango::ELLIPSIZE_MIDDLE: Drops characters from the middle of the label and keeps those at the beginning and the end.

- Pango::ELLIPSIZE_NONE: Turns off ellipsization.

Figure 7-3 shows a label in each of the four ellipsization modes.

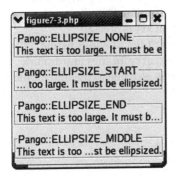

Figure 7-3. *Ellipsized text*

Adding Mnemonics

As far as PHP-GTK is concerned, *mnemonic* is just a fancy word for shortcut key. A mnemonic associates a specific key combination with a particular widget. For instance, most applications have a File menu that can be activated by pressing Alt+F. This shortcut is known as a mnemonic. Mnemonics give the user more options for accessing different elements of an application.

Why on earth is there a section on mnemonics in a discussion about labels? What is the point in having a shortcut for a label? While it is true that labels don't really do anything, they do identify other pieces of information. Since labels are the identifiers, it makes sense to use them to present the shortcuts to the user.

Mnemonics are identified by underlining a given character in the label. The character that is underlined is the key that must be pressed along with the Alt key to activate the mnemonic. That is why, in most applications, the letter *F* is underlined in the File menu. It tells the user that pressing Alt+F will activate the menu.

You can set up a mnemonic in two ways. First, you can add the mnemonic when you construct the label. An optional second argument to the GtkLabel constructor is a Boolean value that tells the constructor whether the label should be created with a mnemonic shortcut. To indicate which key should be used as the shortcut, use an underscore. The shortcut key will be the character after the underscore. For example, if the label is created with the string "_Name", the shortcut will be Alt+N. If the string is "N_ame", the shortcut would be Alt+A. When the label is shown on the screen, the shortcut character will be underlined.

The second way to create a mnemonic is to use set_markup_with_mnemonic (which implicitly sets use_markup to true) or set_text_with_mnemonic. These two methods will set the label's text and inform the application that a mnemonic should be created. Again, an underscore in the string passed to one of these methods indicates which key is the shortcut.

The association of labels and other widgets often goes beyond just the label saying what information the other widget is holding. A label can also be set up so that activating its mnemonic fires a signal in another widget. If the label is part of a button, a menu item, or a notebook tab, the mnemonic will be automatically associated with that button, menu item, or notebook page. Therefore, when the user presses the mnemonic key combination, the button will be clicked or the page will be selected.

If the label is not inside a widget that will automatically connect with the mnemonic, as is the case with the ContributorEdit tool, you can assign a mnemonic widget by using set_mnemonic_widget. This method tells PHP-GTK that when the mnemonic is activated, the mnemonic widget's mnemonic_activate signal should be emitted. If a signal handler has been created for this signal, the callback will be called when the shortcut key is pressed.

In Listing 7-3, which is a modified and abbreviated version of the previous listing, a mnemonic is set up so that when the user presses Alt+N, the GtkEntry for the contributor's first name is given focus. This is the default action when an entry is assigned as the mnemonic widget.

Listing 7-3. *Assigning a Mnemonic Widget*

```php
<?php
    private function _layoutTool()
    {
        // First create the labels that identify the fields.
        $this->firstNameLabel  = new GtkLabel('First _Name');
        // Continue for the rest of the labels...

        // Next add the labels to the table.
        // The labels will be added in two columns.
        // First column.
        $this->attach($this->firstNameLabel,  0, 1, 0, 1, Gtk::FILL, 0);
        // ...
```

```
        // Second column.
        $this->attach($this->street1Label, 2, 3, 0, 1, Gtk::FILL, 0);
        //...

        // Right align all of the labels.
        //...

        // Next create all of the data collection widgets.
        $this->firstNameEntry  = new GtkEntry();

        // Add the entry to the table.
        $this->attach($this->firstNameEntry,  1, 2, 0, 1, 0, 0);

        // Make the entry the mnemonic widget.
        $this->firstNameLabel->set_mnemonic_widget($this->firstNameEntry);
    }
?>
```

Caution Creating a label with two underscores does not give the label two mnemonic keys. It just makes things confusing. The first underscore will be used as the mnemonic, but the character after the second underscore will also be underlined. This means that constructing a label with GtkLabel('_Nam_e') will produce a label whose mnemonic key is Alt+N but has the *e* underlined as well as the *N*. This will definitely confuse the users.

Earlier, in the discussion of Pango markup, I mentioned that using get_text was not the best way to grab a label's text. This is because it strips out Pango formatting and mnemonics. Using get_label preserves the mnemonics. get_label returns the same string that was used to create the label. Just because the return value from a label has an underscore in it doesn't mean that the label has a mnemonic key assigned.

By using set_use_underline, you can force a label to treat the label text literally. If false is passed to set_use_underline, any underscores in the text will appear as underscores instead of underlines. get_use_underline returns a Boolean indicating whether or not the underscore in a label represents a mnemonic key value. Also, just because get_use_underline returns true doesn't mean that there is a mnemonic associated with the label. It simply means that if the label's text has an underscore, it will be used to create a mnemonic key.

To determine if a mnemonic is associated with the label, and if so, which key activates it and which widget it works on, use a combination of get_label, get_use_underline, and get_mnemonic_widget (the opposite of set_mnemonic_widget).

Creating Angled Text

Angled text is any text that is not perfectly horizontal. (Technically, all text is angled, but in GTK 2, angled text refers to any text with an angle other than zero.) Putting text on an angle can improve the use of space in an application. For example, you might use angled text for notebook tabs that run along the side of the pages, column headers in tables, and image credits that appear alongside an image instead of underneath it.

Angled text comes with a few caveats. It is not possible to angle text that has an ellipsize mode other than Pango::ELLIPSIZE_NONE. GTK cannot handle rendering both ellipsized and angled text. Therefore, PHP-GTK can't handle it. Another thing to be careful of when using angled text is that it may not wrap lines. These two rules together mean that angled text that is too long for its container will be cut off.

We'll use angled text in another one of our PIMS application's tools: the category summary tool (CategorySummary). This tool provides a quick look at the products in the inventory grouped by category. Product categories are groups of similar products, such as books or downloadable software. The category summary tool is a table that shows information, such as the number of items in a category, the average price, the average weight, and so on. The categories are listed on the left as row headings, and the category specs are listed along the top as column headings, as shown in Figure 7-4.

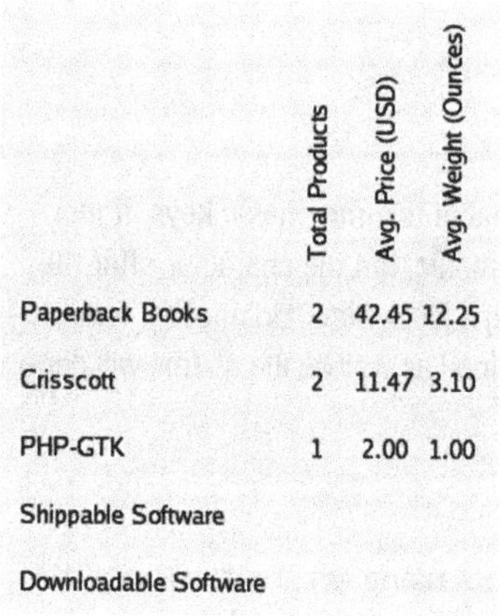

Figure 7-4. *Using angled text in column headings*

Listing 7-4 shows the code for the category summary tool.

Listing 7-4. *Angling Text in a GtkLabel*

```php
<?php
class Crisscott_Tools_CategorySummary extends GtkTable {

    private $lastRow = 0;

    public function __construct($inventory = null)
    {
        // Call the parent constructor.
        // Don't pass any rows or columns because we want the
        // table to grow as we add data.
        parent::__construct();
```

```php
    // Attach the column headers.
    $this->attachColHeaders();

    // If an inventory was passed, add the data to the table.
    if (!empty($inventory)) {
        $this->summarizeInventory($inventory);
    }
}

public function summarizeInventory(Crisscott_Inventory $inventory)
{
    // Clear out the table.
    $this->clear();

    // Reattach the headers.
    $this->attachColHeaders();

    // Add a row for each category.
    foreach ($inventory->categories as $category) {
        $this->summarizeCategory($category);
    }
}

protected function attachColHeaders()
{
    require_once 'Crisscott/Category.php';
    foreach (Crisscott_Category::getCategorySpecs() as $key => $spec) {
        $label = new GtkLabel($spec);
        $label->set_angle(90);
        $label->set_alignment(.5, 1);

        // Leave the first cell empty.
        $this->attach($label, $key + 1, $key + 2, 0, 1, 0, Gtk::FILL, 10, 10);
    }

    // Increment the last row.
    $this->lastRow++;

}

public function summarizeCategory(Crisscott_Category $category)
{
    // First attach the category name.
    $nameLabel = new GtkLabel($category->name);
    $nameLabel->set_alignment(0, .5);
    $this->attach($nameLabel, 0, 1, $this->lastRow,
                $this->lastRow + 1, Gtk::FILL, 0, 10, 10);
```

```
        // Next attach the spec values.
        foreach (Crisscott_Category::getCategorySpecs() as $key => $spec) {
            $value = $category->getSpecValueByName($spec);
            $this->attach(new GtkLabel($value), $key + 1, $key + 2,
                          $this->lastRow, $this->lastRow + 1,
                          0, 0, 1, 1);
        }

        // Increment the last row.
        $this->lastRow++;
    }

    protected function clear()
    {
        foreach ($this->get_children() as $child) {
            $this->remove($child);
        }

        // Reset the last row.
        $this->lastRow = 0;
    }
}
?>
```

To create the CategorySummary table, we add a GtkLabel for each specification. Next, we set the label's angle to 90 degrees using set_angle. The set_angle method takes a float as its only argument and sets the label to that angle. Setting an angle of 90 makes the label read from bottom to top. Setting an angle of 270 makes the label read from top to bottom. Setting an angle of –90 degrees has the same effect as setting an angle of 270 degrees.

After the angle is set, we attach each label to the table. There is no need to worry about the specs being cut off, because the labels are allowed to shrink or expand as needed within their table cells. After the column headers are in place, we add each category to the table along with a value for each column.

Aligning labels can be a little tricky when they are set on an angle. Setting the justification for a label is a little confusing if the label is on an angle of 90 degrees or more. The justification is relative to the text of the label, not to the rest of the application. That is, when a label has an angle of 90 degrees, a justification of Gtk::JUSTIFY_LEFT will cause the text to be aligned to the left of the label as expected, but the left side of the label is actually now parallel to the bottom edge of the screen. When a label has an angle of 180 degrees, the left side of the label is on the right side of the application.

Another factor in aligning labels that becomes more apparent when text is angled is how the label fills or expands within its parent container. Justification tells a label how to align itself within the space available. If a label is not allowed to expand to fill a box or table cell, all justification settings will appear to have the same effect. This is more obvious with angled text because a right justification will appear to be the same as a left justification, unless the label is allowed to at least fill the cell or box, if not also expand.

While justification may be relative to the label's text, alignment of the label itself is relative to the parent container. As you can see in Figure 7-4, the CategorySummary tool has a row of column headers along the top of the table. Each of these labels is set up so that its first character is aligned with the bottom edge of the table row. This was done by not only allowing the labels to fill the table cells, but also by telling them to align themselves as low as possible within their parent container. Notice how the expand and fill settings, justification, and alignment are used in Listing 7-4 to create the application shown in Figure 7-4.

Entry Fields

Displaying information is very important in applications, but most applications are not really considered complete unless they can also collect information from users. One of the easiest ways to collect information from a user is through the GtkEntry widget. GtkEntry is a simple text box, very similar to an HTML input element where the type is set to text.

GtkEntry collects one line of text input. GtkEntry is very useful for getting information such as product titles, people's names, and parts of an address (like the street address and the city). GtkEntry may be simple and versatile, but it is not always the best solution for collecting data. You should not use it when you have a predetermined set of acceptable values, such as ranges of numbers. Other widgets—such as GtkComboBox, GtkVScale, GtkHScale, and GtkSpinButton—are a better fit for those types of tasks, as discussed later in this chapter.

In our PIMS application's contributor editing tool, we will add GtkEntry fields to allow users to input data, as shown in Figure 7-5. If the contributor already has information for a specific field, the GtkEntry will be prepopulated with the correct data. The users are then free to modify any data they wish. When they are finished, the data will be submitted, and the contributor will be updated.

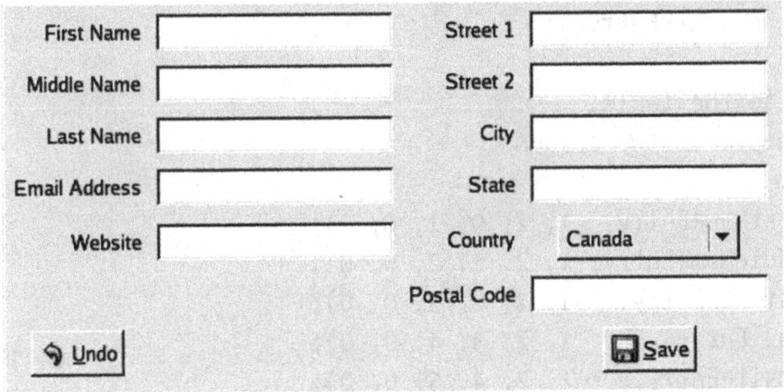

Figure 7-5. *The updated Crisscott contributor editing tool*

Listing 7-5 shows the updated version of the code.

Listing 7-5. *ContributorEdit Tool with GtkEntry Fields*

```php
<?php
    private function _layoutTool()
    {
        // First create the labels that identify the fields.
        $this->firstNameLabel = new GtkLabel('First Name');
        // ...
```

```php
        // Next add the labels to the table.
        // The labels will be added in two columns.
        // First column.
        $this->attach($this->firstNameLabel,  0, 1, 0, 1, Gtk::FILL, 0);
        // ...

        // Right align all of the labels.
        $this->firstNameLabel->set_alignment(1, .5);
        // ...

        // Turn on markup
        $this->firstNameLabel->set_use_markup(true);
        // ...

        // Next create all of the data collection widgets.
        $this->firstNameEntry  = new GtkEntry();
        $this->middleNameEntry = new GtkEntry();
        $this->lastNameEntry    = new GtkEntry();
        $this->emailEntry       = new GtkEntry();
        $this->websiteEntry     = new GtkEntry();
        $this->street1Entry     = new GtkEntry();
        $this->street2Entry     = new GtkEntry();
        $this->cityEntry        = new GtkEntry();
        $this->stateEntry       = new GtkEntry();
        $this->countryEntry     = new GtkEntry();
        $this->postalEntry      = new GtkEntry();

        // Next add the entries to the table.
        // The entries will be added in two columns.
        // First column.
        $this->attach($this->firstNameEntry,  1, 2, 0, 1, 0, 0);
        $this->attach($this->middleNameEntry, 1, 2, 1, 2, 0, 0);
        $this->attach($this->lastNameEntry,   1, 2, 2, 3, 0, 0);
        $this->attach($this->emailEntry,      1, 2, 3, 4, 0, 0);
        $this->attach($this->websiteEntry,    1, 2, 4, 5, 0, 0);

        // Second column.
        $this->attach($this->street1Entry, 3, 4, 0, 1, 0, 0);
        $this->attach($this->street2Entry, 3, 4, 1, 2, 0, 0);
        $this->attach($this->cityEntry,    3, 4, 2, 3, 0, 0);
        $this->attach($this->stateEntry,   3, 4, 3, 4, 0, 0);
        $this->attach($this->countryEntry, 3, 4, 4, 5, 0, 0);
        $this->attach($this->postalEntry,  3, 4, 5, 6, 0, 0);
    }
?>
```

After the labels that identify the individual fields are created and added to the table, GtkEntry widgets are created for all of the contributor values. The constructor of GtkEntry is simple; it doesn't take any arguments and returns a ready-to-use GtkEntry widget.

It is standard practice to put entry widgets to the right of the labels that describe them. This is how users most often encounter input forms like this. Sticking with this standard interface design practice will make the application less confusing for the end user.

The last part of setting up this tool is populating the entry fields with contributor data. If a contributor object is passed to the constructor of ContributorEdit, it will be passed to the populateFields method. The populateFields method can be called at any time to load a new contributor. This method grabs values from the contributor object and calls set_text, which works just as it does for labels. It takes a string argument and sets that as the text in the entry field. After all of the entries have their new values, the method makes sure to assign the contributor that those labels came from as a member variable. This will allow the application to make changes to the contributor or restore the entry values if needed.

set_text is not the only way to control a GtkEntry widget. Two other methods for adding text to an entry are append_text and prepend_text. The two methods insert text at the beginning and end of the current entry text, respectively.

Caution While append_text and prepend_text are very useful, they are deprecated in GTK 2. They should be used with caution, as they may disappear in the future.

Input Box Size and Character Limits

As with GtkLabel, you can also control the number of characters displayed in a GtkEntry input box. set_width_chars sets the width of the input box to the given size in characters. If 10 is passed, the input box will be ten characters wide. This does not mean that the entry cannot accept more then ten characters, but that only ten characters will fit in the visible area. Any additional characters will be pushed out of view to the left or right, but will not be dropped from the entry's value.

To set a character limit on the text value of the entry, use set_max_length. The set_max_length method puts a limit on the number of characters that make up the entry's text. If the maximum length of an entry is set to 10, and a user tries to enter eleven characters, the eleventh character will be ignored. Similarly, if the application itself tries to call set_text with a string more than ten characters long, all characters beyond the tenth will be dropped.

Remember the difference between the two methods. Characters over the limit set by set_width_chars are simply hidden from sight. Characters over the limit imposed by set_max_length are completely ignored or dropped.

Automatic Completion

GtkEntry widgets are excellent tools for allowing users to enter data that cannot necessarily be constrained. Unfortunately, the free-form nature of GtkEntry can sometimes also be a burden. For example, consider the State entry field in the contributor editing tool. While the names of states don't change that often, you wouldn't try to gather a list of all the states, provinces, counties, or parishes in all countries of the world. Therefore, the application must let the user enter values using a GtkEntry widget. This can lead to some very messy data input. There is no guarantee that the users of an application know how to spell Saskatchewan. Fortunately, you can help users supply the correct data.

GtkEntryCompletion is an object that can be associated with a GtkEntry. It tries to match what the user is typing to a predefined list of suggested values, as shown in Figure 7-6. Using a GtkEntryCompletion object can help to reduce the number of errors entered by the user.

GtkEntryCompletion is a helper object, not a widget. It makes no sense to think of a GtkEntryCompletion without an associated GtkEntry.

GtkEntryCompletion is not an end-all solution. It guides the users in the right direction when entering text, but does not force them to pick one of the suggested values. You should use it when there is a set of likely values for a GtkEntry field, but the set of possible values is not finite. The data that is taken from the GtkEntry field must still be checked for invalid values or characters, especially if the data is to be inserted into a database.

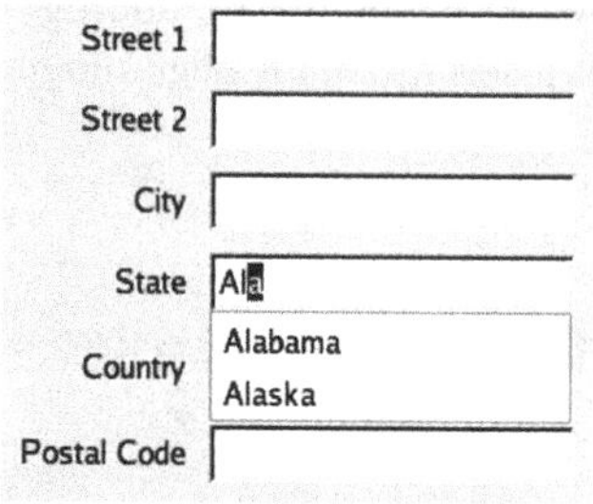

Figure 7-6. *GtkEntryCompletion in action*

GtkEntryCompletion provides a list of suggested values using a GtkListStore. We'll take a closer look at GtkListStore in Chapter 9. For now, you just need to know that GtkListStore is a list of data values and is the main support behind GtkEntryCompletion.

Listing 7-6 shows the code that adds the GtkEntryCompletion to the stateEntry of ContributorEdit.

Listing 7-6. *Creating and Associating a GtkEntryCompletion Object*

```php
<?php
    private function _layoutTool()
    {
        // ...

        // Help the user out with the state by using a GtkEntryCompletion.
        $stateCompletion = new GtkEntryCompletion();
        $stateCompletion->set_model(self::createStateList());
        $stateCompletion->set_text_column(0);
        $this->stateEntry->set_completion($stateCompletion);
        $stateCompletion->set_inline_completion(true);

        // ...
    }
```

```
public static function createStateList()
{
    $listStore = new GtkListStore(Gtk::TYPE_STRING);
    $iter = $listStore->append();
    $listStore->set($iter, 0, 'Alabama');
    $iter = $listStore->append();
    $listStore->set($iter, 0, 'Alaska');
    $iter = $listStore->append();
    $listStore->set($iter, 0, 'Arizona');
    $iter = $listStore->append();
    $listStore->set($iter, 0, 'Arkansas');
    $iter = $listStore->append();
    $listStore->set($iter, 0, 'California');
    $iter = $listStore->append();
    $listStore->set($iter, 0, 'Colorado');
    // ...

    return $listStore;
}
?>
```

The first step, as always, is to create the object. The constructor for GtkEntryCompletion does not take any arguments.

The next step is to set a model for the entry completion using set_model. A *model* is a structured data object. It manages a set of data as a tree or list. In Listing 7-6, the data model being used is a list. The list is created in the createStateList method. This method instantiates a GtkListStore object and adds a value for each state or province that should be suggested. Again, the details of how the GtkListStore object works are discussed in Chapter 9.

Once the list is created and set as the model, the entry completion is told where in the model to look for the completion values. In Listing 7-6, there is only one column of data, so the entry completion must look in column 0. This is done using the set_text_column method.

Finally, the entry completion is associated with the GtkEntry for the state. If the user types the letter *a* in the state entry, he will see something similar to the example shown earlier in Figure 7-6.

Setting the Number of Characters for a Match

GtkEntryCompletion performs a case-insensitive string comparison to find possible matches. That means that if the user enters *a*, he will see the same list of suggestions as he would if he had entered *A*.

The default behavior is to check on every character that is entered. For some lists, in which many values begin with the same few characters, trying to come up with suggested values after only one or two characters have been entered will likely return too many values to be useful, and will probably slow down the application. It is possible to override the default behavior by using set_minimum_key_length. This method changes the number of characters that must be entered before the application tries to find a match for the entry's value.

Using Inline Completion

Another default behavior of GtkEntry is to show suggestions in a pop-up window, like the one shown in Figure 7-6. The pop-up window shows up below the entry. But you don't need to use a pop-up window to guide the user in the right direction. You can turn it off by passing false to set_popup_completion. What is the point of a GtkEntryCompletion without a pop-up list of suggestions? The user can be urged to enter certain characters by using inline completion.

You activate inline completion by passing true to set_inline_completion. For instance, if you have ever used Microsoft Excel, you have probably seen an example of inline completion. Inline completion automatically appends one or more characters to the entry value when at least one matching value is found. The characters that are added are selected, so that the user will overwrite them with the next character typed; the user can continue typing if the value is incorrect. The characters that are added to the entry value depend on the matching items in the list.

With a pop-up completion, comparisons are made with only what the user has entered so far. Inline completion, on the other hand, looks ahead to see what the user could type next. For example, if a user types *a* into the state entry, a pop-up window would show all states that begin with the letter *A*. Inline completion has only one line to work with. The user could type an *l* or an *r* next. Therefore, inline completion does not know which characters to append. If the user types an *l* next, the inline completion can make a suggestion. The only values in the list that begin with *Al* also begin with *Ala*. It is likely that the user is trying to enter either Alaska or Alabama. Therefore, the inline completion will append an *a* to the entry. If the user types *Alab*, the inline completion will find only one match and set the entry's value to Alabama, with the last three characters highlighted. By pressing Enter, the user will select the completion text, and the entry's value will be set to Alabama.

■**Caution** If GtkEntryCompletion is set to use inline completion, the value passed to set_minimum_key_length will be ignored. This may affect performance if the list of possible completions is very large.

Combo Boxes

GtkEntry is a free-form text-entry tool. This means that users can enter any text they like. Of course, the application should check the value to make sure that it not only matches some expected value or pattern, but also that the user is not trying to do something malicious, like perform SQL injection. As noted earlier, sometimes GtkEntry is not the best way to collect data from users. GtkComboBox is a widget that, similar to an HTML select element, provides a list of values from which the user can select. The user may not type in a freehand value. Using a GtkComboBox constrains the user to a given set of possible values. In cases where valid input values can be defined by finite set of data, GtkComboBox is a much better data-entry tool than GtkEntry.

A combo box can show any sort of data, including images, and can show the choices as a flat list or a hierarchical tree. However, in most cases, a combo box just shows a flat list of strings.

Like `GtkEntryCompletion`, `GtkComboBox` uses a model to manage data. This means that the list of possible values needs to be kept in a `GtkListStore` or a `GtkTreeStore`. The model that is chosen for the combo box dictates how the list of values will be shown. If a `GtkListStore` is used, the combo box will show the values as a flat list. If a `GtkTreeStore` is used, the list will be shown as a hierarchical structure. Figure 7-7 shows the difference between the two model views.

Figure 7-7. *Two types of GtkComboBox widgets: GtkListStore gives a flat list (left), and GtkTreeStore presents a hierarchical structure (right)*

Working with a `GtkComboBox` is the same, regardless of which model is used. Here, we will look at using a list store and also using a combo box without a model. We'll discuss creating and manipulating models in Chapter 9.

Flat Text Lists

As noted, most frequently, `GtkComboBox` is used to show a simple, flat list of text values. Because most combo boxes are string lists, PHP-GTK provides a few helper methods to make your life a little easier. These methods are designed specifically for `GtkComboBox` widgets that show a flat text list; they do not work with those that contain multiple levels or values that are not text strings. What is special about this type of combo box is that PHP-GTK knows exactly what the model looks like because PHP-GTK created it. Therefore, you do not need to manage the model.

The most important method when creating a flat text combo box is the static constructor. `GtkComboBox::new_text` returns a combo box that can hold only one level of strings. The combo box that is returned will be set up so that the other helper methods can work on it properly.

To add values, call `prepend_text`, `append_text`, or `insert_text`. These three methods work only on combo boxes that have been created with the `new_text` constructor. PHP-GTK will create the list item and place it properly in the `GtkListStore` that has been automatically created. `prepend_text` and `append_text` add values to the beginning and end of the list, while `insert_text` puts the string in a specific location. `insert_text` expects the position first, followed by the string to insert. To remove a value from the list, call `remove_text` and pass the position of the item that should be removed.

After the user has selected a value from the combo box, you can get the string that the user selected by using the `get_active_text` method.

Listing 7-7 shows how easy it is to create a flat text combo box using `new_text`.

Listing 7-7. *Creating a Flat Text GtkComboBox*

```php
<?php
    private function _layoutTool()
    {
        // ...
```

```
        // The country should be a combo box.
        $this->countryComboBox = GtkComboBox::new_text();
        $this->countryComboBox->append_text('United States');
        $this->countryComboBox->prepend_text('Canada');
        $this->countryComboBox->insert_text(1, 'United Kingdom');
        $this->countryComboBox->set_active(0);

        // ...
    }
?>
```

GtkComboBox with a Custom Model

Occasionally, you may want to manage a GtkComboBox's model instead of letting PHP-GTK take care of it. Perhaps the model has already been created by some class, or the model may not be a flat text list.

When a combo box generated with new_text will not work, you must use the more generic version of GtkComboBox. This version requires you to manage the model independently of the combo box, but offers more flexibility in the model that is accepted.

You can create a GtkComboBox without using new_text by using the classic new GtkComboBox constructor. This method of constructing a combo box returns a combo box with no model. It is just a shell that is ready to be filled.

Once you've created a combo box, you can set or change its model by using set_model. The value given to set_model must represent either a list or a tree; otherwise, a nasty error will be thrown.

Optionally, you can pass a model to the constructor. In this case, it will return a GtkComboBox that already has its mode initialized to the model that is passed in.

Managing the model, including getting and setting the active, or selected item, is your responsibility. You can do that using the methods explained in Chapter 9.

Scales

GtkEntry is excellent for collecting text, and GtkComboBox is good for choosing a value from list, but how does an application collect numerical data? Sure, numerical data could be entered in a GtkEntry field, but that would allow the users to enter any values they like. Using a GtkComboBox to allow the user to select a number between one and one hundred is impractical. Fortunately, PHP-GTK provides widgets designed specifically to allow the user to specify a numeric value. One of those is the scale, or specifically GtkHScale and GtkVScale.

Scales allow the user to select a value within a range by sliding the widget back and forth or up and down. Scrollbars are scales that allow the user to select a relative position of the screen that should be shown. When not used as scrollbars, scales, also known as sliders, are used to visually represent a range of numbers. The values that the scale represents can be integers or floating-point values, and they can have any arbitrary precision that PHP allows.

Scales come in two varieties: horizontal and vertical, as shown in Figure 7-8. Both are controlled and behave exactly the same way. The only difference is in how they are shown on the screen.

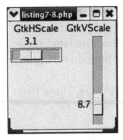

Figure 7-8. *GtkHScale and GtkVScale*

GtkHScale, the horizontal variety, and GtkVScale, the vertical type, are both descendants of GtkScale, which is itself a descendant of GtkRange, a class that extends GtkWidget. This relatively deep ancestry allows each level to focus on specific functionality.

Scales themselves are strictly display widgets. The scale's role is to give the user a visual representation of the value and allow the value to be changed. The scale also controls the precision of the adjustment. Management of the numerical values is handled by a helper object called GtkAdjustment. In fact, the only methods specific to GtkHScale and GtkVScale are the constructors. The standard constructor, new GtkHScale, takes a GtkAdjustment as the only argument.

Scale Adjustment

GtkAdjustment is an object that sets bounds for a range of numbers and also sets the rules for which numbers within those bounds are considered valid values. When an adjustment is created, it must be given five numbers: the initial value, the lower boundary, the upper boundary, the step increment, and the page increment. The value of the adjustment must always be greater than or equal to the lower boundary and less than or equal to the upper boundary. The step increment is the amount the value will be changed when small changes are made. The page increment is used to make moving through the values quicker. It is the amount the value will change when the adjustment is paged.

Paging is what happens when you click the empty space in a scrollbar instead of the arrow at the end. Paging changes the value of the adjustment by a large increment. The adjustment listens to the widget it is helping and makes sure that the value stays within the boundaries.

Scale Precision

Using set_digits, the number of decimal places will be set to the integer value passed in. Passing 0 to set_digits makes the value of the adjustment always stay an integer. get_digits returns the precision. The default precision for scales is one decimal place.

The precision of the adjustment's value is the same as the precision that is shown on the label next to the scale, unless the value is set programmatically. If you set the value programmatically, the value may have any precision, regardless of how many digits are displayed.

Value Display

The slider also controls whether the value appears next to the slider and where the value is shown. set_draw_value takes a Boolean value as the only argument and turns the label on or off. By default, the label is shown on top of the scale.

You can set where the label is shown by using set_value_pos, which expects a GtkPositionType. Listing 7-8 shows the code that was used to create Figure 7-8. Here, set_value_pos is used to move the label of the GtkVScale to the right side of the slider. When possible, the label stays next to the slider. This happens by default for horizontal scales, but doesn't happen for vertical scales unless the label is moved to the left or right.

The methods to get and set the value of the scale are inherited from GtkRange. These two methods are given the rather appropriate names get_value and set_value.

Listing 7-8. *Using GtkHScale and GtkVScale*

```php
<?php
function echoValue($scale)
{
    echo $scale->get_value() . "\n";
}

$window = new GtkWindow();
$window->set_size_request(150, 150);

$hScale = new GtkHScale(new GtkAdjustment(4, 0, 10, 1, 2));
$hScale->connect('value-changed', 'echoValue');

$vScale = new GtkVScale(new GtkAdjustment(4, 0, 10, 1, 2));
$vScale->connect('value-changed', 'echoValue');
$vScale->set_value_pos(Gtk::POS_LEFT);

$hBox  = new GtkHBox();
$vBox1 = new GtkVBox();
$vBox2 = new GtkVBox();

$window->add($hBox);
$hBox->pack_start($vBox1);
$hBox->pack_start($vBox2);

$vBox1->pack_start(new GtkLabel('GtkHScale'), false, false);
$vBox1->pack_start($hScale, false, false);

$vBox2->pack_start(new GtkLabel('GtkVScale'), false, false);
$vBox2->pack_start($vScale);

$window->connect_simple('destroy', array('Gtk', 'main_quit'));
$window->show_all();
Gtk::main();
?>
```

Spin Buttons

The other widget specifically designed to display and collect numerical values is GtkSpinButton. GtkSpinButton is a descendant of GtkEntry.

GtkSpinButton shows its value in an entry field and gives the user controls to increase or decrease the value. Clicking the up or down arrow changes the value. GtkSpinButton uses an adjustment to manage its value, just as scales do. The only difference between a scale and a spin button is how the value is shown and manipulated.

A spin button is useful when there is limited space to put a widget. In general, spin buttons take up less room than sliders. Of course, sliders can be crammed into any space that spin buttons can, but the less space there is, the less usable a scale becomes.

Creating a spin button is similar to creating a scale. It expects an adjustment as the first argument, but unlike scales, a spin button also expects the climb rate and the precision in the constructor. The climb rate is how fast the value will change when the user presses the up or down arrow. The higher the climb rate, the faster the value will change. When the range is large and the precision is relatively small, the climb rate should be high, so that users do not need to click the up arrow too long to get to the value they need. A slower climb rate is useful when the precision is not so great, because the users will move through the values rather quickly.

Listing 7-9 shows the basic usage of a GtkSpinButton. The output of this code is shown in Figure 7-9.

Listing 7-9. *Creating and Using a GtkSpinButton*

```php
<?php
function echoValue($spinButton)
{
    echo $spinButton->get_value() . "\n";
}

$window = new GtkWindow();
$window->set_size_request(100, 100);

$spin = new GtkSpinButton(new GtkAdjustment(4, 0, 10, 1, 2), 1, 0);
$spin->connect('changed', 'echoValue');

$vBox = new GtkVBox();

$window->add($vBox);
$vBox->pack_start(new GtkLabel('GtkSpinButton'), false, false);
$vBox->pack_start($spin, false, false);

$window->connect_simple('destroy', array('Gtk', 'main_quit'));
$window->show_all();
Gtk::main();
?>
```

Figure 7-9. *A typical GtkSpinButton*

Buttons

After users have been prompted for information using GtkLabel widgets and have entered information using GtkEntry widgets, they must be able to notify the application that the information is ready for processing. This is where GtkButton comes in.

GtkButton is designed to tell the application to begin some process—whether it is collecting values that have been supplied by the user, shutting down the application, or anything in between. Buttons are not very useful unless they do something when the user takes an action. The main function of a button is to act as a messenger. The message is transmitted through the use of signal handlers. The most commonly connected event is the clicked event, but buttons are capable of listening for a wide range of user actions.

GtkButton is a unique type of widget. Technically, it is a container, but it reacts to user interactions. Most containers do not actually take up space on the screen, and are therefore not able to be clicked, selected, or otherwise accessed by the user. But GtkButton is specifically designed to be accessed by an application's user. GtkButton is a bin container that holds only a GtkLabel about 70 percent of the time. The other 30 percent of the time, a GtkButton will hold an image or an image and a label. While it is possible to put any non-top-level widget inside a button, it is hard to imagine why an application would need to do that.

Buttons can be simple, containing only a simple label, or they can be complex with icons and mnemonics. A button can be a generic stock button, or it can be so unique that it has a customized shape. (Chapter 12 will go into the details of changing a button's shape). GtkButton is simple but essential. It is hard to imagine any large application that doesn't make use of buttons. The role that buttons play is very specialized. Because of this, constructing a button has been highly specialized. There are two constructor methods for GtkButton: new GtkButton and GtkButton::new_from_stock.

Standard Buttons

A standard empty button, which can contain any widget, can be instantiated in the same way most widgets can: with new GtkButton. You can also create buttons with text already added.

By passing a string as the only argument, the button will automatically create a label widget and add it as the button's child. If you need to access the label the button is created, use the get_label method.

Another typical use of GtkButton involves a GtkLabel with a mnemonic. Instead of creating a button with a label, and then grabbing the label and adding a mnemonic, you can create a button with a mnemonic label automatically. Simply adding an underscore to the button constructor creates a button and uses the string (which should have an underscore to indicate the mnemonic key) to create a mnemonic label and assign the button as the mnemonic widget. The following is an example of creating a button with a mnemonic label:

```
$button = new GtkButton('_Click Me');
```

Stock Buttons

The other method for creating buttons takes advantage of the fact that many applications will need the same type of button. For instance, it is not unlikely that an application will provide a form that the user should fill in. After the user fills in the form, the application must be told that the data is ready for processing. This is usually done with a button that has an OK or Submit label. Since this type of button is so prevalent in PHP-GTK, it exists as one of many stock buttons.

Stock buttons are ready-made buttons that have a default image and label. The label will also often have a mnemonic. PHP-GTK offers dozens of stock buttons that represent common application tasks.

Creating Stock Buttons

You use GtkButton::new_from_stock to create a stock button. This method takes a string that identifies which stock button should be returned. To see a list of all stock buttons and the strings that can be used to create them, fire up the stock item browser from the PHP-GTK /demos directory.

The Crisscott PIMS application's contributor editing tool is a perfect example of a form that can use stock buttons. Listing 7-10 expands on the ContributorEdit class and adds Save and Undo buttons.

Listing 7-10. *Using Stock Buttons*

```php
<?php
    private function _layoutTool()
    {
        // See Listing 7-5 for the rest of this method.

        // Add the save and clear buttons.
        $save  = GtkButton::new_from_stock('Gtk::STOCK_SAVE');
        $reset = GtkButton::new_from_stock('Gtk::STOCK_UNDO);

        // Create signal handlers for the buttons.
        $save->connect_simple('clicked', array($this, 'saveContributor'));
        $reset->connect_simple('clicked', array($this, 'resetContributor'));

        // Attach the buttons to the table.
        $this->attach($reset, 0, 1, 6, 7, 0, 0);
        $this->attach($save,  3, 4, 6, 7, 0, 0);
    }
?>
```

Figure 7-10 shows the buttons added to the form.

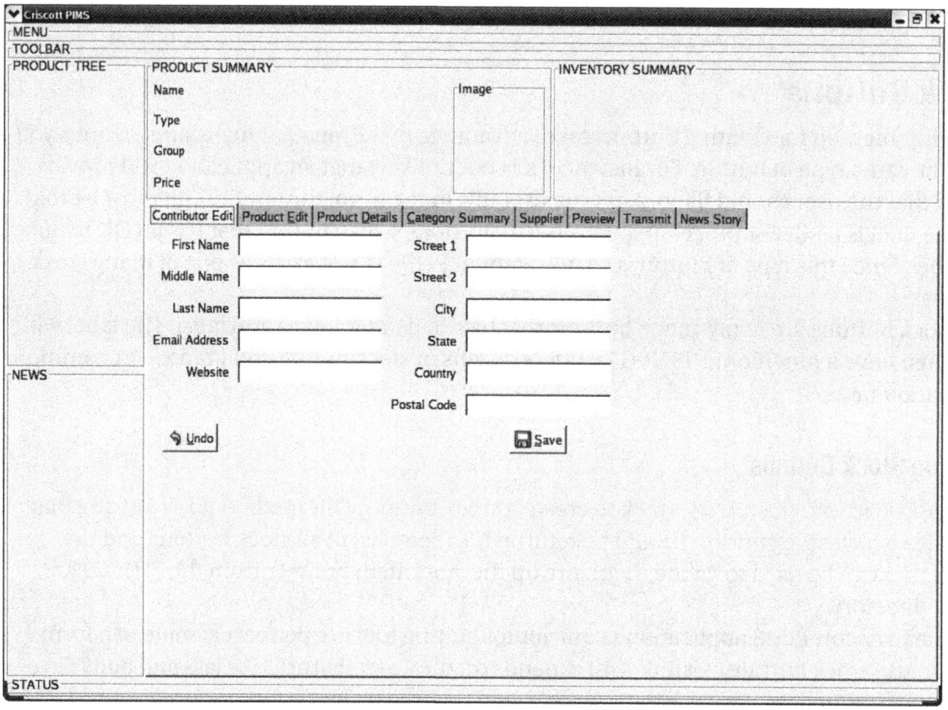

Figure 7-10. *Using stock buttons*

Adding buttons to the ContributorEdit tool is relatively easy. Each button is created using the static GtkButton::new_from_stock method. The first button is a stock Save button. In Figure 7-10, it is the button on the right. The second button is a stock Undo button. Undo is the best choice available for resetting the tool's entry fields.

Both buttons are automatically created with icons, labels, and mnemonic shortcuts. The mnemonic for the button's label will trigger the clicked signal of the button automatically. After the buttons are created, it is essential that their clicked signal is connected to a method. If no signal handler is created, nothing will happen when the button is clicked or the mnemonic shortcut is activated. The final step is to attach the buttons to the table.

Connecting Buttons to a Signal Handler

Having buttons in an application is not very useful unless the buttons are connected to some signal handler. When a button is clicked, it fires a signal handler that tells the application to grab some specific data and do something with it, such as store the data in a database, add a few values together, or send data to a server.

The ContributorEdit tool's buttons are each connected to a signal handler so that something happens when one of them is clicked. Listing 7-11 shows the methods that are used as callback for the two buttons.

Listing 7-11. *Resetting and Saving Contributor Data*

```php
<?php
    public function resetContributor()
    {
        // Make sure we have a contributor already.
        if (!isset($this->contributor)) {
            require_once 'Crisscott/Contributor.php';
            $this->contributor = new Crisscott_Contributor();
        }

        // Reset the fields to the original value.
        $this->populateFields($this->contributor);
    }

    public function saveContributor()
    {
        // First grab all of the values.
        $this->contributor->firstName  = $this->firstNameEntry->get_text();
        $this->contributor->middleName = $this->firstNameEntry->get_text();
        $this->contributor->lastName   = $this->lastNameEntry->get_text();
        $this->contributor->website    = $this->websiteEntry->get_text();
        $this->contributor->email      = $this->emailEntry->get_text();
        $this->contributor->street1    = $this->street1Entry->get_text();
        $this->contributor->street1    = $this->street1Entry->get_text();
        $this->contributor->city       = $this->cityEntry->get_text();
        $this->contributor->state      = $this->stateEntry->get_text();
        $this->contributor->country    = $this->countryCombo->get_active_text();
        $this->contributor->postal     = $this->postalEntry->get_text();

        // Next validate the data.
        $valid = $this->contributor->validate();

        // Create a map of all the values and labels.
        $labelMap = array('firstName'  => $this->firsNameLabel,
                          'middleName' => $this->middleNameLabel,
                          'lastName'   => $this->lastNameLabel,
                          'website'    => $this->websiteLabel,
                          'email'      => $this->emailLabel,
                          'street1'    => $this->street1Label,
                          'street2'    => $this->street2Label,
                          'city'       => $this->cityLabel,
                          'state'      => $this->stateLabel,
                          'country'    => $this->countryLabel,
                          'zip'        => $this->zipLabel
                          );
```

```php
            // Reset all of the labels.
            foreach ($labelMap as $label) {
                $this->clearError($label);
            }

            // If there are invalid values, mark up the labels.
            if (is_array($valid)) {
                foreach ($valid as $labelKey) {
                    $this->reportError($labelMap[$labelKey]);
                }

                // Saving the data was not successful.
                return false;
            }

            // Try to save the data.
            return $this->contributor->save();
        }
?>
```

The Undo button is connected to the resetContributor method of the ContributorEdit class. This method simply overwrites the current GtkEntry values with the values from the last Contributor instance that was passed in. Instead of rewriting the code to populate the fields, the populateFields method is just reused.

The Save button is connected to the saveContributor method. This callback method is slightly more complicated. saveContributor has three jobs to perform. First, it must grab the current values from the GtkEntry elements. This is done by calling get_value on each entry and assigning it to a member of the current contributor instance. After all of the information has been collected, the information is validated. Validating the information is the responsibility of the Crisscott_Contributor class, as is the third step, which is to save the contributor data to the database.

While validating the contributor information is the responsibility of the Crisscott_Contributor class, making the user aware of the invalid data is the job of the ContributorEdit tool. If all the data given to the contributor is not valid, an array indicating which data values failed to validate is returned; otherwise, the validate method returns true. For each value that is returned in the array, the saveContributor method calls the reportError method. The reportError method, the same method shown in Listing 7-2, simply adds Pango markup to the label, which identifies the bad data. In order to reduce confusion, error markup is cleared from all labels before any new markup is added. This way, if the user fixed a previously bad data value, it will no longer be marked as invalid.

Summary

This chapter has explained how to display and collect small amounts of data. GtkLabel can be used to deliver simple text messages or to add formatting to a string of text, making it stand out. Labels can be used to report errors, give instructions, and identify other pieces of the application. Labels are most often used to identify the information that is being collected from the user.

GtkEntry is useful to collect simple text strings from the user. GtkEntry is a free-form widget. The users can enter any value they like. You can use the GtkEntryCompletion helper widget to give the user hints for entering values that the application expects.

GtkComboBox can restrict the set of possible values. The user is only allowed to select from a given set of values, and therefore cannot enter anything the application isn't expecting.

When numerical data is needed, GtkHScale, GtkVScale, and GtkSpinButton are useful. They are designed specifically to display and collect numerical values.

Finally, when all data has been presented and collected from the user, you can use buttons to indicate that data processing should begin.

This chapter showed ways to communicate simple messages. All of these tools allow the application and the user to communicate effectively.

Chapter 8 goes into the details of displaying, editing, formatting, and collecting large amounts of text. With the tools in the next chapter, the Crisscott PIMS application will be able to collect product descriptions and display large amounts of text like RSS news feeds. Editing large amounts of text can be tricky, but the next chapter will give you the tools to make rather complicated changes to a block of text, including copying and pasting blocks of text to and from the clipboard.

CHAPTER 8

■■■

Using Multiline Text

Labels and entries are excellent widgets for displaying small amounts of text, but they are not suitable for larger blocks of text. Their limitations are due to the inherent complications that arise as a block of text grows. While the features of GtkLabel are impressive, its capabilities are unsatisfactory for text blocks such as help pages. GtkEntry obviously doesn't fill all of a user's needs when it comes to text editing, since it allows the user to edit only one simple line of text.

Fortunately, PHP-GTK takes full advantage of the text-editing abilities of GTK+ 2.0, so you have other options for handling text. Using the powerful text-editing features introduced in this chapter, you can build applications capable of creating, manipulating, and displaying large blocks of text with relative ease. Additionally, you can provide end users with the ability to create their own equally complex blocks of text.

The Text-Editing Tool Set

One significant distinction between simple text and multiline text is the way that PHP-GTK handles larger text blocks. One widget, GtkLabel, handles the display of small amounts of text, and another widget, GtkEntry, handles editing. However, for larger amounts of text, both the display and editing are handled by the same collection of widgets and objects.

Each piece involved in multiline text is highly specialized. One object, GtkTextBuffer, holds the text that will be displayed or edited. GtkTextView is a specialized widget for presenting the text to the user. Finally, three other objects—GtkTextMark, GtkTextIter, and GtkTextTag—are used to identify and manipulate groups of characters within the block of text. Combined, these five components make for one very powerful text-editing tool set. The combination of these tools can produce something similar to Figure 8-1.

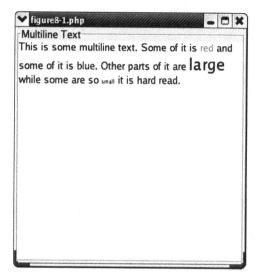

Figure 8-1. *An example of multiline text in an application*

To understand how these tools work together, it is best to start by looking at the objects that work behind the scenes to set up the text display.

Text Marks

The simplest part of the PHP-GTK text-editing tool set is the GtkTextMark object. In this context, a *mark* indicates position. A mark is a location within a block of text that can be used as a point of reference. A mark always references a position located either between two characters or at the beginning or end of the buffer. It never points to a specific character in the text.

Marks are used to preserve locations in a block of text even when the text changes. If the text surrounding a mark is deleted, the mark will still remain. If new text is added at the mark, the mark will reside either to the left or right of the newly inserted text. Which side the mark ends up on depends on its *gravity*.

A mark with left gravity will reside at the beginning of the newly inserted text; a mark with right gravity will reside at the end of the new text. Even though a mark might have right gravity, it could appear to the left of newly inserted text. This is because the gravity is with respect to the direction in which the text is written. For instance, Hebrew text appears from right to left. A mark with right gravity appears at the end of newly inserted text, which in the case of Hebrew, would be on the left.

Referencing Marks

All text buffers are created with two marks:

- The *insertion point*, or the point where text will be inserted in the buffer

- The *selection bound*, which is the block of currently selected characters in the buffer

The text selection is bound on one end by the insertion point and on the other end by the selection bound. If there are no characters located between the insertion point and the selection bound, then no text is selected and the two marks must point to the same location. Furthermore, both of these marks have right gravity, meaning that when new text is inserted into a buffer, both marks will remain at the end of the text unless they are specifically moved.

To make these marks easier to reference, they're named insert and selection_bound. By moving the insert mark, you can change the position that new text will be inserted. If the two marks are separated, the text between them will be selected. When the user selects a block of text, the two marks will be separated. The selection_bound will be at the beginning of the text, and the insert marker will be at the end.

Creating Marks

Marks may exist on their own, but they are not very useful unless they are associated with a GtkTextBuffer. Most of the methods related to marks are actually text buffer methods. Marks also often require the help of another text-editing tool, GtkTextIter. Both GtkTextBuffer and GtkTextIter are discussed in their own sections later in this chapter.

To create a mark requires a method from GtkTextBuffer and the help of a GtkTextIter. The following line demonstrates how to create a text mark:

```
$mark = $buffer->create_mark('endParagraph1', $iter, false);
```

The create_mark method of GtkTextBuffer returns a GtkTextMark object. create_mark expects three arguments: a name for the mark, a GtkTextIter, and whether or not the mark should have left gravity. In this example, the mark has the name endParagraph1. This name will allow you to easily access the mark later. The name may be null. If so, the mark will be anonymous, meaning that while it will not be possible to reference the mark by name, it will be much easier to create on the fly, because mark names within a buffer must be unique. The second argument, $iter, must come from the buffer that called create_mark. By passing false as the last argument, the newly created mark will have right gravity. If text is inserted at the location of this mark, the mark will remain to the right of the text.

Once a mark has been created, it may be retrieved either as the return value from create_mark or by using get_mark. The get_mark method takes a mark name as the only argument and returns the GtkTextMark object identified by that name. Obviously, anonymous marks cannot be returned from this method.

A mark may be removed from a buffer using either delete_mark or delete_mark_by_name. These two methods do not actually delete the mark; they just remove it from its current buffer. delete_mark expects a GtkTextMark instance as its only argument. delete_mark_by_name expects the name of a GtkTextMark.

Moving Marks

You can move a mark with either move_mark or move_mark_by_name. Both of these methods belong to GtkTextBuffer and require the help of a GtkTextIter. The move_mark method expects a GtkTextMark object as the first argument. The move_mark_by_name method expects the mark's name. The second argument to both methods must be a valid GtkTextIter from the same buffer as the mark.

Because moving the insert and selection_bound marks separately selects a region of text, which fires signals and may cause one or more callbacks to be called, there is a special method for moving these two marks together. The place_cursor method or GtkTextBuffer will move both the insert and selection_bound markers to the location at the same time. The location that the marks will be moved to is designated by a GtkTextIter, passed as the only argument.

Even if the end goal is to select a region of text, moving the two marks independently may not be the best idea. Every time either an insert or a selection_bound mark is moved, the text between the two marks is selected. This means that moving the two marks separately selects two regions of text, because one region is selected each time one of the marks is moved. The GtkTextBuffer method select_range moves both the insert and selection_bound marks simultaneously, but to two different places within the text buffer. Using this method selects only one region of text because both marks are moved together. The two arguments for this method are both GtkTextIter objects. The first argument specifies the new location of the insert marker; the second pinpoints the location of the selection_bound marker. Listing 8-1 shows an example of how *not* to move the cursor and select a region of text.

Listing 8-1. *The Wrong Way to Move insert and selection_bound in a GtkTextBuffer*

```php
<?php
function printSelected($buffer, $iter, $mark)
{
    // Get the mark that wasn't moved.
    if ($mark == $buffer->get_mark('insert')) {
        $mark2 = $buffer->get_mark('selection_bound');
    } else {
        $mark2 = $buffer->get_mark('insert');
    }
    // Get the iter at the other mark.
    $iter2 = $buffer->get_iter_at_offset(0);
    $buffer->get_iter_at_mark($iter2, $mark2);



    // Print the text between the two iters.
    echo 'SELECTION: ' . $buffer->get_text($iter, $iter2) . "\n";
}

// Create a GtkTextView.
$text = new GtkTextView();
// Get the buffer from the view.
$buffer = $text->get_buffer();

// Add some text.

$buffer->set_text('Moving a mark is done with either move_mark or ' .
                  'move_mark_by_name.');

// Connect the printSelected method.
$buffer->connect('mark-set', 'printSelected');
```

```php
// How NOT to move the cursor to the beginning of the text.
echo "Move to start\n";
$buffer->move_mark_by_name('insert',           $buffer->get_start_iter());
$buffer->move_mark_by_name('selection_bound', $buffer->get_start_iter());

// How NOT to select a range of text.
echo "Select range\n";
$buffer->move_mark_by_name('selection_bound', $buffer->get_iter_at_offset(7));
$buffer->move_mark_by_name('insert',           $buffer->get_iter_at_offset(16));

?>
```

Notice in Listing 8-1 that the selection_bound and insert markers are moved separately. The connection to the printSelected method gives a clue as to why moving the two marks separately is not such a good idea. Each time move_mark_by_name is called, a mark-set signal is fired, and the printSelected function is called. The following is the output of Listing 8-1. Notice that there are twice as many lines as you would expect. This is because the callback is called when each mark is moved.

```
Move to start
SELECTION: Moving a mark is done with either move_mark or move_mark_by_name.
SELECTION:
Select Range
SELECTION:
SELECTION: a mark is
```

Instead of moving the two marks separately, it is better to move them at the same time. This prevents the signal handler from being called twice. Using place_cursor and select_range moves both the insert and selection_bound marks at the same time, as shown in Listing 8-2.

Listing 8-2. *The Right Way to Move insert and selection_bound in a GtkTextBuffer*

```php
<?php
function printSelected($buffer, $iter, $mark)
{
    // Get the mark that wasn't moved.
    if ($mark == $buffer->get_mark('insert')) {
        $mark2 = $buffer->get_mark('selection_bound');
    } else {
        $mark2 = $buffer->get_mark('insert');
    }
    // Get the iter at the other mark.
    $iter2 = $buffer->get_iter_at_offset(0);
    $buffer->get_iter_at_mark($iter2, $mark2);

    // Print the text between the two iters.
    echo 'SELECTION: ' . $buffer->get_text($iter, $iter2) . "\n";
}
```

```
// Create a GtkTextView.
$text = new GtkTextView();
// Get the buffer from the view.
$buffer = $text->get_buffer();

// Add some text.
$buffer->set_text('Moving a mark is done with either move_mark or ' .
                  'move_mark_by_name.');

// Connect the printSelected method.
$buffer->connect('mark-set', 'printSelected');

// The better way to move the cursor to the beginning of the text.
echo "Move to start\n";
$buffer->place_cursor($buffer->get_start_iter());

// The better way to select a range of text.
echo "Select range\n";
$buffer->select_range($buffer->get_iter_at_offset(7),
                      $buffer->get_iter_at_offset(16));
?>
```

This example uses place_cursor to move the selection_bound and insert markers to the same place simultaneously. At the end of Listing 8-2, a range of text is selected. Instead of moving the selection_bound and insert markers separately, select_range is used to move both marks at once.

The following is the output from this listing. It is much more along the lines of what you would expect. Notice that when the two marks are moved, no text is selected. The mark-set signal is still fired, but only once. The same is true when select_range is called—mark-set is fired only once instead of twice.

```
Move to start
SELECTION:
Select Range
SELECTION: a mark is
```

Iterators

Several of the methods that manipulate GtkTextMarks require the help of another object called GtkTextIter, also known as an *iterator*. GtkTextIter is similar to GtkTextMark in that it is used to mark a position in a text buffer. The main difference between the two objects is that text iterators are not permanent. If the text in a buffer is changed, all of the iterators are no longer valid. Unlike marks, which point to a location between two characters, iterators point to a specific byte in a text buffer, or the beginning or end of the buffer. Iterators indicate where marks should be created or moved.

The position of an iterator is defined by either an *offset* or an *index*. An offset is the number of characters between a position and the start of the buffer. An index is the number of bytes between a position and the start of the buffer. If the buffer contains only ASCII characters, an offset of 8 points to the same location has an index of 8. Text in PHP-GTK is represented using the UTF-8 character set, which means that characters may be represented with two bytes. Therefore, if a buffer consists of Unicode characters, an offset of 8 may point to a different position than an index of 8.

Usually, offsets are used more than indexes, because an index can point to a position between two bytes of one character. Manipulating text by indexes can be dangerous because an iterator may be placed in between two bytes of a given character.

Creating Iterators

Just like marks, iterator objects are created by using GtkTextBuffer. GtkTextIter cannot be instantiated directly, but instead must be returned from a GtkTextBuffer method. The two most commonly used methods for getting iterator instances are get_iter_at_offset and get_iter_at_mark. get_iter_at_offset expects an offset as the only argument and returns an iterator that points to that offset. get_iter_at_mark returns an iterator at the given mark.

Two handy convenience methods are get_start_iter and get_end_iter, which return iterators for the start and end of the buffer, respectively. The start and end of the buffer are excellent reference points from which to start. Listing 8-3 shows several different ways to create and access iterators.

Listing 8-3. *Creating and Moving GtkTextIter Objects*

```php
<?php
// Create a GtkTextView.
$text = new GtkTextView();
// Get the buffer from the view.
$buffer = $text->get_buffer();

// Add some text.
$buffer->set_text('Moving a mark is done with either move_mark or ' .
                  'move_mark_by_name.');

// Get the fifth word from the buffer.
$iter = $buffer->get_start_iter();
$iter->forward_word_ends(5);
$iter2 = $buffer->get_iter_at_offset($iter->get_offset());
$iter->backward_word_start();
echo $buffer->get_text($iter, $iter2) . "\n";

// Get the second to last word.
$iter = $buffer->get_end_iter();
$iter->backward_word_starts(2);
$iter2 = $buffer->get_iter_at_offset($iter->get_offset());
$iter2->forward_word_end();
echo $buffer->get_text($iter, $iter2) . "\n";
```

```
// Figure out how many characters are between the third and sixth words.
$iter = $buffer->get_start_iter();
$iter->forward_word_ends(3);
$endThird = $iter->get_offset();
$iter->forward_word_ends(3);
echo 'There are ' . ($iter->get_offset() - $endThird) . ' ';
echo "characters between the third and sixth words.\n";

// Check to see if the end of the first sentence is the end of the buffer.
$iter = $buffer->get_start_iter();
$iter->forward_sentence_end();
if ($iter == $buffer->get_end_iter()) {
    echo "The buffer only contains one sentence.\n";
} else {
    echo "The buffer contains more than one sentence.\n";
}

// Count the words in the buffer.
$iter  = $buffer->get_start_iter();
$count = 0;
while($iter->forward_word_end()) $count++;
echo 'There are ' . $count . " words in the buffer.\n";
?>
```

All of this iterator manipulation creates the following output:

```
done
by
There are 13 characters between the third and sixth words.
The buffer only contains one sentence.
There are 14 words in the buffer.
```

Aside from being used to define locations and ranges, iterators can return a lot of information about the text. You can use iterators to determine if a location is at the beginning or end of the buffer, a line, a sentence, or a word. The is_start and is_end methods return true if the iterator represents the start or end of the buffer, respectively. The starts_line, starts_sentence, and starts_word methods will return true if the iterator is at the start of a line, sentence, or word. Corresponding methods called ends_line, ends_sentence, and ends_word return true if the iterator points to the end of a line, sentence, or word.

If an iterator is not at the start or end of a word, then it is inside a word. You can test this by using the inside_word method. A similar method called inside_sentence returns true if the iterator is inside a sentence. The break between words and sentences is determined by Pango.

Moving Iterators

Iterators are not necessarily static. You can move them forward or backward by a given number of characters using forward_chars and backward_chars. These two methods expect an integer number of characters to move the iterator. If the iterator should be moved only one character in either direction, use forward_char and backward_char without any arguments. (Notice that the latter two methods are missing an *s* on the end, indicating that they will move the iterator only one character.)

To move the iterator to the next word in the buffer, you could use a loop to move the iterator forward one character at a time and check if the iterator points to the start of a word at each iteration. Fortunately, such a loop isn't necessary. There is a much easier way to jump to the next word. Not only can Pango be used to determine if an iterator points to the start or end of a word, but it can also be used to navigate to a certain number of words from a given location.

The forward_word_ends method will move an iterator forward the given number of word ends. Similar methods are available for moving forward by only one word, moving backward by one or more words, and moving forward and backward by lines and sentences: forward_word_end, backward_word_ends, forward_line_ends, backward_sentence_ends, and so on. Moving forward always goes to the end of the unit of text. The methods for moving backward always go to the start of a text unit. All of these methods return false if there is no next or previous line, sentence, word, or character; they return true if the iterator has moved. This makes looping through a buffer easy.

Listing 8-3 shows several of these methods in action, including a loop that counts the words in the buffer. Notice how even though an iterator is moved, it is still always possible to get an iterator that points to the original location. This is because iterators are simply pointers to a location. Changing the location that an iterator points to has no effect on the buffer itself.

Tags and Tag Tables

Tags allow buffer text to be marked up much like HTML. For instance, you can use tags to change the background color of a block of text, make the text bold, adjust the spacing around the text, and even prevent the user from editing the text. To apply formatting to a range of text within a buffer, you use GtkTextTag, which is a GtkTextBuffer helper object.

Tags can also be used together on the same or overlapping ranges of text, meaning that one tag can be used to make text bold, while another tag is used to make it red. When the two tags overlap, the text affected by both tags will be bold and red.

To be used in a buffer, a tag must be a member of that buffer's tag table. The GtkTextTagTable object is designed to keep tags organized. Each buffer has a tag table, which can be shared among buffers, and only tags from that table may be used in the buffer.

Creating Tags

You can create a tag in two ways. The first method involves instantiating GtkTextTag using the new operator. The second involves returning a tag from the GtkTextBuffer method create_tag. Both of these methods can take an optional string as the tag name, which you can use later to reference the tag.

Tags have a large list of properties that you can set to modify the appearance of a range of text. Table 8-1 shows the properties that can be set, as well as the property type and an example of each.

Table 8-1. *The Properties of GtkTextTag*

Property	Type	Example
background	string	#FFFFFF
background-full-height	boolean	true
background-full-height-set	boolean	true
background-gdk	GdkColor	new GdkColor()
background-set	boolean	true
background-stipple	GdkPixmap	GdkPixmap::new_from_file()
background-stipple-set	boolean	true
direction	GtkTextDirection	Gtk::TEXT_DIR_LTR
editable	boolean	true
editable-set	boolean	true
family	string	Arial
family-set	boolean	true
font	string	Arial Bold 10
font-desc	PangoFontDescription	Pango::font_description_from_string('Serif 15')
foreground	string	#0000FF
foreground-gdk	GdkColor	new GdkColor()
foreground-set	boolean	true
foreground-stipple	GdkPixmap	GdkPixmap::new_from_file()
foreground-stipple-set	boolean	true
indent	integer	8
indent-set	boolean	true
invisible	boolean	true
invisible-set	boolean	true
justification	GtkJustification	Gtk::JUSTIFY_LEFT
justification-set	boolean	true
language	string	EN
language-set	boolean	true
left-margin	integer	5
left-margin-set	boolean	true
paragraph-background	string	#FFFFFF
paragraph-background-gdk	GdkColor	new GdkColor()
paragraph-background-set	boolean	true
pixels-above-lines	integer	4
pixels-above-lines-set	boolean	true
pixels-below-lines	integer	4
pixels-below-lines-set	boolean	true
pixels-inside-wrap	integer	4

Property	Type	Example
pixels-inside-wrap-set	boolean	true
right-margin	integer	4
right-margin-set	boolean	true
rise	integer	4
rise-set	boolean	true
scale	float	1.5
scale-set	boolean	true
size	integer	2
size-points	float	1.5
size-set	boolean	true
stretch	PangoStretch	Pango::STRETCH_NORMAL
stretch-set	boolean	true
strikethrough	boolean	true
strikethrough-set	boolean	true
style	PangoStyle	Pango::STYLE_ITALIC
style-set	boolean	true
tabs	PangoTabArray	new PangoTabArray(3)
tabs-set	boolean	true
underline	PangoUnderline	Pango::UNDERLINE_NONE
underline-set	boolean	true
variant	PangoVariant	Pango::VARIANT_SMALL_CAPS
variant-set	boolean	true
weight	integer	Pango::WEIGHT_BOLD
weight-set	boolean	true
wrap-mode	GtkWrapMode	Gtk::WRAP_WORD
wrap-mode-set	boolean	true

Listing 8-4 shows how to create and manipulate a GtkTextTag object.

Listing 8-4. *Creating a GtkTextTag*

```php
<?php
// Create a named tag.
$tag = new GtkTextTag('red_italic');

// Set the foreground color.
$tag->set_property('foreground', '#FF0000');

// Set the style.
$tag->set_property('style', Pango::STYLE_ITALIC);
?>
```

First, a tag is created using the new operator. When created, the tag is given the name red_italic. This will make referencing the tag easier down the road. Next, a few properties of the tag are set using the set_property method. The foreground color of the tag is set to bright red. When this tag is applied across a range of text, the text will be shown in red instead of black. Lastly, the style property is set to Pango::STYLE_ITALIC. The text that the tag is applied across will be made italic. Of course, nothing will happen until the tag is applied to a region of text. But first, it needs to go in the text buffer's tag table.

Adding Tags to the Tag Table

Before a tag can be used in a buffer, it must be added to the buffer's tag table. A buffer's tag table is returned from the get_tag_table method. You add a tag to a table with the add method, which expects the tag as the only argument.

The remove method will remove a tag from a table. A tag that is not part of a tag table is pretty useless. If a tag is removed from one table, it should be added to another.

Tags that have a name can be retrieved from the tag table using the lookup method. lookup will return the tag with the given name. Not all tags have names, however. Just as with marks, creating tags on the fly is usually done anonymously.

Trying to locate an anonymous tag is a little more difficult. The foreach method of GtkTextTagTable will loop through all of the tags in the table and pass each tag to a callback method. The callback will be called once for every tag in the table. It is up to the function to decide what to do with the tags. The example in Listing 8-5 uses foreach to locate all of the tags that make text bold.

Listing 8-5. *Finding Named and Anonymous GtkTextTag Objects*

```
<?
function checkForBold($tag)
{
    global $bold;

    if ($tag->weight == Pango::WEIGHT_BOLD) {
        $bold[] = $tag;
    }
}

// Create an array to hold the bold tags.
$bold = array();

// Create a GtkTextView.
$text = new GtkTextView();

// Get the buffer from the view.
$buffer = $text->get_buffer();
```

```php
// Add some text.
$buffer->set_text('Moving a mark is done with either move_mark or ' .
                  'move_mark_by_name.');

// Get the buffer's tag table.
$table = $buffer->get_tag_table();

// Create a new tag and set some properties.
$tag = new GtkTextTag();
$tag->set_property('foreground', 'red');
$tag->set_property('background', 'gray');

// Add the tag to the table.
$table->add($tag);

// Create a new tag and set some properties.
$tag = new GtkTextTag();
$tag->set_property('weight', Pango::WEIGHT_BOLD);

// Add the tag to the table.
$table->add($tag);

// Create a new tag and set some properties.
$tag = new GtkTextTag();
$tag->set_property('foreground', 'blue');
$tag->set_property('weight', Pango::WEIGHT_NORMAL);

// Add the tag to the table.
$table->add($tag);

// Create a new tag and set some properties.
$tag = new GtkTextTag();
$tag->set_property('font', 'Arial Bold 10');

// Add the tag to the table.
$table->add($tag);

// Call checkForBold on all tags in the table.
$table->foreach('checkForBold');

var_dump($bold);
?>
```

In this simple example, four tags are created and added to the tag table. Then the checkForBold method is passed to foreach. The checkForBold tag checks the tag's weight property. If the weight is set to Pango::WEIGHT_BOLD, the tag is added to a global array called bold. While the tags in the bold array still don't have names, they are much easier to access.

Applying and Removing Tags

After a GtkTextTag has been created and added to a GtkTextTagTable, the tag can be applied to a region of text. Applying tags is the responsibility of GtkTextBuffer.

There are two methods for applying tags: apply_tag and apply_tag_by_name. Both methods have the same effect, but as apply_tag_by_name implies, this method uses a tag name instead of the tag itself. Tags are applied over a range of text identified by two GtkTextIters. The second argument to apply_tag or apply_tag_by_name is the iterator that indicates where the tag's effects begin. The third argument is an iterator that identifies where the tag's effects will stop.

Because one tag may be applied to several ranges of text, removing a tag also requires starting and ending iterators. The syntax for remove_tag and remove_tag_by_name is the same as add_tag and add_tag_by_name. Removing a tag from the buffer simply means that it will no longer have an effect over the given range of text. The tag will still be part of the buffer's tag table and will still work across any other ranges to which it has been applied.

Tip To remove all tags from a given range in a buffer, use remove_all_tags. remove_all_tags takes two iterators and removes all of the tags that have been applied to the text between them.

As stated earlier, you can apply multiple tags to a given range of text. This can be somewhat problematic when two tags define conflicting values. To help alleviate this problem, you can give tags priority. Each tag in a table has its own unique priority level. Tags with a higher priority will take precedence over tags with lower priority when the same attribute is set by both over the same range of text. No two tags can ever have the same priority in the same tag table, so only one value will be set for a given range. You can determine the priority level of a tag by using the get_priority method. To set the priority, use the set_priority method. Priorities are measured as integers. A tag with a priority of 5 will take precedence over a tag with a priority of 3. The following line is a quick and easy way to make sure that one tag has a higher priority than another.

```
$tag1->set_priority($tag2->get_priority() + 1);
```

Text Buffers

Text editing has two main parts: the widget for display and the text itself. The text is contained in an object called GtkTextBuffer.

The buffer is a manager; its main task is to keep the tags, marks, and iterators organized. The text buffer inserts objects or other text into the current text block, or removes objects or text from the current text block. Part of this job also entails returning information about the objects or pieces of text that make up the buffer. So far, you have seen many of the ways that GtkTextBuffer can be used to manipulate iterators, marks, and tags. This section will focus on using GtkTextBuffer to modify a block of text.

Creating Text Buffers

Text buffers are similar to the tree models that are used with GtkComboBox and GtkEntryCompletion. Text buffers are simply the data behind a view component. It doesn't make much sense to talk about text buffers without an associated GtkTextView. That is why most of the time, a text buffer isn't instantiated directly. Instead, it is created automatically when GtkTextView is instantiated.

While it is perfectly acceptable to create a GtkTextBuffer with new GtkTextBuffer, it is usually easier to grab the buffer that is created when the GtkTextView object is created. The buffer can be retrieved using the get_buffer method of GtkTextView. If a buffer is created with the new operator, it must be added to a view before it can be useful. Buffers returned from get_buffer are already associated with a GtkTextView.

Adding Text to a Buffer

Once the buffer has been created, the next thing you are likely to do is try to add some text. Inserting or deleting text requires the help of at least one iterator or mark. The buffer cannot be manipulated unless it knows where the modifications are supposed to take place.

The most common place text will be inserted is at the cursor. The cursor is just another name for the insert mark. You can add text at the current cursor position with insert_at_cursor, which expects a string of text as the only argument. The string will be inserted into the buffer at the location of the insert marker. After the text is inserted, the insert mark will be to the right of the last character inserted, because the insert mark has right gravity.

If you need to insert a block of text at a location other than the insert mark, use the insert method. The insert method is similar to insert_at_cursor, except it doesn't have a location automatically defined. You must give the location of the insertion using a GtkTextIter. The iterator must be the first argument, followed by the text string and the optional length of the string. This line of code will insert the string "Howdy" after the fifth character of a buffer:

```
$buffer->insert($buffer->get_iter_at_offset(5), "Howdy", -1);
```

Note Moving the cursor was discussed in the "Moving Marks" section of this chapter. Refer to Listing 8-2 for a quick refresher in using place_cursor.

You can also insert text and apply tags to it at the same time. insert_with_tags, just like insert, expects an iterator and a string of text. However, insert_with_tags can take a variable-length list of tags as optional parameters. The tags will be applied across the text that is inserted. If tags are passed to insert_with_tags, pass -1 as the third argument to hold the place of the length parameter. If you know the names of the tags that should be applied, add the tags using insert_with_tags_by_name, which works just like insert_with_tags but expects names instead of GtkTextTag instances.

Removing Text from a Buffer

You can also remove text from the buffer. Removing text requires the help of two iterators. The first iterator indicates the first character to be removed, and the second iterator points to the last character to be removed. All of the characters between the two iterators will also be removed from the buffer. The two iterators must be passed to the delete method. It doesn't matter if the second iterator comes before the first. The underlying GTK method that manipulates the buffer is smart enough to reorder the iterators.

You may want to delete the entire contents of a buffer and replace them with something else. Instead of using delete followed by insert, you can do this in one shot by using set_text. The set_text method clears the buffer and inserts the text passed as the only argument. In Listing 8-6, text is inserted into a buffer and then more text is inserted with some tags. After that, the first word is removed.

Listing 8-6. *Modifying Text in a Buffer Using GtkTextTag*

```php
<?php
// Create a GtkTextView.
$text = new GtkTextView();
// Get the buffer from the view.
$buffer = $text->get_buffer();

// Add some text.
$buffer->insert_at_cursor('Moving a mark is done with either ', -1);

// Create some tags.
$tag = new GtkTextTag();
$tag->foreground = 'red';
$tag2 = new GtkTextTag();
$tag2->weight = Pango::WEIGHT_BOLD;

// Add them to the tag table.
$table = $buffer->get_tag_table();
$table->add($tag);
$table->add($tag2);

// Insert some text as red and bold.
$buffer->insert_with_tags($buffer->get_end_iter(),
                          'move_mark or move_mark_by_name.', -1,
                          $tag, $tag2);

// Get an iter for the end of the first word.
$firstWord = $buffer->get_start_iter();
$firstWord->forward_word_end();

// Remove the first word.
$buffer->delete($buffer->get_start_iter(), $firstWord);
```

```
$window = new GtkWindow();
$window->add($text);
$window->show_all();
gtk::main();
?>
```

Figure 8-2 shows the end result of Listing 8-6.

Figure 8-2. *Text in a buffer with tags applied*

Copying and Pasting Text

Another way to modify a buffer is to copy and paste text. You can use insert_range to copy a range or text and insert it at another point in the buffer. insert_range not only copies the text, but it also brings the tags that have been applied to the text as well.

insert_range uses three iterators to copy and paste the text. The first denotes the location where the text will be inserted. The next two denote the start and end points of the range that will be copied.

Using insert_range, you can even copy text between two buffers. If the last two iterators are both from another buffer, the text and tags from the second buffer will be copied to the first buffer. Before text can be copied between two different buffers, the two buffers must use the same tag table. This is because tags can be applied to a buffer only if they are in the buffer's tag table.

When a buffer is modified, all of the iterators from that buffer become invalid. It cannot be reliably known that a buffer still points to the same place it did before the buffer was modified, so to be safe, GTK invalidates all outstanding iterators every time the buffer changes. Some methods, such as insert and remove, automatically regrab the iterators so it appears as though they are still valid, but the iterators are actually new.

GtkTextBuffer keeps track of whether or not the text has been edited using get_modified and set_modified. Any time the buffer is modified, set_modified is automatically called and passed true. When the text buffer is saved to disk or reaches some known stable state, the code should pass false to set_modified.

Text Views

The final piece of the multiline text puzzle is GtkTextView. GtkTextView is a widget specially designed to display a GtkTextBuffer. GtkTextView not only shows a buffer, but also allows the user to modify the buffer.

Using Multiple Views with a Single Buffer

One text view may show only one text buffer, but the same buffer may be shown by multiple views. If one buffer is shared by two views, changes made in one view are immediately shown

in the other. You have already seen how to get a buffer using get_buffer. If a buffer was created from another view or using the new operator, you can add the buffer to a GtkTextView
using set_buffer.

Why would anyone need to call set_buffer if all views come with a buffer already? Well,
for starters, it is easier to swap out buffers than it is to swap GtkTextView widgets. Also, multiple
views can show the same buffer. Instead of maintaining a block of text in two separate places, it
can be held in one buffer and shown in two places. Listing 8-7 offers a short example of one
buffer being shown (and possibly edited) in two views.

Listing 8-7. *Showing a Buffer in Two Views*

```php
<?php
// Create two GtkTextViews.
$text  = new GtkTextView();
$text2 = new GtkTextView();

// Get the buffer from the view.
$buffer = $text->get_buffer();

// Set the buffer as the buffer for the second view.
$text2->set_buffer($buffer);

// Add some text.
$buffer->insert_at_cursor('Moving a mark is done with either ' .
                          'move_mark or move_mark_by_name.', -1);

// Create a window and a box.
$window = new GtkWindow();
$vBox   = new GtkVBox();

// Add the text views.
$window->add($vBox);
$vBox->pack_start($text);
$vBox->pack_start($text2);

// Show the application.
$window->show_all();
gtk::main();
?>
```

Figure 8-3 shows this code in action.

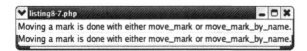

Figure 8-3. *One buffer in two views*

Tip Showing a buffer in two places may allow the buffer to be edited in two places, depending on the setup of each GtkTextView. Try running Listing 8-7 and editing the text in either of the views. Notice how editing one causes the text in the other to change.

Scrolling in a View

The role of GtkTextView is to display a buffer. This includes showing particular parts of the buffer and setting the display properties. Sometimes, the buffer will be too large to fit in the view. This means that not all of the buffer will be shown at one time. The text in the view can be scrolled so that a given mark or iterator is visible.

scroll_to_mark moves the text so that the given mark is on the screen. The mark is not the only argument to scroll_to_mark. The second argument is an imaginary margin that will be applied to the text view. The margin is a percentage of the screen by which the edges will be moved toward the center. A value of 0 means that the margins will be at the edges of the text view. A value of 0.5 (or 50 percent of the height and width) means that the view will have an effective size of zero. If the margin is set to 0.5, the mark will be scrolled to the center of the view. The third argument to scroll_to_mark tells the method whether or not to pay attention to the next two arguments. If the third argument is false, the fourth and fifth arguments are ignored. If it is true, then the fourth and fifth arguments dictate where within the available space the mark will be scrolled to. The scroll_to_iter method works just like scroll_to_mark, but it expects the first argument to be an iterator instead of a mark.

Setting the Buffer Appearance and Editability

The other responsibility of GtkTextView is to control how the buffer is shown and how the buffer appears and how the user interacts with it.

You can set a view's default margins with set_left_margin and set_right_margin. Both methods expect the size of the margins in pixels. Tags in a buffer can override these margins.

Another way to set how the buffer appears is to set the default justification for a view. set_justification expects a justification type and can also be overridden by a buffer's tags.

Whether or not a buffer in a given view can even be edited is controlled by set_editable. Passing false prevents the user from editing the buffer in the view that calls set_editable. set_overwrite can be used to make all user edits overwrite text instead of inserting it when modifying a buffer.

All of these attributes are set on a view level. A buffer that is shared among multiple views may look and act differently, depending on the settings for each view that shows the buffer.

Putting It All Together

Finally, all of the pieces are in place for the Crisscott PIMS application to make use of multiline text. One tool that will use GtkTextView is the news article tool, which shows news and update messages. The messages come into the application via an RSS feed. The headlines are displayed in the News frame on the left side of the application. When a user clicks a headline, the body of the message is shown in the News Story tab of the main application notebook. This tool is primarily used for displaying multiline text.

A tool that will allow the user to edit multiline text is the product editing tool. This tool allows the user to update all of the information for a product, including the description. The description can be more than one line of text, and therefore needs a GtkTextView to be edited properly.

A Multiline Text Display Tool

First, let's look at the News Story tab. Listing 8-8 shows the code for this tab.

Listing 8-8. *The News Article Tool*

```php
<?php
class Crisscott_Tools_NewsArticle extends GtkVBox {

    public $headline;
    public $view;
    public $buffer;

    public function __construct($text = NULL)
    {
        // Call the parent constructor.
        parent::__construct();

        // Lay out the tool.
        $this->_layout();
    }

    private function _layout()
    {
        // Create a label for the headline.
        $this->headline = new GtkLabel();

        // Create a view for the article.
        $this->view = new GtkTextView();

        // Get the buffer from the view.
        $this->buffer = $this->view->get_buffer();

        // Get a tag for making text bold and dark blue.
        $this->tag = new GtkTextTag();
        // Set the tag properties

        // Make the tag part of the buffers tag table.
        $tagTable = $this->buffer->get_tag_table();
        $tagTable->add($this->tag);

        // The text in this view should not be editable.
        $this->view->set_editable(false);
```

```
        // Since the users can't edit the text, there is not point in
        // letting them see the cursor.
        $this->view->set_cursor_visible(false);

        // Pack everything together.
        $this->pack_start($this->headline, false, false, 5);
        $this->pack_start($this->view);
    }

    public function setArticle($headline, $text)
    {
        // Set the headline.
        $this->setHeadline($headline);

        // Set the body.
        $this->setBody($text);
    }

    public function setHeadline($headline)
    {
        // Add some markup to make the headline appear like
        // a headline.
        $headline = '<span weight="' . Pango::WEIGHT_BOLD . '">' . $headline;
        $headline.= '</span>';

        // Set the text of the headline label.
        $this->headline->set_text($headline);

        // Make sure the headline is set to use the markup that was added.
        $this->headline->set_use_markup(true);

    }

    public function setBody($body)
    {
        // Do some special formatting of any instances of
        // Crisscott found in the article body.
        $lastCrisscott = 0;
        while ($pos = strpos($body, 'Crisscott', $lastCrisscott)) {
            $wordStart = $this->buffer->get_iter_at_offset($pos);
            $wordEnd   = $this->buffer->get_iter_at_offset($pos);
            $wordEnd->forward_word_end();

            // Apply the tag.
            $this->buffer->apply_tag($this->tag, $wordStart, $wordEnd);

            // Update the strpos offset.
            $lastCrisscott = $pos;
        }
```

```
        // Set the article text in the buffer.
        $this->buffer->set_text($body);
    }
}
?>
```

This tab displays two pieces of information: the headline and the story body. The two parts are packed together in a GtkVbox. The headline is shown at the top of the tool, where you would expect a headline to be. The headline is a GtkLabel because a headline is just one line. When the headline text is set using setHeadline, it is wrapped in Pango markup. This markup will make the headline appear larger and bolder than the article.

The body of the story is a combination of a GtkTextView and a GtkTextBuffer. The _layout method creates all the pieces of this tool. First, the label for the headline is created. Next, the GtkTextView is created and the buffer is grabbed from the view using get_buffer. A tag is also created for later use. This tag is set to make text appear bold and dark blue. This tag will be used as a sort of marketing tool. Anytime that "Crisscott" appears in the article body, the tag will be applied. The last step of the _layout method is to make the sure that the user cannot edit the article body. This is done by passing false to set_editable. No matter what text is applied to the buffer, the view will not allow it to be edited by the user. Since the text in the view cannot be edited, there is little point in letting the user see the cursor. The cursor is turned off by passing false to set_cursor_visible.

Figure 8-4 shows what the application looks like with an article in place.

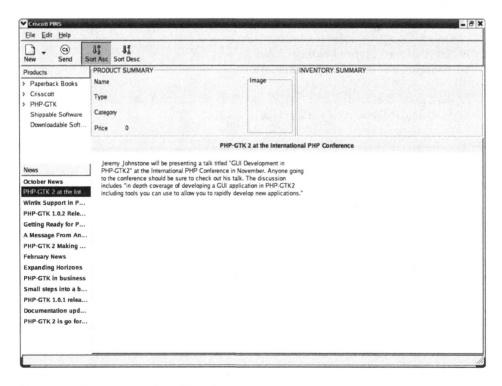

Figure 8-4. *The news article tool in action*

A Text-Editing Tool

Most of the product editing tool (ProductEdit) is built of GtkLabel, GtkEntry, GtkSpinButton, and GtkComboBox widgets, but the product description cannot be properly edited with these tools. The product description needs a GtkTextView in order to allow the user to edit multiple lines of text. The difference between this text view and the news article tool is that this view is to be used for editing a buffer. The text within this view can be changed and saved.

Listing 8-9 shows a slightly abbreviated version of the ProductEdit tool. The repetitive building of all the labels, entries, and combo boxes has been removed to make the code related to GtkTextView easier to follow.

Listing 8-9. *Setting Up a GtkTextView for Editing a Buffer*

```php
<?php
class Crisscott_Tools_ProductEdit extends GtkTable {

    // ...
    public $descView;
    //...


    private function _layout()
    {

        // ...

        // Create the description text view.
        $this->descView = new GtkTextView();

        // ...

        // Set the size of the text view also.
        $this->descView->set_size_request(300, 300);
        // Force the text to wrap lines.
        $this->descView->set_wrap_mode(Gtk::WRAP_WORD);


        // ...

        // Attach the description widgets.
        $this->attachWithAlign($this->descLabel, 2, 3, 0, 1,  Gtk::FILL, 0);
        $this->attachWithAlign($this->descView,  2, 4, 1, 10, Gtk::FILL, 0);

        // Attach the buttons.
        $this->attachWithAlign($reset, 0, 1, 10, 11, Gtk::FILL, 0);
        $this->attachWithAlign($save,  3, 4, 10, 11, Gtk::FILL, 0);
    }
```

```php
/**
 * Attaches a widget to the table inside a GtkAlignment.
 *
 * This method makes it easy to left align items within a table.
 * Simply call this method as you would call attach.
 */
public function attachWithAlign($widget, $row1, $row2, $col1, $col2, $xEF, $yEF)
{
    $align = new GtkAlignment(0,0,0,.5);
    $align->add($widget);
    $this->attach($align, $row1, $row2, $col1, $col2, $xEF, $yEF);
}

// ...

public function resetProduct()
{
    // ...

    // Set the description buffer text.
    $buffer = $this->descView->get_buffer();
    $buffer->set_text($this->product->description, -1);
}

// ...
public function saveProduct()
{
    // ...

    // Get the description from the buffer.
    $this->product->description  = $this->descView->get_buffer()->get_text();


    // ...

    // Try to save the data.
    if ($this->product->save()) {
        // Mark the buffer as saved.
        $this->descView->get_buffer()->set_modified(false);
    } else {
        return false;
    }
}
}
?>
```

The text view in the `ProductEdit` tool is created in the _layout method. Only the view is stored as a member variable because the buffer can be accessed when needed using get_buffer.

The view is sized to 300 pixels square using set_size_request to give the user enough space to type a fairly lengthy description.

Immediately after the text view is sized, the wrap mode is set. The wrap mode determines how the view reacts when the buffer contains more text than can be shown on one line. In this example, the wrap mode is set to Gtk::WRAP_WORD. This means that text will be broken between words and wrapped to the next line. Other options are Gtk::WRAP_NONE, which means the text will not wrap; Gtk::WRAP_CHAR, which breaks the text characters; and Gtk::WRAP_WORD_CHAR, which will first try to break the text between words and then characters if needed.

After the view is set up, it is added to the GtkTable that lays out the tool. Because of the text view's size, it is set to span several rows and columns.

The resetProduct method of the ProductEdit tool is used to set the values of all the data-collection widgets in the tool. The values are taken from the current product.

The last two lines of this method set up the text view. The second-to-last line grabs the buffer from the view. The last line sets the text in the buffer using set_text. Any text that was previously set in the buffer is erased when the new text is set.

The last method in this example that deals directly with the text view is saveProduct. This method is the opposite of resetProduct. The description of the current product is set by calling get_text on the text view's buffer.

After all of the product attributes are set, the new data is validated. If any of the product attributes don't validate, the labels for those attributes are highlighted using Pango markup. If all of the product attributes validate, the product data is saved. If the data is saved properly, the buffer is marked as unmodified. This is done by passing false to set_modified. The end result of all this code is shown in Figure 8-5.

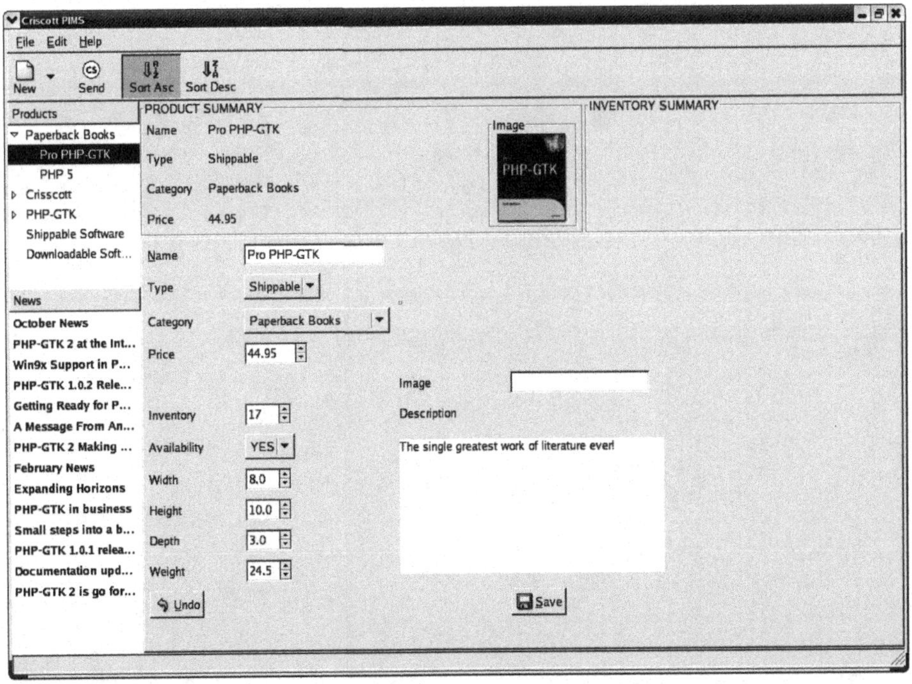

Figure 8-5. *The ProductEdit tool*

Summary

Multiline text is a powerful tool, not only for displaying large amounts of text, but also for collecting large amounts of data from the user. Using multiline text can be simple or rather complex. If plain black text is all you need, you can easily set up a GtkTextView with a buffer. If the text needs to be formatted or modified, GtkTextIter, GtkTextMark, and GtkTextTag allow that to happen. All of these widgets and objects make for a well-designed and specialized tool set.

Text is not the only type of data that comes in large quantities. There are other types of large data sets, such as arrays and trees, that cannot be properly displayed with any of the tools seen so far. In Chapter 9, we will look at how to display large amounts of data. We will look at using trees and lists as the models behind several different ways to display data. Among the types of data that our sample application will display are a list of news headlines and a sortable and expandable list of products.

CHAPTER 9

■ ■ ■

Working with Trees and Lists

In the past two chapters, you've learned how to display and edit both small and large blocks of text. Yet there is still another type of data that requires special handling: collections. Collections are made up of several elements grouped using data structures such as arrays, lists, and trees. For a collection, you may need to show the relationship between individual elements, sort the collection, and filter certain values. The tools that have been introduced so far cannot easily fulfill these needs.

PHP-GTK handles collections of data in a manner similar to how it manages multiline text. One group of objects organizes the data, while another concentrates on the display. This allows you to show one set of data in multiple ways at the same time. Without this separation of responsibility, each piece of the application that wanted to gather information from a data set would have to create and manage its own instance of the data. Using *models* to manage the data and *views* to handle the display allows for more flexibility with less code.

You can use several models to represent data. First, we will examine the unique uses of each type of model. Then we will look at how to use these models to view the collection of data depending on the needs of the application.

Models

Collections of data can be organized into *trees*. A tree is a set of data in which the elements have a parent-child relationship. This relationship may be obvious as it is with a directory listing, or it may be more subtle, such as an array. In a directory listing, a directory is a parent and its files and subdirectories are its children. An array is really a list with multiple columns and elements. A list is just a tree in which each element has at most one child.

Keeping track of this type of data is the responsibility of two types of models: GtkListStore and GtkTreeStore. Each object represents data as a set of rows, where a row is one element in the list or tree but may contain more than one value. This is because a model may have many columns. Each column in a row represents one atomic piece of data. With both trees and lists, data can be prepended, inserted, and appended to a collection. The difference is that elements in trees may have children, but elements in lists cannot. The main objective of both models is the same, but lists are less complex and therefore easier to work with.

The GtkListStore Model

GtkListStore represents a tree of order one, meaning that each element has at most one child. Restricting each element to having only one child makes managing the data a little easier than when there are multiple children. Lists can put data only before or after another piece of data. It is not possible for two pieces of data to occupy the same level in a list. This may sound like a strange restriction to impose on a set of data, but it makes life easier. Lists are well suited as the data behind widgets like GtkComboBox and GtkEntryCompletion, where one value should follow another. In fact, in Chapter 7, we used a GtkListStore to populate both types of widgets. Listing 9-1 shows the portion of GtkEntryCompletion example from Chapter 7 (Listing 7-6) that creates a simple GtkListStore.

Listing 9-1. *Creating a Simple GtkListStore*

```php
<?php
    // ...
    public static function createStateList()
    {
        // Create a new list store.
        $listStore = new GtkListStore(GTK::TYPE_STRING);
        // Get an iterator for appending a value.
        $iter = $listStore->append();
        // Append a value.
        $listStore->set($iter, 0, 'Alabama');
        // Get an iterator for appending a value.
        $iter = $listStore->append();
        // Append a value.
        $listStore->set($iter, 0, 'Alaska');
        // Get an iterator for appending a value.
        $iter = $listStore->append();
        // Append a value.
        $listStore->set($iter, 0, 'Arizona');
        // Get an iterator for appending a value.
        $iter = $listStore->append();
        // Append a value.
        $listStore->set($iter, 0, 'Arkansas');
        // Get an iterator for appending a value.
        $iter = $listStore->append();
        // Append a value.
        $listStore->set($iter, 0, 'California');
        // Get an iterator for appending a value.
        $iter = $listStore->append();
        // Append a value.
        $listStore->set($iter, 0, 'Colorado');
        // ...
```

```
        return $listStore;
    }
    // ...
?>
```

The first step is creating the list store, which represents the model in the Model-View-Controller (MVC) design pattern. This is done in typical PHP fashion using the new operator. In Listing 9-1, one argument is passed to the constructor. The constructor expects a variable list of arguments. Each argument passed in corresponds to a column in the list. The value that is passed for each column defines the expected data type for that column. It may seem odd to have to explicitly give the column type in a loosely typed language, but keep in mind that PHP-GTK is based on GTK+ which is written in C, a strictly typed language. Providing the data type helps the view component determine the best way to show the data and keeps memory usage under control.

There are many acceptable column types, but not all of them are relevant to PHP-GTK. The following are the relevant values:

- Gtk::TYPE_BOOLEAN: For values that have only two states, such as on/off or true/false.

- Gtk::TYPE_LONG: For integers.

- Gtk::TYPE_DOUBLE: For floating-point values, like 1.234.

- Gtk::TYPE_STRING: For text values or values that should be treated like text, such as "crissscott" or "321".

- Gtk::TYPE_OBJECT: For objects that extend from GObject, like GtkObject or GtkButton.

- Gtk::TYPE_PHP_VALUE: For any PHP data type, including user-defined classes, arrays, integers and even resource handles like those used for database connections.

Note If a column is set to type Gtk::TYPE_OBJECT, the value in the column must be a descendant of GObject. You may use your own custom classes only if they extend GObject or some descendant of that class, such as GtkObject or GtkWidget.

Adding Data to a List

After you've created the list with all of its column types, the next task is to add data. First, you add a row to the list, and then you set the data for the row.

After a row is added, the position of the new row is identified by an iterator. This type of iterator is similar to the iterator described in Chapter 8 (GtkTextIter) in that it identifies a location. In this case, the iterator is an instance of GtkTreeIter. GtkTreeIter cannot be instantiated directly using the new operator. GtkTreeIter has two methods: copy and free. The only method you're likely to call is copy. This method simply makes another instance of GtkTreeIter that points to the same location.

You can add rows to the list by using the following methods:

- append: Adds a new row to the end of the list, as in Listing 9-1. The return value is an iterator that points to the newly added row.

- prepend: Puts the new row at the beginning of the list. prepend also returns an iterator pointing to the new row.

- insert: Allows you to insert data into a list at an arbitrary position. insert takes a list position and returns an iterator that points to that position.

The iterators returned from these three methods can then be used to set the new row's data. Listing 9-2 presents code similar to the previous listing, but uses prepend and insert in addition to append.

Listing 9-2. *Another Example of Creating a GtkListStore*

```php
<?php
// Create a list store.
$listStore = new GtkListStore(Gtk::TYPE_STRING, Gtk::TYPE_LONG, Gtk::TYPE_DOUBLE);

// Add some product data.
$iter = $listStore->append();
$listStore->set($iter, 0, 'Crisscott T-Shirts', 1, 10, 2, 19.95);
$iter = $listStore->prepend();
$listStore->set($iter, 0, 'PHP-GTK Bumper Stickers', 1, 37, 2, 1.99);
$iter = $listStore->prepend();
$listStore->set($iter, 0, 'Pro PHP-GTK', 1, 23, 2, 44.95);
$iter = $listStore->insert(2);
$listStore->set($iter, 0, 'Crisscott Pencils', 2, .99, 1, 18);

// Create a view to show the list.
$view = new GtkTreeView();
$view->set_model($listStore);

// Create a column for the product name.
$column = new GtkTreeViewColumn();
$column->set_title('Product Name');
$view->insert_column($column, 0);

// Create a renderer for the column.
$cell_renderer = new GtkCellRendererText();
$column->pack_start($cell_renderer, true);
$column->set_attributes($cell_renderer, 'text', 0);

// Create a column for the inventory quantity.
$column = new GtkTreeViewColumn();
$column->set_title('Inventory');
$view->insert_column($column, 1);
```

```
// Create a renderer for the column.
$cell_renderer = new GtkCellRendererText();
$column->pack_start($cell_renderer, true);
$column->set_attributes($cell_renderer, 'text', 1);

// Create a column for the price.
$column = new GtkTreeViewColumn();
$column->set_title('Price');
$view->insert_column($column, 2);

// Create a renderer for the column.
$cell_renderer = new GtkCellRendererText();
$column->pack_start($cell_renderer, true);
$column->set_attributes($cell_renderer, 'text', 2);

// Create a window and show everything.
$window = new GtkWindow();
$window->add($view);
$window->show_all();
$window->connect_simple('destroy', array('Gtk', 'main_quit'));Gtk::main();
?>
```

You then set the values of the row by using set, which expects an iterator as the first argument followed by one or more column-value pairs. In Listing 9-2, each call to append and prepend is followed by a call to set. In this example, the list has three columns: one for a product name, one for the current inventory, and one for the price. The types for the columns are Gtk::TYPE_STRING, Gtk::TYPE_LONG, and Gtk::TYPE_DOUBLE, respectively.

In each call to set, the first argument is the iterator that identifies the row. The second argument is 0. This means that the next argument passed in will be a value that should be put in column 0 of the row pointed to by the iterator. The next argument is the value that will be assigned to column 0 of the given row. The fourth argument defines the column in which the data value passed as the fifth argument should be placed. The last two arguments follow the same pattern. It doesn't matter in which order the column numbers appear (as can be seen in the last call to set), but each column number must be followed with some data. When executed, Listing 9-2 produces Figure 9-1.

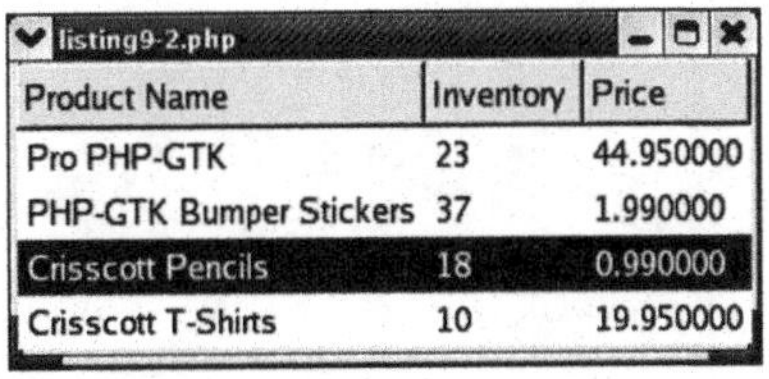

Figure 9-1. *A list with three columns*

Rather than calling set after append, prepend, or insert, as in Listing 9-2, sometimes you can pass the values for the row to these methods. You pass the column values as an array. Listing 9-3 produces the same result as the previous listing but is a little cleaner, making it easier to maintain.

Listing 9-3. *Setting a Row Using append, prepend, and insert*

```php
<?php
// Create a list store.
$listStore = new GtkListStore(Gtk::TYPE_STRING, Gtk::TYPE_LONG, Gtk::TYPE_DOUBLE);

// Add some product data.
$listStore->append(array('Crisscott T-Shirts',       10, 19.95));
$listStore->prepend(array('PHP-GTK Bumper Stickers', 37, 1.99));
$listStore->prepend(array('Pro PHP-GTK',             23, 44.95));

$pencils = array('Crisscott Pencils', 18, .99);
$listStore->insert(2, $pencils);

// Create a view to show the list.
$view = new GtkTreeView();
$view->set_model($listStore);

// Create columns for each type of data.
$column = new GtkTreeViewColumn();
$column->set_title('Product Name');
$view->insert_column($column, 0);

// Create a renderer for the column.
$cell_renderer = new GtkCellRendererText();
$column->pack_start($cell_renderer, true);
$column->set_attributes($cell_renderer, 'text', 0);

// Create columns for each type of data.
$column = new GtkTreeViewColumn();
$column->set_title('Inventory');
$view->insert_column($column, 1);

// Create a renderer for the column.
$cell_renderer = new GtkCellRendererText();
$column->pack_start($cell_renderer, true);
$column->set_attributes($cell_renderer, 'text', 1);

// Create columns for each type of data.
$column = new GtkTreeViewColumn();
$column->set_title('Price');
$view->insert_column($column, 2);
```

```
// Create a renderer for the column.
$cell_renderer = new GtkCellRendererText();
$column->pack_start($cell_renderer, true);
$column->set_attributes($cell_renderer, 'text', 2);

// Create a window and show everything.
$window = new GtkWindow();
$window->add($view);
$window->show_all();
$window->connect_simple('destroy', array('Gtk', 'main_quit'));Gtk::main();
?>
```

You can create the column values array at the time of the call or, as is the case with the call to insert in Listing 9-3, you can use an array that was already initialized somewhere else in the code. When passing data in as an array, the order of the array is important. The indexes are used to place the data in the proper column. The value with index 2 will be assigned to column 2. The return value from these methods can still be valuable, even though data has already been assigned. You can use the iterator returned to reference a particularly significant piece of data or to overwrite the data later by using set.

The append, prepend, and insert methods are ideal if a row needs to be inserted into a specific location in a list. However, sometimes you may need to add a row in a relative position. For example, the list in Listing 9-3 has Crisscott T-Shirts and Crisscott Pencils. Let's say that pencils should always appear in the list right after T-shirts. With a small list such as this, it is easy to manage the order, but with a larger list, it will be much more difficult to keep track of the elements' order. This is where the insert_before and insert_after methods come in handy. Like the insert method, these two methods add rows not based on an index, but rather on other elements in the list. Each method takes an iterator as the first argument and an optional list of row values as the second argument. The value is an iterator pointing to the new row. The row for Crisscott Pencils could be added with code like this:

```
$shirts  = $listStore->insert(3, array('Crisscott T-Shirts', 10, 19.95));
$pencils = $listStore->insert_after($shirts, array('Crisscott Pencils', 18, .99));
```

Keep in mind that lists are not static. Just because the pencil data was inserted after the T-shirt data, it doesn't have to stay there. New values can be added to the list, and existing values can be removed or moved.

Removing Data from a List

Removing elements is easy. Simply pass an iterator pointing to the row that should be removed to the remove method. After removing a row, the iterator passed to remove will be modified to point to the next row in the list. If there are no more rows in the list, the iterator will be *invalidated*, which means that the iterator no longer points to an existing row.

You could test the iterator using iter_is_valid, but it's a rather slow method. It may be useful for debugging applications during the development process, but it is not recommended for production code. Alternatively, you can simply check the return value of remove. If the iterator can be pointed to the next row, remove will return true. If there are no more rows, remove returns false.

You can remove all of the rows from a list from a given point with an empty `while` loop, like this:

```
while($listStore->remove($iter)) ;
```

To remove all rows from a `GtkListStore`, use the `clear` method.

Repositioning Rows

Moving rows that have already been added to a list is similar to inserting a row before or after another row. When a row is moved, it goes to a position relative to another row. The methods `move_before` and `move_after` each expect two iterators as arguments. The first iterator is the row that should be moved. The row will be moved before or after the row identified by the second iterator.

You can also swap rows. Passing two iterators to the `swap` method switchés the position of the two iterators.

Moving and swapping rows should be done with caution. It isn't necessary to reorder rows in a model to make them appear in a particular order on the screen. The view that shows a model can sort the values and display them in a particular order without disturbing the underlying model, as described in the "Model Sorting" section later in this chapter. Changing the order of the rows in a `GtkListStore` will impact all of the views that show the list.

Getting a Value from a List

Now that the values in the list are set, the list can be displayed, as in Listing 9-3, or used as the model behind a widget such as `GtkComboBox`. Eventually, the application will probably need to get a value back from the list, such as when the user makes a selection.

To get a value back from the list requires the same information that was used to set the value: an iterator and a column number. If the iterator returned from `append`, `prepend`, or `insert` was captured, getting the value is straightforward. Simply call `get_value` and pass the iterator followed by the column number. The value in the given column of the row identified by the iterator will be returned.

Searching a List

In some cases, it may be necessary to traverse the list looking for a particular value. You can move through a list by using either the `foreach` method (not to be confused with the `foreach` loop construct) or by grabbing the iterators one by one in a loop.

`foreach` is similar to `array_walk`. `foreach` takes a callback method and an optional array of data. When `foreach` is called, each element in the list is passed to the callback method along with the list, a path to the element, and the array of data, if it is given. The elements are passed to the callback in a *depth-first* manner. As far as lists are concerned, depth-first means starting from the first element and working toward the last. `foreach` will keep passing elements to the callback until it returns `true`. A return value of `true` means that the callback has found what it is looking for and there is no point in processing the rest of the list elements. If the callback returns `false`, or some value that evaluates to `false` such as zero, the callback will be called again and passed the next element in the list. If the callback is designed to process all elements of a list, it should never return `true`.

Listing 9-4 shows how to use foreach to find all of the products that should probably be reordered soon. foreach is called and given the checkInventory function as the callback. The checkInventory function looks at the value of the second column for the given row. If the quantity in stock is less than 15, the item is reordered. Notice that regardless of whether or not the item needs to be reordered, the checkInventory method returns false.

Listing 9-4. *Checking the Values of All Rows in a List*

```php
<?php
function checkInventory($model, $path, $iter, $userData = null)
{
    if ($model->get_value($iter, 1) < 15) {
        echo 'Marking for reordering ' . $model->get_value($iter, 0) . "\r\n";
    }

    return false;
}

// Create a list store.
$listStore = new GtkListStore(Gtk::TYPE_STRING, Gtk::TYPE_LONG, Gtk::TYPE_DOUBLE);

// Add some product data.
$listStore->append(array('Crisscott T-Shirts',       10, 19.95));
$listStore->prepend(array('PHP-GTK Bumper Stickers', 37, 1.99));
$listStore->prepend(array('Pro PHP-GTK',             23, 44.95));

$pencils = array('Crisscott Pencils', 18, .99);
$listStore->insert(2, $pencils);

$listStore->foreach('checkInventory');
?>
```

Listing 9-4 is just an example of how to use the foreach method. Creating a list just to iterate through the rows is pretty silly. The foreach method comes in handy when the data is already stored in a GtkListStore. Why would the data already be in a list store? Well, it may be used for display in some other part of the application, or the list may have been created by the user through the application's interface. The user may drag-and-drop product data from one piece of the application to another.

The other way to move through a list is by grabbing the iterators one by one in a loop. Looping through the iterators requires a starting point. The beginning of the list is a good place to start, and getting the first iterator is pretty easy—just use get_iter_first. Once the first iterator is found, getting the next iterator in the list is a simple matter of calling iter_next. If there is no next iterator in the list, iter_next will return false. You can use these two methods together to move through a list one element at a time. The following for loop will move through a GtkListStore one element at a time.

```
for ($iter = $listStore->get_iter_first(), $continue = true;
     $continue;
     $continue = $listStore->iter_next($iter)
    ) {
        // Do something to each element.
}
```

The GtkTreeStore Model

Data cannot always be properly represented as a list, because a list constrains each row of data to be related to only two others: its predecessor and its successor. However, in some cases, one row of data may have more than one child. Consider a family tree. A person will have one parent row consisting of two columns (one for the mother and one for the father), but a person may have one or more children. Each child in the list may also have one or more children. When this relationship is mapped out, it begins to look like a tree with branches and leaves (rows with no children). In PHP-GTK, a relationship of this nature is stored in an object called GtkTreeStore.

Adding Rows to a Tree

GtkTreeStore is very similar to GtkListStore. The main difference is that when a row is added to a tree, a parent row can be given. The methods for adding rows to a tree are the same as those for adding rows to a list. All of the GtkTreeStore methods take as the first argument an iterator that points to the row that will become the new row's parent. Listing 9-5 shows how to assign a parent row when inserting data.

Listing 9-5. *Adding Rows to a Tree*

```php
<?php
// Create a tree store.
$treeStore = new GtkTreeStore(Gtk::TYPE_STRING, Gtk::TYPE_LONG, Gtk::TYPE_DOUBLE);

// Add two top level rows.
// Capture the return value so that children can be added.
$csMerch     = $treeStore->append(null, array('Crisscott', null, null));
$phpGtkMerch = $treeStore->append(null, array('PHP-GTK',  null, null));

// Add a child row to csMerch.
// Again capture the return value so that children can be added.
$tShirts = $treeStore->append($csMerch, array('T-Shirts', 10, 19.95));

// Add three children to tShirts.
$treeStore->append($tShirts, array('Small',  3, 19.95));
$treeStore->append($tShirts, array('Medium', 5, 19.95));
$treeStore->append($tShirts, array('Large',  2, 19.95));

// Add another child to csMerch.
// Capture the return value so that children can be added.
$pencils = $treeStore->append($csMerch, array(' Pencils', 18, .99));
```

```php
// Add two children to pencils
$treeStore->append($pencils, array('Blue', 9, .99));
$treeStore->append($pencils, array('White', 9, .99));

// Add two children to phpGtkMerch.
$treeStore->prepend($phpGtkMerch, array('PHP-GTK Bumper Stickers', 37, 1.99));
$treeStore->prepend($phpGtkMerch, array('Pro PHP-GTK',            23, 44.95));

// Continue building the view and showing the tree...
?>
```

Figure 9-2 shows the result of this listing.

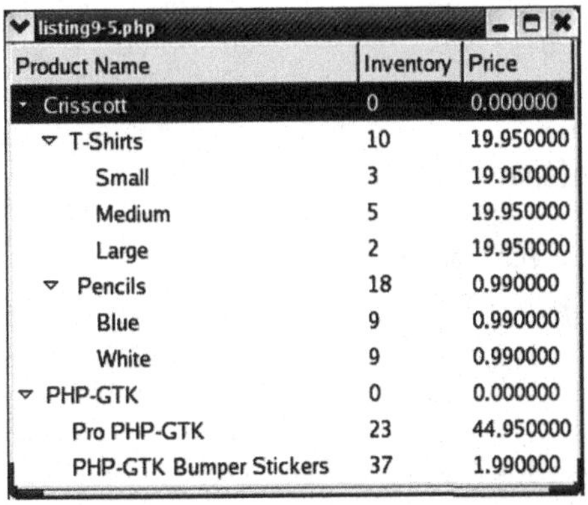

Product Name	Inventory	Price
Crisscott	0	0.000000
▽ T-Shirts	10	19.950000
Small	3	19.950000
Medium	5	19.950000
Large	2	19.950000
▽ Pencils	18	0.990000
Blue	9	0.990000
White	9	0.990000
▽ PHP-GTK	0	0.000000
Pro PHP-GTK	23	44.950000
PHP-GTK Bumper Stickers	37	1.990000

Figure 9-2. *Data represented with a GtkTreeStore*

Moving Through a Tree

Because trees can have multiple levels, moving through all of the rows can be a little more difficult than moving through list rows. Like GtkListStore, GtkTreeStore has a foreach method that moves through the model in a depth-first manner. This means that instead of moving to a row's sibling, foreach will move to the row's children. Only when there are no more descendants will the original row's sibling be passed to the callback.

You can easily move through a list with a for loop, but this isn't as simple with a tree. The for loop shown previously uses iter_next to get the next iterator in the list. With trees, iter_next returns the next iterator at the current level. The next iterator at a given level is a sibling, not a child. This means that iter_next will never return a row's child. Therefore, it is not possible to traverse the tree with this method. Instead, you must use a recursive function, such as the one in Listing 9-6.

Listing 9-6. *Traversing a Tree with a Recursive Function*

```php
<?php
function traverseTree($tree, $iter, $parent, $childNum)
{
```

```
        $dashes = '';
        // Print two dashes for each level.
        for($i = 0; $i < $tree->iter_depth($iter); ++$i) {
            $dashes.= '--';
        }

        // Print out the value of the first column.
        echo $dashes . ' ' . $tree->get_value($iter, 0) . "\n";

        // Go to the children of this iterator.
        if ($tree->iter_has_child($iter)) {
            // The current iterator is the new parent.
            $newParent = $iter->copy();
            // Get the first child iterator.
            $tree->iter_nth_child($iter, $newParent, 0);
            // Call the function again.
            traverseTree($tree, $iter, $newParent, 0);
        } elseif ($childNum < $tree->iter_n_children($parent) - 1) {
            // Go to the next child.
            if ($tree->iter_nth_child($iter, $parent, $childNum + 1)) {
                traverseTree($tree, $iter, $parent, $childNum + 1);
            }
        } elseif ($tree->iter_next($parent)) {
            // Go to the parent's sibling.
            traverseTree($tree, $parent, $iter, $childNum + 1);
        } else {
            // Get the parent of the parent.
            if ($tree->iter_parent($iter, $parent)) {
                // Go to the next iterator.
                $tree->iter_next($iter);
                // Go to that iterator's parent.
                $tree->iter_parent($parent, $iter);
                if ($tree->iter_is_valid($iter)) {
                    traverseTree($tree, $iter, $parent, $childNum);
                }
            }
        }
    }
}
?>
```

In Listing 9-6, the traverseTree function uses several of the GtkTreeStore methods to determine if an iterator has children and to get the next child. iter_has_child takes an iterator and returns true if the iterator has at least one child. iter_n_children returns the number of children for an iterator. iter_nth_child returns the child of an iterator at position *n*. Finally, iter_parent sets the first iterator passed to the parent of the second. As you can see, with trees, using the foreach method is much easier than devising a for loop.

Model Sorting

Trees and lists can be sorted to make data easier to find. Of course, you could sort the model itself, but this would affect every view that shows the data. Sorting the model itself is also very resource-intensive. Sorting just the view requires much less work, as it simply reorders a few references.

Using GtkTreeModelSort allows you to wrap a model and sort the data. Wrapping the model means that the underlying model can be shown in different ways without changing the original data. For example, Figure 9-3 shows two views of the same data. The view on the left shows the data sorted by the Product Name column in descending order, and the view on the right shows the same data sorted by the Price column in ascending order. When sorting trees, the data is sorted at each level. This means that each element of the tree is sorted against its sibling elements, not its children.

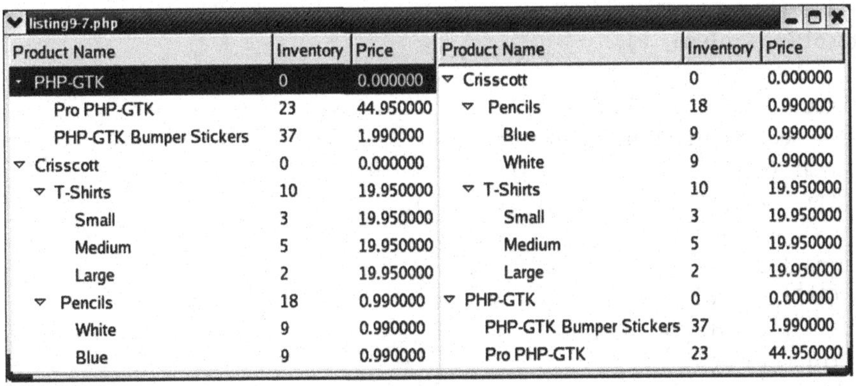

Figure 9-3. *One tree sorted two ways*

Wrapping a model using GtkTreeModelSort is rather easy, consisting of two basic steps:

- Create an instance of GtkTreeModelSort using the new operator. GtkTreeModelSort expects the model to be wrapped as the only argument.

- Set up the sort model so that it can be sorted. This means setting the column that should be sorted and the order in which it should be sorted, using set_sort_column_id. This method expects the column ID as the first argument and the sort type as the second. The sort type must be either Gtk::SORT_ASCENDING or Gtk::SORT_DESCENDING.

Listing 9-7 shows the code that was used to create Figure 9-3. The relevant lines are shown in bold.

Listing 9-7. *Creating Two Sortable Trees from One Tree*

```
<?php
// Build the tree....
```

```
// Create one sortable tree.
$sortable = new GtkTreeModelSort($treeStore);
$sortable->set_sort_column_id(0, Gtk::SORT_DESCENDING);

// Create the other sortable tree.
$sortable2 = new GtkTreeModelSort($treeStore);
$sortable2->set_sort_column_id(2, Gtk::SORT_ASCENDING);

// Create a view to show the tree.
$view = new GtkTreeView();
$view->set_model($sortable);

// Create columns for each type of data.
$column = new GtkTreeViewColumn();
$column->set_title('Product Name');
$view->insert_column($column, 0);

// Create a renderer for the column.
$cell_renderer = new GtkCellRendererText();
$column->pack_start($cell_renderer, true);
$column->set_attributes($cell_renderer, 'text', 0);

// Create columns for each type of data.
$column = new GtkTreeViewColumn();
$column->set_title('Inventory');
$view->insert_column($column, 1);

// Create a renderer for the column.
$cell_renderer = new GtkCellRendererText();
$column->pack_start($cell_renderer, true);
$column->set_attributes($cell_renderer, 'text', 1);

// Create columns for each type of data.
$column = new GtkTreeViewColumn();
$column->set_title('Price');
$view->insert_column($column, 2);

// Create a renderer for the column.
$cell_renderer = new GtkCellRendererText();
$column->pack_start($cell_renderer, true);
$column->set_attributes($cell_renderer, 'text', 2);

// Create a view to show the tree.
$view2 = new GtkTreeView();
$view2->set_model($sortable2);
```

```
// Create columns for each type of data.
$column = new GtkTreeViewColumn();
$column->set_title('Product Name');
$view2->insert_column($column, 0);

// Create a renderer for the column.
$cell_renderer = new GtkCellRendererText();
$column->pack_start($cell_renderer, true);
$column->set_attributes($cell_renderer, 'text', 0);

// Create columns for each type of data.
$column = new GtkTreeViewColumn();
$column->set_title('Inventory');
$view2->insert_column($column, 1);

// Create a renderer for the column.
$cell_renderer = new GtkCellRendererText();
$column->pack_start($cell_renderer, true);
$column->set_attributes($cell_renderer, 'text', 1);

// Create columns for each type of data.
$column = new GtkTreeViewColumn();
$column->set_title('Price');
$view2->insert_column($column, 2);

// Create a renderer for the column.
$cell_renderer = new GtkCellRendererText();
$column->pack_start($cell_renderer, true);
$column->set_attributes($cell_renderer, 'text', 2);

// Create a window and a box to show everything.
$window = new GtkWindow();
$hBox   = new GtkHBox();

// Pack the two views into the box.
$window->add($hBox);
$hBox->pack_start($view);
$hBox->pack_start($view2);

$window->show_all();
$window->connect_simple('destroy', array('Gtk', 'main_quit'));
Gtk::main();
?>
```

As you can see, creating a sortable tree is pretty easy once the original tree has been created.

Model Filtering

Just as a model can be sorted before it is shown, so can it be filtered. Filtering a model hides rows based on a column value or a callback. Filtering out rows is done in much the same way as sorting them. Using GtkTreeModelFilter, you can wrap the model and hide rows. This allows the model to be used in other places in the application without losing any of its data.

For example, you could use one model to represent all of the products in the database. This model could be wrapped by a GtkTreeModelFilter in one piece of the application to show only the items in stock, while in another piece of the application, the model could be wrapped to filter out all but the most expensive product in each category. The same model could even be sorted by price and then filtered to show only those products whose name begins with C.

Listing 9-8 filters a model based on a Boolean column.

Listing 9-8. *Filtering a Model Using GtkTreeFilter*

```php
<?php
// Create a tree store.
$treeStore = new GtkTreeStore(Gtk::TYPE_STRING, Gtk::TYPE_LONG,
                              Gtk::TYPE_DOUBLE, Gtk::TYPE_BOOLEAN);

// Add some product data.
$csMerch     = $treeStore->append(null, array('Crisscott', null, null, true));
$phpGtkMerch = $treeStore->append(null, array('PHP-GTK',  null, null, false));

$tShirts = $treeStore->append($csMerch, array('T-Shirts', 10, 19.95, false));
$treeStore->append($tShirts, array('Small',  3, 19.95, true));
$treeStore->append($tShirts, array('Medium', 5, 19.95, true));
$treeStore->append($tShirts, array('Large',  2, 19.95, true));

$pencils = $treeStore->append($csMerch, array(' Pencils', 18, .99, true));
$treeStore->append($pencils, array('Blue', 9, .99, true));
$treeStore->append($pencils, array('White', 9, .99, true));

$treeStore->append($phpGtkMerch, array('PHP-GTK Bumper Stickers', 37, 1.99, true));
$treeStore->append($phpGtkMerch, array('Pro PHP-GTK',             23, 44.95, true));

// Get a filtered model.
$filtered = $treeStore->filter_new();

// Only show rows that have column three set to true.
$filtered->set_visible_column(3);

// Create a view to show the tree.
$view = new GtkTreeView();
$view->set_model($filtered);
```

```php
// Create columns for each type of data.
$column = new GtkTreeViewColumn();
$column->set_title('Product Name');
$view->insert_column($column, 0);

// Create a renderer for the column.
$cell_renderer = new GtkCellRendererText();
$column->pack_start($cell_renderer, true);
$column->set_attributes($cell_renderer, 'text', 0);

// Create columns for each type of data.
$column = new GtkTreeViewColumn();
$column->set_title('Inventory');
$view->insert_column($column, 1);

// Create a renderer for the column.
$cell_renderer = new GtkCellRendererText();
$column->pack_start($cell_renderer, true);
$column->set_attributes($cell_renderer, 'text', 1);

// Create columns for each type of data.
$column = new GtkTreeViewColumn();
$column->set_title('Price');
$view->insert_column($column, 2);

// Create a renderer for the column.
$cell_renderer = new GtkCellRendererText();
$column->pack_start($cell_renderer, true);
$column->set_attributes($cell_renderer, 'text', 2);

// Create a window and show everything.
$window = new GtkWindow();
$window->add($view);
$window->show_all();
$window->connect_simple('destroy', array('Gtk', 'main_quit'));
Gtk::main();
?>
```

Figure 9-4 shows the result of this filtering.

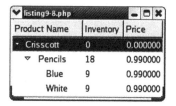

Figure 9-4. *A filtered model*

You can rewrap models wrapped by another filter or sort model. This multilayering allows for incredible flexibility from a single data collection.

Views

In general, data is modeled using a GtkListStore or GtkTreeStore so that it can be shown in at least one part of the application. You can show a model with many widgets. Some are designed for specific purposes, like GtkComboBox and GtkEntryCompletion, but GtkTreeView is the widget most often associated with a model.

GtkTreeView is a generic widget for showing a model and allowing a user to select a row. Despite the name, a tree view is equally well suited for showing a list—after all, a list is really just a simpler version of a tree. GtkTreeView can display any model, even one that has been wrapped many times by a filter or a sort model. You can use multiple views for the same model without disturbing the underlying data. This type of data reuse allows for incredible flexibility within an application.

■**Note** PHP-GTK 1 had separate widgets for displaying lists and trees. PHP-GTK 2 has only one widget— GtkTreeView. Because a list is really just a tree of one level, GtkTreeView can display lists and trees equally well.

A GtkTreeView is the visual representation of a data model, but it cannot fulfill all of the responsibility of displaying the data by itself. GtkTreeView requires the help of GtkTreeViewColumn and GtkCellRenderer. These two classes break down the task of showing a model's data to allow even greater flexibility. GtkTreeViewColumn manages the display properties for a given column in a model. GtkCellRenderer is a base class that is extended in many ways to show different types of data within an individual cell of a row. Together, these three pieces provide an incredibly versatile tool for displaying trees and lists. Let's start at the bottom of the hierarchy and work our way up.

Cell Renderers

Cells are the containers that hold individual pieces of data within a view. A cell is one column within one row of a model. A *cell renderer* is the class that manages the display of a column or a single piece of data.

Before a column can be displayed, it must be assigned a cell renderer. Without the renderer, there is no way to consistently show the data in the column. Cell renderers are used to format numbers and align and color display values. They determine how the column's values will be shown.

Before a renderer can be applied, the type of renderer must be selected. Cell renderers exist for text, progress bars, images, and toggle buttons. Each type of renderer shows its data in a different way:

- GtkCellRendererText: Used for rendering text or values that should be treated like text, such as monetary values.

- GtkCellRendererProgress: Used for graphically showing progress or percentage values.

- GtkCellRendererPixbuf: Used for displaying images.

- GtkCellRendererToggle: Used for showing on/off or true/false values.

Each type of cell renderer has a specific purpose, which can be easily inferred from its name. GtkCellRendererText is the most commonly used renderer, but doesn't always fit the bill. If a value of a column should just be printed in the row, then a GtkCellRendererText is the best fit for that column. However, if the value of a column represents whether or not a product is available, for example, then a GtkCellRendererToggle works better.

Once you've specified the renderer type, you instantiate it using the new operator. That is really all there is to do for cell renderers. The only renderer with methods that are likely to be called in an application is GtkCellRendererToggle.

By default, GtkCellRendererToggle displays its value as a check box. You can change the value display to a radio button by passing true to the set_radio method. You can also change the value of the cell by using the set_active method. If set_active is passed true, the cell will be toggled. This will change the value of the data in the model.

You can see examples of using GtkCellRendererText in Listings 9-2, 9-3, 9-7, and 9-8. For an example of several different types of cell renderers in action, see Listing 9-9 (coming up shortly).

View Columns

One level up from the cell renderer is the *column*. Whereas GtkCellRenderer determines how data is shown in a cell, GtkTreeViewColumn determines how the cells are displayed within the entire column. GtkTreeViewColumn is responsible for managing the column header in the view and the display of the column in the model. It manages attributes such as the width of the column, whether or not the column is visible, and the spacing around cells.

Every column in a model that is to be shown in the view must have a GtkTreeViewColumn associated with it. You create columns by using new GtkTreeViewColumn. After you instantiate a column, you insert it into a view by using the insert_column method of GtkTreeView.

Setting the Column Header

One of the responsibilities of GtkTreeViewColumn is setting the header for the column. You set the column title that will appear by using set_title. If you do not call set_title, the cell for the header will be empty. A header block will still appear at the top of the column, but it will not have any text in it. But note that whether or not the header appears at all is set by the view, not the column.

The header doesn't have to be a label; it can be any widget that you would like to use. If you need to use something other than a simple label, call the set_widget method to set the given widget as the column header. There are no restrictions on what type of widget you can add as the header, but keep in mind what effect setting the widget as the header can have on the usability of your application.

Setting the Column Display Properties

Another responsibility of GtkTreeViewColumn is setting the display properties for the column. The most drastic attribute that can be set is the column's visibility, controlled by using set_visible. As you would expect, passing true to set_visible will make the column appear in the view, and passing false will hide the column.

For example, you may want to allow users to click a column header to hide a column containing data they are not particularly interested in at the moment. Listing 9-9 shows how to use set_visible with the clicked signal. By default, set_clickable is false, so clicking a column header has no effect. Passing true to set_clickable causes the column to emit the clicked signal when a user clicks the header.

Listing 9-9. *Controlling the Display Properties of a GtkTreeViewColumn*

```
<?
function hideColumn($column)
{
        // Toggle the visibility of the column.
        $column->set_visible(!$column->get_visible());
}

// Create a tree store.
$treeStore = new GtkTreeStore(Gtk::TYPE_STRING, Gtk::TYPE_LONG, Gtk::TYPE_DOUBLE);

// Add some product data...

// Create a view to show the tree.
$view = new GtkTreeView();
$view->set_model($treeStore);

// Create columns for each type of data.
$column = new GtkTreeViewColumn();
$column->set_title('Product Name');
$view->insert_column($column, 0);

// Create a renderer for the column.
$cell_renderer = new GtkCellRendererText();
$column->pack_start($cell_renderer, true);
$column->set_attributes($cell_renderer, 'text', 0);
```

```php
// Make the column resizable by the user.
$column->set_resizable(true);
$column->set_sort_column_id(0);

// Create columns for each type of data.
$column2 = new GtkTreeViewColumn();
$column2->set_title('Inventory');
$view->insert_column($column2, 1);

// Create a renderer for the column.
$cell_renderer = new GtkCellRendererProgress();
$column2->pack_start($cell_renderer, true);
$column2->set_attributes($cell_renderer, 'value', 2);

// Make column2 resizable by the user.
$column2->set_resizable(true);
$column2->set_reorderable(true);

// Allow the user to hide the inventory column.
$column2->set_clickable(true);
$column2->connect('clicked', 'hideColumn');
$column->set_sort_column_id(0);

// Create columns for each type of data.
$column3 = new GtkTreeViewColumn();
$column3->set_title('Price');
$view->insert_column($column3, 2);

// Create a renderer for the column.
$cell_renderer = new GtkCellRendererText();
$column3->pack_start($cell_renderer, true);
$column3->set_attributes($cell_renderer, 'text', 2);

// Allow the user to resize the column.
$column3->set_resizable(true);
$column3->set_reorderable(true);
$column3->set_sort_column_id(2);

// Create a window and show everything.
$window = new GtkWindow();
$window->add($view);
$window->show_all();
$window->connect_simple('destroy', array('Gtk', 'main_quit'));
Gtk::main();
?>
```

Figure 9-5 shows the result of Listing 9-9 after the user has clicked the Inventory column to hide it.

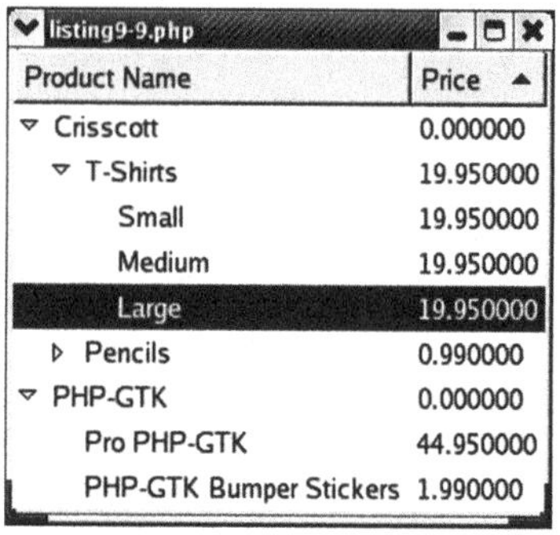

Figure 9-5. *The product tree with the Inventory column hidden*

In Listing 9-9, the clicked signal is used to toggle the visibility of the column. Why is the visibility toggled instead of just set to false? Good question. Once the column is hidden, the user can't click it again, so toggling the visibility doesn't help the user that much. It does make life easier on the application, though. Clicking the header isn't the only way to emit the clicked signal. It can also be emitted programmatically by using the clicked method, which will call the signal handler connected to the clicked signal. For example, the application may have a reset button that goes through all of the columns in a view and checks their current visibility. If the column is hidden, the application could just call the clicked method to make the column visible again.

Listing 9-9 also shows a few other GtkTreeViewColumn methods in action. The columns in the view are set to automatically resize whenever the view of the model is changed. You can set the sizing rules by using set_sizing. This method expects one of the following arguments:

- Gtk::TREE_VIEW_COLUMN_GROW_ONLY: The column will automatically widen to accommodate the largest cell but will never shrink, even if the widest cell is hidden.

- Gtk::TREE_VIEW_COLUMN_AUTOSIZE: The column will automatically resize to fit the widest cell in the column. This is the setting in Listing 9-9.

- Gtk::TREE_VIEW_COLUMN_FIXED: The column will not change size unless explicitly told to do so by the user or the application.

The user can control the size of the column by dragging the outer edge of the column header. Before the user can resize the column, however, the column must be configured properly. The column will be resizable by the user if true is passed to the set_resizable method.

The application can control the size of a column with the help of several methods. You can set the minimum and maximum width of the column by using set_min_width and set_max_width, respectively. You can assign the column a fixed width by using set_fixed_width. Each of these methods requires the number of pixels for the width of the column.

Caution If you set the sizing of a column to Gtk::TREE_VIEW_COLUMN_FIXED, make sure to set the size using set_fixed_width. Otherwise, the column will have a fixed size of zero and will look like it was left out of the view.

Another column attribute that is set in Listing 9-9 is the reorderable attribute. This property of a GtkTreeViewColumn defines whether or not a user may reorder the columns by dragging the column header before or after another column. By default, a user may not reorder the columns. To allow this, pass true to set_reorderable. A reorderable column can be moved to any position in a view. It may even bump columns that have not been made reorderable. There is no way to prevent a user from moving a column to any particular position, but moving a column will cause the view to emit the columns-changed signal. You can set up a view to move a column out of a particular position when a column is moved, as explained in the "Setting GtkTreeView Display Properties" section later in this chapter.

Reordering Rows

The GtkTreeViewColumn is also responsible for ordering rows. Because GtkListStore and GtkTreeStore implement the GtkTreeSortable interface, columns are able to sort the model without help from any other classes.

As you've seen, the default settings for a column restrict the user's options pretty tightly. The user cannot resize the column, hide a column, or reorder the columns. Nor can the user sort the model by clicking the header.

Sorting by a particular column is an extremely useful feature, especially when a tree or list is rather large. Setting up a column in the model to be sorted in the view is actually pretty easy. All it takes is calling set_sort_column_id. This method expects a column number indicating on which column the rows will be sorted. Allowing the user to sort the model by clicking the header of a column requires the column to be clickable. Calling set_sort_column_id automatically makes a column clickable. But be careful, as this can have unforeseen consequences, such as allowing a column to be hidden.

Note Sorting the data is just visual. The underlying model itself has not changed.

In Listing 9-9, each column is set to sort on itself. This is the most common way to sort a column, although it is not required. Applications just tend to be easier to use when clicking a column sorts the data by the values in that column. When a column is sorted, a triangle will appear in the header for that column, indicating the direction that the data has been sorted. A triangle pointing down indicates normal sort order, or ascending order. A triangle pointing up indicates that the data has been sorted in reverse order. If you don't want to show an indicator when the rows are sorted by a particular column, simply pass false to set_sort_indicator. Figure 9-6 shows the code in Listing 9-9 with the model sorted by price in reverse order and with the Inventory column hidden.

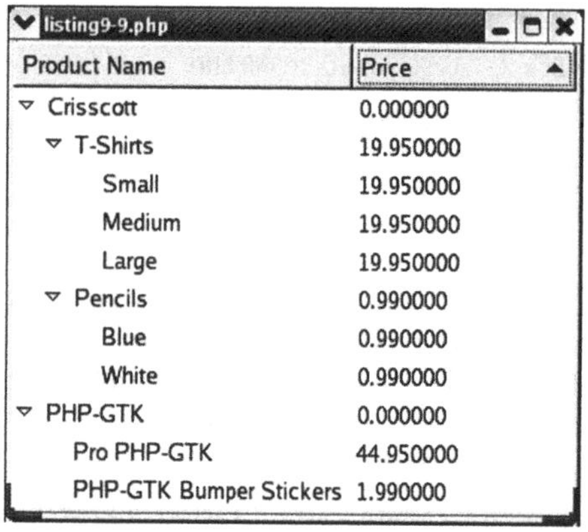

Figure 9-6. *Various adjustments to GtkTreeViewColumn display properties*

Note that a column that is hidden cannot sort a view of the model. In Listing 9-9, column 1 (the Inventory column) is set up so that clicking the header hides the column. Once the column is hidden, it will not sort the view of the model. The column can still be used to sort other views of the model, but its values aren't available to this view until it is shown again.

Adding Cell Renderers

All of the customizations that can be done to a column are basically meaningless unless the column has at least one cell renderer associated with it. Remember that the cell renderer is the class that decides how to show the data.

A column is a special type of container. It is designed to hold only GtkCellRenderer descendants. It may seem odd at first, but a column may hold more than one cell renderer. This will create two cells within each row of the column. This is helpful in cases where the same type of data may be represented in different ways. For example, it may be helpful to show not only the total number of a product sold, but also how that number relates to other products in the same category. This would allow the user to see at a glance the popularity of a product.

You add cell renderers to a column using either pack_end or pack_start. These methods are similar to the GtkVBox and GtkHBox methods of the same name (discussed in Chapter 6), but they have only one optional parameter. This optional argument is a Boolean value that controls whether or not the cell will expand to fill the column. Passing true means the cell with take up as much room as possible; passing false means the cell will use only the space needed.

After you've added a cell renderer to a column, the column must tell the cell renderer not only where to get the data that should be used, but also what to use it for. This is done using add_attribute or set_attributes. add_attribute takes a cell renderer, an attribute, and a column number. This method will tell the cell renderer to take the value from the given column and use it as the value for the attribute. set_attributes, which has been used in earlier listings, is a way to set many attributes at once. This method takes a cell renderer and one or more attribute column pairs. An attribute column pair is an attribute name followed by the column from which the value for that attribute should be taken.

You can tell a cell renderer to get its display values by using a callback method. set_cell_data_func sets a function or method that will be called before the cell is rendered. The callback should set the cell properties. set_cell_data_func expects the cell renderer for the column, followed by the callback and an optional array of other data that should be passed to the callback. The callback should expect to be passed the column the cell renderer is in, the cell renderer, the data model, an iterator pointing to the row being rendered, and the optional user data.

In Listing 9-10, the first column's cell renderer is told to use the value from the first column as the value for the text attribute of the cell renderer. This is how the cells know to display the title as the cell's data. The other two columns are told to get their display values not from a specific column, but instead to use a callback method. The function percentageInventory is used to set the value attribute of GtkCellRendererProgress renderer for column 1. The value that is set is the relative inventory of the given product. This callback also changes another attribute of the cell. If the inventory is below ten, the cell's background color is set to red. This would be useful to indicate to the user that a product might need to be reordered soon.

Listing 9-10. *Using GtkCellRendererProgress and set_cell_data_func*

```php
<?php
function percentageInventory($column, $renderer, $model, $iter, $totalInventory)
{
    // Get the inventory for the individual row.
    $inventory = $model->get_value($iter, 1);
    // Set the value property of the cell renderer.
    $renderer->set_property('value', $inventory / $totalInventory * 100);

    // Check to see if the inventory level is low.
    if ($inventory < 10) {
        // Make the cell background red.
        $renderer->set_property('cell-background', '#F00');
    } else {
        $renderer->set_property('cell-background', 'white');
    }
}

function formatPrice($column, $renderer, $model, $iter)
{
    $price = $model->get_value($iter, 2);
    $renderer->set_propperty('text', number_format($value, 2));
}

// Create a tree store.
$treeStore = new GtkTreeStore(Gtk::TYPE_STRING, Gtk::TYPE_LONG, Gtk::TYPE_DOUBLE);

// Add some product data.
$csMerch     = $treeStore->append(null, array('Crisscott', null, null));
$phpGtkMerch = $treeStore->append(null, array('PHP-GTK',  null, null));
```

```
$tShirts = $treeStore->append($csMerch, array('T-Shirts', 10, 19.95));
$treeStore->append($tShirts, array('Small',  3, 19.95));
$treeStore->append($tShirts, array('Medium', 5, 19.95));
$treeStore->append($tShirts, array('Large',  2, 19.95));

$pencils = $treeStore->append($csMerch, array('Pencils', 18, .99));
$treeStore->append($pencils, array('Blue', 9, .99));
$treeStore->append($pencils, array('White', 9, .99));

$treeStore->append($phpGtkMerch, array('PHP-GTK Bumper Stickers', 37, 1.99));
$treeStore->append($phpGtkMerch, array('Pro PHP-GTK',                23, 44.95));

// Create a view to show the tree.
$view = new GtkTreeView();
$view->set_model($treeStore);

// Create columns for each type of data.
$column = new GtkTreeViewColumn();
$column->set_title('Product Name');
$view->insert_column($column, 0);

// Create a renderer for the column.
$cell_renderer = new GtkCellRendererText();
$column->pack_start($cell_renderer, true);
$column->set_attributes($cell_renderer, 'text', 0);

// Make the column resizable by the user.
$column->set_resizable(true);
$column->set_sort_column_id(0);

// Create columns for each type of data.
$column2 = new GtkTreeViewColumn();
$column2->set_title('Inventory');
$view->insert_column($column2, 1);

// Create a renderer for the column.
$cell_renderer = new GtkCellRendererProgress();
$column2->pack_start($cell_renderer, true);

// Take greater control of how the data is displayed.
$column2->set_cell_data_func($cell_renderer, 'percentageInventory', 88);

// Allow the user to resize the column
$column2->set_resizable(true);
$column2->set_reorderable(true);
```

```
// Create columns for each type of data.
$column3 = new GtkTreeViewColumn();
$column3->set_title('Price');
$view->insert_column($column3, 2);
// Create a renderer for the column.
$cell_renderer = new GtkCellRendererText();
$column3->pack_start($cell_renderer, true);
$column3->set_cell_data_func($cell_renderer, 'formatPrice');

// Allow the user to resize the column.
$column3->set_resizable(true);
$column3->set_reorderable(true);
$column3->set_sort_column_id(2);

// Create a window and show everything.
$window = new GtkWindow();
$window->add($view);
$window->show_all();
$window->connect_simple('destroy', array('Gtk', 'main_quit'));
Gtk::main();
?>
```

Figure 9-7 shows what effect this has on the cell.

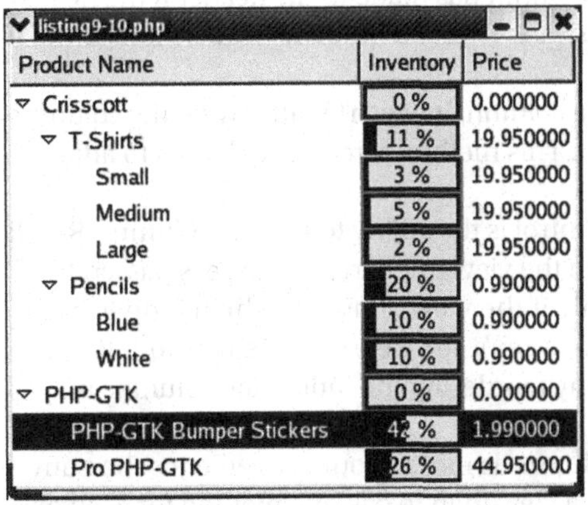

Product Name	Inventory	Price
▽ Crisscott	0 %	0.000000
▽ T-Shirts	11 %	19.950000
Small	3 %	19.950000
Medium	5 %	19.950000
Large	2 %	19.950000
▽ Pencils	20 %	0.990000
Blue	10 %	0.990000
White	10 %	0.990000
▽ PHP-GTK	0 %	0.000000
PHP-GTK Bumper Stickers	42 %	1.990000
Pro PHP-GTK	26 %	44.950000

Figure 9-7. *Setting column display values*

You may have noticed in the figures shown so far that the value of the price displays with far too many decimal places. This is because the GtkCellRendererText instance for the Price column was left to translate the floating-point value of the price into a string all on its own. In order to make the price value appear in a more common monetary format, the application needs to take control by setting the cell's display properties. Just as with the previous column, set_cell_data_func is used to control how the data is displayed in the Price column. Instead of generating new data based on a column value like percentageInventory, the formatPrice callback simply reformats the data before it is set as the cell's text attribute.

Tree Views

Finally, we come to GtkTreeView. This is the first (and only) widget discussed in this chapter. GtkTreeView is the class that puts everything together and makes the list or tree visible in the application.

As with most things in PHP-GTK, GtkTreeView can be very simple to use, but it also allows a great deal of flexibility. The primary role of GtkTreeView is to display a tree or list, but it can also be used to control some of the display properties of the model and to allow the user to select an item. While lists and trees are useful by themselves to model data, GtkTreeView makes them usable by the application's user.

Most of the listings you've seen so far have used GtkTreeView in a very simple way. A view was instantiated using the new operator, and a model was set by calling set_model or the model was passed on construction. Then a few columns were created and inserted into the view. This basic usage should be pretty straightforward by now.

Two methods that you haven't seen yet are append_column and remove_column, but there isn't anything mysterious about these methods. They both expect a column as the only argument and do what their name suggests. (What is somewhat mysterious is that there is no method to prepend a column.)

Setting GtkTreeView Display Properties

When it comes to displaying a model, GtkTreeView is king. GtkTreeViewColumn can set some display properties such as the column header title and whether or not a header can be clicked or reordered, but the view can override some settings and make others basically useless.

For starters, it doesn't matter what settings a column has made for its header if the header is not visible. The GtkTreeView method set_headers_visible will hide the headers altogether if it is passed true.

Also, the view has the final say over the size of a column. It doesn't matter what the column's sizing was set to if the view calls columns_autosize. This method forces all columns to adjust their size to fit the widest cell.

Another column property that the view can control is the ability to reorder columns. Recall that a column can be moved to another position in the view if set_reorderable is passed true. The reality is that the column may be moved only if the view allows it, which it does by default. But you can override this by using GtkTreeView's set_reorderable method. If the view's set_reorderable method is passed false, any reordering the individual columns may permit will be disallowed by the view.

Allowing the view to have control over the columns is more about convenience than anything else. It is much easier to call one method on a view than to call one method for each of the columns.

Navigating the Model

The whole point of creating a GtkTreeView is to allow the user to see a collection of data, but sometimes the data may be too large or complex to show all at once in an understandable manner. For this reason, by default, GtkTreeView starts with the rows collapsed—child rows are not shown.

When the view is originally shown, only the top-level rows are visible. If the row has children, an *expander* icon will be shown next to the row. The expander is normally an arrow or a box with a plus sign in it, depending on the user's settings. When the user clicks the expander, the children of the given row will be shown. Clicking the expander again will hide the children, or collapse the row. All of this collapsing and expanding can make it difficult to find elements within a model. That is why GtkTreeView has plenty of methods to help navigate a model.

Navigating to a specific row normally requires the help of data structure known as a GtkTreePath. A GtkTreePath is really just an array, but it is an array with a special purpose. The elements in a GtkTreePath indicate how to get to a specific row. Think of GtkTreePath as a road map for a tree. The first element in the array tells which top-level row to start with. The next element says which child of the given top-level row to go to. The third array element says which child of the row pointed to by the first two elements to go to. Figure 9-6 is a visual representation of the tree that has been used through most of this chapter. The path for getting to large Crisscott T-Shirts would look like array(0 ,0 ,2).

Using a GtkTreePath, it is possible to find any row in a model. That makes GtkTreePath perfect for navigating a tree.

A quick way to bring the user to a certain row is expand to that row. What this means is to start at the beginning of a path and expand each row until the row at the end of the path has been expanded. You can expand all of the rows in a path by using expand_to_path, which expects a GtkTreePath as the only argument.

If you want to expand only the row pointed to by the path, use expand_row. The same row can be collapsed again by passing the path to collapse_row.

Another method, set_cursor, lets you set the cursor to a given cell. Setting a cursor on a cell will give it the keyboard focus and select the cell's row. set_cursor needs a path to a row and a column. Before the cursor can be set to a given row, the row must be visible. It is a good idea to call expand_to_path before calling set_cursor.

Row Selection

Once a row is selected, either by the application (using set_cursor) or by the user, an application will likely want to do something with the selected row. GtkTreeSelection is an object that is automatically created as part of a view. It cannot be instantiated directly, because it cannot exist without a GtkTreeView. GtkTreeSelection is designed to make it easy to select one or more rows and determine which rows have been selected. Because GtkTreeSelection is part of the view, there can be many selections for the same model. Each selection may have different rows selected. Getting the selection for a model is as easy as calling get_selection on a view.

Setting the Selection Mode

The selection not only manages the currently selected rows, but also controls how many rows may be selected at one time. The selection mode defines how many rows may be selected. You set the selection mode by passing one of the following selection mode constants to GtkTreeSelection's set_mode method:

- Gtk::SELECTION_NONE: No rows of the tree may be selected (none mode).

- Gtk::SELECTION_SINGLE: At most, one row may be selected at a time (single mode).

- Gtk::SELECTION_BROWSE: One row, and only one row, must always be selected (browse mode).

- Gtk_SELECTION_MULTIPLE: One or more rows may be selected at a time (multiple mode).

Depending on the selection mode, a user may or may not be allowed to select one or more rows in a view using the mouse or keyboard. If the selection mode is none, then the rest of this section doesn't really apply. Setting the selection mode to none basically locks the view to be display only. Not even the application can select a row. Browse mode means that once one row has been selected, one row must always be selected. With single or multiple mode, a row may be unselected by holding down the Ctrl key and clicking the row (or by using the methods discussed in the next section). Browse mode is similar to single mode in that only one row may be selected at a time, but a row may not be unselected except by selecting another row. Once a selection has been made, there will always be a selection. Listing 9-11 shows a selection being set to Gtk::SELECT_MULTIPLE.

Listing 9-11. *Setting the Selection Mode*

```php
<?php
function unbold($selection)
{
    // Get the selected rows.
    list($model, $paths) = $selection->get_selected_rows();
    foreach ($paths as $path) {
        // Unbold the selected rows.
        $iter = $model->get_iter($path);
        $model->set($iter, 3, Pango::WEIGHT_NORMAL);
    }
}

// ...

// Create a tree store.
$treeStore = new GtkTreeStore(Gtk::TYPE_STRING, Gtk::TYPE_LONG,
                              Gtk::TYPE_DOUBLE, Gtk::TYPE_LONG);

// Continue with tree setup...

// Create a view to show the tree.
$view = new GtkTreeView($treeStore);

// Set up the columns...

// Set the selection mode to multiple.
$view->get_selection()->set_mode(Gtk::SELECTION_MULTIPLE);
```

```
// Connect a callback to the selection's changed signal.
$selection = $view->get_selection();
$selection->connect('changed', 'unbold');

// Continue with column setup...
?>
```

Figure 9-8 shows what the code in Listing 9-11 produces after the user has selected a few rows.

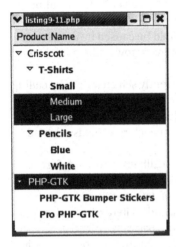

Figure 9-8. *A GtkTreeView that allows multiple selections*

Selecting and Unselecting Rows

If the selection mode is something other than Gtk::SELECTION_NONE, then rows may be selected by the user and the application. An application may use several methods to select a row, but not all of the methods will work all of the time. For instance, the select_all method will attempt to select all of the rows in a view, but if the selection mode is not Gtk::SELECTION_MULTIPLE, not only will the method fail, but an error will be thrown that looks something like this:

```
Gtk-CRITICAL **: gtk_tree_selection_select_all: assertion `selection->type ==
GTK_SELECTION_MULTIPLE' failed
```

Another method that works only when the selection is in multiple mode is select_range. select_range takes two paths as arguments and selects both rows and all of the rows between them. Obviously, there will be problems selecting a range of rows if the selection mode is none, single, or browse. Some methods will work as expected for most modes. These include methods that unselect rows and methods that select a single row.

Unselecting rows can be done by path, by iterator, by range, or by unselecting all currently selected rows. unselect_path and unselect_iter take the arguments you would expect and unselect the given row. If the row is not currently selected, nothing happens. unselect_range works just like select_range. It takes two paths and unselects both rows and everything in between. unselect_all takes no arguments and unselects all rows. None of these methods will work if the selection mode is Gtk::SELECTION_BROWSE. The only way to unselect a row in browse mode is to select a different row.

You can select a single row by using either select_iter or select_path. These two methods select the row identified by the argument passed in. Keep in mind that selecting a row in browse mode automatically unselects the current row.

The selection mode is one way to control the selection, but there is a method that allows very fine control over which rows in a view may be selected. A function or method may be defined to determine if a row may be selected or unselected. The callback should accept the model, the path to the row in question, a Boolean value indicating whether or not the row is currently selected, and an array of user data. If the callback returns true, the row's state will be toggled. This means that if the row was selected, it will be unselected and vice versa. If the callback returns false, the row will stay as it is. To set the callback, use set_select_function. The callback will be called anytime a row's state might change, which could be caused by the user or the application. Calling select_all will fire the callback once for every row in the model (as long as the selection is in multiple mode).

Once a selection has been made, you can determine the currently selected rows by calling get_selected_rows. This method returns an array that contains the model and information about which rows were selected. In the array that is returned, the first element is always the tree or list. The second element is an array of paths. There will be one path for each row that is selected. The application can then do as it pleases with this information.

One way to process the selected rows rather easily is to use a callback. selected_foreach will set up a callback that will be called for every selected row every time the selection changes. selected_foreach requires only the callback and an optional array of data that should be passed to the callback. The callback itself should accept the model, a path, and an iterator, as well as the optional array. Both the path and iterator will point to the current row. Basically, selected_foreach creates a signal handler for the changed signal. The changed signal is emitted anytime a row is selected or unselected, whether by the user or by the application.

Putting It All Together

Two tools in the Crisscott PIMS application can take advantage of the flexibility of GtkTreeView. As mentioned in the previous chapter, the news article tool shows the text of articles that come into the application via an RSS feed. Now you'll see how to set this up. Another segment of the application that makes good use of GtkTreeView is the product tree above the News frame.

The News Article Tool

In Chapter 8, we set up the news article tool to show a given article, but no mention was made of how the article was selected. If you recall from the original mockup of the application, there is a News section in the lower-left corner of the application. This section has been set aside to show a list of news articles that have been pulled in from an RSS feed. The idea is that the RSS feed will be checked periodically, and headlines will be shown in the small News section. When the user selects a headline, the main body of the article will be shown in the area to the right. There are three steps to this plan:

1. Parse the RSS feed for the news items.

2. Display a list (or tree) of news items that can be selected one at a time.

3. Display the selected article.

In the end, the news article tool will end up looking like Figure 9-9.

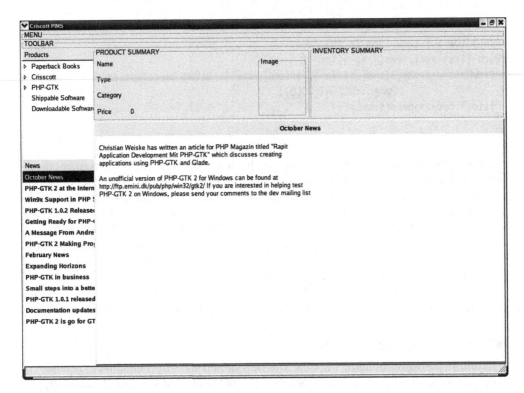

Figure 9-9. *The application with a news feed and article displayed*

Parsing the RSS Feed

The first step will be handled in the `Crisscott_Tools_News` class with the help of `PEAR::XML_RSS`, which is a package designed specifically to deal with RSS feeds. You can install this package using the PEAR installer, like so:

```
$> pear install pear/XML_RSS
```

When the news items are parsed out of the feed, they are put into a model. Listing 9-12 shows the code to take the RSS feed and turn it into a usable model.

Listing 9-12. *Turning an RSS Feed into a GtkListStore*

```php
<?php
// Create the feed parser.
require_once 'XML/RSS.php';
$rss = new XML_RSS('http://gtk.php.net/news.rss');

// Parse the RSS feed.
$rss->parse();
```

```
// Create a model to store the items.
$listStore = new GtkListStore(Gtk::TYPE_STRING, Gtk::TYPE_STRING, Gtk::TYPE_STRING,
                    Gtk::TYPE_LONG );

// Add a row for each item in the feed.
foreach ($rss->getItems() as $item) {
    $rowData = array($item['title'], $item['date'], $item['description'],
                    Pango::WEIGHT_BOLD);
    $listStore->append($rowData);
}
?>
```

For each item in the feed, a new row is appended to the model. The model itself has four columns: the headline, the date, the article body, and an integer that marks whether or not the article has been viewed. This last column can be used to format the headlines in the list for articles that have not yet been read. The value of column 3 will be used as the font weight. A value of Pango::WEIGHT_BOLD, or 800, means that the headline will be bold. Pango::WEIGHT_NORMAL, or 400, will make the headline the normal font weight and will signify that the article has already been viewed. The column will not be shown in the final view and neither will the date. The date is added to the model to make it easy to sort the news items.

Because the articles in an RSS news feed don't have any direct relation to each other, a list is used instead of a tree. This makes the code easier to understand and maintain.

Building the View and Selecting the Article

The second step involves building the view. The view should show the headlines in reverse chronological order and should allow only one article to be selected at a time. Additionally, there is no way to clear an article from the news article tool. Therefore, the currently selected article should not be allowed to be unselected unless another row is selected.

To show the list in reverse chronological order, the list will be wrapped in a GtkTreeModelSort object, which will then be added to the view. The GtkTreeSelection from the view will be set to browse mode so that one article will always be selected. The changed signal of GtkTreeSelection will be used to load the currently selected article into the news article tool. When the article is loaded, it is also marked as read in column 3 by setting the value to Pango::WEIGHT_NORMAL.

Listing 9-13 shows the code for the step of showing an article, as well as the third step, which is just one method call to showArticle in the callback connected to the changed signal. See Figure 9-9, shown earlier, for the results.

Listing 9-13. *Creating the View and Displaying Articles*

```php
<?php
class Crisscott_Tools_NewsFeed extends GtkTreeView {

    // A singleton instance of the class.
    public static $instance;
    // The PEAR::XML_RSS parser.
    public $rss;
```

```php
public function __construct($handle = null)
{
    // Call the parent constructor.
    parent::__construct();

    // Create the parser.
    require_once 'XML/RSS.php';
    $this->rss = new XML_RSS();

    // Set the input if given.
    if (isset($handle)) {
        $this->setInput($handle);
    }

    // Add the tree column.
    $this->addColumn();

    // Set up the selection to load a selected item.
    // When the user picks a headline, the changed signal will be emitted.
    $selection = $this->get_selection();
    $selection->connect('changed', array($this, 'loadArticle'));
}

public function setInput($handle)
{
    $this->rss->setInput($handle);
}

public function createList()
{
    // Parse the feed.
    $this->rss->parse();

    // Create a list store with four columns.
    $listStore = new GtkListStore(Gtk::TYPE_STRING,
                                  Gtk::TYPE_STRING,
                                  Gtk::TYPE_STRING,
                                  Gtk::TYPE_LONG
                                  );

    // Add a row for each item in the feed.
    foreach ($this->rss->getItems() as $item) {
        // Add the title, the release date, and the description
        // and make the headline bold.
        $rowData = array($item['title'],
                         $item['dc:date'],
                         $item['description'],
                         Pango::WEIGHT_BOLD
```

```php
                                );
            // Add the row to the end of the list.
            $listStore->append($rowData);
        }

        // Return the list.
        return $listStore;
    }

    public function showList()
    {
        // Add the list to the view.
        $this->set_model($this->createList());
    }

    protected function addColumn()
    {
        // Create the column.
        $column = new GtkTreeViewColumn();
        $column->set_title('News');

        // Create a cell renderer.
        $cellRenderer = new GtkCellRendererText();

        // Pack the cell renderer.
        $column->pack_start($cellRenderer, true);
        // The text of the cell should be taken from column 0.
        $column->add_attribute($cellRenderer, 'text', 0);
        // The font weight should be taken from column 3.
        $column->add_attribute($cellRenderer, 'weight', 3);

        // Sort the column by date (the value in column 1).
        $column->set_sort_column_id(1);

        // Add the column to the tree.
        $this->append_column($column);
    }

    public function loadArticle($selection)
    {
        // Unbold the selected item to indicate that it has been read.
        // The font weight is stored in column 3.
        list($model, $iter) = $selection->get_selected();
        $model->set($iter, 3, Pango::WEIGHT_NORMAL);

        // Get a singleton news article tool.
        require_once 'Crisscott/Tools/NewsArticle.php';
        $newsArticle = Crisscott_Tools_NewsArticle::singleton();
```

```php
        // Set the article.
        // The headline is found in column 0.
        $headline = $model->get_value($iter, 0);
        // The body of the article is found in column 2.
        $body     = $model->get_value($iter, 2);
        // Add both parts of the article.
        $newsArticle->setArticle($headline, $body);

        // Bring the news story tab to the front.
        require_once 'Crisscott/MainNotebook.php';
        $notebook = Crisscott_MainNotebook::singleton();

        // Get the page index.
        $index = array_search('News Story', array_keys($notebook->pages));
        // Make the news story page move to the front of the notebook.
        $notebook->set_current_page($index);
    }

    public static function singleton()
    {
        // Check to see if the class has been instantiated already.
        if (!isset(self::$instance)) {
            // Create a new instance.
            $class = __CLASS__;
            self::$instance = new $class;
        }
        // Return the static instance.
        return self::$instance;
    }
}
?>
```

The Product Tree

The product tree section provides a quick and easy way for the user to select one product out of the entire inventory. The products are organized into a tree with the product categories as the top-level rows. Each category then has a child for product in that category.

When a category is selected, nothing will happen, because the callback will just return immediately, but when a product is selected, it will be loaded into the product summary section. A product will be added to the product editing tool when the user drags it into the main section of the application, but that is a topic for discussion in Chapter 13.

Just as with the news articles, once the product summary section has been populated, there should be no way to unpopulate it. This means that the product tree selection should be set to browse mode. In Listing 9-14, the tree is built using a Crisscott_Inventory object. The tree stores only the essential data needed to show and organize the information. If products objects were instantiated for each item in the inventory, the application would consume a large amount of memory. After the model is created, the view is set up in a very similar way to the previous

example. Finally, a callback is associated with the changed signal of the tree's selection object.
The callback simply instantiates a product and passes it along to the ProductSummary tool.

Listing 9-14. *Setting Up the Products Section*

```php
<?php
class Crisscott_Tools_ProductTree extends GtkTreeView {

    public static $instance;

    public function __construct()
    {
        // Call the parent constructor.
        parent::__construct();

        // Add/update the model.
        $this->updateModel();
    }

    public function updateModel()
    {
        // Create and set the model.
        $this->set_model($this->_createModel());

        // Next set up the view column and cell renderer.
        $this->_setupColumn();

        // Finally, set up the selection.
        $this->_setupSelection();
    }

    private function _createModel()
    {
        // Set up the model.
        // Each row should have the row name and the product_id.
        // If the row is a category the product_id should be zero.
        $model = new GtkTreeStore(Gtk::TYPE_STRING, Gtk::TYPE_LONG);

        // Get a singleton of the Inventory object.
        require_once 'Crisscott/Inventory.php';
        $inventory = Crisscott_Inventory::singleton();

    // Add all of the categories.
    foreach ($inventory->categories as $category) {
            $catIter = $model->append(null, array($category->name, 0));
            // Add all of the products for the category.
            foreach ($category->getProducts() as $product) {
                $model->append($catIter, array($product['product_name'],
```

```
                                      $product['product_id']));
              }
        }

        return $model;
}

private function _setupColumn()
{
        // Add the name column.
        $column = new GtkTreeViewColumn();
        $column->set_title('Products');

        // Create a renderer for the column.
        $cellRenderer = new GtkCellRendererText();
        $column->pack_start($cellRenderer, true);
        $column->add_attribute($cellRenderer, 'text', 0);

        // Make the column sort on the product name.
        $column->set_sort_column_id(0);

        // Insert the column.
        $this->insert_column($column, 0);
}

private function _setupSelection()
{
        // Get the selection object.
        $selection = $this->get_selection();

        // Set the selection to browse mode.
        $selection->set_mode(Gtk::SELECTION_BROWSE);

        // Create a signal handler to process the selection.
        $selection->connect('changed', array($this, 'sendToSummary'));
}

public function sendToSummary($selection)
{
        // Get the selected row.
        list($model, $iter) = $selection->get_selected();

        // Create a product.
        require_once 'Crisscott/Product.php';
        $product = new Crisscott_Product($model->get_value($iter, 1));
```

```
        // Get the singleton product summary.
        require_once 'Crisscott/Tools/ProductSummary.php';
        $productSummary = Crisscott_Tools_ProductSummary::singleton();
        $productSummary->displaySummary($product);
    }

    public static function singleton()
    {
        if (!isset(self::$instance)) {
            $class = __CLASS__;
            self::$instance = new $class;
        }
        return self::$instance;
    }
}
?>
```

Summary

Trees and lists by themselves are relatively simple objects for modeling, rather than complex data structures. A tree or list can take a collection of data and make it easy to navigate and access individual elements. The organized nature of these models allows them to be used in a myriad of ways when combined with GtkTreeView and its associated objects. The specialization and abstraction of responsibility of these classes make for a very powerful tool set that can provide almost endless flexibility when it comes to how a model should be displayed and accessed.

Now that you have seen how to work with large collections of data, you'll want to know how to display all of that data in a small space. Chapter 10 discusses how to make a section of an application scroll so that the user can access data that cannot fit in the space given for a tool. No longer will the sections of the application be restricted by the size of a container or the user's screen. An endless amount of space will be made available for any piece of the application that needs it by providing scrollbars for both the horizontal and vertical axes.

CHAPTER 10

■ ■ ■

Scrolling

At this point, the Crisscott PIMS application has several tools that may contain large amounts of data. Unfortunately, none of them currently provides a graceful way to handle this data when it exceeds the boundaries of the tool. For instance, if the data contained within the product tree exceeds the space provided by the tree, rows and characters just get pushed out of the visible area. Other tools may stretch to accommodate the oversized data. While this approach doesn't hide data from the user, it can interfere with the layout of the rest of the application, which may be more damaging than hiding values. A better solution enables a tool to extend its data beyond its visible borders, but remain accessible to the users. This is the role of scrolling widgets.

GtkScrolledWindow and GtkViewPort are widgets specifically designed to make data accessible even though it has outgrown its available space within the application. These two widgets provide a means to access data in another widget that is not currently within the widget's visible area. Additionally, you can customize scrolling for a particular widget.

Throughout this chapter, we will examine ways to use scrolling to make better use of the space available in the PIMS application.

Scrolled Windows

Some widgets have been designed with scrolling in mind. These widgets, including GtkTreeView and GtkTextView, will likely display large amounts of data. For example, a tree or list could show many rows from a database. A GtkTextView widget may display a lengthy press release or report. In order to make either of those documents fit on one screen, the font would have to be very small, likely rendering the document unreadable. Instead of asking developers to squeeze data into a restricted space, the designers of these widgets have given them native scrolling support.

Native scrolling support means that the widgets can accept scrollbars and will allow the scrollbars to control which part of the widget is shown in the visible area. GtkScrolledWindow provides the scrollbars that these widgets need.

GtkScrolledWindow is a bin container, a descendant of GtkBin. The scrollbars that it provides make it easier for users to access different parts of the child widget.

For instance, consider Figure 10-1, which depicts the product tree without scrollbars. It is impossible to see all the rows of the tree at once, and there is nothing to indicate to the user that the contents of the view are scrollable.

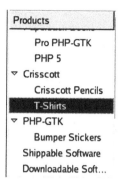

Figure 10-1. *A GtkTreeView without scrollbars*

On the other hand, Figure 10-2 displays the product tree after it has been added to a GtkScrolledWindow. While this doesn't make it possible to see all the rows at once (actually, the scrollbars take up space, making even less information visible), it does make it clear that the contents of the window can be scrolled.

Figure 10-2. *A GtkTreeView with scrollbars*

Adding scrollbars to those widgets that have native scrollbar support is relatively easy. Listing 10-1 presents an excerpt from an updated version of the Crisscott_MainWindow class. In previous iterations of this class, the Crisscott_Tools_ProductTree instance was attached directly to the table. In this example, the instance is added to a GtkScrolledWindow, which is then attached to the table.

Listing 10-1. *Adding Scrollbars to a GtkTreeView*

```php
<?php
    // ...

    // Get a singleton instance of the product tree.
    require_once 'Crisscott/Tools/ProductTree.php';
    $productTree = Crisscott_Tools_ProductTree::singleton();
```

```
// Create a scrolled window for the product tree.
$scrolledWindow = new GtkScrolledWindow();

// Set the size of the scrolled window.
$scrolledWindow->set_size_request(150, 150);

// Set the scrollbar policy.
$scrolledWindow->set_policy(Gtk::POLICY_NEVER, Gtk::POLICY_AUTOMATIC);

// Add the product tree to the scrolled window.
$scrolledWindow->add($productTree);

// Attach the scrolled window to the tree.
$table->attach($scrolledWindow, 0, 1, 2, 3, 0, $expandFill, 0, 0);

// ...
?>
```

Notice that the scrolled window, rather than the product tree instance, is sized. This is because the scrollbars are added to the outside of the scrolled window's child widget. If the product tree were sized to 150 pixels wide and then added to the scrolled window, the layout of the application would be distorted.

In the simplest scrolling use case, adding the child is all that needs to be done. But, as you can see in Listing 10-1, some customizations may be made.

Setting the Scrollbar Policy

One of the most common customizations for a GtkScrolledWindow is setting the *scrollbar policy*. The scrollbar policy determines when scrollbars will appear in the scrolled window. The default is to always show both the horizontal and vertical scrollbars, but this can be changed.

Three policy rules can be applied to horizontal and vertical scrollbars individually:

- Gtk::POLICY_ALWAYS: The scrollbar should be shown, regardless of whether or not there is enough information to scroll in the given direction.

- Gtk::POLICY_AUTOMATIC: The scrolled window shows the scrollbar only when it is needed.

- Gtk::POLICY_NEVER: The scrollbar will never be shown.

You can set the policies for a scrolled window with set_policy. The first argument that set_policy expects is the policy for the horizontal scrollbar, and the second argument is for the vertical scrollbar. The code in Listing 10-1 sets the policy for the horizontal scrollbar to Gtk::POLICY_NEVER, while the vertical scrollbar is set to Gtk::POLICY_AUTOMATIC. The horizontal scrollbar is not needed because the cell renderer for the tree is told to ellipsize the cell text. Even if the policy were set to automatic, the scrollbar would never be shown because the child widget will not expand horizontally.

Not only is it possible to set whether the scrollbars appear in a GtkScrolledWindow, but you can also control where they appear in relation to the child widget.

Controlling Child Placement

Technically speaking, the position of the scrollbars is not changeable, but the placement of the child can be controlled. You can position the child in one of four places relative to the scrollbars: Gtk::CORNER_TOP_LEFT (the default), Gtk::CORNER_TOP_RIGHT, Gtk::CORNER_BOTTOM_LEFT, and Gtk::CORNER_BOTTOM_RIGHT. Figure 10-3 shows the effect each of these placements has on a scrolled window.

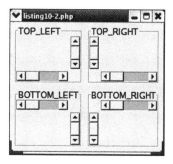

Figure 10-3. *Different child placements in a GtkScrolledWindow*

Setting the placement is a simple matter of passing one of the position types to set_placement. Listing 10-2 shows the code that was used to create Figure 10-3.

Listing 10-2. *Setting Child Placements in a GtkScrolledWindow*

```php
<?php
// Create and set up a window.
$window = new GtkWindow();
$window->connect_simple('destroy', array('gtk', 'main_quit'));

// Add a table to the window.
$table = new GtkTable(2, 2);
$window->add($table);

// Create four scrolled windows.
$sw1 = new GtkScrolledWindow();
$sw2 = new GtkScrolledWindow();
$sw3 = new GtkScrolledWindow();
$sw4 = new GtkScrolledWindow();

// Set each window to a different position.
$sw1->set_placement(Gtk::CORNER_TOP_LEFT);
$sw2->set_placement(Gtk::CORNER_TOP_RIGHT);
$sw3->set_placement(Gtk::CORNER_BOTTOM_LEFT);
$sw4->set_placement(Gtk::CORNER_BOTTOM_RIGHT);

// Create four frames.
$frame1 = new GtkFrame('TOP_LEFT');
```

```
$frame2 = new GtkFrame('TOP_RIGHT');
$frame3 = new GtkFrame('BOTTOM_LEFT');
$frame4 = new GtkFrame('BOTTOM_RIGHT');

// Add the scrolled windows to the frames.
$frame1->add($sw1);
$frame2->add($sw2);
$frame3->add($sw3);
$frame4->add($sw4);

// Attach the frames to the table.
$table->attach($frame1, 0, 1, 0, 1);
$table->attach($frame2, 1, 2, 0, 1);
$table->attach($frame3, 0, 1, 1, 2);
$table->attach($frame4, 1, 2, 1, 2);

// Show everything.
$window->show_all();
gtk::main();
?>
```

In this example, four scrolled windows are created and added to four frames. Each frame is then attached to a table. Each of the four frames is given a different placement by calling set_placement. Along with set_policy, set_placement gives a great degree of control over how and where scrollbars appear in a scrolled window.

Setting a Shadow

The final customization that you can make to a GtkScrolledWindow is to set a shadow around the child widget. Setting a shadow around a scrolled window's child widget helps it to stand out a little from the rest of the application.

You can set the shadow by using set_shadow_type and passing a shadow type constant. These constants are the same as the constants used to set the border on a frame: Gtk::SHADOW_IN, Gtk::SHADOW_OUT, Gtk::SHADOW_ETCHED_IN, and Gtk::SHADOW_ETCHED_OUT. Figure 10-4 shows what each of these shadow types looks like. As you can see from the different windows, the name of the shadow type refers to the position of the window, not the scrollbars.

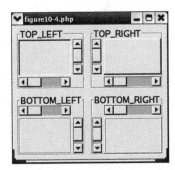

Figure 10-4. *Different shadow types in a GtkScrolledWindow*

View Ports

Just because a widget doesn't have native scrollbar support doesn't mean that it can't be scrolled. Widgets other than GtkTreeView and GtkTextView can extend over their bounds. Containers in particular tend to expand more than the developers originally intended. Unfortunately, widgets without native scrollbar support cannot be added to a GtkScrolledWindow. That is where GtkViewPort steps in.

GtkViewPort is a widget that has native scrollbar support, designed to hold other widgets and make them scrollable. GtkViewPort is a bin container that provides the tools needed to allow its child to be scrolled. You can use the view port within a scrolled window to add scrollbars that determine which part of the child should be shown.

By themselves, view ports do not make a widget scrollable. GtkViewPort is simply a container that implements native scrollbar support, meaning that adding a widget to a view port doesn't accomplish much unless the view port is then added to GtkScrolledWindow.

Creating and using a GtkViewPort is rather easy. Listing 10-3 shows the code needed to add a table to a view port.

Listing 10-3. *Adding Scrollbars Using a GtkViewPort*

```php
<?php
// Create and set up a window.
$window = new GtkWindow();
$window->connect_simple('destroy', array('gtk', 'main_quit'));

// Add a table to the window.
$table = new GtkTable(1, 1);

// Add some stuff to the table that will make it large.
$label = new GtkLabel('This is a rather long label. Hopefully ' .
                      'the table will scroll now.');

// Attach the label.
$table->attach($label, 0, 1, 0, 1);

// Create the view port.
$viewPort = new GtkViewPort();

// Create the scrolled window.
$sWindow = new GtkScrolledWindow();

// Add the table to the view port.
$viewPort->add($table);

// Add the view port to the scrolled window.
$sWindow->add($viewPort);

// Add the scrolled window to the main window.
$window->add($sWindow);
```

```
// Show everything.
$window->show_all();
gtk::main();
?>
```

■Tip Adding scrolling capabilities to a widget doesn't even have to be as complicated as Listing 10-3. The steps of creating a view port and adding it to a scrolled window can be consolidated. GtkScrolledWindow has a method named add_with_viewport. This method takes a widget and creates a view port for it automatically. The widget is then added to the view port, and the view port is added to the scrolled window.

Only two lines are required to add scrollbars to the table. The first adds the table to the view port, and the second adds the view port to a scrolled window. The rest of the code in the example, aside from instantiating the view port and scrolled window, is set up for creating a table that will need to scroll. You determine if and where the scrollbars will appear in the view port in the same way as you do for the tree view, as described in the previous section. Figure 10-5 shows the result of running this code.

Figure 10-5. *A GtkTable inside a GtkViewPort*

■Note GtkViewPort automatically adds a shadow to its child widget of type Gtk::SHADOW_IN. You can change this by calling set_shadow_type on the view port. You can also set a shadow for the GtkScrolledWindow in which the view port resides. This will cause a double border effect.

Custom Scrolling

Everything in PHP-GTK is designed to give flexibility to the developer. Scrolling is no exception. You have total control over how a widget reacts when the user clicks a scrollbar. In fact, you don't even need to use a scrolled window or a view port.

When you use a scrolled window, the widget inside must listen to the scrolled window, but the way that a scrolled window controls a widget may be undesirable. For instance, scrolling the product tree in the previous examples moves the window by fractions of a row each time the user clicks the scroll arrows. Showing a fraction of a row isn't very helpful to the user. It would be better if the widget scrolled by whole rows, so that the user sees the entire text of the first row. That is why GtkScrollbar widgets exist as their own classes and are not built into GtkScrolledWindow.

Let's take a look at what it takes to implement custom scrolling for the Crisscott_Tools_ ProductTree class. To provide scrolling for a widget requires a little bit of insight into how scrollbars actually work.

Creating the Scrollbar

GtkScrollbar is an abstract class that provides the basics for GtkHScrollbar and GtkVScrollbar. Scrollbars are only the visual component to scrolling. They work in conjunction with a GtkAdjustment. The adjustment manages the value and bounds of the scrollbar, while the scrollbar provides the visual representation of the value and communicates with the user. Every scrollbar has an adjustment that keeps track of the value and makes sure that the value stays within a certain range. The adjustment should be passed to the scrollbar on construction.

Listing 10-4 shows how to create a vertical scrollbar. Instantiating the scrollbar is the easy part. It's creating the adjustment that can be tricky.

Listing 10-4. *Creating a GtkVScrollbar*

```php
<?php
// Create an array consisting of the tree path.
function createPathArray($model, $path, $iter, $pathArray)
{
  $pathArray[0][] = $path;
  return false;
}

// Create a reasonably sized window to display the view.
$window = new GtkWindow();
$window->set_size_request(150, 150);
$window->connect_simple('destroy', array('gtk', 'main_quit'));

// First create a model and view.
require_once 'Crisscott/Tools/ProductTree.php';
$view = Crisscott_Tools_ProductTree::singleton();
$view->expand_all();

// Make the headers unclickable.
$view->set_headers_clickable(false);

$pathArray = array();
$view->get_model()->foreach('createPathArray', array(&$pathArray));

// Create the special vscrollbar.
$lower = $value = 0;
$upper = count($pathArray);
$step = 1;
$page = 6;
$size = 1;
```

```
// Create the adjustment and add it to a scrollbar.
$adj = new GtkAdjustment($value, $lower, $upper, $step, $page, $size);
$vScroll = new GtkVScrollbar($adj)
?>
```

An adjustment is nothing more than a collection of numbers that determine how the scrollbar will appear and function. Listing 10-4 shows how these values are collected from the product tree. An adjustment requires six numbers:

- value: The value is simply set to 0 because the initial view should start at the beginning. The value of the adjustment is used to mark a tree path as selected. Look at the call to foreach on the view's model. The callback builds an array of tree paths. Because foreach works in a depth-first manner, the array will be built with the first row shown as the first element and the last row shown as the last element. Changing the scrollbar's value to 5 will scroll to the path defined by the array element with an index of 5.

- lower: The lower bound is set to 0 because that is the lowest index in the array.

- upper: The upper bound is set to the number of elements in the array.

- step: The step size is the amount the value should change when the user clicks the arrows in the scrollbar. This is set to 1.

- page: The page increment is the amount the value should change when the user clicks the empty space in the scrollbar. This is set to 6. This means that the selected row will be six rows up or down when the user pages the view.

- size: The page size is set to 1 so that the scrollbar is allowed to move through the entire list.

With these settings, the custom scrollbar is now ready to control the tree view.

Creating the Signal Handlers

To make the newly created scrollbar control the GtkTreeView, you need a few signal handlers. Listing 10-5 creates a signal handler for the scrollbar created in the previous listing. This signal handler connects the adjustment's value-changed signal to the scrollView function.

Listing 10-5. *Creating the Signal Handler That Makes the View Scroll*

```php
<?php
// Function to scroll to and select a top level row.
function scrollView($adj, $view, $pathArray)
{
  // Create a path to a top level row.
  $path = $pathArray[$adj->get_value()];
  // Set the cursor at that path.
  $view->set_cursor($path, $view->get_column(0), false);
  // Grab focus so that the cell is selected.
  $view->grab_focus();
}
```

```
// Connect the scrollbar to the view so that it scrolls.
$adj->connect('value_changed', 'scrollView', $view, $pathArray);
$adj->value_changed();
?>
```

By default, the callback is passed the adjustment whose value has been changed. The call to connect in this example also passes the view and the array of tree paths created earlier. When the value-changed signal is fired and the callback is called, the cursor of the view is set to the path with the index equal to the adjustment's value. Notice also that the view is told to grab the keyboard focus. This is because the row cannot be selected unless the view has the focus. After the signal handler is created, the value_changed method of the adjustment is called. This method forces the adjustment to emit the value-changed signal whether or not its value has actually changed. Calling value_changed calls the callback method and selects the first row in the view.

It is important not only that the scrollbar communicates with the target widget, but also that the target widget communicates with the scrollbar. If the user selects a different row than the one selected by scrolling, the scrollbar's value needs to be updated so that when the user wants to scroll again, the scrollbar picks up from where the user left off. The scrollbar also needs to know when a row has been added or removed. Changing the model will require changing the adjustment bounds.

Listing 10-6 creates the signal handler to make sure that the adjustment stays in sync with the widget. It listens for the changed signal from GtkTreeSelection. The changed signal is emitted whenever the selection of the view *may* have changed. The changed signal can be emitted even though nothing has changed in the view. This isn't that big of a deal in most cases, including Listing 10-6.

Listing 10-6. *Creating the Signal Handler That Keeps the Widget and Adjustment Synchronized*

```php
<?php
// Update the scrollbar based on the adjustment.
function setScrollValue($selection, $adj, $pathArray)
{
  list($model, $iter) = $selection->get_selected();
  $path = $model->get_path($iter);
  $adj->set_value(array_search($path, $pathArray));
}

// Connect the selection to the scrollbar.
$view->get_selection()->connect('changed', 'setScrollValue', $adj, $pathArray);
?>
```

In Listing 10-6, the changed signal is connected to the setScrollValue. Whenever the selected row might have changed, setScrollValue will be called and passed the selection, the adjustment, and the array of tree paths. setScrollValue then looks for the selected path in the tree path array and sets the adjustment's value to the array index. This signal handler makes sure that the adjustment and target widget are always in sync if the user navigates using the view instead of the scrollbar.

Finally, the adjustment must be modified every time the model is updated. This calls for three more signal handlers: one for when a row is added to the model, one for when a row is removed from the model, and one for when the rows are reordered. When each of these actions occurs, the array of tree paths must be updated to accurately represent the model.

Listing 10-7 begins by first defining a method to create the tree path array. Next, three signal handlers are created: one each for when rows are inserted, deleted, or reordered.

Listing 10-7. *Creating the Signal Handlers to Keep the Model and the Adjustment Synchronized*

```php
<?php
// Update the adjustment to keep in sync with the model.
function updateArrayAdj($model, $array, $adjustment)
{
    // Rebuild the array.
    $model()->foreach('createPathArray', array(&$pathArray));
    // Update the adjustment.
    $adjustment->upper = count($array);
}

// Rebuild the array when a new row is added.
$view->get_model()->connect_simple('row-inserted',  'updateArrayAdj',
                                    $view->get_model(), $pathArray, $adj);
$view->get_model()->connect_simple('row-deleted',   'updateArrayAdj',
                                    $view->get_model(), $pathArray, $adj);
$view->get_model()->connect_simple('rows-reordered', 'updateArrayAdj',
                                    $view->get_model(), $pathArray, $adj);
?>
```

Tip The scrolling that has been implemented in the preceding examples requires the tree to be fully expanded. It would be a good idea when implementing this in a real-world application to scroll only to the rows that are visible or to expand the hidden rows automatically.

These signal handlers connect their respective signals to the createTreePathArray method. It is easier in this case to maintain one method that re-creates the array each time than it is to create three methods that modify the array. If the model becomes very large, this approach may need to be reworked slightly, but for purposes of this example, it works just fine. These three signal handlers ensure that the model and the adjustment stay synchronized when the model is modified.

In summary, when setting up custom scrolling for a widget, you must take three steps:

1. Set up the adjustment to properly represent the target widget (Listing 10-5).

2. Create a signal handler to scroll the target widget when the adjustment's value changes (Listing 10-6).

3. Create one or more signal handlers to make sure that the target widget and the adjustment stay synchronized (Listing 10-7).

It isn't difficult to accomplish these three steps and override the built-in scrolling abilities of many widgets or those added to a view port.

The ability to control how a widget is scrolled is more powerful than it may first appear. Aside from controlling what data appears on the screen, implementing custom scrolling also allows the scrollbar to be separated from the target widget. The scrollbar in the preceding examples is not physically attached to the tree view. It could be placed on the other side of the application. And you don't even need to use a GtkHScrollbar or GtkVScrollbar for this functionality. As long as the adjustment's value can be modified, you could use anything as the scrollbar. For example, a GtkSpinButton could easily be set up to act as a type of scrollbar.

Summary

This chapter was relatively short. Scrolling in PHP-GTK 2 is typically easy to implement. Those widgets that have native scrollbar support can be added to a GtkScrolledWindow. Those that don't can be added to a GtkViewPort. These two widgets can satisfy most scrolling needs.

When a scrolled window or a view port just isn't enough, you can customize scrolling for a particular widget. The three steps for creating custom scrollbars are to set up a GtkAdjustment properly, make the adjustment scroll the target widget, and keep the adjustment and the target widget synchronized.

GtkScrolledWindow and GtkViewPort provide ease of use, while custom scrolling allows for near limitless flexibility.

In Chapter 11, we will add the final components to the main application window. First, we will add the menus that will provide interfaces for many of the applications features, such as saving data, transmitting the information to the Crisscott server, and quitting the application. Then we will move on to adding a toolbar. The toolbar will make some of the actions easily accessible by providing clickable icons that will call certain signal handlers. With these two features in place, the usability of the application will be greatly enhanced.

CHAPTER 11

■ ■ ■

Adding Menus and Toolbars

The final major pieces of the Crisscott PIMS user interface are the menus and toolbars. Menus and toolbars are widgets that provide a means for the user to initiate some action, such as saving a document, closing an application, or copying a block of text. Menus and toolbars are essentially different ways of representing a group of tasks. Menus dynamically hide and show a hierarchical grouping of actions; toolbars tend to be more static. Regardless of whether an action is represented in a menu or a toolbar, the idea is basically to allow the user to activate a segment of the application code.

In this chapter, you will learn how to create several types of menus and how to set up toolbars with various types of buttons. First, let's look at how to create menus, and then we will get into working with toolbars.

Menus

Menus are widgets responsible for organizing user tasks. Most GUI applications will have at least File and Help menus.

What makes a menu different from a toolbar is that a menu provides a hierarchical structure and can hide most of the actions when they are not needed. This makes menus perfect for organizing the user actions in an application, especially those actions that are not used very frequently. Because menus hide the actions when not in use, they can pack a lot of functionality into a relatively small space. In fact, menus can even be set up to detach from the application or seemingly appear out of nowhere.

Let's start with adding a rather simple menu to the Crisscott PIMS application. This menu will allow the users to close the application, save their work, and perform a few other tasks. By the end of this section, the menu will evolve into the menu shown in Figure 11-1.

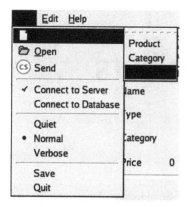

Figure 11-1. *A full-featured menu*

Creating Menu Bars

The most familiar part of an application menu is the menu bar. This is the persistent piece of the menu that doesn't change. Figure 11-2 shows a simple menu bar.

Figure 11-2. *A menu bar (GtkMenuBar)*

GtkMenuBar is a specialized container that holds GtkMenuItem items. A menu bar simply organizes the menu items. GtkMenuBar is a child class of GtkMenuShell, which provides a few methods for adding menu items. GtkMenuBar provides two methods for determining how the newly added items will be shown.

In Listing 11-1, three menu items are added to a menu bar:

- A Help menu item appended to (added to the end of) the menu bar using the append method

- A File menu item prepended to (added to the beginning of) the menu bar using the prepend method

- An Edit menu item added in the second position in the menu bar using the insert method

Listing 11-1. *Adding Items to GtkMenuBar*

```php
<?php
// Create a menu bar.
$menuBar = new GtkMenuBar();
```

```
// Create a help menu item.
$help = new GtkMenuItem('Help');
// Append it to the menu bar.
$menuBar->append($help);

// Create a file menu item.
$file = new GtkMenuItem('File');
// Prepend it to the menu bar.
$menuBar->prepend($file);

// Create an edit menu item.
$edit = new GtkMenuItem('Edit');
// Insert it into the menu bar.
$menuBar->insert($edit, 1);
?>
```

As you can see, the append, prepend, and insert methods each take a GtkMenuItem and add it to the menu bar.

Adding Menus

GtkMenu is similar to GtkMenuBar in that it also extends GtkMenuShell. A GtkMenu is a container that can accept only GtkMenuItem widgets. Whereas a GtkMenuBar is a static fixture, a GtkMenu is not always visible. GtkMenu is often used as a submenu for a menu item (more on menu items in the next section).

Normally, when a menu item from a menu bar is activated, a GtkMenu widget drops down. If a menu item from a GtkMenu is activated, sometimes another GtkMenu pops up. Think of your favorite web browser. Most web browsers have a menu bar at the top with items like File, Edit, and Help. When you click one of those items, a menu drops down with more options. Depending on which browser you use, you may have a View menu with a Zoom or Text Zoom option. In the Mozilla Firefox browser, the Text Zoom option pops up another menu with different zoom options. Both the drop-down and pop-up menus are examples of GtkMenu.

You create a GtkMenu instance by using the new operator. When a GtkMenu is created, it is automatically placed inside a GtkWindow. This window is not a top-level window, but rather a pop-up window. This means that when a menu is created, it should not be added to any other container widgets. Doing so will produce an error message. (Refer to Chapter 5 if you need to review the difference between a pop-up and top-level window.)

After a GtkMenu is created, menu items should be added. You add items to a GtkMenu in the same way that you add items to a GtkMenuBar—by using append, prepend, and insert. GtkMenu also has one additional method for adding menu items called attach.

The attach method functions very similarly to that of GtkTable. Using attach allows you to create menus with multiple rows and columns. Its first argument is the menu item to attach. The next four arguments are the same as those in GtkTable::attach. They define the four rows and columns to which to attach the menu item. Listing 11-2 shows how to attach a menu item.

Listing 11-2. *Creating a GtkMenu Widget and Attaching GtkMenuItem Items*

```php
<?php
// Create a menu bar.
$menuBar = new GtkMenuBar();

// Create a help menu item.
$help = new GtkMenuItem('Help');
// Append it to the menu bar.
$menuBar->append($help);

// Create a file menu item.
$file = new GtkMenuItem('File');
// Prepend it to the menu bar.
$menuBar->prepend($file);

// Create a menu.
$fileMenu = new GtkMenu();
// Create four menu items to be added to the file menu.
$new     = new GtkMenuItem('New');
$open    = new GtkMenuItem('Open');
$save    = new GtkMenuItem('Save');
$edit    = new GtkMenuItem('Edit');

// Attach the four items to the menu.
$fileMenu->attach($new,  0, 1, 0, 1);
$fileMenu->attach($open, 1, 2, 0, 1);
$fileMenu->attach($save, 0, 1, 1, 2);
$fileMenu->attach($edit, 1, 2, 1, 2);

// Add the file menu to the file item.
$file->set_submenu($fileMenu);

// Create an edit menu item.
$edit = new GtkMenuItem('Edit');
// Insert it into the menu bar.
$menuBar->insert($edit, 1);

// Create a window and add the menu.
$window = new GtkWindow();
$window->connect_simple('destroy', array('Gtk', 'main_quit'));
$window->add($menuBar);
$window->show_all();
Gtk::main();
?>
```

Figure 11-3 shows the menu that Listing 11-2 produces. Notice how the menu items in the File menu are positioned in two columns instead of just one.

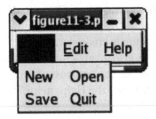

Figure 11-3. *GtkMenu with two columns of GtkMenuItem items*

Creating Menu Items

The real power of menus is in GtkMenuItem. Menu items are the selectable icons and text of the menu. GtkMenuItem widgets are the only valid children of GtkMenu and GtkMenuBar. GtkMenuItem is itself a container. It is a descendant of GtkBin, which was first discussed in Chapter 3. This means that it can take one child widget.

Creating menu items is pretty simple. Listing 11-3 creates a menu bar with three menu items.

Listing 11-3. *Creating GtkMenuItem Items*

```php
<?php
// Create a menu bar.
$menuBar = new GtkMenuBar();

// Create a file menu item.
$file = new GtkMenuItem();
$file->add(new GtkLabel('File'));
// Prepend it to the menu bar.
$menuBar->prepend($file);

// Create an edit menu item.
$edit = new GtkMenuItem('Edit');
// Insert it into the menu bar.
$menuBar->append($edit);

// Create a help menu item.
$help = new GtkMenuItem('_Help');
// Append it to the menu bar.
$menuBar->append($help);

// Create a window and add the menu.
$window = new GtkWindow();
$window->connect_simple('destroy', array('Gtk', 'main_quit'));
$window->add($menuBar);
$window->show_all();
Gtk::main();
?>
```

The first menu item is created using the new operator with no arguments. After it is created, a GtkLabel with the text 'File' is added. The second menu item is created by passing the menu item's label text, 'Edit', at the time of construction. The third menu item is created in a similar manner to the second. The label is passed on construction, but it is also given a mnemonic. Recall from Chapter 7 that a mnemonic is a keyboard shortcut. Therefore, the text passed for the third menu item is '_Help'. This means that pressing Alt+H will activate the Help menu.

Tip By default, the label for a GtkMenuItem is left justified. You can make the label right justified by passing true to set_right_justified for that menu item.

A menu item's primary responsibility is to handle events from the user. Menu items are used to trigger events. When a menu item is clicked, or activated, one of two things usually happens: either some programmatic action is initiated or a submenu appears. Regardless of what the menu item is configured to do, its action is triggered by the activate signal. The activate signal is emitted when the menu item is clicked (or the activate method is called). If the menu item consists of a submenu, PHP-GTK will automatically create a signal handler that shows the submenu when the item is clicked. If there is no submenu, you must create a signal handler to call the method associated with the menu item.

Adding Submenus

Take a look at Listing 11-4, which contains the initial code for the Crisscott PIMS application. First, the menu bar parent constructor is called. Next, two menu items are added to the menu bar. Both items are created with mnemonics to make activating them a little easier. At this stage, activating the items would do nothing. There are no signal handlers created and there are no submenus. Therefore, the next step is to create and add a submenu. The submenu is created by using the new operator and adding a few menu items. Then, set_submenu is called on the File menu item. Another submenu is created and added to the Help menu.

Listing 11-4. *Adding Submenus to GtkMenuItem*

```php
<?php
class Crisscott_Tools_Menu extends GtkMenuBar {


    public $file;


    public $help;

    public function __construct()
    {
        // Call the parent constructor.
        parent::__construct();
```

```
        // Add two menu items.
        $this->file = new GtkMenuItem('_File');
        $this->append($this->file);

        $this->help = new GtkMenuItem('_Help');
        $this->append($this->help);

        // Create the submenus.
        $this->createSubMenus();
    }

    protected function createSubMenus()
    {
        // Create the file menu and items.
        $fileMenu = new GtkMenu();
        $new      = new GtkMenuItem('New');
        $open     = new GtkMenuItem('Open');
        $save     = new GtkMenuItem('Save');
        $quit     = new GtkMenuItem('Quit');

        // Add the four items to the file menu.
        $fileMenu->append($new);
        $fileMenu->append($open);
        $fileMenu->append($save);
        $fileMenu->append($quit);

        // Create the help menu and items.
        $helpMenu = new GtkMenu();
        $help     = new GtkMenuItem('Help');
        $about    = new GtkMenuItem('About');

        // Add both items to the help menu.
        $helpMenu->append($help);
        $helpMenu->append($about);

        // Make the two menus submenus for the menu items.
        $this->file->set_submenu($fileMenu);
        $this->help->set_submenu($helpMenu);
    }
}
?>
```

Now when one of the menu bar's menu items is activated, the attached submenu will drop down. Figure 11-4 shows the menu bar when the File menu has been activated.

Figure 11-4. *An activated menu item (GtkMenuItem) with a submenu*

Creating a Signal Handler for a Menu Item

When activated, a GtkMenuItem doesn't have to pop up a GtkMenu. Instead, it can initiate some method call. This is done by connecting the activate signal of the menu item to a callback.

For example, the Quit menu item in the Crisscott_Tools_Menu class should shut down the application. It should check that the user has saved the work, and then close the application. Listing 11-5 shows the rather simple code for creating the signal handler responsible for closing the application.

Listing 11-5. *Creating a Signal Handler for GtkMenuItem*

```php
<?php
class Crisscott_Tools_Menu extends GtkMenuBar {
    //...
    protected function createSubMenus()
    {
        // Create the file menu and items.
        $fileMenu = new GtkMenu();
        // ...
        $quit    = new GtkMenuItem('Quit');

        // Add the four items to the file menu.
        // ...
        $fileMenu->append($quit);

        // Connect some signal handlers.
        $quit->connect_simple('activate', array('Crisscott_MainWindow', 'quit'));
        // ...
    }
}
```

```
class Crisscott_MainWindow extends GtkWindow {
    // ...
    static public function quit()
    {
        // Check to see if the data has been modified
        // or sent. If it is modified or not sent, don't
        // exit.
        if (!self::$modified && self::$sent) {
            Gtk::main_quit();
            return true;
        }
        return false;
    }
}
?>
```

The callback method first checks a few flags in the main application window before closing the window. If the flags don't show that the user has saved the work and sent the data off to
the Crisscott server, the main loop is not exited. In Chapter 14, we will expand this callback to
pop up a dialog box, instead of just exiting without closing the window.

Using Separator, Image, Check, and Radio Menu Items

Menu items can also improve usability by adhering to standards that users are accustomed to
seeing on application menus. Instead of requiring developers to modify the menu item or create
their own version of standard items, PHP-GTK provides four specialized menu item classes that
you can use: GtkSeparatorMenuItem, GtkImageMenuItem, GtkCheckMenuItem, and GtkRadioMenuItem.
Figure 11-5 shows what each of these items looks like.

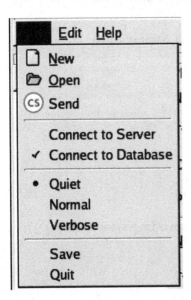

Figure 11-5. *The four specialized GtkMenuItem subclasses*

The classes create the following types of menu items:

Image menu item: The first items in the menu shown in Figure 11-5 are image menu items. An image menu item is an instance of GtkImageMenuItem. A GtkImageMenuItem provides a label like a regular menu item, but also provides a place for a small icon to be shown next to the label. Once created, an image menu item functions just like a regular menu item. It can be activated and can even contain a submenu.

Separator menu item: The simplest class, GtkSeparatorMenuItem, creates a separator item. A separator item is not designed to be activated like other menu items. Instead, it is merely decorative. The menu shown in Figure 11-5 has three separator items. They are the lines that break up the three groups of other menu items.

Check menu item: The next items in Figure 11-5 are a group of check menu items, created with GtkCheckMenuItem. Menu items can not only initiate an action, but they can also represent a current state. A GtkCheckMenuItem is used when the action it initiates is represented by a Boolean state, such as turning on or off an application feature. A check menu item is similar to an image menu item in that it may have an image displayed to the left of the item text. However, the image cannot be set by the developer. The image is a check mark that is toggled every time the menu item is activated. The check mark indicates the menu item's state. If the check mark is visible, the menu item is "on." If the check mark is not visible, the menu item is "off."

Radio menu item: The other type of menu item is GtkRadioMenuItem, which is a descendant of GtkCheckMenuItem. The difference between the two is that if a radio menu item is associated with another radio menu item, only one of the menu items may be checked at a time. If one radio menu item is checked and another in its group is activated, the first becomes unchecked. A group of radio menu items is useful to control a collection of mutually exclusive application features. For instance, Figure 11-5 uses radio menu items for Quiet, Normal, and Verbose options. These control how much output an application produces. Obviously, an application cannot be quiet and verbose at the same time.

Listing 11-6 shows how the menu items shown in Figure 11-5 were created.

Listing 11-6. *Creating Specialized Menu Items*

```php
<?php
    protected function createSubMenus()
    {
        // Create the file menu and items.
        $fileMenu = new GtkMenu();
        $new     = new GtkImageMenuItem(Gtk::STOCK_NEW);
        $open    = new GtkImageMenuItem(Gtk::STOCK_OPEN);
        $send    = new GtkImageMenuItem('Send');
        $send->set_image(GtkImage::new_from_file('Crisscott/images/menuItem.png'));
        $save    = new GtkMenuItem('Save');
        $quit    = new GtkMenuItem('Quit');

        // Add the four items to the file menu.
        $fileMenu->append($new);
```

```php
$fileMenu->append($open);
$fileMenu->append($send);

// Add a separator.
$fileMenu->append(new GtkSeparatorMenuItem());

// Add some check items.
$server   = new GtkCheckMenuItem('Connect to Server');
$database = new GtkCheckMenuItem('Connect to Database');

$fileMenu->append($server);
$fileMenu->append($database);

// Add a separator.
$fileMenu->append(new GtkSeparatorMenuItem());

// Add three noise levels.
$quiet   = new GtkRadioMenuItem(null,   'Quiet');
$normal  = new GtkRadioMenuItem($quiet, 'Normal');
$verbose = new GtkRadioMenuItem($quiet, 'Verbose');

$fileMenu->append($quiet);
$fileMenu->append($normal);
$fileMenu->append($verbose);

// Add a separator.
$fileMenu->append(new GtkSeparatorMenuItem());

// Finish off the menu.
$fileMenu->append($save);
$fileMenu->append($quit);

// Connect some signal handlers.
$quit->connect_simple('activate', array('Crisscott_MainWindow', 'quit'));

// Create the help menu and items.
$helpMenu = new GtkMenu();
$help     = new GtkMenuItem('Help');
$about    = new GtkMenuItem('About');

// Add both items to the help menu.
$helpMenu->append($help);
$helpMenu->append($about);

// Make the two menus submenus for the menu items.
$this->file->set_submenu($fileMenu);
$this->help->set_submenu($helpMenu);
    }
}
?>
```

In most cases, GtkImageMenuItem items are created the same way as the first two in
Listing 11-6—from a stock ID. The static constructor new_from_stock takes a stock ID such as
Gtk::STOCK_SAVE or Gtk::STOCK_QUIT. While creating an image menu item from stock is convenient, it is not the only way to do this. The last image menu item created in Listing 11-6 is
a custom menu item used to send the inventory data to the Crisscott server. The menu item
is first created with just a label by passing the string 'Send' to the constructor. Next, an image is
set using set_image. The end result is a menu item with the Crisscott logo to the left of the label.

A GtkSeparatorMenuItem item comes next. Separator items cannot be activated by the
user, but they can be activated by the application. Using GtkSeparatorMenuItem for anything
other than decoration and to improve usability, while technically possible, is probably not the
best programming practice.

Next in Listing 11-6 are the GtkCheckMenuItem items. When a GtkCheckMenuItem is created,
a signal handler is automatically created. This signal handler connects the activate signal to
an internal method, which toggles the check mark. The basic functionality of this method is to
pass the opposite of get_active to set_active, which takes a Boolean value. If that value is
true, the signal handler makes the check mark visible. If the value is false, the check mark will
be hidden. set_active comes in handy if the state of the menu item doesn't reflect the current
state of the application. This is possible if, for example, a new file is loaded and it has a different setting than the previous file.

The last type of menu item in Listing 11-6 is GtkRadioMenuItem. When a GtkRadioMenuItem
item is created, the first argument the constructor expects is another GtkRadioMenuItem. Notice
in Listing 11-6 that the first radio menu item passes null as the first argument to the constructor.
The other two menu items pass the first menu item as their first argument. Doing so makes the
three radio menu items related. If one is activated, the other two will be deactivated.

These four menu item types allow you to build some very powerful menus with relative
ease. Of course, these classes can be extended to make very custom menus. Listing 11-7 is an
example of a class that extends GtkImageMenuItem.

Listing 11-7. *Creating a Custom Menu Item*

```php
<?php
class CrisscottCheckMenuItem extends GtkImageMenuItem {

    protected $active = true;

    public function __construct($label)
    {
        // Call the parent constructor.
        parent::__construct($label);

        // Create the signal handler that will toggle the image.
        $this->connect_simple('activate', array($this, 'toggle'));

        // Toggle the item to get into a known state.
        $this->toggle();
    }
```

```
    public function toggle()
    {
        // Determine the state.
        if ($this->active) {
            $image = GtkImage::new_from_file('Crisscott/images/menuItemGrey.png');
        } else {
            $image = GtkImage::new_from_file('Crisscott/images/menuItem.png');
        }
        $this->set_image($image);

        // Toggle the state.
        $this->active = !$this->active;
    }
}
?>
```

The class CrisscottCheckMenuItem creates a menu item similar to a GtkCheckMenuItem, but uses two versions of the Crisscott logo to indicate the menu item's state. A grayscale version is used to indicate the item is off, and a full-color version indicates that the item is on. The class doesn't do anything too complicated. It simply creates a signal handler for the activate signal. The callback for this signal handler checks a flag that tracks the state and updates the image accordingly. When this class is put to work in an application, it should be treated in the same way as GtkCheckMenuItem. Because it extends GtkImageMenuItem, it can be added directly to a menu or menu bar. Also, you can create other signal handlers for the activate signal to initiate the programmatic action a normal check menu item would produce.

Creating Tear-Off Menus

One more type of menu item behaves quite differently from the others. GtkTearoffMenuItem is a tear-off menu item that doesn't display any state information or call some application method. Instead, it detaches its parent menu from the application. A tear-off menu item is shown as a dotted line when the menu is activated. When the menu item is activated, the menu will detach from its parent and appear in its own window. When the tear-off menu item is activated again, the menu will disappear and reattach to its original parent. Figure 11-6 shows both states of a menu with a tear-off item.

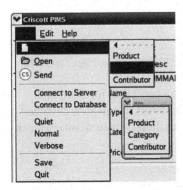

Figure 11-6. *The two states of a tear-off menu*

A tear-off menu is useful when a set of menu options needs to be accessed several times during the course of using an application. With a tear-off menu, the users don't have to dig through several levels of menu items to get to the items they need to use most often. When a menu is torn off, not only is it given its own top-level window, but that window is also set to be above all other application windows. This means that the menu will always be easily accessible until it is reattached.

Listing 11-8 is the code used to create the tear-off menu shown in Figure 11-6. The menu that is able to be torn off is the New menu item's submenu. Making this a tear-off menu allows the user to quickly access the menu items for creating new products, categories, and contacts.

Listing 11-8. *Creating a Tear-Off Menu*

```php
<?php
    protected function createSubMenus()
    {
        // ...

        // Create a submenu for the new item.
        $newMenu  = new GtkMenu();
        $product  = new GtkMenuItem('Product');
        $category = new GtkMenuItem('Category');
        $contrib  = new GtkMenuItem('Contributor');

        // Make the new menu detachable.
        $newMenu->append(new GtkTearoffMenuItem());
        $newMenu->append($product);
        $newMenu->append($category);
        $newMenu->append($contrib);

        // Set the title of the new menu.
        $newMenu->set_title('New');

        // Set the submenu.
        $new->set_submenu($newMenu);

        // ...
    }
?>
```

Making the menu detachable is a simple matter of adding GtkTearoffMenuItem. Once the menu item has been added, PHP-GTK will take care of the rest.

One feature that is useful for menus that can be torn off is the set_title method. This method takes a string that will be set to the title of the new window when the menu is detached. The title will help the user to identify the new window. If the menu item is created using a stock ID, as is the case in Listing 11-8, the title is set automatically.

Creating Context Menus

So far, the menus that we have looked at all start from a menu bar. Even though the menu might have been several levels down or may have been detached, to access it, the user would need to activate an item from a menu bar. As you might suspect, there are other ways to bring up a menu.

In most web browsers, you can right-click a web page to bring up a menu with options such as Save or View Source. This type of menu is called a *context menu* because it comes from and relates to the context of the application. Technically, these menus are no different from any of the GtkMenu widgets you have seen so far. What is different is the method in which the menus are accessed. Instead of starting from some static object on the screen, such as a menu bar, context menus appear to pop up out of nowhere.

Creating a context menu is the same as creating a regular menu. The difference is that a context menu must be popped up using a signal handler. Listing 11-9 shows how a signal handler might be created for a pop-up menu, as well as a callback that can be used to bring the menu to the screen.

Listing 11-9. *Making a Context Menu Pop Up*

```php
<?php
function popupContext($widget, $event, $menu)
{
  // Make sure the event was a button press.
  if ($event->type == Gdk::BUTTON_PRESS) {
    // See if button three was pressed.
    if ($event->button == 3) {
      // Pop up the menu.
      $menu->popup(null, null, null, $event->button, $event->time);
      return true;
    }
  }
  return false;
}

$contextMenu = new GtkMenu();
// Set up the menu...

$contextArea = new GtkTextView();
$contextArea->connect('button-press-event', 'popupContext', $contextMenu);
// ...
?>
```

Notice that the signal handler is not created by the menu itself. The idea is that the user clicks some other part of the application to bring up the menu. Creating the signal handler with the menu object would require the user to click the menu to pop it up. Obviously, that isn't possible.

The callback in Listing 11-9 will be called whenever a button-press-event signal is emitted. Because there are not individual signals for each mouse button, the callback must check to see which button was pressed. This is done by checking the button property of the event object that is automatically passed. In this case, the context menu should be shown only when button 3 is pressed. If button 3 is pressed, the callback then calls the popup method of the menu that has been passed in.

Because popup serves two purposes (user-generated code and system-generated code like GtkMenu widgets), a few arguments are required, but they are not really useful as far as context menus go. The first three arguments to popup are all passed as null because they don't make much sense for context menus. These arguments are used to position the menu in relation to a parent menu and are used by PHP-GTK to bring up child menus. The last two arguments are information about the event that triggered the callback. The second-to-last argument is the number of the button that was pressed to trigger the event. If the callback was triggered by some event other than a button-press-event, this argument should be set to 0. The last argument is the time that the event occurred. The time is taken rather easily from the event's time property.

There is no need for a callback to hide the menu, as this is done automatically when the user clicks somewhere else in the application or activates a menu item (unless that menu item brings up a submenu, in which case the menu will remain visible until the submenu is closed).

Setting up a context menu is pretty simple. In all of Listing 11-9, only one GtkMenu method is called. The callback in this example can be easily applied to any context menu in the application.

Figure 11-7 shows what this simple application looks like with the context menu.

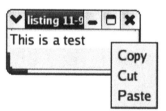

Figure 11-7. *A context menu in action*

Toolbars

A toolbar is similar to a menu in that it exists to give users the ability to initiate some set of predefined actions. Most web browsers have a toolbar near the top of the application that provides items for moving forward or backward in the page history, go to the home page, and print the current page. Another similarity is that GtkToolbar is a special container that can hold only one type of child. In the case of GtkToolbar, the only acceptable widget is GtkToolItem or one of its descendants.

One of the main differences between GtkMenu and GtkToolbar is that a toolbar is generally static. The items in a toolbar do not need to be popped up from another item, as is usually the case with a menu. That isn't to say that a toolbar can't change or be dynamic. In fact, a toolbar can include items that have menus, can have context menus, and can even be detached from the application.

Creating a Toolbar

Adding a toolbar to an application first requires instantiating GtkToolbar. GtkToolbar is the container that is used to lay out and display a collection of GtkToolItem items. The items in a toolbar are displayed one after another. The items that are shown in the toolbar will remain visible and easily accessible. This makes a toolbar a good place to put items for actions that the user is likely to need often. For instance, a Save button is one of the most common items found in a toolbar.

Figure 11-8 shows two instances of GtkToolbar. Both toolbars have the same items, but one toolbar orients them horizontally and the other vertically.

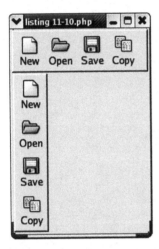

Figure 11-8. *Two GtkToolbar instances*

Creating a toolbar is easy. Simply instantiate a new object using the new operator; the constructor doesn't take any parameters. The more interesting methods of GtkToolbar control how the toolbar is displayed and how it manages the items. As shown in Figure 11-8, a toolbar can display items either horizontally or vertically. You can control the direction in which the items appear by using the set_orientation method. set_orientation takes either a Gtk::ORIENTATION_HORIZONTAL or Gtk::ORIENTATION_VERTICAL argument and displays the items accordingly.

Regardless of how the items are shown, they may not all fit on the toolbar. When there isn't enough room, an overflow menu holds the toolbar items that cannot be shown in the space allotted. An overflow menu looks like a toolbar button with an arrow. You can turn off the overflow menu by passing false to set_show_arrow. If the overflow menu is turned off, the extra items will not be shown.

Listing 11-10 shows how to create a toolbar that shows its items vertically and disables the overflow menu.

Listing 11-10. *Creating a Vertical Toolbar Without an Overflow Menu*

```php
<?php
$window = new GtkWindow();
$window->connect_simple('destroy', array('Gtk', 'main_quit'));
```

```
// Create a vertical toolbar.
$vToolBar = new GtkToolbar();
$vToolBar->set_orientation(Gtk::ORIENTATION_VERTICAL);

// Turn off the overflow.
$vToolBar->set_show_arrow(false);

// Set the toolbar to show icons next to text.
$vToolBar->set_style(Gtk::TOOLBAR_BOTH_HORIZ);

// Add a new item.
$new = GtkToolButton::new_from_stock(Gtk::STOCK_NEW);
$vToolBar->add($new);

// Add an open item.
$open = GtkToolButton::new_from_stock(Gtk::STOCK_OPEN);
$vToolBar->add($open);

// Add a save item.
$save = GtkToolButton::new_from_stock(Gtk::STOCK_SAVE);
$vToolBar->add($save);

// Add a copy item.
$copy = GtkToolButton::new_from_stock(Gtk::STOCK_COPY);
$vToolBar->add($copy);

// Pack the toolbar into a box.
$hBox = new GtkHBox();
$hBox->pack_start($vToolBar, false, false);

// Show everything.
$window->add($hBox);
$window->show_all();
Gtk::main();
?>
```

A toolbar shows toolbar items, which can include both icons and text. The toolbar can control which parts of the item are shown; that is, the toolbar can show only the items, only the text, or both. You can control which piece of the item is shown by using the set_style method. set_style takes a toolbar style as the only argument, as follows:

- Gtk::TOOLBAR_ICONS: Shows only the icons of the items.
- Gtk::TOOLBAR_TEXT: Shows only the text of the items.
- Gtk::TOOLBAR_BOTH: Displays the text beneath the icon.
- Gtk::TOOLBAR_BOTH_HORIZ: Displays the text to the right of the icon.

In Listing 11-10, the toolbar is set to display both text and icons horizontally.

Caution If the toolbar style is not overridden using `set_style`, the user's system preferences will be used. Keep in mind that by using `set_style`, you are overriding the user's preferred display style.

Adding Tooltips

When a toolbar is set to show only the item icons, it can be difficult for a user to know exactly what clicking the icon will do. You can help users by adding tooltips. A *tooltip* is a small label that pops up to provide a more verbose description of an object.

You can apply a tooltip to many different type of widgets, as long as the widget has its own GtkWindow. You create tooltips by first instantiating a new GtkTooltips object. A GtkTooltips object is a group of tooltips. Next, you add a tooltip to the group for each toolbar item using set_tip. The set_tip method takes the item the tip is for, the tip to be shown, and an optional string containing more information that might be helpful for the user.

Unfortunately, tooltips for toolbar items are created slightly differently than they are for most widgets. GtkToolItem does not have its own GtkWindow. This means that it cannot receive enter and leave events. Without these events, it is impossible for an application to know when to show a tooltip. Fortunately, the widgets within a GtkToolItem item can receive enter and leave events. This means that they can be used to show the tooltip. Instead of requiring users to dig through the children of the tool item, GtkToolItem provides a method that makes it much easier to assign a tooltip to a button. The set_tooltip method takes a GtkTooltips object and a string as arguments. The string is the tooltip to be displayed.

Listing 11-11 creates a toolbar and adds tooltips for each item.

Listing 11-11. *Creating a Toolbar with Tooltips*

```php
<?php
$window = new GtkWindow();
$window->connect_simple('destroy', array('Gtk', 'main_quit'));

// Create a horizontal toolbar.
$hToolBar = new GtkToolbar();

// Add a new item.
$new = GtkToolButton::new_from_stock(Gtk::STOCK_NEW);
$hToolBar->add($new);

// Add an open item.
$open = GtkToolButton::new_from_stock(Gtk::STOCK_OPEN);
$hToolBar->add($open);

// Add a save item.
$save = GtkToolButton::new_from_stock(Gtk::STOCK_SAVE);
$hToolBar->add($save);
```

```php
// Add a copy item.
$copy = GtkToolButton::new_from_stock(Gtk::STOCK_COPY);
$hToolBar->add($copy);

// Add tooltips.
$tooltips = new GtkTooltips();

// Create a tooltip for each item.
$new->set_tooltip($tooltips,  'New',  'Creates a new product.');
$open->set_tooltip($tooltips, 'Open', 'Open an existing inventory file.');
$save->set_tooltip($tooltips, 'Save', 'Saves the current inventory.');
$copy->set_tooltip($tooltips, 'Copy', 'Copies a product.');

// Make sure the toolbar is set to display tooltips.
$hToolBar->set_tooltips(true);

// Only show the icons, not the text.
$hToolBar->set_style(Gtk::TOOLBAR_ICONS);

// Pack the toolbar into a box.
$vBox = new GtkVBox();
$vBox->pack_start($hToolBar, false, false);

// Show everything.
$window->add($vBox);
$window->show_all();
Gtk::main();
?>
```

Figure 11-9 shows what this toolbar looks like with the tooltip for the Save item displayed.

Figure 11-9. *A toolbar with tooltips*

Adding Tool Buttons

As with menus, the real workhorse of toolbars is not the container but the items that go in it. The only items allowed in a GtkToolbar are those that extend GtkToolItem. The most powerful of these objects is the GtkToolButton. A tool button is basically an icon with a label that can be added to a toolbar. Tool buttons are clickable and are most often used to initiate some programmatic action, just as menu items are used.

The easiest way to create a tool button is to use a stock ID. Just as menu items and buttons can be created from stock items, so can toolbar items. Using stock items makes it easy to adhere to common practices that will help users to use and understand the application. You create a stock tool button by calling the static constructor new_from_stock and passing a stock ID such as Gtk::STOCK_SAVE.

After you've created a tool button, you can add it to a toolbar by passing it to the toolbar's add method. However, adding a tool button to a toolbar is not the last step. At this point, if the user were to click the button, nothing would happen. You must create a signal handler that connects the button's clicked signal to a callback.

Listing 11-12 shows the code that creates a stock item, adds it to a toolbar, and creates a signal handler.

Listing 11-12. *Creating a Stock Tool Button and an Appropriate Signal Handler*

```php
<?php
// Create a new toolbar.
$toolbar = new GtkToolbar();

// Add a stock quit item.
$quit = GtkToolButton::new_from_stock(Gtk::STOCK_QUIT);
$toolbar->add($quit);

// Create a signal handler.
$quit->connect_simple('clicked', array('Gtk', 'main_quit'));
?>
```

Creating Custom Tool Buttons

You don't have to create tool buttons from stock. To create a unique tool button, just add an icon and label to an empty tool button. Listing 11-13 creates a custom Send tool button using a Crisscott logo icon. The button will be used in the application to allow the users to transmit their inventory data to the Crisscott server.

Listing 11-13. *Creating a Custom Tool Button*

```php
<?php
// Create a new toolbar.
$toolbar = new GtkToolbar();

// Create an empty button.
$crisscott = new GtkToggleToolButton();

// Add an icon.
$icon = GtkImage::new_from_file('Crisscott/images/menuItemGrey.png');
$crisscott->set_icon_widget($icon);

// Create a special label.
$crisscottLabel = new GtkLabel('Send data to Crisscott');
$crisscottLabel->set_ellipsize(Pango::ELLIPSIZE_START);
```

```
// Set the label widget.
$crisscott->set_label_widget($crisscottLabel);

// Add the tool button.
$toolbar->add($crisscott);
?>
```

Creating the button is a simple three-step process:

1. Create an empty tool button using the new operator and passing no arguments.

2. Add an icon by passing a small Crisscott logo image to set_icon_image.

3. Add a label with set_label.

The label could have been set to a widget instead of a string using set_label_widget. In most cases, when set_label_widget is called, it is to create a more interesting text label, not to add a button or a container, although adding a button or container is possible. For instance, you could add a GtkLabel with an ellipsization mode set to allow the label to take up less space. This would allow the toolbar to show more items without resorting to an overflow menu.

Using Menu, Toggle, and Radio Tool Buttons

As with menu items, PHP-GTK provides a few specialized toolbar widgets, which can expand a toolbar item or represent a state. The classes are GtkMenuToolButton, GtkToggleToolButton, and GtkRadioMenuItem. Figure 11-10 shows these types of tool buttons.

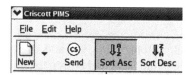

Figure 11-10. *A toolbar with several types of tool buttons*

The classes create the following types of tool buttons:

Menu tool button: GtkMenuToolButton is just like a normal tool button, but also has an additional "mini-button" attached to the side or bottom. The mini-button is represented with an arrow, which pops up a GtkMenu widget when clicked. A menu tool button is useful to group similar actions into one button. In Figure 11-10, the New button is a menu tool button.

Toggle tool button: GtkToggleToolButton is similar to GtkCheckMenuItem. GtkToggleToolButton uses a shadow and a color change to indicate the state of the button. When the button is active, the background will be darker and a drop shadow will be added. When the button is not active, the background will match the rest of the toolbar and the border will not be shown. This visual representation works equally as well regardless of the toolbar style (whether the buttons show only text, only icons, or both). In Figure 11-10, the Send button is a toggle tool button.

Radio tool button: GtkRadioToolButton is similar to GtkRadioMenuItem in that only one of a group of buttons may be active at any given time. When activated, a GtkRadioToolButton button will deactivate the other button in the group that is currently activated. In Figure 11-10, the Sort Asc and Sort Desc buttons are radio tool buttons.

Listing 11-14 shows how the toolbar buttons shown in Figure 11-10 were created.

Listing 11-14. *Creating a GtkToolbar Widget with Several Types of Tool Buttons*

```php
<?php
class Crisscott_Tools_Toolbar extends GtkToolbar {

    public function __construct()
    {
        // Call the parent constructor.
        parent::__construct();

        // Create the submenus.
        $this->createButtons();
    }

    protected function createButtons()
    {
        // Create a button to make new products, categories and
        // contributors.
        $img = GtkImage::new_from_stock(Gtk::STOCK_NEW,
                                        Gtk::ICON_SIZE_SMALL_TOOLBAR);
        $new = new GtkMenuToolButton($img, 'New');
        $newMenu = new GtkMenu();

        // Create the menu items.
        $product = new GtkMenuItem('Product');
        $newMenu->append($product);
        $category = new GtkMenuItem('Category');
        $newMenu->append($category);
        $contrib = new GtkMenuItem('Contributor');
        $newMenu->append($contrib);

        // Set the menu as the menu for the new button.
        $newMenu->show_all();
        $new->set_menu($newMenu);

        // Add the button to the toolbar.
        $this->add($new);

        // Create the signal handlers for the new menu.
        require_once 'Crisscott/MainWindow.php';
        $application = Crisscott_MainWindow::singleton();
```

```
            $new->connect_simple('clicked', array($application, 'newProduct'));
            $product->connect_simple('activate', array($application, 'newProduct'));
            $category->connect_simple('activate', array($application, 'newCategory'));
            $contrib->connect_simple('activate', array($application, 'newContrib'));

            // Create a toggle button that will connect to the database.
            $database = GtkToggleToolButton::new_from_stock(Gtk::STOCK_CONNECT);
            $database->set_label('Connect to Database');

            // Add the button to the toolbar.
            $this->add($database);

        // Create two buttons for sorting the product list.
        $sortA = new GtkRadioToolButton(null, 'Ascending');
        $sortA->set_icon_widget(GtkImage::new_from_stock(Gtk::STOCK_SORT_ASCENDING,
                                              Gtk::ICON_SIZE_LARGE_TOOLBAR));
        $sortA->set_label('Sort Asc');

        $sortD = new GtkRadioToolButton($sortA, 'Descending');
        $sortD->set_icon_widget(GtkImage::new_from_stock(Gtk::STOCK_SORT_DESCENDING,
                                              Gtk::ICON_SIZE_LARGE_TOOLBAR));
        $sortD->set_label('Sort Desc');

            // Add the two buttons.
            $this->add($sortA);
            $this->add($sortD);
        }
    }
?>
```

Listing 11-14 creates one button with a menu that allows the user to create a new product, category, or contributor. First, the menu button is created using the new operator. The icon and text are passed to the constructor. Afterward, the menu is created and added with set_menu. Signal handlers need to be created for all of the menu items as well as for the button itself. It is a good idea to connect the button to the same callback as one of the menu items, because the user will most likely expect something to happen when the button is clicked.

Next is the GtkToggleToolButton. Note that you could change the icon associated with a toggle button to represent different states of the button by extending GtkToggleToolButton and creating a signal handler for the toggled signal.

The last type of toolbar button shown in Listing 11-14 is GtkRadioToolButton, created using the new operator. When instantiated, a radio button requires one of the other buttons in the group or null. In Listing 11-14, the first radio button is given null as the first argument. The second button is given the first button to make a group.

The toolbar created in Listing 11-14 and shown in Figure 11-10 will be used as the PIMS application's toolbar.

> **Note** The only other type of widget that can be added to a toolbar is `GtkSeparatorToolItem`. A separator item doesn't normally serve any purpose except to visually group tool items. For example, a group of radio tool buttons might be surrounded by two separator items to make it clear that they are one radio group.

Summary

Menus and toolbars provide ways for users to trigger actions in an application. They provide structured ways to represent abstract user tasks. A menu provides a hierarchical method for organizing tasks into several groups, while a toolbar creates a more persistent means to show tasks with an icon, a label, or both. When either a menu item or a tool button is clicked, or activated, it usually triggers some action or pops up another menu. While a toolbar is mostly static and is constantly shown, menus can appear from almost any location. When a menu seemingly appears from nowhere with options relating to a particular piece of the application, the menu is known as a context menu. Menus can also be detached from the application. Using a `GtkTearoffMenuItem`, it is possible to put a menu in its own top-level window that can then be moved around the user's desktop.

Several listings in this chapter used images to create icons for menu items or toolbar buttons but didn't provide any explanation. Chapter 12 goes into the details of using images in an application. Not only will the next chapter look at how to display images of varying types, but it will also go into the details of creating images on the fly and using images to shape other widgets. Using images, the PIMS application can take on a unique look and feel.

CHAPTER 12

■ ■ ■

Adding Images

As the old saying goes, "A picture is worth a thousand words." The same holds true for GUI applications. Sometimes the best way to get an idea across is to use an image instead of text. Furthermore, adding images can give the application a unique look and feel. For instance, in our sample application, adding a logo to the Crisscott splash screen uniquely identifies the application as a Crisscott product.

In Chapter 11, you saw how to create menu items and toolbar buttons from stock images, which are widely understood for certain functions. In this chapter, we will look at how to use images in the Crisscott PIMS application not only to enhance usability and present data, but also to shape the application itself.

Images

GtkImage is a widget that displays an image—any image that can be loaded into memory. It may be a product photo, a company logo, or a stock image. GtkImage is a descendant of GtkMisc (introduced in Chapter 7), which means that an image can be aligned and given padding just like a label. But before you can assign an alignment or padding, you must create a GtkImage object.

Creating an Image Object

Images can be created from many sources and data types. For each of these types, PHP-GTK provides a function to load the image.

Referencing the File Location

The most commonly used method for loading an image is to reference its location. Several examples in previous chapters have shown the use of GtkImage::new_from_file. This static constructor takes a path to a file and returns a GtkImage.

You can open most common file types, such as JPEG, PNG, and BMP, with new_from_file. If the file cannot be found or opened, a default broken image icon will be returned instead. Depending on the user's system, a broken image icon may look like Figure 12-1. If it is important for the application to know whether or not the image was loaded successfully, you should use another method to add the image.

```
┌PRODUCT SUMMARY──────────────────────────────────────
│  Name      Pro PHP-GTK                    ┌Image──────┐
│                                           │           │
│  Type      Shippable                      │           │
│                                           │    [x]    │
│  Category  Paperback Books                │           │
│                                           │           │
│  Price     44.95                          └───────────┘
└─────────────────────────────────────────────────────
```

Figure 12-1. *A broken image icon*

Using a Stock ID

In previous examples, you have seen how to create images for buttons and menu items by using stock IDs. A stock ID is a shortcut that identifies a commonly used image. You can also create a regular image from a stock ID by using new_from_stock. This static constructor takes the stock ID plus a size. The size is defined by a GtkIconSize constant. Stock images come in different sizes so that they can be used for different purposes. Each use has its own size constant, as follows:

- Gtk::ICON_SIZE_MENU: A small image normally used in menus.

- Gtk::ICON_SIZE_SMALL_TOOLBAR: A small version of the icon used for toolbars.

- Gtk::ICON_SIZE_LARGE_TOOLBAR: A larger version of the toolbar icon.

- Gtk::ICON_SIZE_BUTTON: The version normally used for buttons.

- Gtk::ICON_SIZE_DND: The icon size used when an item is dragged.

- Gtk::ICON_SIZE_DIALOG: The version normally used in dialog windows.

Using a Pixel Buffer

Another way to create an image is from data in memory. An image stored in memory can usually be found in a GdkPixbuf. A pixel buffer (or *pixbuf*) is simply a representation of the image in memory. It cannot be displayed on its own; it is just data. You can put an image into a pixbuf when an application is started to allow commonly used images to be loaded more quickly.

A pixbuf can be created from a file, just as an image can be created. To create a pixbuf from a file, call the static constructor new_from_file and pass a file path. Listing 12-1 creates a pixbuf from a file and then creates an image from the pixbuf using the static constructor new_from_pixbuf.

Listing 12-1. *Loading an Image into a GdkPixbuf and Then a GtkImage*

```php
<?php
// Create a window to display the image.
$window = new GtkWindow();
// Close the application cleanly.
$window->connect_simple('destroy', array('Gtk', 'main_quit'));

// Load a pixbuf from a file.
$pb = GdkPixbuf::new_from_file('Crisscott/images/logo.png');
```

```php
// Create the image from the pixbuf.
$image = GtkImage::new_from_pixbuf($pb);

// Add the image to the window.
$window->add($image);

// Show the image and the window.
$window->show_all();
// Start the main loop.
Gtk::main();
?>
```

Using GdkPixbuf and GtkImage, we can now add product images to the Crisscott PIMS application. Product images should appear in two places: in the product summary area and in the product editing tool.

Listing 12-2 shows the code added to the Crisscott_Tools_ProductEdit class to allow the user to add or change a product image. The added lines include a GtkEntry for entering the path to the image file and the code to display the images. In this example, the creation of the pixbuf is wrapped in a try/catch block. That is because if the file for the pixbuf is not found, an exception will be thrown. This allows the application to detect a failure to load an image.

Listing 12-2. *Adding Product Images to the Application*

```php
<?php
// The added lines from the product summary area.
class Crisscott_Tools_ProductSummary extends GtkTable {
    // ...
    public function displaySummary(Crisscott_Product $product)
    {
        // Set the product.
        $this->product = $product;

        // Set the attribute labels to the values of the product.
        $this->productName->set_text($product->name);
        $this->productType->set_text($product->type);

        // Get the category information.
        require_once 'Crisscott/Inventory.php';
        $inv = Crisscott_Inventory::singleton();
        $cat = $inv->getCategoryById($product->categoryId);
        // Set the category name.
        $this->productCategory->set_text($cat->name);

        // Set the product price.
        $this->productPrice->set_text($product->price);

        // Remove the current product image.
        $this->productImage->remove($this->productImage->get_child());
```

```
            // Try to add the product image.
            try {
                // Create a pixbuf.
                $pixbuf = GdkPixbuf::new_from_file($product->imagePath);
                // Create an image from the pixbuf.
                $this->productImage->add(GtkImage::new_from_pixbuf($pixbuf));
                // Show the image.
                $this->productImage->show_all();
            } catch (Exception $e) {
                // Just fail silently.
            }
        }
        // ...
}
class Crisscott_Tools_ProductEdit extends GtkTable {
    // ...
    private function _layout()
    {
        // Set up the data entry widgets.
        // ...
        $this->imageContainer = new GtkFrame();
        $this->imagePathEntry = new GtkEntry();

        // ...
        // Set up the labels.
        // ...
        $this->imageLabel     = new GtkLabel('Image');

        // Set the labels' size.
        // ...
        $this->imageLabel->set_size_request(100, -1);

        // ...

        // Next align each label within the parent container.
        // ...
        $this->imageLabel->set_alignment(0, .5);

        // Make all of the labels use markup.
        // ...
        $this->imageLabel->set_use_markup(true);

        // ...
```

```
        // Attach the image widgets.
        $this->attachWithAlign($this->imageContainer, 2, 4, 0, 4,  Gtk::FILL, 0);
        $this->attachWithAlign($this->imageLabel,     2, 4, 4, 5,  Gtk::FILL, 0);
        $this->attachWithAlign($this->imagePathEntry, 3, 4, 4, 5,  Gtk::FILL, 0);

        // ...
    }

    public function resetProduct()
    {
        // Make sure that there is a product.
        if (!isset($this->product)) {
            require_once 'Crisscott/Product.php';
            $this->product = new Crisscott_Product();
        }

        // Update the tools in the widget.
        // ...
        $this->imagePathEntry->set_text($this->product->imagePath);

        // Remove the current image.
        $this->imageContainer->remove($this->imageContainer->get_child());
        // Try to load the product image.
        try {
            // Load the image into a pixbuf.
            $pixbuf = GdkPixbuf::new_from_file($this->product->imagePath);
            // Load the pixbuf into an image.
            $this->imageContainer->add(GtkImage::new_from_pixbuf($pixbuf));
            // Show the image.
            $this->imageContainer->show_all();
        } catch (Exception $e) {
            // Fail silently.
            // The product object will verify if the image exists.
        }

        // ...
    }
}
?>
```

Figure 12-2 shows the new version of the application. In Chapter 14, we will expand on this even further to make it easier to find a valid file path.

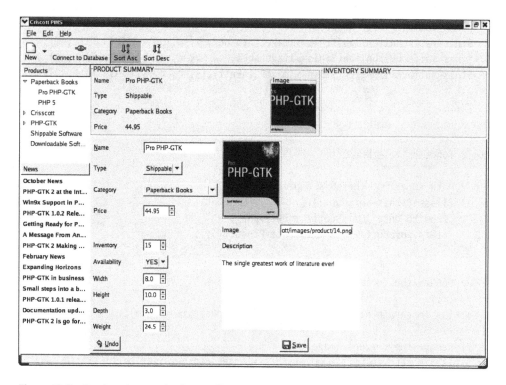

Figure 12-2. *Product images in the application*

Note that in Figure 12-2, the image in the product summary area is not quite right. The image is cropped because it doesn't fit in the area provided. Instead of resizing the application to fit the image, it is more reasonable to resize the image to fit the application.

Scaling Images

Resizing an image is also known as *scaling*. The quick and easy way to scale a GdkPixbuf is by using scale_simple. scale_simple takes a pixbuf, a new height, and a new width, and returns a new pixbuf with the given dimensions.

■**Caution** scale_simple scales the buffer exactly as it is told. It does not respect the aspect ratio of the original buffer. Make sure that the new dimensions you choose do not distort the buffer beyond your acceptable limits.

---

scale_simple also requires one more argument, which tells GDK how to create the new image. Each of the following methods tells the pixbuf to scale the new image in a different manner, using a different algorithm. The faster the algorithm, the lower the quality of the scaled image.

- Gdk::INTERP_NEAREST: This is the fastest way to scale an image, but the quality of the new image will likely be unacceptable, especially when making the image smaller.

- Gdk::INTERP_HYPER: This produces the best-quality image, but may be too slow for some applications or for large images.

- Gdk::INTERP_TILES: This method is probably best when you are not certain if the buffer is being scaled up or being scaled down. It resembles Gdk::INTERP_NEAREST when scaling up and Gdk::INTERP_BILINEAR when scaling down.

- Gdk::INTERP_BILINEAR: This offers the best balance of quality and speed.

In Listing 12-3, the product image for the product summary area is scaled to fit in the 100 × 100 pixel area set aside for the image.

Listing 12-3. *Scaling a GdkPixbuf*

```php
<?php
class Crisscott_Tools_ProductSummary extends GtkTable {
    // ...
    public function displaySummary(Crisscott_Product $product)
    {
        // ...
        // Remove the current product image.
        $this->productImage->remove($this->productImage->get_child());

        // Try to add the product image.
        try {
            // Create a pixbuf.
            $pixbuf = GdkPixbuf::new_from_file($product->imagePath);

            // Scale the image.
            $pixbuf = $pixbuf->scale_simple(80, 100, Gdk::INTERP_BILINEAR);

            // Create an image from the pixbuf.
            $this->productImage->add(GtkImage::new_from_pixbuf($pixbuf));
            // Show the image.
            $this->productImage->show_all();
        } catch (Exception $e) {
            // Just fail silently.
        }
    }
    // ...
}
?>
```

Figure 12-3 shows the product summary area with the scaled image.

Figure 12-3. *A scaled product image*

■**Tip** Another method for scaling an image is named scale. scale is a very powerful method for manipulating images. Like scale_simple, it scales an image, but it also can take a portion of the new image and
paste it onto an existing image. This method allows for some rather creative image manipulations, but is a little
too complicated for use in most applications. For more details about using scale, consult the GdkPixbuf
documentation at http://gtk.org.

Setting Transparency

Images can not only define visible pixels, but they also can define pixels that cannot be seen.
These pixels are transparent. Transparent pixels allow the user to see through parts of an image.
Transparent pixels are useful in cases where an image is a unique shape and you do not want
to have a solid-colored background.

For example, let's say that the products can be rated from zero to five stars based on how
well they sell. In order to make the application look clean and professional, the star icons
depicting the rating should appear in the application without a background. The actual data
that defines an image always defines a rectangular region. To show only the star shape, you
can make some of the pixels in the rectangular region transparent and leave the pixels that
represent the star as opaque.

Most graphic editors, like The GIMP and Photoshop, allow you to create an image with
transparent pixels built in. GdkPixbuf will respect transparent pixels that are built into an image
file. However, it is sometime necessary to work with images that have been created without
transparency. This doesn't present too much of a problem, because you can add transparency
to any GdkPixbuf that doesn't have transparency already. You do this by creating an *alpha channel*
for the GdkPixbuf. An alpha channel defines a particular color in an image to make transparent.
The following line makes all white pixels in an image transparent:

```
$newPixbuf = $pixbuf->add_alpha_channel(true, 255, 255, 255);
```

The first argument to add_alpha_channel is a Boolean that tells the pixbuf to make the
color transparent. The next three arguments define the color to make transparent. The color
values here are 8-bit values for red, green, and blue (as opposed to the 16-bit values used by
GdkColor). Now when the image shown, all white pixels will be transparent, and the color of
the widget behind the image (usually a GtkButton or GtkWindow) will show through.

Animations

Static images are not the only type of images that you can use with PHP-GTK. You can also load animations. An *animation* is a series of static images where the images are displayed one after another.

An animation is useful to draw attention to an image. Something moving on the screen will be much more eye-catching than a static image. An animation can also be used as a sort of progress indicator. While work is being performed, you can display an animation. When the work is done, the animation can be replaced with a static image again.

Working with animations is just like working with static images. In fact, an animation (most likely in .gif format) can even be loaded with GtkImage::new_from_file. When an animation is loaded into a GtkImage, it creates a GdkPixbufAnimation instead of a regular GdkPixbuf. A GtkImage that contains an animation can be added to a container just like any other widget.

Widget Shaping

You can use images for more than just adding pictures to an application. Using images, you can define shapes that you can then apply to windows and other widgets. An image can be used to turn a normal rectangular button into a symbol such as a plus sign, a star, or any other shape.

Setting a widget's shape is like trimming the widget using a stencil. The stencil defines which parts should be left and which parts should be removed. After the stencil is applied, all that is left of the widget are the parts the stencil did not say to trim.

For example, Figure 12-4 shows a GtkTextView that has been modified to remove some parts from the middle. Notice how only the display of the widget is affected, not the actual shape of the widget. The text still flows as if the GtkTextView were square.

Figure 12-4. *A GtkTextView with pieces missing*

■**Caution** Users often associate particular shapes with specific actions. For instance, they often expect buttons and entries to be rectangular. Make sure that your modifications will have a positive impact on the usability of the application before straying from the customary shapes and sizes.

To shape a widget, you use a pixel map (pixmap) in combination with a bitmap. GdkPixmap is another format for storing image data in memory. The difference between a pixmap and a pixbuf is that a pixmap can be drawn onto by other GDK objects.

A GdkPixmap is basically a way to map colors to a given pixel. The number of bits used to represent each color in the pixmap is called the *depth*. The greater the depth, the more colors a pixmap contains. One of the values that can be represented in a pixmap is transparency. Transparent pixels are basically pixels that do not exist. GdkBitmap, also known as a *bitmask*, is pixmap that has a depth of 1. In a bitmap, each bit does not represent a color, but rather indicates an on or off state. Pixels that are off are transparent. When a bitmap is laid over a GtkWindow, the bits that are off will not allow the window to show through. This is how a widget is shaped.

The window in Figure 12-4 was created from the code in Listing 12-4.

Listing 12-4. *Changing the Shape of a GtkWindow*

```php
<?php
// Create a window.
$window = new GtkWindow();
// Set up the window to exit cleanly.
$window->connect_simple('destroy', array('Gtk', 'main_quit'));

// Create a pixbuf from an image file.
$pb = GdkPixbuf::new_from_file('Crisscott/images/inverse.png');

// Get the objects that will shape the widget.
list($pixmap, $mask) = $pb->render_pixmap_and_mask();

// Create a GtkTextView and add some text.
$text = new GtkTextView();
$text->get_buffer()->set_text('This is a test. There is a whole ' .
                              'in the middle of this text view widget.');

// Wrap the text.
$text->set_wrap_mode(Gtk::WRAP_WORD);

// Change the shape of the text view.
$text->shape_combine_mask($mask, 0, 0);

// Add the text view to the window.
$window->add($text);
// Show the window and image.
$window->show_all();
// Start the main loop.
Gtk::main();
?>
```

The first step in creating the "see-through" text view is to create a regular GtkWindow. Next, a pixbuf is created from an image file. After the pixbuf is created, it is used to generate two objects, one of which will be used as the stencil for shaping the window. The GdkPixbuf method render_pixmap_and_mask takes no arguments and returns an array containing a GdkPixmap and a GdkBitmap.

The GdkBitmap is then passed to the window's shape_combine_mask method. This method applies the mask to the GtkTextView, starting from the offset given by the last two arguments. In this case, the mask is not offset because both the x offset (second argument) and y offset (last argument) are 0. The rest of the example is pretty standard. The text view is added to the window, the window is shown, and the main loop is started.

Summary

Images are an essential for almost all applications. Simply displaying an image is rather easy. Once created, a GtkImage can be added to any container. All of the methods for GtkImage are either constructors for creating the image from different sources or methods for setting the contents of a previously created image.

To work with the contents of an image, you must edit a pixel buffer, or pixbuf. GdkPixbuf stores an image and allows the image to be manipulated. A pixbuf can be scaled to a different size or turned into a pixel map (pixmap) and bitmask. You can use a GdkBitmap to give widgets a custom shape. This way, the use of images in an application not only makes the application more visually appealing, but can also shape the application itself.

Chapter 13 looks at what it takes to allow users to drag objects in an application and move them to another part of the application. This is known as *drag-and-drop*. You will learn not only how to make an item draggable, but also how to make a widget accept or reject items for dropping.

CHAPTER 13

■ ■ ■

Drag-and-Drop

Drag-and-drop, or DnD for short, refers to using the mouse to move an element on the screen to another location. Most people are familiar with DnD—moving an icon from one place on their desktop to another, dragging a file from one folder to another, and so on.

But DnD is not just about moving files around the file system. It is actually a metaphor for interprocess communication. This means that DnD is a way for the user to supply a particular piece of an application with information that is stored in a different part of the application or comes from an entirely different process. For example, most web browsers will display an HTML file when you drag it from your desktop and drop it over an open browser window.

Adding DnD to an application can help make its use more intuitive. DnD makes the answer to "How do I get this data from here to there?" as simple as "Drag it and drop it."

There are two parts to every DnD operation. First there is the source, or the item being dragged, and then there is the destination, which is the place the item will be dropped. Of the two, creating a destination is easier and so, we will consider that task first.

Drag-and-Drop Destinations

A *destination* is a widget that is configured to accept the information provided by dropped data and do something with it. Any widget can be a destination for a drop. For example, a GtkEntry widget used to collect the path of an image file may be configured to accept image files that are dropped onto it. This allows users to drag an image file from their file system onto the widget. Depending on the setup of the GtkEntry, the path to the file may be set as the GtkEntry's text, or maybe the image will be loaded into another widget.

Setting the Drag Destination

A few usability enhancements can be added to the Crisscott PIMS application by way of DnD. To start, let's look at what it takes to allow users to add product images simply by dragging an icon from their desktop and dropping it in the product editing tool's image path GtkEntry widget. Listing 13-1 shows the code that sets the GtkEntry as a drop location.

Listing 13-1. *Making a GtkEntry Accept Drops*

```php
<?php
class Crisscott_Tools_ProductEdit extends GtkTable {
    // ...
    private function _layout()
    {
        // Set up the data entry widgets.
        $this->nameEntry = new GtkEntry();
        // ...
        $this->imagePathEntry = new GtkEntry();

        // Make the image path entry accept file drops.
        $this->acceptDrops($this->imagePathEntry);
    }

    public function acceptDrops($widget)
    {
        // Set the widget as a drop location.
        $widget->drag_dest_set(Gtk::DEST_DEFAULT_ALL,
                               array(array('text/uri-list', 0, 0)),
                               Gdk::ACTION_COPY | Gdk::ACTION_MOVE
                               );

        // Connect the drag-data-received signal.
        $widget->connect('drag-data-received', array($this, 'dragDataReceived'));
    }

    // ...
}
?>
```

Making a widget accept drops is a pretty quick process. Calling the drag_dest_set method of GtkWidget is all it takes to make a widget accept drops. The method takes three arguments:

- flags: Flags that indicate what should happen when data is dragged over the widget.

- targets: An array that determines the drop types the widget will accept.

- actions: The possible actions the destination can take when data is dropped.

Drag Destination Flags

The first argument to drag_dest_set (flags) is bitmask of values that determines how the widget should react when potential drop data is dragged over the widget. The following are the possible flag values:

- `Gtk::DEST_DEFAULT_MOTION`: Causes the widget to check to see if data being dragged over the widget is acceptable to be dropped onto the widget.

- `Gtk::DEST_DEFAULT_HIGHLIGHT`: Causes the widget to be highlighted while acceptable drop data is held over the widget.

- `Gtk::DEST_DEFAULT_DROP`: Causes the widget to call `drag_get_data` when acceptable data is dropped on the widget.

- `Gtk::DEST_DEFAULT_ALL`: Combines all three flags. `Gtk::DEST_DEFAULT_ALL` is used a vast majority of time.

In Listing 13-1, the flag value passed to `drag_dest_set` is `Gtk::DEST_DEFAULT_ALL`.

Drag Destination Targets

The second argument to `drag_dest_set` (`targets`) is an array of targets that the widget should accept. The targets are not specific items, but rather types of items. Each element of the array is called a *target entry*. Each target entry is itself an array consisting of a string and two integers.

The string indicates the MIME type of the data that is acceptable to drop in the destination widget. Listing 13-1 sets this to `text/uri-list`. This means that only lists of URIs (strings that give the location of files either on the local host or on a remote machine) are allowed to be dropped on the widget. When a file from the user's desktop is dragged over the widget, the data type will be `text/uri-list`. This means that the user can drag an icon onto the widget and it will respond when the data is dropped. If other types of data, such as highlighted text from a website (`text/plain`), are dropped onto the widget, the data will be ignored.

The second element of a target entry array is a flag that can be used to further restrict the data that may be dropped onto the widget. In Listing 13-1, this value is set to 0 because no other restrictions are needed. However, it could be set to either of the following:

- `Gtk::TARGET_SAME_APP`: Only data dragged from within the same application as the destination widget will be accepted. For example, using this value will mean that the user may not drag items from the desktop and drop them onto the destination widget.

- `Gtk::TARGET_SAME_WIDGET`: Only data from the same widget will be accepted as drop data. This value is useful for widgets such as `GtkTextView`. It can be used to allow text to be moved within the widget but restrict text from being pulled in from outside resources.

The final element of the target entry array is an integer used to identify the entry type. This value will be passed to any callbacks used to handle the DnD events. The value should be unique for each target entry. Using the integer ID is faster than comparing the data types, and its main purpose it to save time.

Drag Destination Actions

The last argument of `dest_drag_set` (`actions`) is a bitmask value that defines what the destination widget should do with the dragged data. As in Listing 13-1, the values may be combined to allow more than one type of action to happen when data is dropped. Possible values for this argument are any combination of the following:

- Gdk::ACTION_COPY: Copy the dragged data. The location of a file should be copied when a file is dragged onto the destination widget.

- Gdk::ACTION_MOVE: Move the data from the drag source to the destination. For example, when dragging text from one part of a GtkTextView to another, it should be moved not copied.

- Gdk::ACTION_LINK: Add a link to the data. Note that this is useful only if the source and destination agree on what it means.

- Gdk::ACTION_PRIVATE: Indicate to the source that the destination will do something with the data that the source will not understand.

- Gdk::ACTION_ASK: Ask the user what to do with the data. This is useful only if the source allows multiple actions that the destination accepts.

Calling drag_dest_set is all that is needed to make a widget accept drops. Of course, that is not all there is to DnD. Once a widget accepts drops, it must be set up to do something with the data. That is what we will look at next.

Note A widget can be unset as a drag destination using drag_dest_unset. Calling this method will clear any drag destination information set using drag_dest_set. This is useful to limit the number of times a widget is allowed to accept dragged data.

Handling the drag-data-received Signal

When data is dropped onto a drag destination, the drag-data-received signal is emitted. This signal indicates not only that data was dropped on the widget, but also that it matches one of the target entry arrays used when setting up the destination. When this signal is fired, the application should do something with the drag data. Listing 13-2 shows the creation of the signal handler and the signal handler itself.

Listing 13-2. *Creating a drag-data-received Signal Handler*

```php
<?php
class Crisscott_Tools_ProductEdit extends GtkTable {
    // ...

    public function acceptDrops($widget)
    {
        // Set the widget as a drop location.
        $widget->drag_dest_set(Gtk::DEST_DEFAULT_ALL,
                               array(array('text/uri-list', 0, 0)),
                               Gdk::ACTION_COPY | Gdk::ACTION_MOVE
                               );
```

```php
        // Connect the drag-data-received signal.
        $widget->connect('drag-data-received', array($this, 'dragDataReceived'));
    }

    public function dragDataReceived($widget, $context, $x, $y, $data,
                                     $info, $time, $userData)
    {
        // Get the dropped file's path.
        $path = trim($data->data);

        // Strip off the "file://localhost/" from the path.
        // See the CAUTION note below!
        $path = substr($path, 17);

        // Check the mime type to make sure the file is an image.
        if (strpos(mime_content_type($path), 'image') === false) {
            return false;
        }

        // Set the current product's image path.
        $this->product->imagePath = $path;

        // Reset the product.
        $this->resetProduct();
    }

    // ...
}
?>
```

■**Caution** File URIs are seldom implemented correctly. The correct format is `file://hostname/path/ to/file`. Because of the many different implementations of this URI, it is a good idea to do a few checks to make sure that the data points to an actual file. Take a look at PEAR::Gtk_FileDrop (http://pear.php. net/package/Gtk_FileDrop) for a more complete example of working with file URIs. For a quick and easy way to set a destination to accept file drops, check out PEAR::Gtk2_FileDrop (http://pear.php.net/ package/Gtk2_FileDrop).

The signal handler created in Listing 13-2 is set up to receive eight arguments:

- destWidget: The destination widget where data was dropped. This is passed because the signal handler was created with connect, rather than connect_simple.

- context: The drag context—information related to the data being dropped. The drag context is an object that contains information such as the action that will happen (Gdk::ACTION_COPY, Gdk::ACTION_MOVE, and so on), the data types offered by the drag source, and the GdkWindow of the source and destination widgets.

- x: The horizontal coordinate of the cursor position when the data is dropped.

- y: The vertical coordinate of the cursor position when the data is dropped.

- data: An object containing information about the dragged data.

- info: The target entry ID number.

- time: The timestamp of the event.

- userData: An optional array of user data passed to the callback.

The data argument is a GtkSelectionData object, which contains information about the dropped data. In Listing 13-2, the only property that is used is the data property, which contains the data that is dropped. In the case of Listing 13-2, this is the path to the file that is dropped on the GtkEntry. The path is a URI that pinpoints the file that was dropped on the widget. Notice that a little work is needed to obtain a usable value. First, the string "file://localhost" needs to be stripped off the beginning of the path. (Don't forget that the file URI needs to point to an actual file!) Next, any white space must also be removed from the end of the path.

Tip If multiple data types are accepted by the destination, you can check the type of the dropped data by inspecting the type property of the GtkSelectionData object. However, if an appropriate ID was set in the target entry, it is easier to simply check the info argument.

Drag-and-Drop Sources

Just as widgets can accept data that has been dropped onto them, they can also be used to provide data by being dragged. Users may try to drag a list item to make it part of another list, or they may drag a product to a part of the application, expecting that the application will allow them to edit that product's data. A widget that can be dragged from one part of the application to another, or even to another application, is called a DnD *source*.

Setting the Drag Source

Listing 13-3 shows the Crisscott PIMS application's product summary tool being turned into a drag source.

Listing 13-3. *Turning a Widget into a Drag Source*

```php
<?php
class Crisscott_MainWindow extends GtkWindow {
    // ...

    private function _populate()
    {
        // Create the layout table.
        $table = new GtkTable(5, 3);
```

```php
    // A shortcut for setting both the expand and fill properties.
    $expandFill = Gtk::EXPAND|Gtk::FILL;

    // ...

    // Create a frame to hold the product summary tool.
    $productSummary = new GtkFrame('PRODUCT SUMMARY');
    $productSummary->set_size_request(-1, 150);

    // Add the product summary tool.
    require_once 'Crisscott/Tools/ProductSummary.php';
    $this->productSummary = Crisscott_Tools_ProductSummary::singleton();
    $productSummary->add($this->productSummary);

    // Make the widget a drag source.
    // It must be wrapped in a GtkEventBox.
    $eb = new GtkEventBox();

    // The data will be plain text and the user must use
    // the first mouse button to drag.
    $eb->drag_source_set(Gdk::BUTTON1_MASK, array(array('text/plain', 0, 0)),
                         Gdk::ACTION_COPY);

    // Create a signal handler to get the appropriate data.
    $eb->connect('drag-data-get',
                 array($this, 'getSummaryDragData'),
                 $this->productSummary);

    // Add the product summary to the event box.
    $eb->add($this->productSummary);

    // ...
    }

    // ...
}
?>
```

One of the key things to notice about Listing 13-3 is that the ProductSummary tool itself is
not made a drag source. This is because no-window widgets—those without a GdkWindow—
cannot be made into drag sources. Because the ProductSummary tool extends GtkTable, it must
be wrapped inside a GtkEventBox if it is to be used as a drag source. This is not usually a big
deal for most applications.

Making a widget DnD source is very similar to making a widget a DnD destination. You
use the drag_source_set method, which takes three arguments:

- `buttonMask`: A bitmask of buttons that will initiate the drag operation.

- `targets`: An array that determines the drop types the widget will accept.

- `actions`: The possible actions the destination can take when data is dropped.

Drag Source Button Masks

The first argument to `drag_source_set` (`buttonMask`) is a mask of buttons that can be used to start the drag operation. This bitmask determines which mouse buttons the user must hold down in order to drag the widget. The bitmask should be a combination of one or more of the masks for each button, as follows:

- `Gdk::BUTTON1_MASK`: The first mouse button.

- `Gdk::BUTTON2_MASK`: The second mouse button.

- `Gdk::BUTTON3_MASK`: The third mouse button.

- `Gdk::BUTTON4_MASK`: The fourth mouse button.

- `Gdk::BUTTON5_MASK`: The fifth mouse button.

For example, to allow either the first or second mouse button to be used to start a drag operation, use `Gdk::BUTTON1_MASK | Gdk::BUTTON2_MASK`.

Note PHP-GTK has support for mice with up to five buttons, but most users' mice have only three buttons. You should carefully consider your target audience before deciding to restrict drag operations to the fourth or fifth mouse button.

Drag Source Targets and Actions

The next two arguments to `drag_source_set` are an array of targets and a bitmask of possible actions. These two arguments take the same form as the corresponding arguments for `drag_dest_set`. The `targets` argument is an array of target entries and defines the ways that the data for the source may be represented. The `actions` bitmask determines what will happen to the data when it is dropped.

Handling the drag-data-get Signal

Notice also that a signal handler is created for the `drag-data-get` signal. This signal is emitted when the data is dropped. The callback should be used to set the data that will be passed on to the drag destination. The data is set by modifying the `GtkSelectionData` object that is passed in as one of the callback arguments. Listing 13-4 shows a callback that is connected to the `drag-data-get` signal. It expects the same arguments as the signal handler used for the `drag-data-received` signal (Listing 13-2).

Listing 13-4. *Setting Drag Data*

```php
<?php
class Crisscott_MainWindow extends GtkWindow {
    // ...

    private function _populate()
    {
        // ...

        // Create a signal handler to get the appropriate data.
        $eb->connect('drag-data-get',
                    array($this, 'getSummaryDragData'),
                    $this->productSummary)

        // ...
    }

    public function getSummaryDragData($widget, $context, $selection,
                                       $info, $time, $summary)
    {
        // Set the product id as the selection's data value.
        $selection->set_text($summary->product->productId);
    }

    // ...
}
?>
```

In Listing 13-4, the set_text method is used to set the data property of the GtkSelectionData object to the product ID of the ProductSummary tool's current product. When the GtkSelectionData object is passed on to the drag destination, the product ID can be retrieved from the data property of the selection object.

Setting Drag Source Icons

When data is dragged from one place to another, the cursor turns into an icon representing the type of data being moved. Normally, this is determined by the target entry value of the drag source, but you can control which icon appears. This adds another level of customization to an application. For example, if the drag source is a Crisscott product, the drag icon could be set to a small version of the Crisscott logo. This lets the users know that they are moving product data and not just an image or chunk of text.

Setting a custom icon is a simple matter of passing a GdkPixbuf object to a widget's drag_source_set_icon_pixbuf. Listing 13-5 shows a simple example.

Listing 13-5. *Setting a Custom Drag Source Icon*

```php
<?php
class Crisscott_MainWindow extends GtkWindow {
    // ...

    private function _populate()
    {
        // ...

        // Make the widget a drag source.
        // It must be wrapped in a GtkEventBox.
        $eb = new GtkEventBox();

        // Set a drag source icon.
        $pixbuf = GdkPixbuf::new_from_file('Crisscott/images/menuItem.png');
        $eb->drag_source_set_icon_pixbuf($pixbuf);

        // ...
    }

    // ...
}
?>
```

In this example, a new pixbuf is created using GdkPixbuf::new_from_file and is passed directly to drag_source_set_icon_pixbuf. When the source is dragged, the cursor changes to a small Crisscott logo. The end result can be seen in Figure 13-1.

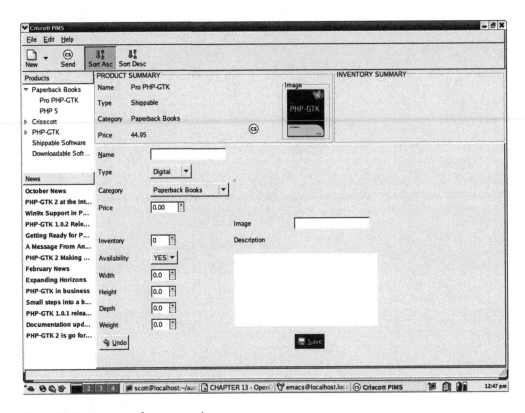

Figure 13-1. *A custom drag source icon*

Summary

To receive drop data, a widget must be set as a destination. This is a simple matter of calling drag_dest_set. Of course, the widget must also be set up to handle the incoming data, and that can be done by creating a signal handler for the drag-data-received signal. A source of drop data is created using drag_source_set. The data that a source gives to the destination needs to be set in the signal handler for the drag-data-get signal.

DnD is a powerful means to make an application more intuitive. It allows users to achieve complex operations by simply dragging data from one place to another. DnD can be used to communicate data from one part of an application to another or to send and receive data from other applications. DnD empowers users to move or copy data by picking it up and dropping it in another location, just as they would move a piece of paper from their desk to their filing cabinet.

In Chapter 14, we will look at other ways to collect data from the user in the form of selectors and dialogs. These are windows that pop up and present the users with a message or ask them to make a choice. Selectors and dialogs allow the application to break specialized tasks out from the rest of the application to maximize space and hide functionality that isn't always needed.

CHAPTER 14

■ ■ ■

Using Selectors & Dialogs

Ⅴser decisions are ultimately responsible for determining the course of an application's actions. For instance, a user is often prompted to confirm a pending action, such as closing a file without saving, or choosing a particular value such as a filename or color. Normally, such prompts do not need to appear within the interface but will appear in their own window, preventing the user from interacting with other parts of the application until the request has been satisfied. Prompts that pose a specific question are known as *dialogs*, while those that ask the user to make a selection are known as *selectors*. For example, the prompt to confirm the closure of a file without first saving it is known as a dialog, while the prompt to choose a specific filename is a selector.

PHP-GTK 2 offers several widgets that make the process of creating and displaying dialogs and selectors rather simple. Dialogs and selectors are really just GtkWindows, which are already filled with a collection of widgets and emit certain signals. Instead of building a window and filling it with buttons, labels, and lists, a developer can instantiate one of the dialog or selector widgets, provide a few hints as to what the contents should be, and wait for the pop-up to return information regarding the user's choice. This chapter examines what is required to set up and communicate with the many types of dialogs and selectors available in PHP-GTK 2.

Dialogs

GtkDialog is a widget designed to prompt the user to answer a question using a top-level window that displays a message, providing a means for the user to respond. An example of such a window is presented in Figure 14-1. The dialog asks the user to confirm that they want to close the application even though their work has not been saved. Note that these windows are made up of two pieces: the top with the message or question, and the bottom containing buttons that allow the user to provide some sort of feedback.

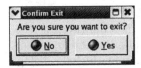

Figure 14-1. *A simple GtkDialog window*

Listing 14-1 contains the code used to create the dialog in Figure 14-1. This listing only shows the code that actually instantiates the class. Later examples will show how to use the dialog in an application.

Listing 14-1. *Creating a GtkDialog*

```php
<?php

// Set up the options for the dialog
$dialogOptions = 0;

// Make the dialog modal.
$dialogOptions = $dialogOptions | Gtk::DIALOG_MODAL;

// Destroy the dialog if the parent window is destroyed.
$dialogOptions = $dialogOptions | Gtk::DIALOG_DESTROY_WITH_PARENT;

// Don't show a horizontal separator between the two parts.
$dialogOptions = $dialogOptions | Gtk::DIALOG_NO_SEPARATOR;

// Set up the buttons.
$dialogButtons = array();

// Add a stock "No" button and make its response "No".
$dialogButtons[] = Gtk::STOCK_NO;
$dialogButtons[] = Gtk::RESPONSE_NO;

// Add a stock "Yes" button and make its response "Yes".
$dialogButtons[] = Gtk::STOCK_YES;
$dialogButtons[] = Gtk::RESPONSE_YES;

// Create the dialog.
$dialog = new GtkDialog('Confirm Exit', null, $dialogOptions, $dialogButtons);

// Add the warning message.
$dialog->vbox->pack_start(new GtkLabel('Are you sure you want to exit?'));

?>
```

A GtkDialog requires four pieces of information when it is created. The first is a string that will be used as the title for the dialog window. In Listing 14-1, the title is "Confirm Exit." The dialog window in Figure 14-1 shows the title in the title bar of the window. The next argument for the GtkDialog constructor is the parent window. This is a GtkWindow from which the dialog was generated. If a GtkWindow is passed, the dialog will be associated with that window. When it appears on the screen it will appear over the parent window. Depending on the value passed as the third argument, the dialog can also be modal for the parent, meaning that the user must answer the dialog's question before continuing with the main application. If the value for the second argument is null, the dialog will not be associated with any particular window. It will pop up in the center of the screen and will not be able to restrict the user from interacting with the original window.

The third argument passed to the GtkDialog constructor is an integer that determines the properties of the new dialog. There are three properties that can be set with this value. In Listing 14-1 all are set to on:

- Gtk::DIALOG_MODAL: This value determines whether the dialog will be modal. If the dialog is modal, the parent window may not be accessed until the dialog has been closed.

- Gtk::DIALOG_DESTROY_WITH_PARENT: If destroy with parent is turned on, the dialog window will be destroyed when the parent window is destroyed.

- Gtk::DIALOG_NO_SEPARATOR: This is a horizontal decoration line that can appear between the two sections of a dialog. Listing 14-1 sets the dialog to be modal and to be destroyed with its parent. The separator is turned off.

The final argument for the GtkDialog constructor is an array of buttons and responses. In Listing 14-1 the array consists of four constants. The first and third elements are stock button IDs. The GtkDialog constructor will turn these IDs into buttons. The second and fourth elements are responses. The array that is passed as the last argument to the constructor must have an even number of elements and the elements must alternate between strings for buttons, and integers for responses. If the string is a stock ID, a stock button will be created; otherwise, the string will be used as the label for a new button. The response for each button can be any integer value but there are a few values that are already defined.

Table 14-1 shows the constants for these values along with their integer values. All of the predefined response values are negative. This doesn't mean they should be interpreted as false. These values are negative as a convenience for the developer. Any positive response value can be set for a button without the fear that it will be interpreted as a predefined response. In Listing 14-1, two buttons are added, one for no and one for yes. Each is given a corresponding response value.

Table 14-1. *Predefined GtkDialog Responses*

Constant	Integer Value
Gtk::RESPONSE_NONE	-1
Gtk::RESPONSE_REJECT	-2
Gtk::RESPONSE_ACCEPT	-3
Gtk::RESPONSE_DELETE_EVENT	-4
Gtk::RESPONSE_OK	-5
Gtk::RESPONSE_CANCEL	-6
Gtk::RESPONSE_CLOSE	-7
Gtk::RESPONSE_YES	-8
Gtk::RESPONSE_NO	-9
Gtk::RESPONSE_APPLY	-10
Gtk::RESPONSE_HELP	-11

Note The return value from a GtkDialog will be Gtk::RESPONSE_DELETE_EVENT if the dialog is closed without clicking a button. This might be because its parent window was destroyed or because the user clicked the X in the upper right-hand corner.

Displaying a Dialog

After a GtkDialog is created, it remains hidden until needed. A dialog is normally shown in response to some user action. This means that some sort of signal handler is responsible for creating and displaying the dialog. Just like any other widget, the dialog can be shown using show or show_all (show_all is probably the better choice for most applications). Calling show_all will cause the window to appear and, depending on the settings, may block the user from accessing the parent window. When the user clicks one of the dialog buttons or exits the dialog window, the dialog will fire a response signal. A signal handler should be created to capture the user's response.

Managing the User's Response

When a dialog is set to be modal, the user may not interact with the rest of the application until he or she has closed the dialog, either by clicking a button or by closing the window. This essentially blocks the rest of the application until the dialog is closed. There is a slightly more elegant way to block the main window while a dialog is visible. The run method of GtkDialog creates a separate GTK loop just for the dialog. This loop is inside the initial main loop. Until the dialog is closed, nothing will happen in the main loop. When the dialog is closed, run will return the response ID for the button that is clicked, or Gtk::RESPONSE_NONE if the dialog is closed. While run will call show on the dialog, it will not show the children. It is up to the application to show the children before calling run.

Listing 14-2 shows the run method in action. In this example, the quit method of Crisscott_MainWindow uses a GtkDialog to confirm the closing of the window if the user hasn't saved the current inventory and transmitted to the Crisscott server.

Listing 14-2. *Verifying the User's Action with a GtkDialog*

```php
<?php
class Crisscott_MainWindow extends GtkWindow {
    // ...
    static public function quit()
    {
        // Check to see if the data has been modified
        // or sent. If it is modified or not sent, don't
        // exit.
        if (self::$modified || !self::$sent) {
            // Create a dialog to make sure the user wants to quit.
            // Set up the options for the dialog
            $dialogOptions = 0;
```

```php
        // Make the dialog modal.
        $dialogOptions = $dialogOptions | Gtk::DIALOG_MODAL;
        // Destroy the dialog if the parent window is destroyed.
        $dialogOptions = $dialogOptions | Gtk::DIALOG_DESTROY_WITH_PARENT;
        // Don't show a horizontal separator between the two parts.
        $dialogOptions = $dialogOptions | Gtk::DIALOG_NO_SEPARATOR;

        // Set up the buttons.
        $dialogButtons = array();

        // Add a stock "No" button and make its response "No".
        $dialogButtons[] = Gtk::STOCK_NO;
        $dialogButtons[] = Gtk::RESPONSE_NO;

        // Add a stock "Yes" button and make its response "Yes".
        $dialogButtons[] = Gtk::STOCK_YES;
        $dialogButtons[] = Gtk::RESPONSE_YES;

        // Create the dialog.
        $dialog = new GtkDialog('Confirm Exit', $window,
                                $dialogOptions, $dialogButtons);

        // Add a question to the top part of the dialog.
        $message = "The current inventory has not been saved\n";
        $message.= "and transmitted to Crisscott. Are you sure\n";
        $message.= "you would like to quit?\n";

        $label   = new GtkLabel($message);
        $dialog->vbox->pack_start($label);

        // Show the top part of the dialog (The bottom
        // will be shown automatically).
        $dialog->vbox->show_all();

        // Run the dialog and check the response.
        if ($dialog->run() !== Gtk::RESPONSE_YES) {
            // Destroy the dialog and return false.
            $dialog->destroy();
            return false;
        }
    }
    // Exit the application.
    Gtk::main_quit();
    return true;
    }
}
?>
```

Adding Items to the Top of a Dialog

The top section of a GtkDialog is just a GtkVBox. As seen in the two previous examples, the box can be accessed as the vbox property of the dialog. Any widget can be packed into the dialog's vbox. It is common practice to pack an icon into the vbox. This icon can help to draw the user's attention and give him an idea of what the message is about before he has a chance to read the message. In Listing 14-3, a stock warning icon is added to the dialog.

Listing 14-3. *Adding a Stock Image to a GtkDialog*

```php
<?php
class Crisscott_MainWindow extends GtkWindow {
    // ...
    static public function quit()
    {
        // Check to see if the data has been modified
        // or sent. If it is modified or not sent, don't
        // exit.
        if (self::$modified || !self::$sent) {
            // Create a dialog to make sure the user wants to quit.
            // Set up the options for the dialog
            // ...

            // Set up the buttons.
            // ...

            // Create the dialog.
            $dialog = new GtkDialog('Confirm Exit', $window, $dialogOptions,
                            $dialogButtons);

            // Add an image and a question to the top part of the dialog.
            $hBox = new GtkHBox();
            $dialog->vbox->pack_start($hBox);

            // Pack a stock warning image.
            $warning = GtkImage::new_from_stock(Gtk::STOCK_DIALOG_WARNING,
                                        Gtk::ICON_SIZE_DIALOG);
            $hBox->pack_start($warning, false, false, 5);

            $message = "The current inventory has not been saved\n";
            $message.= "and transmitted to Crisscott. Are you sure\n";
            $message.= "you would like to quit?\n";

            $label   = new GtkLabel($message);
            $label->set_line_wrap();

            $hBox->pack_start($label);
```

```
        // Show the top part of the dialog (The bottom
        // will be shown automatically).
        $dialog->vbox->show_all();

        // Run the dialog and check the response.
        if ($dialog->run() !== Gtk::RESPONSE_YES) {
            $dialog->destroy();
            return false;
        }
    }
    // Exit the application.
    gtk::main_quit();
    return true;
    }
}
?>
```

In order to make the dialog appear as it does in Figure 14-2, you must first pack
a GtkHBox into the dialog's vbox. Then add the icon and the label to the hbox. Figure 14-2
shows the Gtk::STOCK_DIALOG_WARNING image.

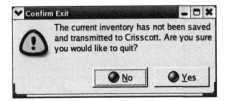

Figure 14-2. *A GtkDialog with a Stock Image*

When the image is created from the stock ID, it is given the appropriate size, Gtk::ICON
_SIZE_DIALOG. There are four other stock images specifically designed for GtkDialog windows.
They are Gtk::STOCK_DIALOG_AUTHENTICATION, Gtk::STOCK_DIALOG_ERROR, Gtk::STOCK_DIALOG
_INFO, and Gtk::STOCK_DIALOG_QUESTION. Each of these simply creates a different icon that will
be displayed in the dialog window. They offer a visual queue to help the user quickly understand
the dialog's message. You can see these icons by starting up the stock-browser2.php demo that
comes with the PHP-GTK 2 source or Window binaries.

Adding Items to the Bottom of a Dialog

Just as items can be added to the top section of a dialog, they can be added to the bottom section,
which is also known as the *action area*. The action area can be accessed as the action_area
property of a dialog. The action area is really just a GtkHButtonBox, and should only be used to
hold buttons for the dialog even though it is possible to add any widget to a button box. You can
add buttons using the button box methods of add, pack_start or pack_end, which were discussed
in Chapter 6. Unfortunately, these methods only add the button to the box. They do not allow
the button to close the dialog and emit the response signal with a response ID.

While the application could create the needed signal handlers, there is a better way to add items to the action area. The proper way to add a button to a GtkDialog is by using one of the following:

- add_button: The add_button method takes a string and an integer as arguments. The string should be either a stock ID or the label for a new button. The integer should be the response ID for the new button. These arguments are similar to those given in the array that is the last argument to the GtkDialog constructor.

- add_buttons: This adds multiple buttons to the action area at once. It takes only one argument, an array which is of the same format as the array passed to the GtkDialog constructor. The elements must be alternating strings and integers. The strings will be used to create the buttons and the integers will be the response IDs.

- add_action_widget: This takes two arguments—a widget and a response ID. The widget must be "activatable." This means that the widget must be able to emit the activate signal. Activatable widgets include buttons, entries, and menu items. Listing 14-4 shows an example using add_action_widget.

Listing 14-4. *Adding a Button to a GtkDialog Using add_action_widget*

```php
<?php
class Crisscott_MainWindow extends GtkWindow {
    // ...
    static public function quit()
    {
        // Check to see if the data has been modified
        // or sent. If it is modified or not sent, don't
        // exit.
        if (self::$modified || !self::$sent) {
            // Create a dialog to make sure the user wants to quit.
            // Set up the options for the dialog
            // ...

            // Set up the buttons.
            // ...

            // Create the dialog.
            $dialog = new GtkDialog('Confirm Exit', $window, $dialogOptions);

            // Add the buttons to the action area.
            $noButton  = GtkButton::new_from_stock(Gtk::STOCK_NO);
            $yesButton = GtkButton::new_from_stock(Gtk::STOCK_YES);

            $dialog->add_action_widget($noButton,  Gtk::RESPONSE_NO);
            $dialog->add_action_widget($yesButton, Gtk::RESPONSE_YES);

            // ...
        }
```

```
    }
}
?>
```

A GtkDialog is an excellent tool for prompting the user for some information. It is flexible and easy to use. One of the drawbacks to a GtkDialog is its simplicity. Getting more than just a simple response from a dialog is difficult. Luckily, there are some classes that act like dialogs but are slightly more powerful.

Selectors

Selectors are more complex versions of dialogs. Like dialogs they are top-level windows, but unlike dialogs, selectors return something other than an integer response. Selectors can be used to return such things as fonts, colors, or file paths. Selectors also come with buttons that can be used to launch the dialog window.

Color Selection Dialogs

Some applications may need to allow the user to select a color. A GtkColorSelectionDialog widget is a dialog window with a GtkColorSelection widget in the dialog vbox. The action area is packed with three buttons. Figure 14-3 shows a GtkColorSelectionDialog in action. A GtkColorSelection allows a user to pick a color using one of five methods. The large color wheel on the left of the window allows the user to select a color by clicking in the triangle in the center of the wheel. If the desired color can't be found in the triangle, clicking the outer ring will change the colors in the triangle. Below the color wheel is a small window showing the original color and the current selection. To the right of this window is an eyedropper tool. The eyedropper can be used to select a color from any part of the screen. On the right of the dialog window, there are three methods to identify a color. The color can be named using a hue, a saturation, a value combination, an RGB value, or a hex value. The buttons packed into the action area are a cancel button and an OK button.

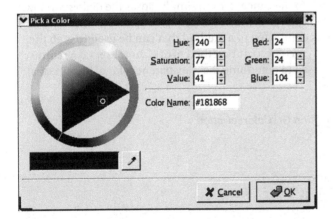

Figure 14-3. *A GtkColorSelectionDialog*

Creating and showing a GtkColorSelectionDialog isn't all there is to the story. You can access the color selection from the dialog via the colorsel property and then set the properties for the color selection. Additionally, there are two extra tools you can add to the default color selection. You can add an opacity tool by passing true to set_has_opacity_control. The opacity control determines how transparent the selected color will be. The other tool you can add is a color palette, which is a selection of colors. You can add a palette by passing true to set_has_palette. Figure 14-4 shows a GtkColorSelection with an opacity control and a color palette.

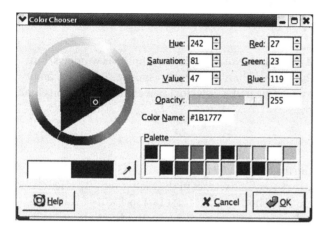

Figure 14-4. *A GtkColorSelection with an opacity control and a color palette*

Signal Handlers

Once you've created the color selection interface, you should create the signal handlers. Without them, the color selection will not be very useful. The signal handlers should be connected to the three buttons in the action area. The buttons can be accessed using the ok_button, cancel_button, and help_button properties. Listing 14-5 shows what the signal handlers may look like. The signal handler connected to the cancel button simply closes the dialog window. The signal handler for the help button calls a method that will open up a new window with helpful information. The OK button is connected to a method that can be used to grab the color from the color selection. The get_current_color method of GtkColorSelection returns a GdkColor object. This object can be used to determine the transparent color of a GdkPixmap among other things.

Listing 14-5. *Creating Signal Handlers for a GtkColorSelection*

```php
<?php

// Create and show the color dialog.
$color = new GtkColorSelectionDialog('Color Chooser');
$color->show_all();

// Create a signal handler for the cancel button.
$color->cancel_button->connect_simple('clicked', array($color, 'destroy'));
```

```php
// Create a signal handler to show a help window.
$color->help_button->connect_simple('clicked', 'showHelp');

// Create a signal handler to grab the selected color.
$color->ok_button->connect_simple('clicked', 'getColor', $color);

?>
```

Color Buttons

Setting up a GtkColorSelectionDialog can be a somewhat tedious process. First, all of the properties for the GtkColorSelection must be set. Then signal handlers must be created for each of the buttons. For more complicated uses, this flexibility is very helpful; but for more typical uses, such as selecting color for a block of text, the needs are much simpler. All that needs to be returned is a color. There is no need for a help window or a color palette. To make life a little easier there is GtkColorButton, a subclass of GtkButton, which displays a color swatch. When clicked, the button starts up a GtkColorSelectionDialog. After the user selects a color, the dialog is closed and the new color is shown in the button. The dialog that appears is slightly different from a normal GtkColorSelectionDialog. It has no help button. Also, the OK and cancel buttons are already connected to appropriate signal handlers. When the user clicks the cancel button, the dialog is closed. When the user clicks the OK button, a color-set signal is fired. In Listing 14-6, the color-set signal is connected to a method that applies a tag to a block of text. The color button's get_color method grabs the color shown in the button.

Listing 14-6. *Using GtkColorButton*

```php
<?php

function applyTag($colorButton, $text)
{
    // Create a color object to hold the color.
    $color = new GdkColor();

    // Get the color from the button.
    $colorButton->get_color($color);

    // Create a new tag to modify the text.
    $tag = new GtkTextTag();

    // Set the tag color.
    $tag->set_property('foreground-gdk', $color);

    // Get the buffer.
    $buffer = $text->get_buffer();

    // Get iters for the start and end of the selection.
    $selectionStart = $buffer->get_start_iter();
    $selectionEnd   = $buffer->get_start_iter();
```

```
        // Get the iters at the start and end of the selection.
        $buffer->get_iter_at_mark($selectionStart, $buffer->get_insert());
        $buffer->get_iter_at_mark($selectionEnd,  $buffer->get_selection_bound());

        // Add the tag to the buffer's tag table.
        $buffer->get_tag_table()->add($tag);

        // Apply the tag.
        $buffer->apply_tag($tag, $selectionStart, $selectionEnd);
    }

    // Create a window and set it to close cleanly.
    $window = new GtkWindow();
    $window->connect_simple('destroy', array('gtk', 'main_quit'));

    // Create a vBox to hold the window's contents.
    $vBox = new GtkVBox();

    // Create an hBox to hold the buttons.
    $hBox = new GtkHBox();

    // Create the color button and pack it into the hBox.
    $color = new GtkColorButton();
    $hBox->pack_start($color, false, false);

    // Pack the hBox into the vBox.
    $vBox->pack_start($hBox, false, false, 3);

    // Create the text view.
    $text = new GtkTextView();
    $text->set_size_request(300, 300);

    // Create a signal handler for the color button.
    $color->connect('color-set', 'applyTag', $text);

    // Add the text view to the vBox.
    $vBox->pack_start($text);

    // Add the vBox to the window and show everything.
    $window->add($vBox);
    $window->show_all();
    gtk::main();
?>
```

Figure 14-5 shows a simple text editor that makes use of GtkColorButton. The image also shows the dialog that GtkColorButton pops up.

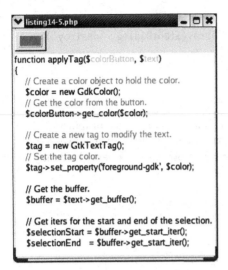

Figure 14-5. *GtkColorButton in a very simple text editor*

Font Selection Dialogs

GtkFontSelectionDialog is a widget designed to provide a consistent interface for selecting text fonts. A GtkFontSelectionDialog is similar to a GtkColorSelectionDialog. It is simply a GtkDialog window that is prepopulated with widgets needed to perform a given task. In this case, the task is selecting a font and its attributes. The top portion of a GtkFontSelectionDialog is a GtkFontSelection widget. A GtkFontSelection contains widgets needed to select the font family, style (bold, italic, etc.), and size. The GtkFontSelection also has an area to preview the selected font. The action area of the font selection dialog has a cancel button, an apply button, and an OK button. Just like GtkColorSelectionDialog, the buttons in the action area of a GtkFontSelectionDialog must be connected to signal handlers. Listing 14-7 creates a font selection dialog and the appropriate signal handlers.

Listing 14-7. *Creating a GtkFontSelectionDialog*

```php
<?php

// Create a font dialog.
$fontDialog = new GtkFontSelectionDialog('Font Selection');

// Create a signal handler for the cancel button.
$fontDialog->cancel_button->connect_simple('clicked',
                                           array($fontDialog, 'destroy'));

// Create a signal handler to apply the font.
$fontDialog->apply_button->connect_simple('clicked', 'applyTag', $textBuffer);

// Create a signal handler to apply the font.
$fontDialog->ok_button->connect_simple('clicked', 'applyTag', $textBuffer);
```

```
// Create a signal handler to close the dialog.
$fontDialog->ok_button->connect_simple('clicked', array($fontDialog, 'destroy'));

// Show the dialog.
$fontDialog->show_all();
?>
```

The callbacks are not implemented in this example, but they aren't that complicated. The apply button and OK button both apply the font to a text buffer. The difference between the two is that the OK button closes the dialog, and the apply button leaves it open. The dialog created in Listing 14-7 can be seen in Figure 14-6.

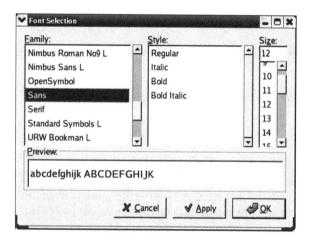

Figure 14-6. *A GtkFontSelectionDialog*

You can access the GtkFontSelection widget of a GtkFontSelectionDialog via the fontsel property. A GtkFontSelection widget has a few methods you can call to customize the tool. First, you can select the default font by using the set_font_name method. This method will preselect a font family name if it is available on the user's system. The text used to preview the font is also configurable. The set_preview_text method takes a string and puts it in the preview area of the GtkFontSelection widget. This method is particularly handy if the user is setting a font over a selection of text. The selected text can be set in the preview area to give users a better idea of the change they are about to make.

Font Buttons

Creating a GtkFontSelectionDialog and setting up all the signal handlers can be just as tedious as with a GtkColorSelectionDialog. Using a GtkFontButton is an easy way to set up a GtkFontSelection. A font button can display the font family, style, and size of the currently selected font. When clicked, the button will launch a font selection dialog. The dialog created by the button will have all the signal handlers for the buttons created. The only signal handler that needs to be set up by the developer is the font-set signal. This signal is emitted when the user clicks the apply or OK buttons.

Listing 14-8 shows a callback method that could be connected to a font button's font-set signal to change the font of a selected region of text in a GtkTextBuffer. The font-set signal automatically passes the font button to the callback. The selected font can be returned using get_font_name. This method returns the font family, style, and size as one string. The value of get_font_name is then used to set the font property of a GtkTextTag object. This tag is then applied across the selection to modify the font of the text.

Listing 14-8. *A Callback for a GtkFontButton's Font-Set Signal*

```php
<?php
function applyTag($fontButton, $text)
{
    // Create a new tag to modify the text.
    $tag = new GtkTextTag();

    // Set the tag font.
    $tag->set_property('font', $fontButton->get_font());

    // Get the buffer.
    $buffer = $text->get_buffer();

    // Get iters for the start and end of the selection.
    $selectionStart = $buffer->get_start_iter();
    $selectionEnd   = $buffer->get_start_iter();

    // Get the iters at the start and end of the selection.
    $buffer->get_iter_at_mark($selectionStart, $buffer->get_insert());
    $buffer->get_iter_at_mark($selectionEnd,   $buffer->get_selection_bound());

    // Add the tag to the buffer's tag table.
    $buffer->get_tag_table()->add($tag);

    // Apply the tag.
    $buffer->apply_tag($tag, $selectionStart, $selectionEnd);
}
?>
```

By default, a font button displays the font family and size of the currently selected font. The display properties of the button can be controlled. The style (bold, italic, etc.) can be added to the button's label by passing true to set_show_style. Passing false to this method will turn the style off again. Passing false to set_show_size will hide the size in the button's label. The size can be shown again by passing true to the same method. In addition to showing the font description, you can control the font of the button's label. A button can be told to use the currently selected font, style, or size in its label.

In Figure 14-7, the GtkFontButton is told to use the font and style that has been selected. This is done using the set_use_font method. This method expects a Boolean value and changes the font and style of the button's label if it is given true. The button's label will not use the selected size unless true is passed to set_use_size. Be careful when using set_use_size because the button can become unreadable or distort the appearance of the application, depending on how it is packed into its parent container.

Figure 14-7. *A GtkFontButton set to use the selected font and style*

File Chooser Dialogs

GtkColorSelectionDialog and GtkFontSelectionDialog are rather specialized widgets. They are most commonly used with text editing applications or pieces of an application that can edit text. GtkFileChooserDialog, on the other hand, has much broader appeal. Many different types of applications will need to access the file system in one way or another. For example, an application may need to open or save files, or an email client might need to attach a file to a message. These actions require the user to select a file and tell the application where it can be found. This is the purpose of GtkFileChooserDialog. It provides an interface for the user to browse the file system and pick one or more files.

A GtkFileChooserDialog is very similar to the other selectors. It consists of a dialog window that has the top portion populated with a GtkFileChooserWidget. The action area is prepopulated with different buttons depending on the intended use of the dialog. When a file chooser dialog is created it expects not only a title and a parent window but also an action type. The action type defines the expected behavior of the dialog. The different types are Gtk::FILE_CHOOSE_ACTION_OPEN, Gtk::FILE_CHOOSER_ACTION_SAVE, Gtk::FILE_CHOOSER_ACTION_SELECT_FOLDER, and Gtk::FILE_CHOOSER_ACTION_CREATE_FOLDER.

Figure 14-8 shows a save and an open file chooser dialog. The create folder and select folder dialogs are very similar in appearance. After passing the action type, the constructor for GtkFileChooserDialog expects an array of buttons and responses. These buttons and their responses will be added to the action area. Signal handlers should be created for these just as with the other selector dialogs.

Just as with the other selector widgets, there is a button that makes using a file selector quite easy. GtkFileChooserButton will launch a GtkFileChooserDialog. The constructor for the button requires a title for the dialog window and an action type. A GtkFileChooserButton can only accept Gtk::FILE_CHOOSER_ACTION_OPEN and Gtk::FILE_CHOOSER_ACTION_SELECT_FOLDER as its action type. This means that a file chooser button can only be used to open files or folders. It cannot be used to save files or create folders. Figure 14-9 shows what a GtkFileChooserButton might look like in an application. To determine which filename is selected, a signal handler needs to be created for the open button of the dialog. The dialog can be accessed using the dialog property. A GtkFileChooserButton is a quick and easy way to set up a file chooser.

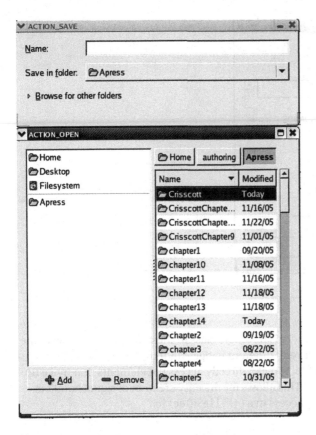

Figure 14-8. *Two types of GtkFileChooserDialog*

Figure 14-9. *A GtkFileChooserButton*

File Selection

A GtkFileChooserDialog is a very specialized tool for allowing users to select a file. Its form and function changes depending on what the dialog will be used for. A more practical and standard approach to allow the user to select a file from the file system is to use a GtkFileSelection. This selector is much more similar to the other types of selectors we have seen so far. The interface, which can be seen in Figure 14-10, is probably more recognizable and easier to use.

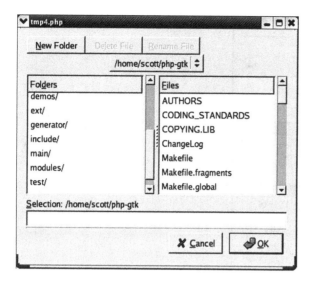

Figure 14-10. *A GtkFileSelection*

Unlike the other types of selectors, there is no single class in the dialog's vbox. Instead, the top section of the dialog is made up of several different widgets that together provide the functionality needed to let the user select a file. You can directly access the elements that make up both the top section and the action area. This allows for the easy creation of signal handlers. Table 14-2 shows the properties you can access in a GtkFileSelection.

Table 14-2. *GtkFileSelection Properties*

Property	Description
ok_button	The dialog's OK button. A signal handler should be connected to this button to get the filename.
cancel_button	The dialog's cancel button. A signal handler should be connected to this button to close the dialog.
fileop_c_dir	A button to allow the user to create a directory. No signal handler needs to be created.
fileop_del_file	A button to allow the user to delete a file. No signal handler needs to be created.
fileop_ren_file	A button to allow the user to rename a file. No signal handler needs to be created.
fileop_dialog	The GtkDialog holding all the other widgets.
history_pulldown	A GtkOptionMenu showing the directory history.

As you can see by the list of properties, a GtkFileSelection allows the user to do much more than select a file. The file operation buttons that appear at the top of the dialog can be used to create directories, delete files or directories, and rename files or directories. This amount of freedom may be undesirable in some circumstances. Therefore, these buttons can be hidden from the user by calling hide_fileop_buttons. Calling show_fileop_buttons will show these buttons again. If the buttons are left visible, not much else needs to be done. The buttons come equipped with the signal handlers needed to perform their specified tasks. Of course, a new signal handler could be created if, for instance, the application wants to know when a new directory is created. If the application has a tree view of the file system, knowing when a new directory is created or deleted would allow the application to know when to rebuild the underlying model.

Listing 14-9 presents the code from the Crisscott_MainWindow class. The code is used to retrieve a filename that contains the XML for an inventory. This example is only for the file open function. Saving files requires a different dialog. A GtkFileSelection is created and then run using the run method. The return value of the run method is checked to see if a file was selected. The filename is taken from the dialog using the get_filename method. If the file cannot be found, a new dialog is popped up and the open method is called again. If the filename is valid, a static method for the main window is called to load the information found in the given file.

Listing 14-9. *Connecting a GtkFileSelection for Opening a File*

```php
<?php
class Crisscott_MainWindow extends GtkWindow {
    // ...
    public function open()
    {
        // Create the file selection dialog.
        $fileSelection = new GtkFileSelection('Open');

        // Make sure that only one file is selected.
        $fileSelection->set_select_multiple(false);

        // Filter the files for XML files.
        $fileSelection->complete('*.xml');

        // Show the dialog and run it.
        $fileSelection->show_all();
        if ($fileSelection->run() == Gtk::RESPONSE_OK) {
            // Make sure the file exists.
            if (@is_readable($fileSelection->get_filename())) {
                // Load the file.
                self::loadFile($fileSelection->get_filename());
            } else {
                // Pop up a dialog warning...
                // ...
                // Run this method again.
                self::open();
            }
        }
    }
}
?>
```

In Listing 14-9, two adjustments are made to the file selection before it is shown. First, the file selection is told not to allow multiple selections. This is done by passing false to set_select_multiple. This is really just a precaution because selection of multiple files is disabled by default. Next, a pattern is set using the complete method. The pattern is used to check for a possible default filename. If a file matches the pattern, it will be selected by default. If there is more than one file that matches the pattern, those files will be the only ones listed in the files list of the dialog. In Listing 14-9 the pattern is set to *.xml. This will limit the initial list of files to only XML files.

About Dialogs

The final dialog we will consider in this chapter is GtkAboutDialog. It presents information about the application in a pop-up window but doesn't ask any questions. A GtkAboutDialog is normally popped up from an about menu item in the help menu. The about dialog shows information, such as the application name and version, the copyright, and the application authors. Listing 14-10 shows the code that creates the Crisscott about dialog. The end result of this code can be seen in Figure 14-11.

Listing 14-10. *The GtkAboutDialog for the Crisscott PIMS Application*

```php
<?php
class Crisscott_AboutDialog extends GtkAboutDialog {

    public function __construct()
    {
        // Call the parent constructor.
        parent::__construct();

        // Set the elements of the dialog.
        $this->init();
    }

    public function init()
    {
        // Set the logo image.
        $this->set_logo(GdkPixbuf::new_from_file('Crisscott/images/logo.png'));
        // Set the application name.
        $this->set_name('Crisscott PIMS');
        // Set the copyright notice.
        $this->set_copyright('2005 Crisscott, Inc.');
        // Set the license.
        $this->set_license(file_get_contents('Crisscott/license.txt'));
        // Set the URL to the Crisscott website.
        $this->set_website('http://www.crisscott.com/');
        // Set the version number.
        $this->set_version('1.0.0');
        // Set the description of the application.
```

```
        $this->set_comments('An application to manage product information '.
                            'for distribution through Crisscott.com');
    }
}
?>
```

Figure 14-11. *The Crisscott about dialog*

The preceding listing sets the many different parts of the about dialog. The first thing that is set is the logo. The logo is set with set_logo that expects a GdkPixbuf as the only argument. Next, the name of the application is set using set_name. The copyright information is set using set_copyright. The license is set using set_license. The copyright and license methods expect a string as the only argument. There are several different pieces of information that can be set and each has its own method:

- set_name: Sets the name of the application.

- set_copyright: Sets the copyright notice.

- set_comments: Adds a description of the application.

- set_license: Adds a line describing the license the application is released under. It adds a button to the dialog that opens another window with the contents of the license.

- set_website: Can be used to add a URL where more information can be found.

- set_website_label: Sets a string used as the text for the website link. If no label is set, the link defaults to the URL.

- set_authors: Adds each author in the given array to the list of authors.

- set_artists: Adds each artist in the given array to the list of artists.

- set_documenters: Adds each documenter in the given array to the list of documenters.

- set_translator_credits: Adds a line for the translator who worked on the current language version.

Summary

Dialogs and selectors allow large functional components to be hidden until needed. These components can be used to confirm a user's action or to gather more complicated information, such as colors, fonts, and filenames. Using a dialog is a simple matter of showing the dialog and connecting the needed signal handlers. In some cases, it is possible to automate the process using a specially designed button. Color, font, and file selectors have buttons that can open up the dialog and connect most of the signal handlers. When a button is used, normally, only one signal handler needs to be created. This signal handler can then return the needed value.

Dialogs and selectors are the last major functional widgets I will talk about. Chapter 15 talks about doing work in the background. It will show how to allow the user to continue working while an application does other work. You will also see how to report the progress of background tasks using progress bars. Finally, you will see how to repeat tasks over an interval of time. Chapter 15 makes the Crisscott PIMS application more automated.

■ ■ ■

Doing Background Work

A typical Web-based application uses a very rigid process for communicating with the user. The user makes a request and the server sends a response. In a Web-based application the server can't initiate contact with the user, whereas a GUI application can notify the user when an event has occurred. This simple distinction allows for one of the more interesting features of PHP-GTK: background work.

Background work goes on while the user is working on something else, allowing for much greater efficiency. Contrast this with a Web application where the user must wait for each, often time-consuming, process. For example, consider a travel website. When a user submits a search request for airline tickets, normally a graphic is loaded asking the user to be patient while the search is conducted. Until the user is taken to the results page, he or she can't access any other information. But in a GUI application, long running processes can occur behind the scenes while the user continues to work. When the process is finished, the application can notify the user. In this chapter we will see how to allow the user to continue working while the application is doing work in the background.

Progress Bars

Before discussing the details of how an application can perform background work, it is a good idea to discuss how the user will be notified of the application's progress. One method, as we have seen with the splash screen, is to offer continuously updated messages in the interface. Another method is to use a progress bar. GtkProgressBar is a widget designed to keep the user informed about the status of a long running process. The process can be anything that has a definite beginning and end, such as uploading a file, writing information to a database, or even collecting information from the user in several steps. If the progress of something can be measured, then a GtkProgressBar can relay that information to the user.

Progress bars can be used to display information about two distinct types of processes:

- *Progress mode*: This mode describes a process where the amount of work completed, as well as the total amount of work to be completed, is known. To tell the user how much work has been done and how much work is left to do, the progress bar grows from one end to the other.

- *Activity mode*: This mode can only tell the user that work is in progress. When the progress bar is in activity mode, the bar bounces back and forth. Activity mode is useful if, for example, the application is waiting for a response from a remote server.

Figure 15-1 shows an example of each type of progress bar.

Figure 15-1. *A GtkProgressBar in progress mode and in activity mode*

Creating a Progress Bar

Creating a progress bar is a simple matter of using the new operator, regardless of the type of progress bar you need. The type of progress bar that is used is decided at runtime and is dependent upon which GtkProgressBar method is called.

For progress mode, the set_fraction method is called. With set_fraction a fraction of the progress bar between zero and one (inclusive) is filled. When called repeatedly, set_fraction makes the progress bar appear to grow or shrink from one end to the other.

You can put a progress bar into activity mode by calling the pulse method, which takes no arguments. This method moves the bar one *pulse step*, which is the relative distance the activity indicator will travel with each pulse. The pulse step can be set using the appropriately named set_pulse_step method. This method takes one argument, which is similar to the value passed to set_fraction. The value passed to set_pulse_step must be a number between zero and one (inclusive) and will determine how far the indicator will move with each pulse. For example, if the value passed to set_pulse_step is .2, each pulse will cause the indicator to move one-fifth of the total length of the progress bar. After five pulses, the indicator would reach the end of the progress bar. The next pulse will cause the indicator to move one-fifth of the way back toward the beginning of the progress bar.

■**Note** If there is not a full step between the indicator and the end of the progress bar, the indicator will only move to the end of the progress bar. It will not rebound in the opposite direction in a single step.

Listing 15-1 is a class that sends product data to the Crisscott server using a SOAP interface. In this class, data is transmitted one product at a time. This allows the method to know how much work has been done and to update the progress bar after sending the data for each product. The progress bar will be displayed in progress mode because the set_fraction method is being called. Notice also the call to the set_text method of the progress bar. The set_text method superimposes text over the progress bar. The text appears centered over the entire progress bar, not just the portion that has been filled in.

Listing 15-1. *Creating and Updating a GtkProgressBar*

```php
<?php
class Crisscott_Tools_ProgressDialog extends GtkDialog {

    public $progress;
```

```php
    public function __construct($title = 'Progress', $parent = null)
    {
        // Set up the flags for the dialog.
        $flags = Gtk::DIALOG_NO_SEPARATOR;

        // Set up the buttons for the action area.
        // We only want one button, close.
        $buttons = array(Gtk::STOCK_CLOSE, Gtk::RESPONSE_CLOSE);

        // Call the parent constructor.
        parent::__construct($title, $parent, $flags, $buttons);

        // Any response should close the dialog.
        $this->connect_simple('response', array($this, 'destroy'));

        // Add a progress bar.
        $this->progress = new GtkProgressBar();
        $this->vbox->pack_start($this->progress);
    }
}

class Crisscott_Inventory {

    // ...

    public static function transmitInventory()
    {
        // Create a SOAP client.
        require_once 'Crisscott/SOAPClient.php';
        $soap = new Crisscott_SOAPClient();

        // Collect all of the products.
        $products = self::getAllProducts();

        // Create a progress dialog for showing the progress.
        require_once 'Crisscott/Tools/ProgressDialog.php';
        $dialog = new Crisscott_Tools_ProgressDialog('Sending Inventory');

        // Show the progress dialog.
        $dialog->show_all();

        // We need to know the total to know the percentage complete.
        $total = count($products);
        // Transmit each product one at a time.
        foreach ($products as $key => $product) {
```

```
                $soap->sendProduct($product);
                // Update the progress bar.
                $percentComplete = ($key + 1) / $total;
                $dialog->progress->set_fraction($percentComplete);

                // Display the percentage as a string over the bar.
                $percentComplete = round($percentComplete * 100, 0);
                $dialog->progress->set_text($percentComplete . '%');
            }
        }

    public static function getAllProducts()
    {
        $products = array();
         // Loop through categories in the inventory.
        foreach (self::$instance->categories as $category) {
            // Loop through the products in each category.
            foreach ($category->products as $product) {
                $products[] = $product;
            }
        }

        return $products;
    }
}
?>
```

In this example, the text is used as another way to communicate with the user. The super-imposed text shows the percentage of the work completed. It doesn't have to simply reiterate the progress; it could be a string that identifies what the progress bar is indicating. For example, it might show "Uploading Products." The text message could also be the current action being taken, similar to the text message in the splash screen. An example of the progress dialog can be seen in Figure 15-2.

As with most text displayed in PHP-GTK, the text shown on a progress bar may extend beyond its boundaries. When a GtkLabel is too large for the area it is being shown in, it can be ellipsized to trim off some characters and indicate to the user that some information is being lost. The same can be done for the text in a GtkProgressBar. The set_ellipsize method takes a Pango ellipsization mode constant (like those used for labels seen in Chapter 4) and ellipsizes the text if needed. Ellipsizing the text on a progress bar comes in particularly handy when the orientation of the progress bar has been changed.

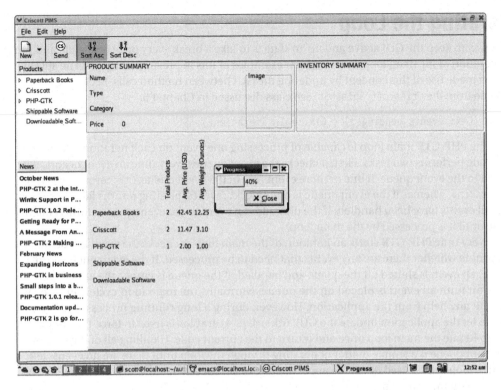

Figure 15-2. *A progress bar in a dialog pop-up*

Using set_orientation

A progress bar doesn't have to move from left to right. Using set_orientation, the progress bar can be set to move from right to left, which isn't much of an advantage, especially for progress bars in activity mode, or from top to bottom or bottom to top. The value passed to set_orientation determines which way the progress indicator will move or grow. Passing Gtk::PROGRESS_LEFT_TO_RIGHT makes the progress bar move from left to right, which is the default. A value of Gtk::PROGRESS_RIGHT_TO_LEFT will cause the progress bar to behave the opposite. Gtk::PROGRESS_TOP_TO_BOTTOM or Gtk::PROGRESS_BOTTOM_TO_TOP will make the progress bar move or grow vertically. You can only change the orientation by using set_orientation. Any text added using set_text will still be presented horizontally. This is when set_ellipsize is helpful. Any string more than a few characters long will quickly overextend the standard width of a vertically displayed GtkProgressBar.

Progress bars are a very nice way to let the user know that some task, which may take a while, is in progress. However, in order to be truly useful, a progress bar must update incrementally. A progress bar that sits still and then suddenly shows the work is done with no intermediate steps doesn't offer much assistance to the user. Updating the progress bar in the middle of a function or loop is only slightly better. Yes, the progress bar may indicate several steps of progress, but the user isn't able to interact with the application until the function or loop exits. In order to allow the progress bar to be updated and to keep the GUI responsive, a long running task must be broken into discrete chunks. Each chunk can then be executed and the GUI can be updated. The next few sections show how to ask the application to do work without locking up the GUI.

Iterating the Loop

One way to keep the GUI active and up-to-date is to take a break every once in a while and run an iteration of the main loop. We have seen examples of this in previous chapters. The splash screen made use of this concept by updating the GUI between method calls. Recall the following line from the `Crisscott_SplashScreen` class discussed in Chapter 5:

```
while (Gtk::events_pending()) { Gtk::main_iteration(); }
```

The PHP-GTK main loop is capable of processing one event on each iteration. The previous code performs two tasks. First, it checks the event queue. Every time an event occurs, it is added to the event queue. If one or more events are in the event queue, `Gtk::events_pending` returns true, whereas if the event queue is empty, `Gtk::events_pending` returns false, meaning that all events have been handled. If the user adds an event to the event queue, it will remain there until it is processed by the main loop.

Every time PHP-GTK starts an iteration of the main loop, it checks the event queue to determine whether there are any events that need to be processed. If the event queue is not empty, an event is shifted off the queue and handled. If the queue is empty, the application will wait until an event is placed on the queue. Normally, the main loop cycles on its own without any help from the application. However, during a long running process it is a good idea to let the application update the GUI. `Gtk::main_iteration` is used to force the application to iterate the main loop once and return to the current code. Handling all of the events in the event queue is a simple matter of iterating through the loop until there are no events left. A `while` loop can be used to tell the application to check for and handle any events before continuing with the rest of the currently executing code.

Adding this loop to the `transmitInventory` method shown in Listing 15-1 is all that is required to make the progress bar update in real time. Listing 15-2 shows exactly where it should be added. The `while` loop is added right after the progress bar is updated. This makes sure that the new progress is shown right away. With this addition, when the `transmitInventory` method is called, the user will not only be shown the progress of the transfer, but will also be able to continue working with the rest of the application. For instance, the user can open menus, click buttons, and even make changes to the inventory data while it is being sent.

Listing 15-2. *Updating the GUI While Data Is Being Transmitted*

```php
<?php
class Crisscott_Inventory {

    // ...

    // A flag that indicates products are being transmitted.
    static public $transmitting = false;
    public static function transmitInventory()
    {
        // Create a SOAP client.
        require_once 'Crisscott/SOAPClient.php';
        $soap = new Crisscott_SOAPClient();
```

```php
    // Collect all of the products.
    $products = self::getAllProducts();

    // Create a progress dialog for showing the progress.
    require_once 'Crisscott/Tools/ProgressDialog.php';
    $dialog = new Crisscott_Tools_ProgressDialog('Sending Inventory');

    // Show the progress dialog.
    $dialog->show_all();

    // Set a flag that indicates transmission has started.
    self::$transmitting = true;

    // We need to know the total to know the percentage complete.
    $total = count($products);
    // Transmit each product one at a time.
    foreach ($products as $key => $product) {
        $soap->sendProduct($product);
        // Update the progress bar.
        $percentComplete = ($key + 1) / $total;
        $dialog->progress->set_fraction($percentComplete);

        // Display the percentage as a string over the bar.
        $percentComplete = round($percentComplete * 100, 0);
        $dialog->progress->set_text($percentComplete . '%');

        // Update the GUI.
        while (Gtk::events_pending()) { Gtk::main_iteration(); }
    }

    // Unset the flag, now that transmitting has finished.
    self::$transmitting = false;
    }
    // ...
?>
```

Of course, allowing the user to change the inventory while it is being modified is probably not the best idea. That is why a flag (the static property $transmitting) is set before the loop starts and unset after the loop finishes. The Crisscott_Product class can check this flag before allowing the user to make any changes. Listing 15-3 shows the code that can be used to alert the user that data is being transmitted and should not be changed. To get the user's attention a dialog is popped up.

Listing 15-3. *Alerting the User When Products Are Being Updated and Transmitted at the Same Time*

```php
<?php
class Crisscott_Tools_ProductEdit extends GtkTable {

    // ...
```

```php
    public function saveProduct()
    {
        // Don't save the product if data is being transmitted.
        require_once 'Crisscott/Inventory.php';
        if (Crisscott_Inventory::$transmitting) {

            // Dialog flags.
            $flags = Gtk::DIALOG_MODAL | Gtk::DIALOG_DESTROY_WITH_PARENT;

            // Create the message.
            $message = "Products cannot be updated while\n";
            $message.= "data is being transmitted.";

            // Popup a dialog to alert the user.
            $dialog = new GtkMessageDialog(null, $flags,
                                        Gtk::MESSAGE_WARNING,
                                        Gtk::BUTTONS_CLOSE, $message);

            // Close the dialog when the user clicks the button.
            $dialog->connect_simple('response',
                                array($dialog, 'destroy'));

            // Run the dialog.
            $dialog->run();

            // Return false to indicate that the product wasn't updated.
            return false;
        }
        // ...
    }
    // ...
}
?>
```

Timeouts

Using Gtk::main_iteration allows a function or a method to take a short break and return control to the main loop. Yet one of the drawbacks to using Gtk::events_pending and Gtk::main_iteration is that the application must explicitly call these two methods. Basically the developer is playing the role of PHP-GTK. Instead of letting the application manage itself, the developer has added hints forcing the application to stop working and update the GUI. If the work to be done can be broken up into several smaller chunks, the application can take back the responsibility of managing the GUI and user interactions. This lets the application focus on the issue it was meant to solve.

Transmitting an entire inventory listing to the Crisscott server simply involves transmitting information regarding all of the products. However, instead of sending all the products during one method call, as shown in Listing 15-1, each product can be sent individually.

Listing 15-4 modifies the Crisscott_Inventory class slightly, this time using a class to send products one at a time rather than using a foreach loop to cycle through the inventory. Each time the transmitInventory method is called, a new product is sent to the server. When all the products have been sent, transmitInventory returns false. The method returns true while there are still products that haven't been sent.

Listing 15-4. *Breaking Up transmitInventory to Send One Product at a Time*

```php
<?php
class Crisscott_Inventory {

    // ...

    public static $products;
    public static $currentProduct = 0;

    public static function transmitInventory()
    {
        // Create a SOAP client.
        require_once 'Crisscott/SOAPClient.php';
        $soap = new Crisscott_SOAPClient();

        // Collect all of the products.
        if (empty(self::$products)) {
            self::getAllProducts();
        }

        // Create a progress dialog for showing the progress. (From Listing 15-1)
        require_once 'Crisscott/Tools/ProgressDialog.php';
        $dialog = Crisscott_Tools_ProgressDialog::singleton('Sending Inventory');

        // Show the progress dialog.
        $dialog->show_all();

        // We need to know the total to know the percentage complete.
        $total = count(self::$products);

        // Transmit the current product.
        $soap->sendProduct(self::$products[self::$currentProduct]);

        // Update the progress bar.
        $percentComplete = (++self::$currentProduct) / $total;
        $dialog->progress->set_fraction($percentComplete);

        // Display the percentage as a string over the bar.
        $percentComplete = round($percentComplete * 100, 0);
        $dialog->progress->set_text($percentComplete . '%');
```

```
        // Return true if there are more products to send.
        $count = count(self::$products);
        if (self::$products[self::$currentProduct] == self::$products[$count - 1]) {
            $dialog->destroy();
            return false;
        } else {
            return true;
        }
    }

    public static function getAllProducts()
    {
        self::$products = array();
        // Loop through categories in the inventory.
        foreach (self::$instance->categories as $category) {
            // Loop through the products in each category.
            foreach ($category->products as $product) {
                self::$products[] = $product;
            }
        }
    }
}
?>
```

Breaking up the process of sending the inventory data means you don't have to worry about inserting any code that isn't directly related to sending data. This makes the code cleaner and easier to maintain. It also makes the code more portable. This class can now be used with some other type of front end because it doesn't have any code specific to PHP-GTK.

Adding a Timeout

Having nice clean code is great but isn't very useful unless there is a way to call it. Something needs to be set up that will call transmitInventory periodically to make sure the next product gets sent to the server. To do this, we will use *timeouts*. A timeout is a way to call a method at regular intervals. A timeout is similar to a signal handler in which the event is the passing of a certain amount of time. Created using timeout_add, the first argument is the number of milliseconds between calls to the callback method. The second argument is the callback itself.

timeout_add can also take a variable list of arguments that will be passed to the callback. For example, Listing 15-5 shows how a timeout can be set up to call transmitInventory. In this case, transmitInventory is called every half second until the timeout is removed or the callback returns a value that can't evaluate to true. This is why Listing 15-4 returns true while there are more products to send. Doing so ensures that the callback will be called again. When there are no more products left to send, false is returned. This stops the callback from being called.

Listing 15-5. *Calling transmitInventory with a Timeout*

```php
<?php
require_once 'Crisscott/Inventory.php';
Gtk::timeout_add(500, array('Crisscott_Inventory', 'transmitInventory'));
?>
```

Removing a Timeout

When a timeout is added, it returns an ID number, similar to a signal handler ID. The number uniquely identifies the created timeout. This allows an application to keep track of the timeouts that are created, but, more importantly, it allows a timeout to be removed. When this value is passed to timeout_remove it is similar to destroying a signal handler. The callback will not be called anymore. In most cases, using timeout_remove isn't necessary because the function can simply return false if it should not be called again. But sometimes there may be other forces at work. For example, the user may decide to stop sending data in the middle of transmitting the inventory.

In Listing 15-6, the creation and removal of a timeout is controlled by a GtkToggleToolButton.

Listing 15-6. *Creating and Destroying a Timeout at the User's Request*

```php
<?php
class Crisscott_Tools_Toolbar extends GtkToolbar {

    // ...

    protected function createButtons()
    {
        // Create a button to make new products, categories and
        // contributors.
        // ...

        // Create the signal handlers for the new menu.
        // ...

        // Create a button that will transmit the inventory.
        $send = new GtkToggleToolButton();

        // Identify the button with a Crisscott logo.
        $icon = GtkImage::new_from_file('Crisscott/images/menuItem.png');
        $send->set_icon_widget($icon);

        // Label the button "Send".
        $send->set_label('Send');

        // Add the button to the toolbar.
        $this->add($send);
```

```
            // Connect a method to start and stop sending the data.
            $send->connect_simple('toggled', array($this, 'toggleTransmit'), $send);

            // Create two buttons for sorting the product list.
            // ...
        }

        public function toggleTransmit(GtkToolButton $button)
        {
            // Check to see if data is currently being transmitted.
            require_once 'Crisscott/Inventory.php';
            if (isset(Crisscott_Inventory::$transmitId)) {
                // Remove the timeout.
                Gtk::timeout_remove(Crisscott_Inventory::$transmitId);

                // Remove the handler ID.
                Crisscott_Inventory::$transmitId = null;

                // Hide the dialog.
                require_once 'Crisscott/Tools/ProgressDialog.php';
                $dialog = Crisscott_Tools_ProgressDialog::singleton();
                $dialog->hide_all();

                // Turn off the button.
                $button->set_active(false);
            } else {
                // Create a new timeout and capture the handler ID.
                $tid = Gtk::timeout_add(500, array('Crisscott_Inventory',
                                                   'transmitInventory'));
                Crisscott_Inventory::$transmitId = $tid;

                // Make sure the button is active.
                $button->set_active(true);
            }
        }
    }
}
?>
```

This example will be applied to the PIMS application so the user can simply click on
a button or menu item to start sending data to the Crisscott server. When the user switches
the button on, a timeout is created that calls the transmitInventory method. When the user
clicks the button again, the timeout is removed. Figure 15-3 is a screenshot with the toggle
button depressed and the progress dialog visible.

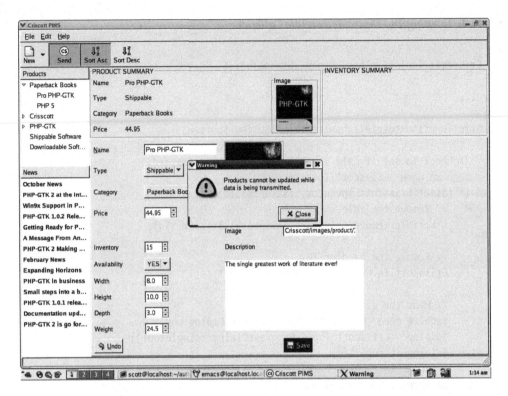

Figure 15-3. *The PIMS application in the middle of transmitting data*

Idle Work

One of the drawbacks to using a timeout is the rigidity with which the callback is called. It will be called every time at the interval defined so long as the callback returns true and the timeout is not removed. It doesn't matter what else needs to be done; the callback will be called. This can be somewhat troublesome if the response time of the application is very important. During iterations when the callback is called, the application must first process one event from the event queue then call the callback. Other events in the queue will have to wait until after the callback has finished processing. It might be nicer to only call the callback when there are no events pending, but timeouts don't care about what is going on around them.

Fortunately, Gtk::idle_add is at your disposal. It is similar to Gtk::timeout_add in that it sets up a callback, but it only sets up a callback when there is nothing else to do. There is no scheduled time interval for an idle callback. idle_add only requires one argument, the callback. Other optional arguments may be passed also. These values will be passed to the callback each time it is called.

Listing 15-7 is a modified version of Listing 15-6, using idle_add instead of timeout_add. On every iteration of the main loop, the event queue will be checked. If there are events in the queue, they will be handled. If there are no events in the queue, the callback will be called. This is a better use of resources and increases the response time for the user. Instead of automatically calling the callback every half second, it is only called when the user (or application) is not doing anything else.

Listing 15-7. *Creating and Destroying an Idle Callback*

```php
<?php
class Crisscott_Tools_Toolbar extends GtkToolbar {

    // ...

    public function toggleTransmit(GtkToolButton $button)
    {
        // Check to see if data is currently being transmitted.
        require_once 'Crisscott/Inventory.php';
        if (isset(Crisscott_Inventory::$transmitId)) {
            // Remove the idle.
            Gtk::idle_remove(Crisscott_Inventory::$transmitId);

            // Remove the handler ID.
            Crisscott_Inventory::$transmitId = null;

            // Hide the dialog.
            require_once 'Crisscott/Tools/ProgressDialog.php';
            $dialog = Crisscott_Tools_ProgressDialog::singleton();
            $dialog->hide_all();

            // Turn of the button.
            $button->set_active(false);
        } else {
            // Create a new idle and capture the handler ID.
            $tid = Gtk::idle_add(array('Crisscott_Inventory', 'transmitInventory'));
            Crisscott_Inventory::$transmitId = $tid;

            // Make sure the button is active.
            $button->set_active(true);
        }
    }
}
?>
```

Notice in Listing 15-7 that the return value of idle_add is captured in a variable. This value is just like that returned from timeout_add or any of the connect methods. It is used to identify the new handler that was just created. This value is passed to idle_remove when the button is toggled off. This is the only way to destroy an idle callback. Unlike a timeout callback, returning false will not stop the method from being called again.

Summary

Forcing a user to wait while a long running process completes is not only a waste of resources but can leave the user confused and frustrated. Most users are not patient enough to understand that their mouse click can't be processed because there is a method in the middle of running. They simply want the application to do its work in the background while they continue with theirs. Allowing the interface to be updated and handle user events is much more effective for long running processes. By using Gtk::events_pending paired with Gtk::main_iteration certain points in a method can be designated to allow the application to be updated. Using Gtk:: timeout_add allows the application to manage the display itself by calling a method at regular intervals. While the method is not processing, the GUI can be updated and interacted with. Gtk:idle_add goes one step further by only calling the method when there are no events to process. Gtk::idle_add makes the user the priority. Anytime they trigger an event, their event is handled. The callback is only processed after all the events have been taken care of.

Now that you have most of the substance for your application defined, Chapter 16 will look at style. Changing the look and feel of an application allows it to take on a more personal appearance. Changing colors of certain widgets is not always about style; it can also serve a rather practical purpose, such as indicating that something has gone wrong or pointing the user in the right direction. Chapter 16 shows how to change the appearance of a widget, groups of widgets, or the entire application.

CHAPTER 16

■ ■ ■

Changing the Look and Feel

So far, we've focused on how widgets and objects function. Yet in order for an application to be truly successful, you'll also need to spend some time tweaking how it looks. While appearance may not seem to be as important as function, the look and feel of an application sometimes has a greater impact on usability than the widgets it uses. For example, making a widget stand out by changing its color or using a mouse-over effect can draw the users' attention and let them know that the widget serves some important purpose.

In general, changing the appearance of an application provides a level of uniqueness that will separate your application from others like it. And it just makes your application look cool! Let's face it, making the application look good can sometimes be just as important as making it work properly. For instance, in Chapter 12, you learned how to use a mask to change the shape of a widget. Perhaps this could be vital to the function of an application, but in most cases, it just makes the application appear more interesting. Even though shaping a widget doesn't have much practical use, I'll have to admit that it is my favorite feature in PHP-GTK.

In this chapter, we will look at how to affect the appearance of an application. First, we will look at resource files, which are a sort of style sheet similar to CSS, but intended for a client-based application. Then we will discuss GtkStyle, an object that controls its parent widget's appearance. While working through this chapter, try to keep in mind not only how these techniques can make an application look good, but also how they can impact the usability of an application.

Resource Files

Resource files are used to define how individual widgets, groups of widgets, or a widget class appear. A resource file (RC file) is an external file that is parsed at runtime and functions like a CSS file referenced in an HTML document. An RC file defines rules that determine which widgets should be modified from their default appearance and specifies how they should be modified.

The RC files are listed in the variable $_ENV['GTK2_RC_FILES']. The value of $_ENV['GTK2_RC_FILES'] defaults to /usr/local/etc/gtk-2.0/gtkrc (C:\Program Files\Common Files\gtkrc on Windows systems) and .gtkrc-2.0 in the user's home directory. These files are created by GTK.

To modify the appearance of widgets, you need to create an RC file that will be parsed when the application starts up. By default, at least one RC file is always parsed when the application starts. With RC files, when two or more rules match the same widget, the last rule is the one that is applied. So any RC file parsed at runtime will override the matching rules in any RC file parsed so far.

Creating an RC File

An RC file is just a text file that contains RC style rules and definitions. An RC file can be edited with any text editor.

Listing 16-1 is a simple RC file that sets some display properties for the splash screen. Using this file allows the display settings to be removed from the splash screen code and put into a separate file. Now to change the look and feel, you simply change the RC file instead of editing the code. This is another example of separation of work, which makes it easier to maintain your applications.

Listing 16-1. *The Contents of an RC File*

```
style "crisscott-splash"
{
  bg[NORMAL]      = "#FFFFFF"
  fg[NORMAL]      = "#0A0A6A"

  fg[ACTIVE]      = "#FFFFFF"
  bg[ACTIVE]      = "#0A0A6A"

  font_name       = "Arial Bold 10"
}

widget "splash*" style:highest "crisscott-splash"
```

Let's take a closer look at the RC file in Listing 16-1. The first ten lines are a *style definition*, and the last line is a *style rule*.

Style Definition

The style definition defines how the different properties of a widget will appear. The first line in Listing 16-1 defines a style named crisscott-splash by using the keyword style followed by a quoted name. Next, the RC file sets different display properties. Table 16-1 shows the properties that you can modify with an RC file style definition.

Table 16-1. *Resource File Style Properties*

Property	Description	Example
bg[state]	The background color of the widget	bg[ACTIVE] = { "#0A0A06" }
fg[state]	The foreground color of the widget	fg[ACTIVE] = { "#FFFFFF" }
base[state]	The background color of editable text (GtkEntry, GtkTextView, and so on)	base[NORMAL] = { "#FFFFFF" }
text[state]	The color of editable text (GtkEntry, GtkTextView, and so on)	text[NORMAL] = { "#000000" }
xthickness	Horizontal padding in pixels	xthickness = { 3 }
ythickness	Vertical padding in pixels	ythickness = { 3 }
bg_pixmap[state]	Background image to be used instead of a color	bg[INSENSITIVE] = "image.png"
font_name	The Pango font name to use for all text	font_name = "Arial Bold 10"
stock[stockId]	Used to create a stock item for use in buttons, menu items, and so on	stock["myStock"] = { {"stockButton.png", *, *, "gtk-button"} }
engine	Used to set properties for the theme engine	engine "bluecurve" { contrast = 1.0 }
class::property	Used to set a default value for the given property of the given class	GtkScrollbar::min_slider _length = 30

Of these properties, bg, fg, base, text, and bg_pixmap can have different values for each state, as follows:

- NORMAL: The state of a widget when no other state applies.

- ACTIVE: The state for a widget such as a GtkRadioToolButton that has been selected.

- PRELIGHT: The state for a widget such as a button or menu item that the user has moved the mouse over. Setting a value for this state creates an effect similar to a mouse-over effect in an HTML document.

- SELECTED: The state used when data is selected. For example, it's used for the selection in a GtkTextView or the selected elements in a GtkTreeView.

- INSENSITIVE: The state of a widget that has had false passed to set_sensitive.

In the crisscott-splash style, the background in the NORMAL state is set to white. The foreground in the NORMAL state is set to a dark blue. When a widget is in the ACTIVE state, the colors for the background and foreground are switched.

The last property set in the style definition is the font name to be used. In this case, the font is set to 10-point bold Arial.

Style Rules

The last line in Listing 16-1 is a style rule that defines which styles apply to which widgets:

```
widget "splash*" style:highest "crisscott-splash"
```

A style rule has two pieces: the rule type and path, followed by the style that is to be applied.

The rule type can be `class`, `widget`, or `widget_class`. The rule type defines which widgets will match the rule, as follows:

- `class`: The rule will match parts of the GUI based on the name of the class, such as `GtkButton` or `GtkBox`. A `class` rule means that widgets of a given class will be used.

- `widget`: The rule will match parts of the GUI based on a name applied to a widget using `set_name`. A `widget` rule means that widgets matching a path of named widgets will be used.

- `widget_class`: The rule will match parts of the GUI based on a path of widget class names. If a `widget_class` rule is defined, widgets matching a path of classes will be used.

The `class` rules are pretty simple. They are created by using the keyword `class` followed by a quoted class name, such as `"GtkButton"` or `"GtkBox"`, as the path. However, the `widget` and `widget_class` rules require a more complicated path element.

A `widget` rule's path must consist of widget names. You assign widget names by using the `set_name` method. The path to a button named `myButton` inside a `GtkHBox` named `myHBox` inside a window named `myWindow` would look like this: `"myWindow.myHBox.myButton"`.

A `widget_class` path is similar, except that each element must be a class name. The same button used in the previous example would be reached by the class path of `"GtkWindow.GtkHBox.GtkButton"`. The difference between the two is that the widget path will match any widget that follows the names in the path. Say a label was added to the same `GtkHBox` and given the name `myButton` (names don't need to be unique). Using the `widget_class` path, the label and the button would have the same rule applied to them. On the other hand, if the `class` path were used, the label would not have the style applied, but any other button in any `GtkHBox` in any window would.

To make rules more generic, you can use the wildcards * and ? to take the place of either a class or a name. For example, `*.GtkButton` will match any path that ends in `GtkButton`.

In Listing 16-1, the style will be applied to any widget named `splash`, as well as any widgets contained at any level within a widget named `splash`.

The second half of the style rule determines what should be applied to the widgets that match the given path. Listing 16-1 applies the style named `"crisscott-splash"`. In this rule, the keyword `style` is followed by a colon and a priority. The priority is optional. In this case, the priority is set to `highest`. Other values, in order of priority, are `rc`, `theme`, `application`, `gtk`, and `lowest`. The priority setting is useful when multiple rules may apply to the same widget. Normally, if two styles that set different values for the same property are applied to the same widget, the style defined later takes priority. By manually setting the priority, you can override this behavior.

Applying the RC File to the Application

Now that this RC file has been defined, it must be applied to the application. Listing 16-2 shows the splash screen code before and after it has been modified to use the RC file.

Listing 16-2. *Crisscott_SplashScreen Before and After Using an RC File*

```php
<?php
/*** BEFORE ***/
class Crisscott_SplashScreen extends GtkWindow {

    // A label to display the status message.
    public $status;

    public function __construct()
    {
        // Call the parent constructor.
        parent::__construct();

        // Turn off the window borders and title bar.
        $this->set_decorated(false);

        // Center the window.
        $this->set_position(Gtk::WIN_POS_CENTER);

        // Set the background using a style.
        $style = $this->style->copy();
        // Make the background white.
        $style->bg[Gtk::STATE_NORMAL] = $style->white;
        // Set the style.
        $this->set_style($style);

        // Fill the window with the needed pieces.
        $this->_populate();

        // Make the window stay above other windows.
        $this->set_keep_above(true);

        // Call a method when the class is shown.
        $this->connect_simple_after('show', array($this, 'startMainWindow'));
    }

    private function _populate()
    {
        // Create the needed pieces.
        $frame     = new GtkFrame();
        $hBox      = new GtkHBox();
        $vBox      = new GtkVBox();
        $logoBox   = new GtkHBox();
        $statusBox = new GtkHBox();

        // Set the shadow type for the splash screen.
        $frame->set_shadow_type(Gtk::SHADOW_ETCHED_OUT);
```

```php
            // Create a label for the title.
            // Mark up the text to change its color to dark blue.
            $title = new GtkLabel('<span foreground="#0A0A6A">' .
                    '<b>Crisscott Product Information Management ' .
                    'System</b></span>');
            // Tell the label widget that the text contains Pango markup.
            $title->set_use_markup(true);

            // Finish creating the elements and packing everything...
        }

    // ...
}
/*** AFTER ***/
class Crisscott_SplashScreen extends GtkWindow {

    // A label to display the status message.
    public $status;

    public function __construct()
    {
        // Call the parent constructor.
        parent::__construct();

        // Turn off the window borders and title bar.
        $this->set_decorated(false);

        // Center the window.
        $this->set_position(Gtk::WIN_POS_CENTER);

        // Set the name for rules in the RC file.
        $this->set_name('splash');

        // Fill the window with the needed pieces.
        $this->_populate();

        // Make the window stay above other windows.
        $this->set_keep_above(true);

        // Call a method when the class is shown.
        $this->connect_simple_after('show', array($this, 'startMainWindow'));

        // Parse the application's RC file.
        // The path to the RC file is a constant defined by the Crisscott_MainWindow class.
        require_once 'Crisscott/MainWindow.php';
        // The RC file is the same as Listing 16-1.
        Gtk::rc_parse(Crisscott_MainWindow::RC_PATH);
    }
```

```
private function _populate()
{
    // Create the needed pieces.
    $frame     = new GtkFrame();
    $hBox      = new GtkHBox();
    $vBox      = new GtkVBox();
    $logoBox   = new GtkHBox();
    $statusBox = new GtkHBox();

    // Set the shadow type for the splash screen.
    $frame->set_shadow_type(Gtk::SHADOW_ETCHED_OUT);

    // Create a label for the title.
    $title = new GtkLabel('Crisscott Product Information Management System');

    // Finish creating the elements and packing everything...
}

// ...
}
?>
```

In the before section of Listing 16-2, the class manually sets a GtkStyle object to make the window background white. The "Styles" section later in this chapter describes how to use GtkStyle objects. The text color is set using Pango markup (see Chapter 7 for a refresher on Pango markup).

In the after section of Listing 16-2, the GtkStyle and Pango markup are removed and two lines are added. The first line gives the window object the name splash. This widget will now match the style rule defined in the RC file. The second line parses the RC file. While the end result of the after section is the same as the before section, the difference, aside from the cleaner code, is that you can now update the style of the splash screen without modifying the PHP code.

Figure 16-1 shows the new splash screen. Notice that it isn't much different from the previous version.

Figure 16-1. *The splash screen using an RC file*

Because the application's look and feel is no longer hard-coded into the application, it is even possible to change the styles on the fly. You could allow users to edit resource files to suit their personal preferences. If an RC file is edited, Gtk::rc_reparse_all should be called. If the modification time of any RC file that has been parsed previously has changed, all files will be reparsed. You can determine whether the files were reparsed by the return value. Gtk::rc_reparse_all

returns true if the files were reread and false if they were not or if there was an error
rereading the files.

As another example, Listing 16-3 shows an RC file that uses different types of style rules
and some more interesting style definitions.

Listing 16-3. *Another Resource File*

```
# Set a path to find images.
pixmap_path "/home/scott/authoring/Apress/Crisscott/images"

# A style for the splash screen.
style "crisscott-splash"
{
  # Make the background white and the text blue.
  bg[NORMAL]      = "#FFFFFF"
  fg[NORMAL]      = "#0A0A6A"

  # Set the font.
  font_name       = "Arial Bold 10"
}

# The main style builds off of the splash screen style.
style "crisscott-main" = "crisscott-splash"
{
  # Make active elements the opposite of normal elements.
  fg[ACTIVE]      = "#FFFFFF"
  bg[ACTIVE]      = "#0A0A6A"

  # Do the same for selected elements.
  bg[SELECTED]    = "#0A0A06"
  fg[SELECTED]    = "#FFFFFF"
  base[SELECTED]  = "#0A0A06"
  text[SELECTED]  = "#FFFFFF"

  # Give insensitive elements a checkered background.
  bg_pixmap[INSENSITIVE] = "insensitiveCheckered.png"

  # We don't need the font to be bold anymore.
  font_name       = "Arial 10"
}

# Make all widgets use the crisscott-main style.
class "*" style "crisscott-main"

# Any widget named or inside of a widget named splash.
widget "splash*" style "crisscott-splash"
```

Notice the addition of comments in Listing 16-3. Comments must begin with the hash
character (#). Any text following the hash character will be ignored.

The next addition to this file is a `pixmap_path` value, which tells the application where to look for any images that are used in the RC file. A `pixmap_path` definition begins with the keyword `pixmap_path`. The value that follows must be a collection of absolute paths separated by colons (or semicolons on Windows systems). Relative paths are not allowed in `pixmap_path` value. It functions and looks just like the `include_path` in a `php.ini` file.

Next in Listing 16-3 is a style definition for the splash screen. This isn't much different from Listing 16-1, except the colors for the active state have been removed. There isn't much point in defining anything for the active state of the splash screen because none of the widgets can be activated.

After this, another style is defined. This style, `crisscott-main`, builds on the `crisscott-splash` style. Instead of redefining the same properties, this style uses those already defined by a previous style. That is why the definition has `= crisscott-splash`. This means that the style being defined should inherit properties from the style specified after the equal sign. Properties that are inherited can be overridden. This can be seen in the definition of the `font_name` property. Even though it was defined in the parent style, it is overridden in the `crisscott-main` style. This style definition sets a few other properties besides the font name. The most unique of these is `bg_pixmap`. This property defines an image to be used as the background for a given state. This example sets the background of widgets that have been made insensitive to a simple checkered pattern. The image will be tiled across the background of the widget.

The `crisscott-main` style is applied to all widgets in the application by using a wildcard for the class name in the class rule. All widgets in the application will match this rule.

Figure 16-2 shows what the Crisscott PIMS application looks like after the RC file in Listing 16-3 has been applied.

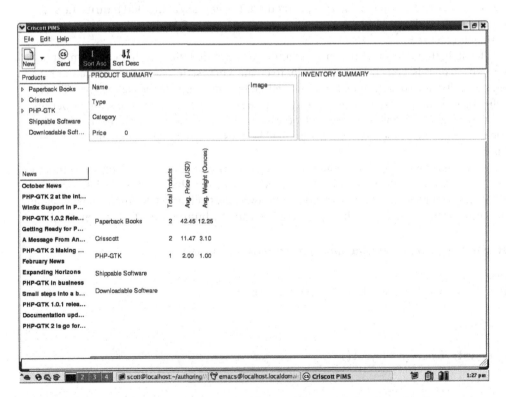

Figure 16-2. *The Crisscott PIMS application after the new RC file has been applied*

The RC file in Listing 16-3 isn't very complex. It defines only two styles and two rules. It isn't one that I would recommend applying to the PIMS application, but it does serve as a good example of how an application can be changed by loading an RC file.

In a more realistic application development environment, one team member might create the RC file while other developers worked on producing the rest of the application. When both sides were finished, the RC file could simply be plugged into the application to see the final product.

Styles

While RC files are well suited for defining styles that can be applied to a broad range of widgets, you might want to create styles on the fly or apply them to specific widgets regardless of their path. To solve this problem, PHP-GTK offers the GtkStyle class.

All widgets have a style property that is a GtkStyle object. When an object is created, a GtkStyle class is created at the same time. The GtkStyle object defines the look and feel for its parent widget. Because GtkStyle objects are created at runtime and are attached to individual widgets, they are excellent for modifying the look and feel of widgets on the fly.

Modifying a Style

You can use GtkStyle to control the way a widget is displayed on the screen. You can access a widget's GtkStyle object in two ways: through the style property of a widget using $widget->style or by using the get_style method. The get_style method returns the style property of the calling widget. The get_style method is part of the GtkWidget class; therefore, all widgets can use it.

The style that comes with a widget cannot be modified directly. Instead, it must be replaced. To do this, you create a new style. To create a new style, use the new operator or the copy method of an existing style. The copy method returns a copy of the calling style. This is useful if you want to make changes to a style without having to set all of the style properties.

A style that is built along with a widget will have some properties already set. When the style is created, the properties from the applied RC files are used to populate the GtkStyle object.

Regardless of how a GtkStyle object was created, you can modify it by writing to its properties. A GtkStyle object has all of the same properties available to it that an RC style definition does.

Listing 16-4 presents a small example that shows how to copy a style, modify it, and reapply it to a button. In this example, the style is copied from the button using the copy method.

Listing 16-4. *Copying, Modifying, and Applying a GtkStyle Object*

```php
<?php
class Crisscott_Tools_ProductEdit extends GtkTable {

    // ...

    private function _layout()
    {
        // ...
```

```
    // We need save and cancel buttons.
    $save  = GtkButton::new_from_stock('gtk-save');
    $reset = GtkButton::new_from_stock('gtk-undo');

    // Modify the button's style.
    $style = $save->style->copy();

    // Change the normal state.
    // Set the background color to dark blue.
    $blue = new GdkColor::parse('#0A0A6A');
    $style->bg[Gtk::STATE_NORMAL] = $blue;

    // Make the prelight color white.
    $style->bg[Gtk::STATE_PRELIGHT] = $style->white;

    // Set the style.
    $save->set_style($style);

    // The label inside the button must be changed too.
    $style = new GtkStyle();
    // Change the normal and prelight states.
    $style->fg[Gtk::STATE_NORMAL]   = $style->white;
    $style->fg[Gtk::STATE_PRELIGHT] = $blue;

    // Root through the button's children and grandchildren.
    foreach ($save->get_child()->get_children() as $child) {
        foreach($child->get_children() as $c) {
            // Set the style.
            $c->set_style($style);
        }
    }

    // Connect the buttons to useful methods.
    // ...
    }
}
?>
```

In Listing 16-4, after the style is copied, the background of the button in the normal state is changed to dark blue. When assigning colors to a GtkStyle property, simple strings are not enough. Instead, you need to use a GdkColor object. A GdkColor object is a helper object that defines a color for the screen. You create a new GdkColor by using the new operator and providing RGB values. The values must be an integer in the range of 0 to 65535. This allows for a wide range of colors because each color value is represented by 16 bits instead of the normal 8 bits. Calculating these values can be quite difficult, however, especially for developers used to using hex values, as in HTML. In Listing 16-4, the color is created in a slightly easier manner. Instead of figuring out the integer RGB values for dark blue, a GdkColor object is created using the static

Gdk::parse method. This method can take a string representation of a color, such as #0A0A6A for dark blue, as used here, or #FF0000 for red, and will return a GdkColor object. The string in this case is a hexadecimal value.

Properties that have multiple states, such as bg (used in this example), fg, and text, are represented by arrays. You can access each state by using a different array index. To access the value for the normal state, Listing 16-4 uses Gtk::STATE_NORMAL. If you wanted to modify the active state, you would use Gtk::STATE_ACTIVE as the array index. The other states follow the same pattern.

Next, Listing 16-4 changes the prelight background to white. Styles have two properties, black and white, which can be used as shortcuts when defining colors for other properties. In Listing 16-4, the prelight background is set to be the same color as the style's white property.

Then the style for the button is set. Notice that set_style is used to set the button's style. Trying to assign a value to the style property will not work.

Simply setting the button's style, and not the style of its children, is not quite enough for this example. The idea here is that the button will stand out. To do this, the style is set so that the background color is dark blue. Unfortunately, if you stopped here, the button's label would be the same color as the background, making it impossible to read. To rectify the situation, the label's style must also be changed. This is a complicated process that requires digging through the children and grandchildren of the button. In this case, using an RC style rule, as described in the previous section, would be a better way to achieve the desired effect.

Figure 16-3 shows the new look of the button after the modified style has been applied.

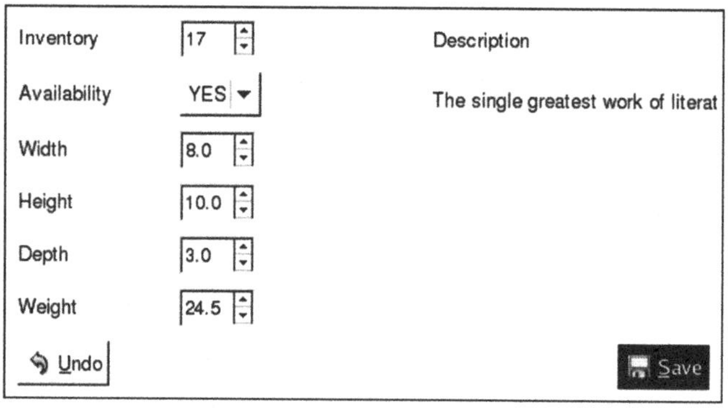

Figure 16-3. *A button with a modified style applied*

Setting a Background Pixmap for a Style

As when assigning colors to a GtkStyle property, the bg_pixmap property also requires more than just a string pointing to a file. bg_pixmap must be assigned a GdkPixmap object. Recall from Chapter 12 that a pixmap can be returned by calling render_pixmap_and_mask on a GdkPixbuf object.

Listing 16-5 shows a small example that sets the background pixmap for a style. In this example, a checkered pattern is used for widgets that are insensitive.

Listing 16-5. *Setting the Background Pixmap for a GtkStyle*

```php
<?php
// Create a window and set it up to shut down
// cleanly.
$window = new GtkWindow();
$window->connect_simple('destroy', array('Gtk', 'main_quit'));

// Create a new style object.
$style = new GtkStyle();

// Create a pixbuf.
$file    = 'Crisscott/images/insensitiveCheckered.png';
$pixbuf = GdkPixbuf::new_from_file($file);

// Get a pixmap from the pixbuf.
list($pixmap) = $pixbuf->render_pixmap_and_mask();

// Assign the pixmap to the normal bg_pixmap.
$style->bg_pixmap[Gtk::STATE_INSENSITIVE] = $pixmap;

// Create two buttons.
$button1 = new GtkButton('Active');
$button2 = new GtkButton('Inactive');

// Set the style for both buttons.
$button1->set_style($style);
$button2->set_style($style);

// Make button two inactive.
$button2->set_sensitive(false);

// Add a button box to the window.
$buttonBox = new GtkHButtonBox();
$window->add($buttonBox);

// Add the buttons to the box.
$buttonBox->pack_start($button1);
$buttonBox->pack_start($button2);

// Show the window and start the main loop.
$window->show_all();
Gtk::main();
?>
```

Figure 16-4 shows the result of this small script. One button appears normally, while the other (which has been made insensitive using set_sensitive) has a checkered background.

Figure 16-4. *Using GtkStyle to Change a Background Pixmap*

Summary

Even the most unique application can end up with an appearance that is ordinary and routine. Modifying the look and feel of an application can not only give it life, but also improve its usability. Changing a widget's appearance by using RC files or GtkStyle objects can make a widget stand out, so that it is more noticeable, or can give the user clues about the state of the widget.

In an RC file, definitions and rules are set up similar to a CSS file in an HTML page. The rules determine which styles will be applied to each widget. GtkStyle objects are similar, but are used for real-time style modifications. Using a GtkStyle object allows a widget to change colors or fonts based on an event. Regardless of how styles are applied, they provide a level of customization that can enhance the application.

This and the previous chapters have taken you through the process of building an application. But simply creating an application is not enough. The application must be distributed to its various users, and those users must be able to install and update the application as needed. In the next, and final, chapter we will look at ways to distribute the application to many users even if they don't have PHP-GTK installed. You will also learn a few strategies for automatically updating the application behind the scenes.

## CHAPTER 17

Distributing PHP-GTK Applications

Developing an application is only part of a project's life cycle. Unless the application is designed purely for individual use, it will also need to be distributed to the end user. After all, an application cannot be considered successful unless someone is making good use of it.

When you're considering how to offer an application to the end user, the deciding factor should be which method will allow the most people to install it with a minimum of fuss. By far, the most widely available means to distribute a PHP application is using PEAR. While it may not be the best solution for all applications, it is available to almost everyone who uses PHP-GTK applications and therefore will be the focus of this chapter. At the end of the chapter, we'll take a quick look at using a PHP-GTK "compiler" to distribute a single executable file.

Downloading and Installing an Application

These days, simply offering a zip file for the user to download may not be enough. While it is the simplest way to distribute an application, it requires the end user to select the right location and move files around. Users want, and in some cases need, applications that are easily installable without requiring them to move files from place to place or extract archives.

Another issue that many users struggle with is dependencies. Requiring the user to install a long chain of dependencies will almost surely result in some level of frustration. While depending on other packages can make a developer's life much easier, asking the user to manually download and install the dependencies could discourage widespread adoption of your application.

To hide much of the installation tedium, consider using PEAR, available for both Windows and Linux environments and bundled with most PHP installations. Any application can be packaged using PEAR and distributed using the Chiara_PEAR_Server package. The flexibility of the PEAR package format allows the application to be installed painlessly, while at the same time letting users customize the application to fit their preferences. Users can specify where the application will be installed and can even make substitutions in the installed code. This gives the users control over the installation process without requiring them to do a lot of work.

Setting Up the Channel Server

The first step in distributing an application using PEAR is to configure a *channel server*. A channel server is a web interface that allows the user to browse, download, and install packages. It also provides an interface for the PEAR installer that helps to make sure the user installs the most recent version of a package.

A channel server consists of two components: a MySQL database and a web server. Once these two requirements are met, installation is a simple two-step process. First, install the package using the PEAR installer, using the following commands:

```
$> pear channel-discover pear.chiaraquartet.com
$> pear install -a chiara/Chiara_PEAR_Server
```

The first command gathers information from the Chiara channel server and makes its packages available to the local PEAR installer. The Chiara channel server is a PEAR channel server maintained by Greg Beaver, the maintainer of the PEAR installer. This server is used to distribute the channel server application. The second command installs the Chiara_PEAR_ Server package. The -a flag tells the PEAR installer to also download and install any dependencies needed for the channel server package. These two steps are similar to those users will need to follow to download packages on your channel server.

Note The -a flag should have triggered the installation of the CRTX_PEAR_Server_Frontend package. This package provides a web interface for the channel server. If it was not installed automatically, you should install it.

Next, you'll need to configure the server by running the *post-install scripts*. As the name implies, post-install scripts are PHP scripts that are run after the package is installed. These scripts are often used to configure a package specifically for the user who has installed the package. In the case of the channel server, post-install scripts are used to configure the database and set up the file that describes the new server. To run the post-install scripts, issue the following command:

```
$> pear run-scripts chiara/Chiara_PEAR_Server
```

You will then be prompted to answer about a dozen questions. When all of the questions have been answered, the new channel server will be ready. You will be able to reach the administration pages via a web browser on your local host.

Creating the Package

The *package* is the file that the users will download and install on their computer. A package contains all of the files needed for the application in addition to an XML file that tells the PEAR installer where to place each file. When a user installs a package, the PEAR installer downloads and unpacks the package file. Then it reads the XML file and moves the files to their proper location according to the instructions found in the XML file. After that, the application is ready for use.

To package the application, you need to create the XML file that tells the PEAR installer where to place each file, called the package.xml file. You can create this file in a few different ways:

- Write it by hand. This can be a long process even for applications that consist of only a few files. If an application has many files, creating the XML by hand quickly becomes impractical.

- Use the PEAR_PackageFileManager class. This PEAR package provides a class to help create and update package.xml files. While this approach is definitely easier than creating the XML by hand, it requires a new script to be written for each application that is packaged. Creating the individual scripts saves only a little time over writing the XML by hand.

- Use one of the GUI front ends for the PEAR_PackageFileManager. The PEAR_PackageFileManager_GUI_Gtk2 application is a PHP-GTK 2 wrapper around the PEAR_PackageFileManager class.

Tip There is also a PEAR_PackageFileManager_GUI_Web front end for creating package.xml files via a web browser.

Since it's the easiest way to create a package XML file, we'll go through the steps of using PEAR_PackageFileManager_GUI_Gtk2 (http://pear.php.net/package/PEAR_PackageFileManager_GUI_Gtk2).

The first step in using PEAR_PackageFileManager_GUI_Gtk2 is to enter the information about the application, as shown in Figure 17-1. You'll need to tell the package file where to find the application files. You can click the browse buttons next to the Package File Directory and Package Output Directory fields to browse to the correct directories. Next, enter the name of the package. This is the name by which users will download and install the application. The third piece of information you need to supply is the base installation directory. This is the directory where the files will be installed. The final two fields on this page are for a summary and a description of the package. The channel server will display these pieces of information when the user is browsing the website.

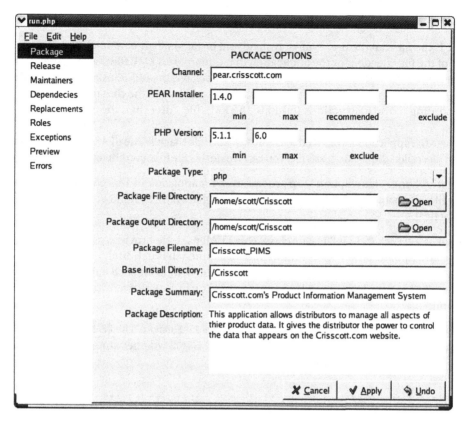

Figure 17-1. *The first page of the PEAR_PackageFileManager_GUI_Gtk2 application*

The next step in creating a package.xml file is to provide a list of maintainers. A *maintainer* is someone who has in some way contributed to the package. To add a maintainer, simply enter a handle (or user name), a real name, an email address, and a role for the maintainer, as shown in Figure 17-2. Those maintainers who are designated as leads can release new versions of the package. Other roles are used to give credit to and provide contact information for those people who have helped develop the package.

Once you've added all of the maintainers, there are only a few remaining steps to complete. The first is to save the XML (select File ➤ Save). This will create two files: package.xml and package2.xml. The package.xml file is used by earlier versions of PEAR and allows for relatively simple installations. package2.xml is used by newer versions of PEAR and allows for greater flexibility, including handling dependencies from other channel servers.

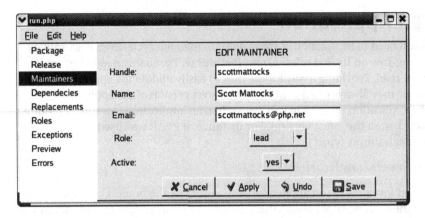

Figure 17-2. *The Maintainers page of the PEAR_PackageFileManager_GUI_Gtk application*

Next, the application needs to be packaged. Packaging the file is a simple matter of issuing the following command:

```
$> pear package package2.xml
```

This command will create a gzipped tar archive (.tgz). This file is called a *package file* and contains all of the information PEAR needs to install the application.

The last step is to upload the new package file to the channel server using the administrator interface provided by Chiara_PEAR_Server. Once the package has been uploaded, users can download and install the application.

■**Note** The PEAR package XML format is very powerful. You can use different elements and attributes to control how an individual file is handled at installation. The PEAR_PackageFileManager_GUI_Gtk2 application can create the XML needed for most of these customizations. For more details, refer to the PEAR manual (http://pear.php.net/manual/en/guide.developers.package2.php).

Users can now install the application by first discovering your channel server and then telling PEAR to install the application:

```
$> pear channel-discover <your channel server>
$> pear install <your channel server>/<application>
```

■**Tip** The Gnope installer (http://www.gnope.org) is an open source application used to install PHP-GTK. Because this application is open source, anyone is free to take the code and modify it to suit their needs. Visit the forums on the Gnope website for more information.

Updating an Application

Most applications will need to be updated at some point in their life cycle. Even if an application is completely bug-free on its first release, new features will probably need to be added somewhere down the road. Providing a way for the user to easily update the application will help to ensure that the user always has the latest and greatest version of the application.

You can handle application updates in two ways. First, an application can simply require the user to manually install the latest version. For instance, if PEAR was used to install the application, the user can simply type:

```
$> pear upgrade <channel>/<application>
```

The other method for updating an application is to automate the process and upgrade the application behind the scenes. Applications that require a manual update process are much less likely to remain up-to-date than those that are updated automatically. Automating the update process not only makes life easier on the user, but also makes life easier on the support team, because there are likely to be fewer versions of an application in wide distribution at one time.

Automatically updating an application is a four-step process:

1. Determine if an upgrade is needed.

2. If an upgrade is needed, obtain the user's permission.

3. Download the new version.

4. Install the new version.

Just as PEAR is the easiest way to reliably distribute an application, it is also the easiest way to automatically update an application. Here, we'll look at how to use PEAR to check for a new version of the application and download and install it if needed.

Checking for Updates

Checking to see if the application needs to be updated is normally done when the application is started. At some point during the startup process (usually the very beginning), a request can be made to the channel server to see if an upgrade is needed. If the package is listed on a PEAR channel server, then the tools for checking for an upgrade are already in place. Using them is just a matter of knowing which classes are needed and which methods to call.

Listing 17-1 shows just how easy it is to check for a new version of the Crisscott PIMS application. This code is added to the splash screen to ensure that the new version check is done every time the application is started.

Listing 17-1. *Checking for a New Version of a Package*

```php
<?php
class Crisscott_SplashScreen extends GtkWindow {
    // ...
    public function startMainWindow()
    {
```

```php
    // Update the GUI.
    while (gtk::events_pending()) gtk::main_iteration();
    // Give the user enough time to at least see the message.

    // Check for a new version first.
    $newVersion = $this->checkNewVersion();
    if ($newVersion === true) {
        $this->status->set_text('New Version');
        // A new version was found!
        $this->askForInstall();
    } else {
        // Let the user know what happened.
        $this->status->set_text($newVersion);
    }
    // ...
}

public function checkNewVersion()
{
    // Create a config object.
    require_once 'PEAR/Config.php';
    $config = new PEAR_Config();

    // Get the config's registry object.
    $reg = $config->getRegistry();

    // Parse the package name.
    $parsed = $reg->parsePackageName('crisscott/Crisscott_PIMS');

    // Check for errors.
    if (PEAR::isError($parsed)) {
        return 'Error: ' . $parsed->getMessage();
    }

    // Get a PEAR_Remote instance.
    $r = $config->getRemote();

    // Get the package info.
    $info = $r->call('package.info', $parsed['package']);

    // Check to make sure the package was found.
    if (PEAR::isError($info)) {
        return 'Could not find package on server. Unable to ' .
                'automatically update.';
    }
```

```
        // Get the installed version of the package.
        $instVersion = $reg->packageInfo($parsed['package'], 'version',
                                    $parsed['channel']);

     if (version_compare(reset(array_keys($info['releases']))),
                       $instVersion,
                       '>')
        ) {
           return true;
      } else {
           return 'No updates found.';
      }
    }
    // ...
  }
?>
```

This small piece of code uses the same classes that the PEAR installer uses to upgrade packages. The first step is to create a PEAR_Config instance. PEAR_Config manages the user's preferences and helps to instantiate other classes properly.

Once the PEAR_Config object is created, it is used to create a PEAR_Registry object using getRegistry. You can use the PEAR_Registry object to access information about packages that are already installed on the user's computer. In this case, it is used to verify that the name of the package to be updated is valid and parse it into different segments.

After parsing the package name (crisscott/Crisscott_PIMS) into a channel and package name, a PEAR_Remote object is created by calling the PEAR_Config object's getRemote method. PEAR_Remote allows the code to access the remote server and query for package information. Passing package.info to the remote object's call method returns a host of information about the package. The relevant information in this case is the version number. If the version number on the channel server is greater than the installed version (which is returned from the registry object's packageInfo method), then a new version of the package is available.

Obtaining the User's Permission to Upgrade

If a new version of the application is available, the responsible thing to do is to ask the user for permission before upgrading the application. As you may have guessed, the best way to ask permission is to use a GtkDialog, as shown in Figure 17-3. The dialog window displays a message and two buttons. If the user clicks the Yes button, the application will be upgraded. If the user clicks No or closes the dialog window, the application is not updated and will be loaded as usual.

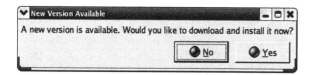

Figure 17-3. *A dialog window requesting permission to upgrade the application*

Listing 17-2 shows the code used to create the dialog window shown in Figure 17-3.

Listing 17-2. *A Dialog to Ask Permission Before Upgrading the Application*

```php
<?php
class Crisscott_SplashScreen extends GtkWindow {
    // ...
    public function askForInstall()
    {
        // Set up the flags for the dialog.
        $flags = Gtk::DIALOG_NO_SEPARATOR;

        // Set up the buttons for the action area.
        // We only want one button, close.
        $buttons = array(Gtk::STOCK_NO, Gtk::RESPONSE_NO,
                                Gtk::STOCK_YES, Gtk::RESPONSE_YES);

        // Call the parent constructor.
        $dialog = new GtkDialog('New Version Available', null, $flags, $buttons);

        // Set a message as the dialog label.
        $dialog->vbox->add(new GtkLabel("A new version is available. \n" .
                        'Would you like to download and install it now?'));

        // Show the dialog.
        $dialog->show_all();

        // Any response should close the dialog.
        $dialog->connect_simple_after('response', array($dialog, 'destroy'));
        // If the user clicks the X in the corner, close the dialog.
        $dialog->connect_simple('destroy', array($dialog, 'destroy'));

        // Run the dialog and check the response.
        if ($dialog->run() === Gtk::RESPONSE_YES) {

            // The user wants to update the application.
            if ($this->doUpdate()) {
                // Let the user know that the application must be restarted.
                $this->status->set_text('The application must be restarted.');

                // Update the message and give the user some time to read it.
                while (gtk::events_pending()) gtk::main_iteration();
                sleep(2);
```

```
                    // Quit the application so that the user must restart.
                    exit;
                } else {
                    // There was a problem.
                    // Let the user know but continue with the startup.
                    $this->status->set_text('Error uploading application.');
                    while (gtk::events_pending()) gtk::main_iteration();
                }
            }
        }
    }
    // ...
?>
```

Performing the Upgrade

The final step is to actually upgrade the application, as shown in Listing 17-3. Just as with the
two previous listings, Listing 17-3 takes advantage of the classes and methods provided by PEAR.

Listing 17-3. *Upgrading the Application*

```
<?php
class Crisscott_SplashScreen extends GtkWindow {
    // ...
    public function doUpdate()
    {
        // Create a config object.
        require_once 'PEAR/Config.php';
        $config = new PEAR_Config();

        // Create a command object to do the upgrade.
        require_once 'PEAR/Command.php';
        $upgrade = PEAR_Command::factory('upgrade', $config);

        // Try to upgrade the application.
        $result = $upgrade->doInstall('upgrade', array(),
                                array('crisscott/Crisscott_PIMS'));

        // Return true if the upgrade was successful.
        return !PEAR::isError($result);
    }
}
?>
```

The first step in upgrading the application is to create a PEAR_Config instance. Again, this
class holds user-defined configuration settings. Next, a PEAR_Command instance is created with
the PEAR_Command::factory methods. This method requires the name of a command and the
configuration object created earlier. It will return an object capable of completing the upgrade.

The call to the doInstall method tells the command object to upgrade the application. If the process is successful, the doInstall method will return true. If an error occurs, the method will return a PEAR_Error object.

Uninstalling an Application

Part of being a responsible developer is not only providing an easy way to install an application, but also providing an easy way to uninstall an application. Regardless of how wonderful an application is, people may need to remove it from their computer. Unfortunately, in too many cases, this requires the users to manually remove all of the files associated with the application. To make life easier on the end user, all applications should come with a way to uninstall them.

The method used for uninstalling an application usually depends on the method that was used to install it in the first place. Some installation tools have the ability to remove a previously installed package. For example, any package installed with PEAR can be uninstalled by simply issuing an uninstall command, like this:

```
$> pear uninstall crisscott/Crisscott_PIMS
```

This command will remove all files that came in the original package. Files that were added by the application later, such as data files or custom resource files, will not be removed.

Of course, as with the upgrade step, this simple PEAR command can be integrated into the application. Alternatively, you can create a separate smaller application as an uninstaller. Listing 17-4 is a simple yet effective application that prompts the user for confirmation and then uninstalls the application if requested, by using the classes provided by PEAR.

Listing 17-4. *An Uninstall Application*

```php
<?php
class Uninstall extends GtkDialog {

    public function __construct()
    {
        // Set up the flags for the dialog.
        $flags = Gtk::DIALOG_NO_SEPARATOR;

        // Set up the buttons for the action area.
        // We only want one button, close.
        $buttons = array(Gtk::STOCK_NO, Gtk::RESPONSE_NO,
                         Gtk::STOCK_YES, Gtk::RESPONSE_YES);

        // Call the parent constructor.
        parent::__construct('Uninstall Crisscott PIMS', null, $flags, $buttons);

        // Any response should close the dialog.
        $this->connect_simple('response', array($this, 'destroy'));
        // The static properties must also be unset.
        $this->connect_simple('destroy', array($this, 'destroy'));
```

```php
        // Add an image and a question to the top part of the dialog.
        $hBox = new GtkHBox();
        $dialog->vbox->pack_start($hBox);

        // Pack a stock warning image.
        $warning = GtkImage::new_from_stock(Gtk::STOCK_DIALOG_WARNING,
                                            Gtk::ICON_SIZE_DIALOG);
        $hBox->pack_start($warning, false, false, 5);

        // Add a message
        $message = new GtkLabel('Are you sure you want to remove the ' .
                    'Crisscott PIMS application?');
        $message->set_line_wrap();
        $hBox->pack_start($message);
    }

    public function run()
    {
        // Show the dialog.
        $this->show_all();

        // Run the dialog and wait for the response.
        if (parent::run() === Gtk::RESPONSE_YES) {
            // Uninstall the application.
            $this->_doUninstall();
        }
    }

    private function _doUninstall()
    {
        // Create a config object.
        require_once 'PEAR/Config.php';
        $config = new PEAR_Config();

        // Create a command object.
        require_once 'PEAR/Command.php';
        $uninstall = PEAR_Command::factory('uninstall', $config);

        // Uninstall the application.
        $result = $uninstall->doInstall('uninstall', array(),
                                        array('crisscott/Crisscott_PIMS'));

        // Report any errors.
        if (PEAR::isError($result)) {
            echo $result->getMessage() . "\n";
        }
    }
}
```

```
// Create an uninstall instance
$unInst = new UnInstall();

// Run the dialog.
$unInst->run();
?>
```

Using PHP Compilers

All PHP-GTK applications have one thing in common: they need PHP-GTK in order to work. This can make it difficult to distribute an application to users who do not have PHP-GTK installed on their computers. The users must download and install PHP-GTK before attempting to run a PHP-GTK application. As you saw in Chapter 2, this can sometimes be a difficult process. One solution is to use a PHP "compiler."

A PHP compiler is an application that takes PHP code and turns it into an executable program. Once compiled, a PHP script can be run by any user, regardless of whether or not they have PHP installed.

A few different PHP compilers are available. Some are commercial applications such as Roadsend's Compiler for PHP (http://www.roadsend.com) and PriadoBlender, but there is one open source, freely available PHP compiler called bcompiler (http://pecl.php.net).

Unfortunately, as of the time of this writing, most of these applications or extensions do not work well enough with PHP-GTK 2 to allow a thorough description of their use. However, Roadsend's Compiler for PHP does allow a majority of applications to be compiled into executables.

Roadsend's Compiler for PHP is available as a command-line application on Linux and as both a command-line application and GUI front end on Windows. Since the command-line application is available on both major platforms, we will focus on that version here. PHP Compiler can turn PHP-GTK source code into an executable with one command:

```
$> pcc --gui Crisscott/run.php
```

This command creates a file named run. This file can be executed on any system that has PHP-GTK installed. Of course, this is not quite what we are looking for. Our end goal is to create an application that can be run without installing PHP-GTK. To do this, you need to use the following command:

```
$> pcc --gui --static Crisscott/run.php
```

This command produces a file with the same name. However, this file, which is much larger than the previous version, includes the PHP and GTK binaries necessary to run without PHP-GTK being installed.

Note I strongly encourage everyone to give these compilers a try and provide as much feedback for the developers as possible. A fully functioning PHP-GTK 2 compiler will allow applications to reach a much greater audience. In the end, a little time spent testing can help to create a better product for everyone.

Summary

Distribution of an application is arguably just as critical as its development and testing. The decision to use one distribution method over another depends greatly on the target users and the goals of the project. If the target users are PHP-GTK developers, then a relatively simple distribution method, such as a channel server, is appropriate, because PHP-GTK does not need to be distributed along with the package. Other groups of users are likely to need PHP-GTK to be distributed and installed along with the application. With any luck, these users will not have to wait much longer for a fully functional PHP compiler.

Index

You Need the Companion eBook

Your purchase of this book entitles you to its companion eBook for only $10.

We believe this Apress title will prove so indispensable that you'll want to carry it with you everywhere, which is why we are offering the companion eBook for $10 to customers who purchase this book now. Convenient and fully searchable, the eBook version of any content-rich, page-heavy Apress book makes a valuable addition to your programming library. You can easily find, copy, and apply code—and then perform examples by quickly toggling between instructions and the application. Even simultaneously tackling a donut, diet soda, and complex code becomes simplified with hands-free eBooks!

Once you purchase this book, getting the $10 companion eBook is simple:

❶ Visit **www.apress.com/promo/tendollars/**.

❷ Complete a basic registration form to receive a randomly generated question about this title.

❸ Answer the question correctly in 60 seconds and you will receive a promotional code to redeem for the $10 eBook.

2560 Ninth Street • Suite 219 • Berkeley, CA 94710

Offer valid through 10/06.